Lecture Notes in Computer Science 4691

Commenced Publication in 1973
Founding and Former Series Editors:
Gerhard Goos, Juris Hartmanis, and Jan van Leeuwen

T0223248

Theo Dimitrakos   Fabio Martinelli
Peter Y. A. Ryan   Steve Schneider (Eds.)

Formal Aspects in Security and Trust

Fourth International Workshop, FAST 2006
Hamilton, Ontario, Canada, August 26-27, 2006
Revised Selected Papers

 Springer

Volume Editors

Theo Dimitrakos
BT Group Chief Technology Office, Ipswich IP5 3RE, UK
E-mail: Theo.Dimitrakos@bt.com

Fabio Martinelli
National Research Council - C.N.R., Pisa, Italy
E-mail: fabio.martinelli@iit.cnr.it

Peter Y. A. Ryan
University of Newcastle, UK
E-mail: peter.ryan@ncl.ac.uk

Steve Schneider
University of Surrey, UK
E-mail: S.Schneider@surrey.ac.uk

Library of Congress Control Number: Applied for

CR Subject Classification (1998): C.2.0, D.4.6, E.3, K.4.4, K.6.5

LNCS Sublibrary: SL 4 – Security and Cryptology

ISSN   0302-9743
ISBN-10   3-540-75226-9 Springer Berlin Heidelberg New York
ISBN-13   978-3-540-75226-4 Springer Berlin Heidelberg New York

Springer is a part of Springer Science+Business Media

springer.com

© Springer-Verlag Berlin Heidelberg 2007
Printed in Germany

Typesetting: Camera-ready by author, data conversion by Scientific Publishing Services, Chennai, India
Printed on acid-free paper   SPIN: 12164677   06/3180   5 4 3 2 1 0

Preface

The present volume contains the post-proceedings of the 4th International Workshop on Formal Aspects in Security and Trust (FAST2006), held in Hamilton, Ontario, Canada, August 26–27, 2006. FAST is an event affiliated with the Formal Methods 2006 Congress (FM06). FAST 2006 was held under the auspices of the IFIP WG 1.7 on Foundations of Security Analysis and Design.

FAST2006 aimed at continuing the successful effort of the previous three FAST workshop editions for fostering the cooperation among researchers in the areas of security and trust. The new challenges offered by the so-called ambient intelligence space, as a future paradigm in the information society, demand for a coherent and rigorous framework of concepts, tools and methodologies to provide users with trust and confidence in the underlying communication/interaction infrastructure. It is necessary to address issues relating to both guaranteeing security of the infrastructure and the perception of the infrastructure being secure. In addition, user confidence in what is happening must be enhanced by developing trust models effectively but that are also easily comprehensible and manageable by users.

FAST sought for original papers focusing on formal aspects in: security and trust policy models; security protocol design and analysis; formal models of trust and reputation; logics for security and trust; distributed trust management systems; trust-based reasoning; digital assets protection; data protection; privacy and ID issues; information flow analysis; language-based security; security and trust aspects in ubiquitous computing; validation/analysis tools; Web service security/trust/privacy; GRID security; security risk assessment; and case studies.

The FAST2006 post-proceedings collect the revised versions of 18 papers, selected out of 47 submissions. Each paper was reviewed by at least three members of the Program Committee.

We wish to thank the the Program Committee members for their valuable efforts in properly evaluating the submissions, and the FM06 organizers for accepting FAST as an affiliated event and for providing a perfect environment for running the workshop.

Thanks are also due to the Center for Software Reliability (CSR) of Newcastle University and IIT-CNR for sponsoring FAST2006.

February 2007

Theo Dimitrakos
Fabio Martinelli
Peter Y.A. Ryan
Steve Schneider

Organization

Workshop Organizers

Theo Dimitrakos, BT
Fabio Martinelli, IIT-CNR
Peter Y.A. Ryan, University of Newcastle
Steve Schneider, University of Surrey

Invited Speakers

Joshua D. Guttman, MITRE, USA

Program Committee

Gilles Barthe, INRIA Sophia-Antipolis, France
Stefano Bistarelli, University of Pescara, Italy
Gregor v. Bochmann, University of Ottawa, Canada
John A. Clark, University of York, UK
Frédéric Cuppens, ENST Bretagne, France
Roberto Gorrieri, University of Bologna, Italy
Joshua D. Guttman, MITRE, USA
Masami Hagiya, University of Tokyo, Japan
Chris Hankin, Imperial College (London), UK
Christian Jensen, DTU, Denmark
Audun Jøsang, DSTC, Australia
Jan Jürjens, TU München, Germany
Yuecel Karabulut, SAP, Germany
Igor Kotenko, SPIIRAS, Russia
Heiko Krumm, University of Dortmund, Germany
Ninghui Li, Purdue University, USA
Steve Marsh, Institute for Information Technology, NRC, Canada
Catherine Meadows, Naval Research Lab, USA
Ron van der Meyden, University of New South Wales, Australia
Mogens Nielsen, University of Aarhus, Denmark
Flemming Nielson, Danish Technical University, Denmark
Indrajit Ray, Colorado State University, USA
Babak Sadighi Firozabadi, SICS, Sweden
Pierangela Samarati, University of Milan, Italy
Jean-Marc Seigneur, University of Geneva, Switzerland
Paul Syverson, Naval Research Laboratory, USA
Ketil Stolen, SINTEF, Norway
William H. Winsborough, George Mason University, USA

Local Organization

Alessandro Falleni, IIT-CNR

Table of Contents

Strategic Games on Defense Trees 1
  Stefano Bistarelli, Marco Dall'Aglio, and Pamela Peretti

Timed Calculus of Cryptographic Communication 16
  Johannes Borgström, Olga Grinchtein, and Simon Kramer

A Semantic Paradigm for Component-Based Specification Integrating a
Notion of Security Risk 31
  Gyrd Brændeland and Ketil Stølen

Game-Based Criterion Partition Applied to Computational Soundness
of Adaptive Security 47
  M. Daubignard, R. Janvier, Y. Lakhnech, and L. Mazaré

Measuring Anonymity with Relative Entropy 65
  Yuxin Deng, Jun Pang, and Peng Wu

Formalizing and Analyzing Sender Invariance 80
  Paul Hankes Drielsma, Sebastian Mödersheim, Luca Viganò, and
  David Basin

From Simulations to Theorems: A Position Paper on Research in the
Field of Computational Trust 96
  Karl Krukow and Mogens Nielsen

A Tool for the Synthesis of Controller Programs 112
  Ilaria Matteucci

Where Can an Insider Attack? 127
  Christian W. Probst, René Rydhof Hansen, and Flemming Nielson

Maintaining Information Flow Security Under Refinement and
Transformation 143
  Fredrik Seehusen and Ketil Stølen

A Classification of Delegation Schemes for Attribute Authority 158
  Ludwig Seitz, Erik Rissanen, and Babak Sadighi

Program Partitioning Using Dynamic Trust Models 170
  Dan Søndergaard, Christian W. Probst,
  Christian Damsgaard Jensen, and René Rydhof Hansen

Locality-Based Security Policies 185
  Terkel K. Tolstrup, Flemming Nielson, and René Rydhof Hansen

A Theorem-Proving Approach to Verification of Fair Non-repudiation
Protocols 202
    Kun Wei and James Heather

A Formal Specification of the MIDP 2.0 Security Model............... 220
    Santiago Zanella Béguelin, Gustavo Betarte, and Carlos Luna

A Comparison of Semantic Models for Noninterference................ 235
    Ron van der Meyden and Chenyi Zhang

Hiding Information in Multi Level Security Systems 250
    Danièle Beauquier and Ruggero Lanotte

A New Trust Model Based on Advanced D-S Evidence Theory for P2P
Networks 270
    Chunqi Tian, Shihong Zou, Wendong Wang, and Shiduan Cheng

Author Index 285

Strategic Games on Defense Trees*

Stefano Bistarelli[1,2], Marco Dall'Aglio[1], and Pamela Peretti[1]

[1] Dipartimento di Scienze, Università degli Studi "G. d'Annunzio", Pescara, Italy
{bista,maglio,peretti}@sci.unich.it
[2] Istituto di Informatica e Telematica, CNR, Pisa, Italy
Stefano.Bistarelli@iit.cnr.it

Abstract. In this paper we use defense trees, an extension of attack trees with countermeasures, to represent attack scenarios and game theory to detect the most promising actions attacker and defender. On one side the attacker wants to break the system (with as little efforts as possible), on the opposite side the defender want to protect it (sustaining the minimum cost).

As utility function for the attacker and for the defender we consider economic indexes (like the Return on Investment (ROI) and the Return on Attack (ROA)). We show how our approach can be used to evaluate effectiveness and economic profitability of countermeasures as well as their deterrent effect on attackers, thus providing decision makers with a useful tool for performing better evaluation of IT security investments during the risk management process.

Keywords: Security, Risk Analysis, Game Theory.

1 Introduction

Security has become today a fundamental part of the enterprise investment. In fact, more and more cases are reported showing the importance of assuring an adequate level of protection to the enterprise's assets.

In order to focus on the real and concrete threats that could affect the enterprise's assets, a risk management process is needed in order to identify, describe and analyze the possible vulnerabilities that must be eliminated or reduced. The final goal of the process is to make security managers aware of the possible risks, and to guide them toward the adoption of a set of countermeasures which bring the overall risk under an acceptable level.

The determination of the acceptable risk level and the selection of the best countermeasure is unfortunately not an easy task. There are no standard methodologies for the process, and often security managers have to decide among too many alternatives.

To model the attack scenario and the defender possibilities we use *defense trees* [1], an extension of attacks trees with countermeasures. The vulnerabilities are represented as leaf nodes of the tree and are decorated with the countermeasures able to mitigate the damage of threats using such a vulnerability.

---

* Partially supported by the MIUR PRIN 2005-015491.

T. Dimitrakos et al. (Eds.): FAST 2006, LNCS 4691, pp. 1–15, 2007.

Moreover, economic indexes are used as labels for countermeasures and attacks. The *Return on Investment* (ROI) [18,17] index gives a measure of the efficacy of a specific security investment in a countermeasure w.r.t. a specific attack. The *Return on Attack* (ROA) [3] is instead an index that is aimed at measuring the convenience of attacks, by considering the impact of a security solution on the attacker's behavior.

The computed ROI and ROA function are then considered as utility functions (payoffs) in a two player strategic game. On one side the system administrator wants to protect the system by buying and adopting countermeasures; on the other side the attacker wants to exploit the vulnerabilities and obtain some profit by breaking the system.

We solve the games by looking at their Nash equilibria with both pure and mixed strategies. Our results show that is always worth installing countermeasures for the defender; however, it is not true that increasing the number of countermeasure gives an overall better benefit to the enterprise (as showed in [7] investing in security measure is not profitable beyond a certain level). This is not completely surprising, since more and more sophisticated protection may be accompanied by escalating marginal costs, while the probability that any given type of protection will be needed (that is, its expected benefit) may remain constant. Also interesting is the fact that the strategies of *no-attacks* and *no-countermeasures* is not (unfortunately) a point of equilibrium.

After an introduction to the concepts of security risk management and of defense trees (Section 2) we study the selection of the most promising countermeasures by interpreting the scenario as a game with two players: the defender and the attacker (Section 3). Section 4, instead, shows a realistic example where the attacker wants to steal information about customers maintained in a server. Finally, Section 5 summarizes the paper results and sketches some directions for future work.

2   Security Risk Management and Defense Trees

Defending an IT system is hard because many are the risks that can affect each asset of the system. Organizations need a process that enable to identify, describe and analyze the possible vulnerability that can be exploited by an adverse individual, and identify the security measures necessary to reduce the risks.

In [1] we propose the use of the *defense tree* (extension of *attack trees* [15,16]), an instrument for representing an attack against a system and how it can be mitigated by a set of countermeasures.

The difference between an attack tree and a defense tree is that the first represents only the attack strategies that an attacker can perform, while the second adds the set of countermeasures that can be introduced into the system to mitigate the possible damages produced by an attack.

Integrating countermeasures into threat trees, and more generally into directed acyclic graphs, is not new. In the early 90s researchers used "threat countermeasure diagrams". One may also see examples of countermeasures in DAGs in both Nathalie Foster's thesis [4] and Stuart Schechter's thesis [14], both of which include discussions and histories of the evolution of these structures. Even in the popular Microsoft text by Howard and LeBlanc, "Writing Secure Code", one can find threat trees (another name for attack trees) in which countermeasures are integrated [8].

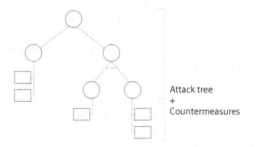

Attack tree
+
Countermeasures

Fig. 1. A defense tree

Figure 1 shows an example of a defense tree: round nodes form the attack tree and square nodes represent the corresponding countermeasures. The root of the tree is associated with an asset of the IT system under consideration and represents the attacker's goal. Leaf nodes in the attack tree represent simple subgoals which lead the attacker to (partially) damage the asset by exploiting a single vulnerability. Non-leaf nodes (including the tree root) can be of two different types: or-nodes and and-nodes. Subgoals associated with or-nodes are completed as soon as any of its child nodes is achieved, while and-nodes represent subgoals which require all of its child nodes to be completed (in Figure 1 we draw an horizontal line between the children of an and-node to distinguish it from the or-node).

We consider defense trees [1] enriched with economic indexes that quantify the cost of attacks and the return on security investments in any branch of the tree. We interpret such indexes as utility functions for the system administrator and for the attacker, by viewing the scenario as a classical game with two player looking for different and usually opposite results (see Section 3).

In particular we label the tree with:

1. the *Return On Investment* (*ROI*) [17] measuring the return that a defender expects from a security investment over the costs he sustains for countermeasures. It is calculated with the formula:

$$ROI = \frac{ALE \times RM - CSI}{CSI}$$

where:
   - the *Annualized Loss Expectancy* (*ALE*) [9] measures the expected annual financial loss which can be ascribed to a threat to the organization. It is calculated as $ALE = AV \times EF \times ARO$, where:

- the *Asset Value* (*AV*) is a measure of the cost of creation, development, support, replacement and ownership values of an asset,
- the *Exposure Factor* (*EF*) represents a measure of the magnitude of loss or impact on the value of an asset arising from a threat (expressed as a percentage of the asset value),
- the *Annualized Rate of Occurrence* (*ARO*) is a number that represents the estimated number of annual occurrences of a threat.
  - the *Risk Mitigated* by a countermeasure (*RM*) represents the effectiveness of a countermeasure in mitigating the risk of loss deriving from exploiting a vulnerability (*RM* is a numeric value in [0,1] that measures the proportion of reduced risk),
  - the *Cost of Security Investment* (*CSI*) is the cost that an enterprise sustains for implementing a given countermeasure.
2. the *Return On Attack* (*ROA*) [3] measures the gain that an attacker expects from a successful attack over the losses that he sustains due to the adoption of security measures by his target. It is calculated as:

$$ROA = \frac{GI \times (1 - RM) - (cost_a + cost_{ac})}{cost_a + cost_{ac}}$$

where:
  - *GI* is the expected gain from the successful attack on the specified target,
  - $cost_a$ is the cost sustained by the attacker to succeed,
  - $cost_{ac}$ is the additional cost brought by the countermeasure c adopted by the defender to mitigate the attack a.

We will see in Section 3 that other choices for the utility functions are possible. For instance we could consider ROI and ROA without dividing the gain by the costs (CSI and $cost_a + cost_{ac}$ respectively), or by considering the damage of an attack without considering its (often unknown) rate of occurrence (ARO).

3   Defense Trees as Strategic Games

In this section we will show how game theory can be used to analyze the possible strategies of the system administrator and of the attacker. In our scenario we consider a strategic game [6] that consists of:

- n players (n is usually just 2, but we plan to extend it to the case of 1 defender and k attackers),
- a set of strategies S_i for each player i,
- the utility function (or payoff) u_i for each player i.

We consider here the case with $n = 2$ players: the *defender* (Bob) and the *attacker* (Alice) of a system. The set of defender's strategies is the set of countermeasures that he can introduce into the systems while the set of attacker's strategies is the set of vulnerability that she can exploit. The payoff functions we will consider are the Return on Investment (ROI) for the defender and the

Return on Attack (ROA) for the attacker. Notice that ROI and ROA represent normalized payoffs; in some cases a not normalized utility function could be used instead, that may lead to different equilibrium strategies (because each player is trying to maximize its return rather than its payoff).

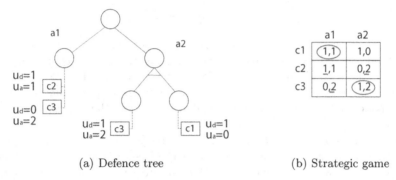

(a) Defence tree   (b) Strategic game

Fig. 2. Defense tree and the corresponding strategic game (with a pure strategy Nash Equilibrium)

As an example consider the defense tree depicted in Figure 2(a). It can be modeled as the strategic game in Figure 2(b), where:

- the players of the game are the defender of the enterprise that can select actions represented in the rows, and the attacker that can choose possible attacks (represented as columns in the table),
- the defender's set of strategies is $S_d = \{c_1, c_2, c_3\}$, that consists of the possible countermeasures that he can enforce to protect the system,
- the attacker's set of action is $S_a = \{a_1, a_2\}$ that represents the two possible attack strategies (the columns in Figure 2(b));
- the goal of each player is to maximize his/her own payoff function (the number in each box of Figure 2(b)). The payoffs associated to a strategy (c_i, a_i) are $u_d(c_i, a_i)$ for the defender, and $u_a(c_i, a_i)$ for the attacker.

Each player chooses the best available action given his belief about the other player's action.

The solution of the game is the (set of) countermeasure that the defender is more likely to adopt, and the (set of) vulnerability that the attacker feels more suitable to exploit. In some special cases the best strategy of the attacker and of the defender converges to a specific action profile s^* with the property that the defender cannot do better by choosing an action different from s_d^*, given that the attacker adopt s_a^*, and viceversa. In this case we say that the game admits a *Nash Equilibrium* [13].

Definition 1 (Nash Equilibrium [6]). *In a strategic game with 2 players, consider the sets S_1, S_2 and the functions u_1, u_2 that are the set of possible* *strategies and the utility functions of players 1 and 2 respectively. The combination of strategy (s_1^*, s_2^*) with $s_1^* \in S_1$ and $s_2^* \in S_2$ is a Nash Equilibrium if and only if, for each player i, the action s_i^* is the best response to the other player:*

$$u_1(s_1^*, s_2^*) \geq u_1(s_1, s_2^*) \text{ for any } s_1 \in S_1$$

$$u_2(s_1^*, s_2^*) \geq u_2(s_1^*, s_2) \text{ for any } s_2 \in S_2$$

Figure 2(a) shows an example of defense tree where two possible attacks are represented: a_1 and a_2. The first one can be mitigated by two countermeasure c_2 and c_3, the second one can be mitigated by c_1 and c_3. Figure 2(b) shows the corresponding strategic game, where the numbers in the bimatrix are the payoffs associated to each player (associated as label to the tree as we will see in Section 3).

Using Definition 1 we can calculate the possible Nash Equilibria of the game. Notice that if the attacker plays strategy a_1 the best response for the defender is to play the strategies c_1 or c_2 (by looking at the first column on the left we can see that he can gain 1 instead of 0), while if the attacker plays strategy a_2 the best response is to play the strategies c_1 or c_3.

Conversely if the defender plays the strategy c_1 the best response for the attacker is play strategy a_1, if the defender plays the strategy c_2 the best response is to play strategy a_2 and if the defender plays strategy c_3 the best response for the attacker is to play strategies a_1 or a_2. The game admits two different Nash Equilibria (the circled payoffs): the couple of strategies $\{c_1, a_1\}$ and $\{c_3, a_2\}$.

The Nash Equilibrium represents the best strategies for both the attacker and the defender (with the hypothesis that neither the attacker nor the defender have any knowledge of the other). In the case depicted in Figure 2, the defender will select, if possible, both countermeasure $c1$ and $c3$. However if the financial resources available to the system administrator are limited, only countermeasure $c3$ will be selected (because it will cover both strategy of the attacks). In Section 4 a complete more realistic example will be presented where the economic indexes will be used for the selection.

Sometimes in a strategic game it is impossible to find a Nash Equilibrium. Moreover we often need to take into account the uncertainty of the player's behavior. In this case a player may consider a *mixed strategy*.

Definition 2 (Mixed strategy [6]). *Consider a strategic game with 2 players, $G = \{S_1, S_2; u_1, u_2\}$ where $S_i = \{s_{i1}, \ldots, s_{ik}\}$ the strategies of player i. A mixed strategy for player $1 \leq i \leq 2$ is a probability distribution $p_i = (p_{i1}, \ldots, p_{ik})$, where $0 \leq p_{ik}$.*

In our context the use of mixed strategies finds a justification in the fact that a player, especially the defender, deals with a single attacker, whose behavior is not known. He may assume, however, that this players is drawn from a population of attackers whose actions can be estimated as frequencies from previous attacks (leading to the notion of *repeated games* where the players can randomize their strategies).

What we obtain is shown in Figure 3. The Attacker A can play the strategy a_1 with probability p_{a_1}, and the strategy a_2 with probability p_{a_2}, whilst the Defender D plays the strategy c_i with probability p_{c_i}, with $1 \leq i \leq 3$.

		p_{a_1}	p_{a_2}
		a_1	a_2
p_{c_1}	c_1	$u_d(c_1,a_1), u_a(c_1,a_1)$	$u_d(c_1,a_2), u_a(c_1,a_2)$
p_{c_2}	c_2	$u_d(c_2,a_1), u_a(c_2,a_1)$	$u_d(c_2,a_2), u_a(c_2,a_2)$
p_{c_3}	c_3	$u_d(c_3,a_1), u_a(c_3,a_1)$	$u_d(c_3,a_2), u_a(c_3,a_2)$

Fig. 3. Mixed strategies

We can compute payoffs in presence of mixed strategies by taking into account probability distributions and computing expectations. If the defender uses a pure strategy[1] in response to a mixed strategy of the attacker, the resulting payoffs for each possible countermeasure c_i is:

$$u_d(c_i) = u_d(c_i, a_1) \times p_{a_1} + u_d(c_i, a_2) \times p_{a_2}$$

If the attacker uses a pure strategy in response of a mixed strategy of the defender the resulting payoffs for each attack a_i is:

$$u_a(a_i) = u_a(c_1, a_i) \times p_{c_1} + u_a(c_2, a_i) \times p_{c_2} + u_a(c_3, a_i) \times p_{c_3}$$

Definition 3. *Given a game with 2 players, and 2 sets of strategies $S_1 = \{s_{11}, \ldots, s_{1K_1}\}$ and $S_2 = \{s_{21}, \ldots, s_{2K_2}\}$, if player i believes that player j will play the strategies $(s_{j1}, \ldots, s_{jK_j})$ with probability $(p_{j1}, \ldots, p_{jK_j})$, the expected payoff for player i obtained with the pure strategy s_{ij} is:*

$$\sum_{k=1}^{K_j} p_{jk} u_i(s_{ij}, s_{jk})$$

We can use Definition 3 to solve the game in Figure 2 by using the mixed strategies. In particular suppose that the defender uses a pure strategy and the attacker plays a mixed strategy $\{a_1, a_2\}$ with probability (p_{a_1}, p_{a_2}) (as shown in Figure 4). The expected payoff for the defender, if the attacker plays a mixed strategy are:

$$1 \cdot p_{a_1} + 1 \cdot p_{a_2} = p_{a_1} + p_{a_2} \text{ for countermeasure } c_1$$
$$1 \cdot p_{a_1} + 0 \cdot p_{a_2} = p_{a_1} \qquad \text{ for countermeasure } c_2$$
$$0 \cdot p_{a_1} + 1 \cdot p_{a_2} = p_{a_2} \qquad \text{ for countermeasure } c_3$$

---

[1] A pure strategy is a strategy that a player plays with probability 1.

	p_{a1} a_1	p_{a2} a_2
p_{c1} c_1	1,1	1,0
p_{c2} c_2	1,1	0,2
p_{c3} c_3	0,2	1,2

Fig. 4. Example of mixed strategy

Conversely, if the attacker uses a pure strategy and the defender plays a mixed strategy $\{c_1, c_2, c_3\}$ with probability $(p_{c_1}, p_{c_2}, p_{c_3})$, the expected payoff for the defender are:

$$1 \cdot p_{c_1} + 1 \cdot p_{c_2} + 2 \cdot p_{c_3} = p_{c_1} + p_{c_2} + 2p_{c_3} \text{ for attack } a_1$$
$$0 \cdot p_{c_1} + 2 \cdot p_{c_2} + 2 \cdot p_{c_3} = 2p_{c_2} + 2p_{c_3} \qquad \text{for attack } a_2$$

Definition 4. *If the players 1 and 2 play respectively the strategies $(s_{11}, \ldots, s_{1J})$ with probability $p_1 = (p_{11}, \ldots, p_{1J})$, and $(s_{21}, \ldots, s_{2K})$ with probability $p_2 = (p_{21}, \ldots, p_{2K})$, the expected payoff for the players are computed as follows:*

$$v_1(p_1, p_2) = \sum_{j=1}^{J} p_{1j} \left[\sum_{k=1}^{K} p_{2k} u_1(s_{1j}, s_{2k}) \right] = \sum_{j=1}^{J} \sum_{k=1}^{K} p_{1j} \cdot p_{2k} u_1(s_{1j}, s_{2k})$$

$$v_2(p_1, p_2) = \sum_{k=1}^{K} p_{2k} \left[\sum_{j=1}^{J} p_{1j} u_2(s_{1j}, s_{2k}) \right] = \sum_{j=1}^{J} \sum_{k=1}^{K} p_{1j} \cdot p_{2k} u_2(s_{1j}, s_{2k})$$

The mixed strategies (p_1^*, p_2^*) are a Nash Equilibrium only if the mixed strategy for each player is the best response to the mixed strategy of the other player:

$$v_1(p_1^*, p_2^*) \geq v_1(p_1, p_2^*) \text{ for any } p_1$$

$$v_2(p_1^*, p_2^*) \geq v_2(p_1^*, p_2) \text{ for any } p_2.$$

By applying Definition 4 we can now compute the Nash Equilibrium when the defender and the attacker adopt mixed strategies(Figure 4).

The utility of the defender u_d and of the attacker u_a are respectively:

$$u_d = 1p_{c_1}p_{a_1} + 1p_{c_1}p_{a_2} + 1p_{c_2}p_{a_1} + 1p_{c_3}p_{a_2}$$

$$u_a = 1p_{c_1}p_{a_1} + 1p_{c_2}p_{a_1} + 2p_{c_2}p_{a_2} + 2p_{c_3}p_{a_1} + 2p_{c_3}p_{a_2}.$$

Figure 5 shows an equilibrium with mixed strategy for the game: the defender plays the strategy c_1 with probability $\frac{1}{2}$ and c_2 with probability $\frac{1}{2}$, the attacker plays a_1 with probability 1.

	a₁	a₂
$\frac{1}{2}$ c₁	1,1	1,0
$\frac{1}{2}$ c₂	1,1	0,2
c₃	0,2	1,2

Fig. 5. Example of mixed strategy

4 Using Economic Indexes as Payoffs

In this section we show how to model a security problem by using the results highlighted in the previous section. An enterprise's server is used to store information about customers. Consider the defense tree depicted in Fig. 6 reflecting attacks to the server (the asset) and the corresponding mitigation countermeasures.

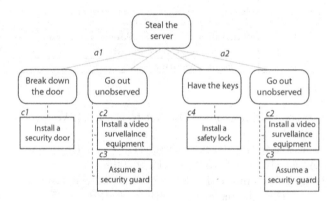

Fig. 6. Example of defense tree: theft of a server

In the example we consider a server with a value of 100.000 €. The Exposure Factor (EF) and the Annualized Rate of Occurrence (ARO) of each attack are shown in Table 1. Notice that associated to the risk management process is the lack of reliable statistical data to use in a quantitative analysis. In our paper we use (when available) statistics collected in [12] that combine the information from two surveys: a magazine survey in Information Week (October 1996) that asked "What Security Problems have resulted in financial losses?", and another magazine survey, in InfoSecurity News May 1997 that asked "In the past 12 months, which of the following breaches have you experienced?".

We need now to compute ALE for each of the possible attacks. Considering the first attack of Figure 6 we can notice that for a successful attack we need both to break down the door and to go out unobserved. So, the EF and ARO

Table 1. Computation of ROI

Attack	EF	ARO	Countermeasures	RM	CSI	ROI
a1 Break down	90%	0,1	c1 Install a security door	0,7	1500	3.20
the door			c2 Install a video surveillance equip.	0,1	3000	-0.70
and go out			c3 Employ a security guard	0,5	12000	-0.63
unobserved			c4 Install a security lock	0	300	-1
a2 Open the door	93%	0,1	c1 Install a security door	0	1500	-1
with keys			c2 Install a video surveillance equip.	0,1	3000	-0.69
and go out			c3 Employ a security guard	0,5	12000	-0.61
unobserved			c4 Install a security lock	0,2	300	5.20

Table 2. Computation of ROA

Attack	$Cost_a$	Countermeasures	$Cost_{ac}$	ROA
a1 Break down	4000	c1 Install a security door	2000	0.50
the door		c2 Install a video surveillance equipment	1000	4.40
and go out		c3 Employ a security guard	1500	1.73
unobserved		c4 Install a security lock	0	6.50
a2 Open the door	4200	c1 Install a security door	0	6.14
with keys		c2 Install a video surveillance equipment	1000	4.19
and go out		c3 Employ a security guard	1500	1.63
unobserved		c4 Install a security lock	200	4.45

are associated to the pair of actions (and not to the leaf). We proceed similarly for the second attack.

The ALE associated to the attack are, respectively, $ALE =100.000 € \times 0.9 \times 0.1 =9.000 €$ and $ALE =100.000 € \times 0.93 \times 0.1 =9.300 €$.

The second step is to compute the ROI for each countermeasure by considering the cost (CSI) and the amount of risk mitigated (RM) of Table 1. Notice that the countermeasures c_1 and c_4 have two different RM values: in Figure 6 we can see that c_1 is used only to mitigate the attack a_1 in this case the value of RM is 0.7, but if it is used to mitigate the attack a_2 the value of decreases to 0. The same is true for the countermeasure c_4, if it is used to mitigate the attack a_2 the value of RM is 0.2 but if it is used for the attack a_1 RM is 0.

For the first countermeasure (installing a security door to mitigate the threat of breaking down a door), we have $ROI = \frac{(ALE \times RM) - CSI}{CSI} = \frac{(9.000 € \times 0.7) - 1.500 €}{1.500 €} = 3.20$. Similarly we can compute the ROI for all the other countermeasure as shown in Table 1.

For ROA we analyze the scenario from the attacker perspective. Let us suppose that the attacker has an advantage that can be economically quantified as 30.000 € for a successful attack to the server. By using the data in Table 2 we compute the ROA for each countermeasure.

Notice that the cost an attacker has to pay depends on the attack and on the countermeasure installed. In Table 2, for instance, the fixed cost to be sustained by the attacker from stealing the server is different ($4.000\,€$ or $4.200\,€$): the variable costs instead depends on the specific countermeasure ($2.000\,€$ when encountering a security door vs $1.000\,€$ for a video surveillance installation).

The data in the table are used to compute ROA for all the countermeasures in the tree. So, for instance when installing a security door we can obtain a $ROA = \frac{GI \times (1-RM) - (cost_a + cost_{ac})}{cost_a + cost_{ac}} = \frac{30.000\,€ \times (1-0.7) - (4.000\,€ + 2.000\,€)}{4.000\,€ + 2.000\,€} = 0.50$. In a similar manner we can compute ROA for all the other countermeasures as shown in Table 2.

The resulting defense tree labeled with ROI and ROA for each countermeasure and attack is depicted in Figure 7.

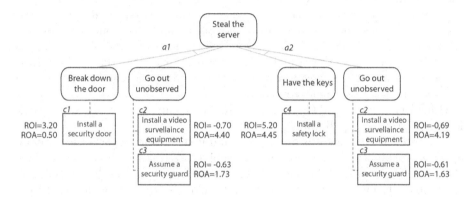

Fig. 7. The defense tree of Fig. 6 decorated with ROIs and ROAs

4.1   Selection of a Single Countermeasure/Attack

To model the defense tree as a strategic game we consider the set of strategies for the defender as composed by single countermeasures as represented in Figure 6. In a similar manner the strategies for the attacker are just a_1 (the left hand side of the tree) and a_2 (the right hand side). The utility functions are the indexes ROI and ROA introduced in Section 2 as described in the bimatrix of Figure 8.

Now, using Definition 1, we look for a Nash Equilibrium of the game. From the attacker's viewpoint: if the defender plays the strategy c_1 the best response of the attacker is to play the strategy a_2, if he plays strategies c_2, c_3 or c_4 the best response is strategy a_1. Instead, from the defender's viewpoint: if the attacker plays strategy a_1 the defender's best response is to play c_1, while if she plays a_2 or a_3 the defender plays c_4.

As consequence there are no Nash Equilibrium with pure strategies. In fact, our game is similar to a constant sum game where the payoffs of the two players have opposite rewards. The absence of so-called equilibrium points or saddle points (optimal for all players at once) means that there are no optimal situations in the sense that they provide to each participant the maximum of what he/she can get given the acts of the other players.

	a1	a2
c1	3.20,0.50	-1.00,6.14
c2	-0.70,4.40	-0.69,4.19
c3	-0.63,1.73	-0.61,1.63
c4	-1.00,6.50	5.20,4.45

Fig. 8. Bimatrix for the attacker/defender game with single selection of countermeasures/attacks

So there are no stable strategies to follow for the defender and the attacker in the game. In spite of the absence of a rational choice (some advice can be however given following other approaches [1]), when the game is repeated many times, some optimal lines of behavior can be found. To find them one must extend the analysis to include the adoption of mixed strategies by the players. As the criterion for the choice of optimal mixed strategies one takes the mathematical expectation value of the payoff which shows how much one can win on average by repeating the game many times.

Using Definition 4 (and Gambit [11], a tool for computing equilibria[2]) we look for mixed strategy equilibria.

The result is that there is one equilibrium if the defender plays the strategy c_1 with probability $\frac{205}{769}$ and c_4 with probability $\frac{564}{769}$, and if the attacker plays the strategy a_1 with probability $\frac{31}{52}$ and a_2 with probability $\frac{21}{52}$. We see that the probability for the two attacks are pretty close, so the system administrator cannot consider to reduce the attention to only one of the two branches. Moreover, it seems that the best that a system administrator can do is to invest in the countermeasure c_1 to avoid the first attack *and* in the countermeasure c_4 to avoid the second attack.

Notice however that this strategy is not so natural; in fact, why not to invest in countermeasure c_3 to be able to partially cover both the attacks? In the example studied here we do not study indeed the possibility to have both the attacks occurring simultaneously and to have more then one countermeasure implemented.

4.2   Selection of Set of Countermeasures/Attacks

In the previous strategic game we considered only one attack/countermeasure strategy by each players. Here, instead, each player can play any set of countermeasures/attacks together (but we have also the possibility to select no attack or countermeasure).

In order to avoid some technical problems (division by 0) when dealing with empty sets of countermeasures or attacks we change the utility functions for the two players. We retain the numerator from the old utility functions.

$$u_d = ALE \times RM - CSI$$
$$u_a = GI \times (1 - RM) - (cost_a + cost_{ac})$$

---

[2] Available at http://econweb.tamu.edu/gambit/

	∅	a1	a2	{a1,a2}
∅	0, 0	0, 26.000	0, 25.800	0, 21.800
c1	-1.500, 0	4.800, 3.000	-1.500, 25.800	11.310, -1.200
c2	-3.000, 0	-2.100, 22.000	-2.070, 21.800	-1.170, 17.800
c3	-12.000, 0	-7.500, 9.500	-7.350, 9.300	-2.850, 5.300
c4	-300, 0	-300, 26.000	1.560, 19.600	3.360, 15.500
{c1,c2}	-4.500, 0	1.800, 2.000	-3.570, 21.800	8.310, -2.200
{c1,c3}	-13.500, 0	-7.200, 1.500	-8.850, 9.300	-690, -2.700
{c1,c4}	-1.800, 0	4.500, 3.000	60, 18.600	11.010, -1.500
{c2,c3}	-15.000, 0	-10.500, 8.500	-10.350, 8.300	-5.850, 4.300
{c2,c4}	-3.300, 0	-2.400, 22.000	-1.440, 18.600	360, 14.500
{c3,c4}	-12.300, 0	-7.800, 9.500	-7.650, 9.100	-3.150, 5.000
{c1,c2,c3}	-16.500, 0	-10.200, 500	-11.850, 8.300	-3.690, -3.700
{c1,c2,c4}	-4.800, 0	1.500, 2.000	-2.940, 18.600	8.010, -2.500
{c1,c3,c4}	-13.800, 0	-7.500, 1.500	-9.150, 9.100	-990, -3.000
{c2,c3,c4}	-15.300, 0	-10.800, 8.500	-10.650, 8.100	-6.150, 4.000
{c1,c2,c3,c4}	-16.800, 0	-10.500, 500	-12.150, 8.100	-3.990, -4.000

Fig. 9. Bimatrix for the attacker/defender game with a set selection of countermeasures/attacks

Using the new utility functions we obtain the strategic game of Figure 9.

Once again there are no Nash Equilibria with pure strategy, but Gambit computes a mixed equilibrium where the defender plays the strategy c_4 with probability $\frac{39}{55}$ and $\{c_1, c_4\}$ with probability $\frac{16}{55}$, and the attacker plays the strategy a_1 with probability $\frac{5}{21}$ and a_2 with probability $\frac{16}{21}$.

As a side result we note that two compound strategies by the attacker, namely ∅ and $\{a_1, a_2\}$, are uniformly dominated by the simple strategies a_1 and a_2. This shows that the attacker has no interest in combining the actions together.

5   Conclusions and Future Work

The use of game theory, allow us to model the interaction between the attacker and the defender: they represent two players with opposite goals. The tactical choices of each one of the player strictly depends from the moves of the other. In particular, when an attacker has to select a possible attack for an asset, he/she has to consider necessarily the possible countermeasure that the defender have introduced into the system; vice-versa, when a system administrator has to select which countermeasure introduce in order to protect the system, he has to consider the possible attacks that the attacker could perform.

Using the Nash Equilibria allow us to model the above situation where attacker and defender need to take some decision. The Nash equilibrium has been used [10][5] to determine the best move of the two players, by considering the fix point of the interactions between attacker and defender.

In this paper we first, used defense trees as extension of attack trees with countermeasures and economic quantitative indexes for modeling attack scenarios.

Then such scenarios are analyzed as strategic games. The strategies of the two players (the defender can select countermeasures and the attacker can choose among several vulnerabilities to exploit) lead to different payoffs represented as economic indexes. In particular ROI and ROA are used. The study confirms that investments beyond a certain level do not produce any beneficial effect after a certain point are not anymore useful [7] (so, only a subset of the countermeasure usually has to be considered).

The methodology presented in this paper provides a basis for future work along several research directions.

While it may seem obvious to compute the solution cost of a set $C = \{c_1, c_2\}$ of countermeasures as the sum $CSI_C = CSI_{c_1} + CSI_{c_2}$ of the costs of the single countermeasures in C, it should be noticed that the total cost of implementing a set of countermeasures could realistically be less than CSI_C (e.g. discounted price of bundled security solutions) or greater than CSI_C (e.g. when countermeasures must be managed by different employees, due to the existence of separation of duty constraints [2]).

On the other hand, it is not clear how to compute the value of the Risk Mitigated attribute for a set of countermeasures $\{c_1, c_2\}$, as any value between $\max(RM_{c_1}, RM_{c_2})$ (one countermeasure strictly entails the other) and $(RM_{c_1} + RM_{c_2})$ (completely independent countermeasures) appears to be acceptable depending on the type and nature of countermeasures and the asset being protected.

We plan to extend this work by considering n player games (where we have 1 defender and $n-1$ attackers). This could lead to interesting discussion about the amount of cooperation between the attacker. Usually attackers try to cooperate, unless the cooperation reduces their gain too much (that is, the benefit coming from the attack has to be divided among them).

When considering several attackers also notions of *types* (and bayesian games) could be important. From which type of attacker we expect to have the attack? We can differentiate between attacker w.r.t. their propension/aversion to risk?

Dynamic games provide another source for extension. Repeat games with the normal games described above as a stage game could be considered. As well a game when both players refine their information as the sequence of attacks and countermeasures progress.

We hope our work can help encourage research and experimentation with the use of economic indexes and combined development of attacker/defender perspectives during evaluation of alternative security investments.

References

1. Bistarelli, S., Fioravanti, F., Peretti, P.: Defense tree for economic evaluations of security investment. In: 1st International Conference on Availability, Reliability and Security (ARES'06), pp. 416–423 (2006)
2. Clark, D.D., Wilson, D.R.: A comparison of commercial and military computer security policies. In: IEEE Symposium on Computer Security and Privacy (1987)

3. Cremonini, M., Martini, P.: Evaluating information security investments from attackers perspective: the Return-On-Attack (ROA). In: Fourth Workshop on the Economics of Information Security (June 2005)
4. Foster, N.L.: The application of software and safety engineering techniques to security protocol development. PhD thesis, University of York, Department of Computer Science (2002)
5. Fudenberg, D., Tirole, J.: Game Theory. MIT Press, Cambridge (1991)
6. Gibbons, R.: A Primer in Game Theory. Pearson Higher Education (1992)
7. Gordon, L.A., Loeb, M.P.: The economics of information security investment. ACM Trans. Inf. Syst. Secur. 5(4), 438–457 (2002)
8. Howard, LeBlanc.: Writing Secure Code. Microsoft Press, Redmond (2002)
9. Krutz, R.L., Vines, R.D., Stroz, E.M.: The CISSP Prep Guide: Mastering the Ten Domains of Computer Security. Wiley, Chichester (2001)
10. Liu, Y.: Intrusion Detection for Wireless Networks. PhD thesis, Stevens Institute of Technology (2006)
11. McKelvey, R.D., McLennan, A.M., Turocy, T.L.: Gambit: Software tools for game theory (version 0.2006.01.20) (2006), http://econweb.tamu.edu/gambit
12. Meritt, J.W.: A method for quantitative risk analysis. In: Proceedings of the 22nd National Information Systems Security Conference (October 1999)
13. Osborne, M.J.: An introduction to game theory. Oxford Univ. Press, Oxford (2003)
14. Schechter, S.E.: Computer Security Strength & Risk: A Quantitative Approach. PhD thesis, Harvard University (May 2004)
15. Schneier, B.: Attack trees: Modeling security threats. Dr. Dobb's Journal (1999)
16. Schneier, B.: Secrets & Lies: Digital Security in a Networked World. John Wiley & Sons, Chichester (2000)
17. Sonnenreich, W., Albanese, J., Stout, B.: Return On Security Investment (ROSI): A practical quantitative model. In: Security in Information Systems, Proceedings of the 3rd International Workshop on Security in Information Systems, WOSIS 2005, pp. 239–252. INSTICC Press (2005)
18. Stoneburner, G., Goguen, A., Feringa, A.: Risk management guide for information technology systems. Nist special publication 800–830, NIST, National Institute of Standard Technology (July 2002)

Timed Calculus of Cryptographic Communication

Johannes Borgström[1], Olga Grinchtein[2], and Simon Kramer[3]

[1] EECS, Technical University of Berlin
jobo@cs.tu-berlin.de
[2] IT, Uppsala University
olgag@it.uu.se
[3] Ecole Polytechnique Fédérale de Lausanne (EPFL)
simon.kramer@a3.epfl.ch

Abstract. We extend the (core) Calculus of Cryptographic Communication (C^3) with real time, e.g., time stamps and timed keys. We illustrate how to use this extended calculus (tC^3) on a specification and verification case study, namely the failure of the Wide-Mouthed-Frog protocol in its original, i.e., timed, version.

Keywords: Applied process calculi, timed cryptographic protocols, formal modelling, model-based specification and verification.

1 Introduction

Timed — as opposed to untimed — cryptographic protocols have received comparatively little attention from the formal methods community so far. The only timed formalisms for the modelling, specification, and verification of such protocols we are aware of are Timed CSP [1], tock-CSP [2], tCryptoSPA [3], the timed Spi-Calculus [4], and the (unnamed) process model from [5] (which we will refer to as tBEL). (Although Timed CSP and tock-CSP are special-purpose w.r.t. the temporal aspect, they — like core CSP — are actually not special-purpose w.r.t. the cryptographic aspect.) For practical usability, special-purpose models of timed cryptographic protocols are preferable over their general-purpose counterparts because (untimed) general-purpose models tend to create considerable (en)coding overhead: "[...] the coding up required would make the complex behaviour difficult to understand, and it is preferable to use a language designed to express such real-time behaviour." [2].

In tock-CSP, tCryptoSPA, and timed Spi-Calculus time is *natural*-number valued. tock-CSP and tCryptoSPA provide local processes that globally synchronise through so-called tock events resp. tick actions, which represent the passage of one unit of time. And the timed Spi-Calculus provides a process constructor for querying a global clock. Thus, tock-CSP, tCryptoSPA, and the timed Spi-Calculus lack local clocks that potentially advance at different rates across different processes/locations. However [6], "[c]locks can become unsynchronized due to sabotage on or faults in the clocks or the synchronization mechanism, such as overflows and the dependence on potentially unreliable clocks on remote sites [...]". Moreover [6], "[e]rroneous behaviors are generally expected during clock failures [...]" Hence, a faithful model of timed cryptographic protocols must allow for potentially desynchronised, local clocks.

T. Dimitrakos et al. (Eds.): FAST 2006, LNCS 4691, pp. 16–30, 2007.

In tBEL, time — in particular, a time stamp — is *real*-number valued, yielding a *dense* time domain. We contend that real-valued time-stamps are too fine-grained because protocol messages have finite length, which implies that real numbers are not transmittable as such. Moreover, real clocks only have finite precision. tBEL does provide local clocks, yet they "advance at the same rate as time." [5, Page 2]. Further, adversarial break of short-term keys is modelled only indirectly with a parallel process rather than directly as part of the adversary model. Furthermore, tBEL lacks a process equivalence. On the other hand, tBEL comes with a (third-order) special-purpose logic for reasoning about tBEL models, and a decision procedure for a class of reachability properties of bounded protocols based on syntactic control points. In our opinion, tBEL and its associated logic are unnecessarily domain-specific. They seem to have been built from scratch rather than as Occham's-razor extensions of untimed formalisms. Adding real-time to a model or logic without explicit time can be simple [7].

In contrast to the models discussed, tC^3 extends C^3 [8] with (1) *rational*-number valued time (which still is dense), (2) local clocks that may progress at different rates across different locations, and (3) adversarial break of short-term keys based on ciphertext-only attacks enabled by key expiration. Moreover, tC^3 comes with a notion of observational process equivalence for model-based protocol specification and verification. As a property-based complement, we have also *co-designed* a logic, namely tCPL [9,10], for tC^3. The three primary features of the co-design of tC^3 and tCPL are that (1) tC^3's notion of execution is a temporal accessibility relation for tCPL's temporal modalities, (2) tC^3's notion of observational equivalence and tCPL's notion of propositional knowledge have a common definitional basis, namely an epistemic accessibility relation defined in terms of structurally indistinguishable protocol histories, and (3) execution constraints of tC^3-processes are checkable via tCPL-satisfaction. These three features, especially Feature 2, are the result of our wholistic conception of model-based (process algebra) and property-based (modal logic) specification and verification as two truly complementary approaches. Other important features of C^3, and thus of tC^3, are explicit out-of-band communication and history-based key (and for tC^3, clock value) lookup. C^3 neatly extends to tC^3 by maintaining backwards compatibility. Essentially, only two additional axioms (and no modified axioms/rules!) are needed in its operational semantics.

2 Definition

Our timed Calculus of Cryptographic Communication is a conservative extension of a core calculus [8]. Core C^3 consists of a language of distributed processes and an associated notion of concurrent execution in the style of structural operational semantics (SOS). Its *modelling hypotheses* are those of abstract ideal cryptography and interleaving concurrency. Cryptography is abstract in the sense that communicated information atoms (names) are logical constants and communicated information compounds are syntactic terms. We use pattern matching as a linguistic abstraction for cryptographic computation. Cryptography is ideal in the sense that cryptographic primitives are assumed to be perfect, i.e., unbreakable. Process execution engenders the activity of protocol participants and the standard Dolev-Yao adversary **Eve**, i.e., the generation of a history of legitimate resp. illegitimate protocol events, and the evolution of their respective knowledge computed from that history.

We extend C^3 to tC^3 according to the following two *design principles*: first, for every legitimate participant and the adversary, we introduce a rational-number valued local clock with an associated drift rate, where the adversary's clock always displays the actual time; and second, we model the passage of (real) time by means of the adversary, who, at any (logical) time of protocol execution, may advance the time by an arbitrary but always finite amount by advancing her local clock. In this way, the adversary is in full control of time (subject to monotonicity). Adding communication and/or computation delays imposes non-zero lower bounds on the advancement of time between certain pairs of actions, and could be handled by only considering traces where the adversary respects these bounds.

2.1 Syntax

The syntactic novelties in tC^3 w.r.t. C^3 are the following. A set $\mathcal{TV} := \mathbb{Q} \cup \{\infty, -\infty\}$ of *time values* t with the associated sort TV; *temporal expressions* $E ::= t \mid E + E \mid E - E$ for the calculation of temporal intervals and bounds; a binary relational symbol $E @ a$ for testing the clock of a participant a with the time value E; *temporal inequalities* $E \leq E'$ for the comparison of time values; and an *action* Set E for clock (re)setting.

The full, sorted alphabet for information atoms in tC^3 is the following.

Definition 1 (Sorted names). *Names n are participant names $c, d \in \mathcal{P}$, the adversary's name Eve, symmetric keys $k \in \mathcal{K}$, private keys $p \in \mathcal{K}^-$, and nonces $x \in \mathcal{X}$ (also used as session identifiers). We assume that given a private key, one can compute the corresponding public key, as in DSA and Elgamal.*

The sorts σ corresponding to these kinds of names are P, Adv, K, K$^-$, *and* X, *respectively.* K, K$^-$, *and* X *are the sorts ς of freshly generable names.*

These sorted names (logical constants) are part of the language $\mathcal{M}$ of communicated messages in tC^3. $\mathcal{M}$ contains, besides the usual cryptographic constructions, a distinguished abstract message ■. This message is a computational artifice to represent the absence of *intelligibility*, just as the number zero is a computational artifice to represent the absence of *quantity*. The abstract message is very useful for doing knowledge-based calculations (e.g., as effectuated by tC^3's observational equivalence, cf. Section 2.3) just as the number zero is very useful (to say the least) for doing number-based calculations. The abstract message is also very useful for adding *backwards-compatible extensions* to the core calculus as we will show on the example of the present (real-time) extension in the sequel. Symmetric keys may be *compound* for key *agreement* (in addition to mere key *transport*).

Definition 2 (Messages and Message forms). *The structure of protocol messages $M \in \mathcal{M}$ is defined in Table 1. Message forms F are messages with variables $v \in \mathcal{V}$, and are used in process terms where they may instantiate to (transmittable) messages. Sorts of compound messages are macro-definable (cf. [8]).*

tC^3-processes are parallel compositions of *located threads*. A non-idle thread T located at the participant c and session x, written $c.x[\,T\,]$, has either an action prefix or a lookup

Table 1. Protocol messages

$$
\begin{aligned}
M ::= \ & n & \text{(names)} \\
| \ & \blacksquare & \text{(the abstract message)} \\
| \ & t & \text{(time values)} \\
| \ & p^+ & \text{(public keys)} \\
| \ & \lceil M \rceil & \text{(message hashes)} \\
| \ & \{\!|M|\!\}_M & \text{(symmetric message ciphers)} \\
| \ & \{\!|M|\!\}_{p^+}^+ & \text{(asymmmetric message ciphers)} \\
| \ & \{\!|M|\!\}_p^- & \text{(signed messages)} \\
| \ & (M, M) & \text{(message tuples)}
\end{aligned}
$$

prefix. The action prefixes $\mathsf{Out}_a\, F$ and $\mathsf{sOut}_a\, F$ express insecure (intercepted by the adversary) resp. secure (unobservable by the adversary) output of F to a; $\mathsf{In}\, \Pi$ **when** φ and $\mathsf{sIn}_a\, \Pi$ **when** φ express insecure resp. secure input (from a) of a message matching the pattern Π and having the property φ; $\mathsf{New}\,(v : \varsigma, (O, V))$ expresses the generation and binding to the variable v of a fresh name of type ς *tagged* with (O, T), where O (a tuple of participant names) stipulates intended ownership and V (a pair of temporal expressions) validity of the generated name; and $\mathsf{Set}\, E$ expresses the (re)setting of the local clock to the value E. The lookup prefix $\mathsf{Get}_a\,(v : \varsigma, O)$ in expresses the lookup and binding to v of a name of type ς generated by a with ownership tag O.

Observe that thanks to sorts, tags, and the abstract message the new-name and the lookup-prefix can also elegantly handle timed information: new-timed-key generation as $\mathsf{New}\,(v : \mathsf{K}, (O, V))$, timed-key lookup as $\mathsf{Get}_a\,(v : \mathsf{K}, O)$ in, and clock lookup as $\mathsf{Get}_a\,(v : \mathsf{TV}, \blacksquare)$ in. Finally, our communication model is based on participants rather than channels for separating specification from implementation concerns.

Definition 3 (Processes). *The structure of protocol processes $P \in \mathcal{P}$ is defined in Table 2. There, $a, b \in \mathcal{P} \cup \mathcal{V}$; $\cup$ means "freshly generated", : "has sort", k "knows", and $\preccurlyeq$ "is a subterm of". A process P is* epistemically local *:iff for all located threads $c.x[\,T\,]$ in P and for all $a.x \cup n.(O, V)$, $a\ \mathsf{k}\ F$, and $t@a$ in T, $a = c$. Implementation processes must be epistemically local, whereas specification processes need not be. In addition, in implementation processes $\forall v$ must not bind v in any F, whereas in specification processes this need not be.*

Action prefixes π, as opposed to the lookup prefix, generate events when executed. Action prefixes for secure I/O generate unobservable events; they model out-of-band communication such as trusted couriers, personal contact between communicating parties, and dedicated communication links. The same prefixes can also be used for (1) encoding extensions to the core calculus, such as *vertical composition* (i.e., sub-protocol calls), *conditionals* (i.e., execution guards); (2) defining *specification processes* relied upon by equivalence-based specification of secrecy; and (3) defining *initialisation traces* (cf. Section 3). The purpose of including session ids x in locations $c.x[\,T\,]$ is to enable the factorisation of the history of a protocol execution into individual sessions (cf. *strands* in strand spaces).

Table 2. Protocol processes

$$P ::= c.x[\,T\,] \mid P \parallel\!\parallel P$$

$$T ::= 1 \mid \pi.T \mid \mathsf{Get}_a\,(v : \varsigma, O)\ \text{in}\ T$$

$$\pi ::= \mathsf{Out}_a\,F \mid \mathsf{sOut}_a\,F \mid \mathsf{In}\,\Pi\ \text{when}\ \varphi \mid \mathsf{sIn}_a\,\Pi\ \text{when}\ \varphi \mid \mathsf{New}\,(v : \varsigma, (O, V)) \mid \mathsf{Set}\,E$$

$$\Pi ::= F \mid (\Pi, \Pi) \mid \langle\!\langle \Pi \rangle\!\rangle_{\overline{F}} \mid \langle\!\langle \Pi \rangle\!\rangle_{\overline{F}}^{+} \mid \langle\!\langle \Pi \rangle\!\rangle_{\overline{F}}^{-}$$

$$\varphi ::= E@a \mid E \le E \mid a.x \cup n.(O, V) \mid n : \sigma \mid a\,\mathsf{k}\,F \mid F \preccurlyeq F \mid \neg\varphi \mid \varphi \wedge \varphi \mid \forall v(\varphi)$$

2.2 Semantics

The semantic novelties in tC^3 w.r.t. C^3 are the following. *Calculation with temporal expressions*: a (partial) evaluation function $[\![\cdot]\!]$ takes temporal expressions to time values (where $[\![\infty - \infty]\!]$ and suchlike are undefined). *Protocol events*: we add events $\mathsf{S}(c, x, t)$ for the setting of c's clock to clock value t by c in session x. By convention, these events are unobservable by the adversary, i.e., they are secure. *Clock setting*: we add the rule SET (cf. Table 6) to the operational semantics. *Clock drifting*: we assume the existence of a total function δ from participants to drift rates (rational numbers). *Advancement of time*: we add the rule TIME (cf. Table 6) to the operational semantics.

tC^3 is a reduction calculus on protocol states $(P, \mathfrak{h})$, i.e., pairs of a process term $P \in \mathcal{P}$ and a protocol history $\mathfrak{h} \in \mathcal{H}$. Protocol histories are records of past protocol events ε, comprising: generation of a fresh name n with intended ownership O and (absolute) temporal validity V in session x by c, written $\mathsf{N}(c, x, n, (O, V))$; insecure input of M [...], written $\mathsf{I}(c, x, M)$; secure input of M from d [...], written $\mathsf{sI}(c, x, M, d)$; insecure output of M to d [...], written $\mathsf{O}(c, x, M, d)$; secure output of M to d [...], written $\mathsf{sO}(c, x, M, d)$; and setting of a clock to some time value, as mentioned above. Protocol histories $\mathfrak{h} \in \mathcal{H}$ are simply finite words of protocol events ε, i.e., event traces: $\mathfrak{h} ::= \epsilon \mid \mathfrak{h} \cdot \varepsilon$ where ϵ denotes the empty protocol history. tC^3 employs pattern matching as a linguistic abstraction for cryptographic computation, which is straightforward to implement [11]. When a message matches a pattern, the result is a substitution relating variables to matched subterms. Substitutions are partial functions from variables to messages, and are lifted to terms as usual. Matching is computed by the partial function match defined in Table 3. There, $\uplus$ denotes composition, if the domains of the operands are disjoint, and is otherwise undefined. Input guards φ are expressed in a decidable sub-language of our co-designed logic CPL. Their satisfaction is history dependent. Specifically, the knowledge of a participant depends only on the preceeding events witnessed by the participant in question. As an example, this lets us easily express that keys to be looked up must already be known to the participant looking them up.

Definition 4 (Satisfaction). *Satisfaction is defined in Table 4. There* data$_c(\mathfrak{h})$ *denotes the set of data that c has generated, received, or sent in $\mathfrak{h}$; and* analz$_{\mathfrak{h}}$ *and* synth *denote message analysis resp. synthesis [12,8]. Our analysis has the additional rule "if* $\mathfrak{h} \models t_{\mathsf{Eve}}@\mathsf{Eve} \wedge \exists v \exists v' \exists v''(v.v' \cup k.(v'', (t_b, t_e)))$ *and* $\mathfrak{h}' \models \exists m(\mathsf{Eve}\,\mathsf{k}\,\{\!|m|\!\}_k) \wedge \exists t(t@\mathsf{Eve} \wedge t_e - t_b < t_{\mathsf{Eve}} - t)$ *for some prefix $\mathfrak{h}'$ of $\mathfrak{h}$ then $k \in$ analz$_{\mathfrak{h}'}(\mathcal{K})$" for some set $\mathcal{K}$ of data known to the adversary. This rule models adversarial break of short-term keys based*

Table 3. Pattern matching

$$\text{match}(v, M) := \{{}^{M}/_{v}\}$$
$$\text{match}(M, M) := \emptyset$$
$$\text{match}((\Pi, \Pi'), (M, M')) := \text{match}(\Pi, M) \uplus \text{match}(\Pi', M')$$
$$\text{match}(\{\!|\Pi|\!\}_{\overline{M'}}, \{\!|M|\!\}_{M'}) := \text{match}(\Pi, M)$$
$$\text{match}(\{\!|\Pi|\!\}_{\overline{p}}^{+}, \{\!|M|\!\}_{p^{+}}^{+}) := \text{match}(\Pi, M)$$
$$\text{match}(\{\!|\Pi|\!\}_{\overline{p^{+}}}^{-}, \{\!|M|\!\}_{p}^{-}) := \text{match}(\Pi, M)$$

on ciphertext-only attacks enabled by key expiration $(t_e - t_b < t_{\text{Eve}} - t)$. Finally, our synthesis has the additional axiom "$t \in \text{synth}(\mathcal{K})$" for some set $\mathcal{K}$ of data known to the concerned agent.

Table 4. Satisfaction

$\mathfrak{h} \models E@a$:iff $[\![E]\!] = t + \delta_a \cdot \Delta$ where
- t denotes the time value of a's last clock-set event in $\mathfrak{h}$, i.e., there are $\mathfrak{h}_1, \mathfrak{h}_2, x$ s.t. $\mathfrak{h} = \mathfrak{h}_1 \cdot S(a, x, t) \circ \mathfrak{h}_2$ and there is no x', t' s.t. $S(a, x', t') \in \mathfrak{h}_2$
- $\delta_a \in \mathcal{TV}$ denotes the drift rate of a's local clock
- Δ denotes the temporal difference between Eve's last clock-set event before $S(a, x, t)$ and Eve's last clock-set event so far in $\mathfrak{h}$, i.e., $\Delta =$
$$\begin{cases} t_2 - t_1 & \text{if for } i \in \{1, 2\} \text{ there are } \mathfrak{h}_{i'}, \mathfrak{h}''_i, t_i \text{ s.t.} \\ & \mathfrak{h}_i = \mathfrak{h}'_i \cdot S(\text{Eve}, \blacksquare, t_i) \circ \mathfrak{h}''_i \text{ and there is no } t'_i \text{ s.t.} \\ & S(\text{Eve}, \blacksquare, t'_i) \in \mathfrak{h}''_i, \text{ and} \\ 0 & \text{otherwise.} \end{cases}$$

$\mathfrak{h} \models E \leq E'$:iff $[\![E]\!]$ is smaller than or equal to $[\![E']\!]$

$\mathfrak{h} \models c.x \cup n.(O, V)$:iff $N(c, x, n, t, (O, V)) \in \mathfrak{h}$

$\mathfrak{h} \models c \,\mathsf{k}\, M$:iff $M \in \text{synth}(\text{analz}_{\mathfrak{h}}(\text{data}_c(\mathfrak{h})))$

$\mathfrak{h} \models M \preccurlyeq M'$:iff M is a subterm of M'

$\mathfrak{h} \models n : \sigma$:iff n has sort σ

$\mathfrak{h} \models \neg \phi$:iff not $\mathfrak{h} \models \phi$

$\mathfrak{h} \models \phi \wedge \phi'$:iff $\mathfrak{h} \models \phi$ and $\mathfrak{h} \models \phi'$

$\mathfrak{h} \models \forall v(\phi)$:iff for all $M \in \mathcal{M}$, $\mathfrak{h} \models \{{}^{M}/_{v}\}\phi$

The key and clock store of each participant are induced by protocol events. Keys and clocks are looked up in the protocol history w.r.t. the local view of each participant. Lookup of keys additionally refers to their creator and the tag they were given at creation. We assume that the creator and the tag associated with a key are authentic and universally available (given possession of the key). This gives an approximation of certificate-based key lookup, where we explicitly model key distribution but key metadata is magically protected. A lookup succeeds when the desired tag is a subterm of the one used at the creation of the key. This lets us model cases where the same shared key is to be used whenever two participants take part in a protocol, independently of their roles, as well as making more complex key-sharing arrangements possible. We model lookup with the predicate $\mathsf{looksUp}(c, x, n, \varsigma, d, O)$ pronounced "c in session x looks up n of type ς generated by d with a tag containing O" and defined in Table 5. The conditions enforce that the retrieved name n is either the local time ($n@c$) or is a key which (1) has the desired type ($n : \varsigma$); (2) was known by c ($c \ \mathsf{k} \ n$); (3) was generated by d ($d.x' \cup v.(o, (t_b, t_e))$); (4) has a compatible, intended ownership ($O \leqslant o$); and (5) is perceived as timely by c ($\exists t_c(t_c@c \wedge t_b \leq t_c \leq t_e)$).

Table 5. Lookup predicate

$$\mathsf{looksUp}(c, x, n, \varsigma, d, O) := n : \varsigma \wedge c \ \mathsf{k} \ n \wedge (n@c \ \vee$$
$$\exists x' \exists v \exists o \exists t_b \exists t_e (d.x' \cup v.(o, (t_b, t_e)) \wedge$$
$$(n = v \vee n = v^+) \wedge O \leqslant o \wedge \exists t_c(t_c@c \wedge t_b \leq t_c \leq t_e)))$$

We are now ready to define our (process) reduction calculus tC^3.

Definition 5 (Process calculus). *Let* $\longrightarrow \subseteq (\mathcal{P} \times \mathcal{H}) \times (\mathcal{P} \times \mathcal{H})$, *defined in Table 6, denote reduction of protocol states* $\mathsf{s} \in \mathcal{P} \times \mathcal{H}$. *Then* tC^3 *denotes the Timed Calculus of Cryptographic Communication as defined below.*

$$tC^3 := \langle \mathcal{P} \times \mathcal{H}, \longrightarrow \rangle$$

The generation of a new name (Rule NEW and NEW-EVE) is possible only if that name has not been generated yet, i.e., names are always *fresh* w.r.t. the current state. The adversary Eve may generate a new name at any time. Insecure input (Rule IN) is generated by the adversary and may consist in any message from her knowledge that matches the input pattern Π and that satisfies the input constraint φ. Successful input results in the substitution of the matching message parts for the matched variables in the receiving thread. Secure communication (Rule sOUT, sIN and sCOM-L, with sCOM-R being tacit) is synchronous. To achieve this, we introduce two auxiliary transition relations $\xrightarrow{\mathsf{sI}}$ and $\xrightarrow{\mathsf{sO}}$ not visible on the top level. Insecure communication between two legitimate participants is asynchronous because it goes through the adversary, and secure communication is synchronous because it does not. Execution of parallel processes happens via *interleaving concurrency* (Rule PAR-L, PAR-R being tacit). Finally, observe how *non-determinism* abstracts away four determining choices in the execution of a protocol, i.e., the choice of (1) the time value by which the adversary advances the time, (2) the message sent by the adversary in an insecure input, (3) the new name selected at name generation time, and (4) the scheduling of located threads.

2.3   Process Equivalence

We define a notion of observational equivalence for tC^3-processes based on the concepts of *cryptographic parsing* (inspired by [13]) and *structurally indistinguishable protocol histories*. Cryptographic parsing captures an agent's capability to understand the structure of a cryptographically obfuscated message. The idea is to parse unintelligible messages to the abstract message ■.

Table 6. Process and thread execution

Below, $\overset{\alpha}{\longrightarrow} \in \{\longrightarrow, \overset{sO}{\longrightarrow}, \overset{sI}{\longrightarrow}\}$.

$$\text{TIME} \; \frac{\mathfrak{h} \models \exists t'(t' @ \text{Eve} \wedge t' \leq t < \infty)}{\begin{pmatrix} P \\ \mathfrak{h} \end{pmatrix} \longrightarrow \begin{pmatrix} P \\ \mathfrak{h} \cdot \text{S}(\text{Eve}, \blacksquare, t) \end{pmatrix}} \qquad \text{SET} \; \frac{}{\begin{pmatrix} a.x[\text{ Set } t.T\,] \\ \mathfrak{h} \end{pmatrix} \longrightarrow \begin{pmatrix} a.x[\,T\,] \\ \mathfrak{h} \cdot \text{S}(a, x, t) \end{pmatrix}}$$

$$\text{NEW} \; \frac{\mathfrak{h} \models n : \varsigma \wedge \neg \exists a \exists x \exists o \exists v (a.x \cup n.(o, v))}{\begin{pmatrix} c.x[\text{ New }(v : \varsigma, (O, V)).T\,] \\ \mathfrak{h} \end{pmatrix} \longrightarrow \begin{pmatrix} c.x[\,\{^n\!/_v\}T\,] \\ \mathfrak{h} \cdot \text{N}(c, x, n, (O, V)) \end{pmatrix}}$$

$$\text{NEW-EVE} \; \frac{\mathfrak{h} \models \text{Eve k }(O, V) \wedge \neg \exists a \exists x \exists o \exists v (a.x \cup n.(o, v))}{\begin{pmatrix} P \\ \mathfrak{h} \end{pmatrix} \longrightarrow \begin{pmatrix} P \\ \mathfrak{h} \cdot \text{N}(\text{Eve}, \blacksquare, n, (O, V)) \end{pmatrix}}$$

$$\text{OUT} \; \frac{}{\begin{pmatrix} c.x[\text{ Out}_d\ M.T\,] \\ \mathfrak{h} \end{pmatrix} \longrightarrow \begin{pmatrix} c.x[\,T\,] \\ \mathfrak{h} \cdot \text{O}(c, x, M, d) \cdot \text{I}(\text{Eve}, \blacksquare, M) \end{pmatrix}}$$

$$\text{IN} \; \frac{\mathfrak{h} \models \text{Eve k } M \wedge \text{match}(\Pi, M)\varphi}{\begin{pmatrix} c.x[\text{ In } \Pi \text{ when } \varphi.T\,] \\ \mathfrak{h} \end{pmatrix} \longrightarrow \begin{pmatrix} c.x[\text{ match}(\Pi, M)T\,] \\ \mathfrak{h} \cdot \text{O}(\text{Eve}, \blacksquare, M, c) \cdot \text{I}(c, x, M) \end{pmatrix}}$$

$$\text{sOUT} \; \frac{}{\begin{pmatrix} c.x[\text{ sOut}_d\ M.T\,] \\ \mathfrak{h} \end{pmatrix} \overset{sO}{\longrightarrow} \begin{pmatrix} c.x[\,T\,] \\ \mathfrak{h} \cdot \text{sO}(c, x, M, d) \end{pmatrix}}$$

$$\text{sIN} \; \frac{\mathfrak{h} \models \text{match}(\Pi, M)\varphi}{\begin{pmatrix} d.x[\text{ sIn}_c\ \Pi \text{ when } \varphi.T\,] \\ \mathfrak{h} \cdot \text{sO}(c, x', M, d) \end{pmatrix} \overset{sI}{\longrightarrow} \begin{pmatrix} d.x[\text{ match}(\Pi, M)T\,] \\ \mathfrak{h} \cdot \text{sO}(c, x', M, d) \cdot \text{sI}(d, x, M, c) \end{pmatrix}}$$

$$\text{sCOM-L} \; \frac{\begin{pmatrix} P \\ \mathfrak{h} \end{pmatrix} \overset{sO}{\longrightarrow} \begin{pmatrix} P' \\ \mathfrak{h}' \end{pmatrix} \qquad \begin{pmatrix} Q \\ \mathfrak{h}' \end{pmatrix} \overset{sI}{\longrightarrow} \begin{pmatrix} Q' \\ \mathfrak{h}'' \end{pmatrix}}{\begin{pmatrix} P \;|\!|\!|\; Q \\ \mathfrak{h} \end{pmatrix} \longrightarrow \begin{pmatrix} P' \;|\!|\!|\; Q' \\ \mathfrak{h}'' \end{pmatrix}}$$

$$\text{LOOKUP} \; \frac{\begin{pmatrix} c.x[\,\{^n\!/_v\}T\,] \\ \mathfrak{h} \end{pmatrix} \overset{\alpha}{\longrightarrow} \begin{pmatrix} c.x[\,T'\,] \\ \mathfrak{h}' \end{pmatrix} \qquad \mathfrak{h} \models \text{looksUp}(c, x, n, \varsigma, d, O)}{\begin{pmatrix} c.x[\text{ Get}_d\ (v : \varsigma, O) \text{ in } T\,] \\ \mathfrak{h} \end{pmatrix} \overset{\alpha}{\longrightarrow} \begin{pmatrix} c.x[\,T'\,] \\ \mathfrak{h}' \end{pmatrix}}$$

$$\text{PAR-L} \; \frac{\begin{pmatrix} P \\ \mathfrak{h} \end{pmatrix} \overset{\alpha}{\longrightarrow} \begin{pmatrix} P' \\ \mathfrak{h}' \end{pmatrix}}{\begin{pmatrix} P \;|\!|\!|\; Q \\ \mathfrak{h} \end{pmatrix} \overset{\alpha}{\longrightarrow} \begin{pmatrix} P' \;|\!|\!|\; Q \\ \mathfrak{h}' \end{pmatrix}}$$

Definition 6 (Cryptographic parsing). *The cryptographic parsing function* $(\!|\cdot|\!)_a^{\mathfrak{h}}$ *associated with an agent* $a \in \mathcal{P}$ *and a protocol history* $\mathfrak{h} \in \mathcal{H}$ *(and complying with the assumptions of perfect cryptography) is an identity on names, the abstract message, time values, and public keys; and otherwise acts as defined in Table 7.*

Table 7. Parsing on cryptographic messages

$$
(\!|\lceil M \rceil|\!)_a^{\mathfrak{h}} := \begin{cases} \lceil (\!|M|\!)_a^{\mathfrak{h}} \rceil & \text{if } \mathfrak{h} \models a \mathsf{\,k\,} M, \text{ and} \\ \blacksquare & \text{otherwise.} \end{cases}
$$

$$
(\!|\{\!|M|\!\}_{M'}|\!)_a^{\mathfrak{h}} := \begin{cases} \{\!|(\!|M|\!)_a^{\mathfrak{h}}|\!\}_{(\!|M'|\!)_a^{\mathfrak{h}}} & \text{if } \mathfrak{h} \models a \mathsf{\,k\,} M', \text{ and} \\ \blacksquare & \text{otherwise.} \end{cases}
$$

$$
(\!|\{\!|M|\!\}_{p^+}^+|\!)_a^{\mathfrak{h}} := \begin{cases} \{\!|(\!|M|\!)_a^{\mathfrak{h}}|\!\}_{p^+}^+ & \text{if } \mathfrak{h} \models a \mathsf{\,k\,} p \vee (a \mathsf{\,k\,} M \wedge a \mathsf{\,k\,} p^+), \text{ and} \\ \blacksquare & \text{otherwise.} \end{cases}
$$

$$
(\!|\{\!|M|\!\}_{p}^-|\!)_a^{\mathfrak{h}} := \begin{cases} \{\!|(\!|M|\!)_a^{\mathfrak{h}}|\!\}_{p}^- & \text{if } \mathfrak{h} \models a \mathsf{\,k\,} p^+, \text{ and} \\ \blacksquare & \text{otherwise.} \end{cases}
$$

$$
(\!|(M, M')|\!)_a^{\mathfrak{h}} := ((\!|M|\!)_a^{\mathfrak{h}}, (\!|M'|\!)_a^{\mathfrak{h}})
$$

For notational convenience, we subsequently write $\varepsilon(a)$ for any protocol event as defined in Section 2.2, $\varepsilon(a, n)$ for any of these name-generation events, $\varepsilon(a, M)$ for any of these communication events, and $\hat{\varepsilon}(a)$ for any of these secure events.

Definition 7 (Structurally indistinguishable protocol histories). *Two protocol histories* $\mathfrak{h}$ *and* $\mathfrak{h}'$ *are structurally indistinguishable from the viewpoint of* *an agent* a, *written* $\mathfrak{h} \approx_a \mathfrak{h}'$, :iff a *observes the same* event pattern *and the same* data patterns *in* $\mathfrak{h}$ *and* $\mathfrak{h}'$. *Formally, for all* $\mathfrak{h}, \mathfrak{h}' \in \mathcal{H}$, $\mathfrak{h} \approx_a \mathfrak{h}'$:iff $\mathfrak{h} \approx_a^{(\mathfrak{h}, \mathfrak{h}')} \mathfrak{h}'$ *where,*

- *given that a is a legitimate participant or the adversary* Eve,

1. $$\dfrac{}{\epsilon \approx_a^{(\mathfrak{h}, \mathfrak{h}')} \epsilon}$$

2. $$\dfrac{\mathfrak{h}_l \approx_a^{(\mathfrak{h}, \mathfrak{h}')} \mathfrak{h}_r}{\mathfrak{h}_l \cdot \varepsilon(a, n) \approx_a^{(\mathfrak{h}, \mathfrak{h}')} \mathfrak{h}_r \cdot \varepsilon(a, n)}$$

3. $$\dfrac{\mathfrak{h}_l \approx_a^{(\mathfrak{h}, \mathfrak{h}')} \mathfrak{h}_r}{\mathfrak{h}_l \cdot \varepsilon(a, M) \approx_a^{(\mathfrak{h}, \mathfrak{h}')} \mathfrak{h}_r \cdot \varepsilon(a, M')} \quad (\!|M|\!)_a^{\mathfrak{h}} = (\!|M'|\!)_a^{\mathfrak{h}'}$$

- *given that a is a legitimate participant,*

4. $$\dfrac{\mathfrak{h}_l \approx_a^{(\mathfrak{h}, \mathfrak{h}')} \mathfrak{h}_r}{\mathfrak{h}_l \cdot \varepsilon(b) \approx_a^{(\mathfrak{h}, \mathfrak{h}')} \mathfrak{h}_r} \ a \neq b \qquad \dfrac{\mathfrak{h}_l \approx_a^{(\mathfrak{h}, \mathfrak{h}')} \mathfrak{h}_r}{\mathfrak{h}_l \approx_a^{(\mathfrak{h}, \mathfrak{h}')} \mathfrak{h}_r \cdot \varepsilon(b)} \ a \neq b$$

- *given that a is the adversary* Eve,

4. $\dfrac{\mathfrak{h}_l \approx_{\mathrm{Eve}}^{(\mathfrak{h},\mathfrak{h}')} \mathfrak{h}_r}{\mathfrak{h}_l \cdot \hat{\mathcal{E}}(b) \approx_{\mathrm{Eve}}^{(\mathfrak{h},\mathfrak{h}')} \mathfrak{h}_r}$ Eve $\neq b$ $\dfrac{\mathfrak{h}_l \approx_{\mathrm{Eve}}^{(\mathfrak{h},\mathfrak{h}')} \mathfrak{h}_r}{\mathfrak{h}_l \approx_{\mathrm{Eve}}^{(\mathfrak{h},\mathfrak{h}')} \mathfrak{h}_r \cdot \hat{\mathcal{E}}(b)}$ Eve $\neq b$

5. $\dfrac{\mathfrak{h}_l \approx_{\mathrm{Eve}}^{(\mathfrak{h},\mathfrak{h}')} \mathfrak{h}_r}{\mathfrak{h}_l \cdot \mathrm{I}(b, x, M) \approx_{\mathrm{Eve}}^{(\mathfrak{h},\mathfrak{h}')} \mathfrak{h}_r \cdot \mathrm{I}(b, x, M')}$ $(\!|\, M \,|\!)_{\mathrm{Eve}}^{\mathfrak{h}} = (\!|\, M' \,|\!)_{\mathrm{Eve}}^{\mathfrak{h}'}$

6. $\dfrac{\mathfrak{h}_l \approx_{\mathrm{Eve}}^{(\mathfrak{h},\mathfrak{h}')} \mathfrak{h}_r}{\mathfrak{h}_l \cdot \mathrm{O}(b, x, M, c) \approx_{\mathrm{Eve}}^{(\mathfrak{h},\mathfrak{h}')} \mathfrak{h}_r \cdot \mathrm{O}(b, x, M', c)}$ $(\!|\, M \,|\!)_{\mathrm{Eve}}^{\mathfrak{h}} = (\!|\, M' \,|\!)_{\mathrm{Eve}}^{\mathfrak{h}'}$

Note that the observations at the different (past) stages $\mathfrak{h}_l$ and $\mathfrak{h}_r$ in $\mathfrak{h}$ and $\mathfrak{h}'$ respectively must be made with the whole (present) knowledge of $\mathfrak{h}$ and $\mathfrak{h}'$ (cf. $\mathfrak{h}_l \approx_{}^{(\mathfrak{h},\mathfrak{h}')} \mathfrak{h}_r$). Learning new keys may render intelligible past messages to an agent a in the present that were not intelligible to her before.

Remark 1. For all agents a including **Eve**, $\approx_a \subseteq \mathcal{H} \times \mathcal{H}$ is

1. an equivalence with an infinite index due to fresh-name generation
2. not a right-congruence due to the possibility of learning new keys
3. a refinement on the projection $\mathcal{H}|a$ of $\mathcal{H}$ onto a's view [14]
4. decidable

We lift structural indistinguishability from protocol histories to protocol states, i.e., tuples of a protocol term and a protocol history.

Definition 8 (Structurally indistinguishable protocol states). *Let P_1 and P_2 denote two tC^3-processes. Then two protocol states $(P_1, \mathfrak{h}_1)$ and $(P_2, \mathfrak{h}_2)$ are structurally indistinguishable from the viewpoint of an agent a, written $(P_1, \mathfrak{h}_1) \approx_a (P_2, \mathfrak{h}_2)$, :iff $\mathfrak{h}_1 \approx_a \mathfrak{h}_2$.*

This relation coincides with the relation of epistemic accessibility defining the epistemic modality of CPL [9], which reflects the intimate co-design of C^3 and CPL. We are finally ready to define observational equivalence for tC^3-processes.

Definition 9 (Trace-equivalent cryptographic processes). *For all agents a including* **Eve** *and for all $\mathfrak{s}_1, \mathfrak{s}_2 \in \mathcal{P} \times \mathcal{H}$,*

- *$\mathfrak{s}_2$ trace-refines $\mathfrak{s}_1$ from the viewpoint of a, written $\mathfrak{s}_1 \gtrsim_a^* \mathfrak{s}_2$, :iff for all $\mathfrak{s}_2' \in \mathcal{P} \times \mathcal{H}$, if $\mathfrak{s}_2 \longrightarrow^* \mathfrak{s}_2'$ then there is $\mathfrak{s}_1' \in \mathcal{P} \times \mathcal{H}$ s.t. $\mathfrak{s}_1 \longrightarrow^* \mathfrak{s}_1'$ and $\mathfrak{s}_2' \approx_a \mathfrak{s}_1'$; and*
- *$\mathfrak{s}_1$ and $\mathfrak{s}_2$ are trace-equivalent from the viewpoint of a, written $\mathfrak{s}_1 \approx_a^* \mathfrak{s}_2$, :iff $\mathfrak{s}_1 \gtrsim_a^* \mathfrak{s}_2$ and $\mathfrak{s}_2 \gtrsim_a^* \mathfrak{s}_1$.*

3 Case Study

We illustrate how to use tC^3 on a specification and verification case study, namely the failure of the Wide-Mouthed-Frog protocol (WMF), a server-based key-transport protocol employing symmetric cryptography, (cf. Table 8).

We recall that model-based (e.g., process algebraic) correctness statements of cryptographic protocols enunciate an observational equivalence that is supposed to hold

Table 8. Protocol narration for WMF

$1a$. $\texttt{Alice} \rightarrow \texttt{Trent}$: $\texttt{Alice}$
$1b$. $\texttt{Alice} \rightarrow \texttt{Trent}$: $\{\!|((t_{\texttt{Alice}}, \texttt{Bob}), k_{(\texttt{Alice},\texttt{Bob})})|\!\}_{k_{(\texttt{Alice},\texttt{Trent})}}$
$2.$ $\texttt{Trent} \rightarrow \texttt{Bob}$: $\{\!|((t_{\texttt{Trent}}, \texttt{Alice}), k_{(\texttt{Alice},\texttt{Bob})})|\!\}_{k_{(\texttt{Bob},\texttt{Trent})}}$

between two process models (terms) of the protocol under scrutiny. The choice of the actual process terms depends on the cryptographic goal that the correctness statement is intended to encode. For example, authenticity goals for a cryptographic protocol can be encoded as an observational equivalence between, on the one hand, an obviously (via different kinds of "magic") correct specification process and, on the other hand, an implementation process expressing the protocol as it would be coded in a realistic implementation. In our case, we are interested in a timeliness goal for WMF, namely that the responder only accepts the session key within a fixed interval of time. It is well known that WMF fails to meet this goal (cf. Table 9). As it turns out, this goal can be checked in a similar set-up as for authenticity properties, i.e., as an equivalence from Eve's viewpoint ($\approx^*_{\text{Eve}}$) between an implementation and a specification term (cf. Table 10).

Table 9. Attack narration for WMF

$1a'$. $\texttt{Eve}_{\texttt{Bob}} \rightarrow \texttt{Trent}$: $\texttt{Bob}$
$1b'$. $\texttt{Eve}_{\texttt{Bob}} \rightarrow \texttt{Trent}$: $\{\!|((t_{\texttt{Trent}}, \texttt{Alice}), k_{(\texttt{Alice},\texttt{Bob})})|\!\}_{k_{(\texttt{Bob},\texttt{Trent})}}$
$2'$. $\texttt{Trent} \rightarrow \texttt{Eve}_{\texttt{Alice}}$: $\{\!|((t'_{\texttt{Trent}}, \texttt{Bob}), k_{(\texttt{Alice},\texttt{Bob})})|\!\}_{k_{(\texttt{Alice},\texttt{Trent})}}$
$1a''$. $\texttt{Eve}_{\texttt{Alice}} \rightarrow \texttt{Trent}$: $\texttt{Alice}$
$1b''$. $\texttt{Eve}_{\texttt{Alice}} \rightarrow \texttt{Trent}$: $\{\!|((t'_{\texttt{Trent}}, \texttt{Bob}), k_{(\texttt{Alice},\texttt{Bob})})|\!\}_{k_{(\texttt{Alice},\texttt{Trent})}}$
$2''$. $\texttt{Trent} \rightarrow \texttt{Bob}$: $\{\!|((t''_{\texttt{Trent}}, \texttt{Alice}), k_{(\texttt{Alice},\texttt{Bob})})|\!\}_{k_{(\texttt{Bob},\texttt{Trent})}}$

The "magic" in our specification process is the non-trivial and *epistemically non-local* input guard of the last input of the responder process. In the implementation, we only check the types of the atoms in the message and that the time stamp is recent. In the specification, we additionally check that the key has been created by the initiator for communication with the responder and that the local time is within the validity interval of the key, as expressed by the formula $\exists t \exists t' \exists x (oth.x \cup key.((slf, oth), (t, t')) \wedge \exists t_s (t_s @ slf \wedge t \leq t_s \leq t'))$. It is possible to have the simple time stamp check succeed but the "more obviously correct" validity check fail, as evidenced below.

Observe that lookup of local time is done in two different ways, namely imperatively by means of the get-prefix, and declaratively by means of the @-predicate. We assume that the local clocks are accurate, i.e., all drift rates are 1.

WMF presumes that the server shares a symmetric long-term key with each corresponding client. We model this a priori knowledge by name-generation and subsequent secure-communication events, recorded in the initialisation trace shown in Table 11.

Table 10. Specification ($\varphi \stackrel{\text{def}}{=} \exists t \exists t' \exists x(oth.x \cup key.((slf, oth), (t, t')) \wedge \exists t_s(t_s@slf \wedge t \leq t_s \leq t'))$) and implementation ($\varphi \stackrel{\text{def}}{=} \top$) process template for WMF

$\text{WMF}_{\text{INIT}}(slf, srv, oth, \delta) \stackrel{\text{def}}{=}$	$\text{WMF}_{\text{SERV}}(slf, \delta) \stackrel{\text{def}}{=}$	$\text{WMF}_{\text{RESP}}(slf, srv, \delta) \stackrel{\text{def}}{=}$
$\text{Get}_{slf}(t_s : \text{TV}, \blacksquare)$ in $\text{New}(k_{so} : \text{K}, ((slf, oth), (t_s, t_s + \delta + \delta))).$ $\text{Get}_{srv}(k_{ss} : \text{K}, (slf, srv))$ in $\text{Out}_{srv}\, slf.$ $\text{Out}_{srv}\, \|((t_s, oth), k_{so})\|_{k_{ss}}.1$	$\text{In}\, fst$ when $fst : \text{P}.$ $\text{Get}_{slf}(k_{sf} : \text{K}, (slf, fst))$ in $\text{In}\, \|((t, snd), key)\|_{k_{sf}}^{\leftarrow}$ when $t : \text{TV} \wedge$ $\exists t_s(t_s : \text{TV} \wedge t_s@slf \wedge t + \delta \leq t_s) \wedge$ $snd : \text{P} \wedge$ $key : \text{K}.$ $\text{Get}_{slf}(k_{ss} : \text{K}, (slf, snd))$ in $\text{Out}_{snd}\, \|((t_s, fst), key)\|_{k_{ss}}.1$	$\text{Get}_{srv}(k_{ss} : \text{K}, (slf, srv))$ in $\text{In}\, \|((t, oth), key)\|_{k_{ss}}^{\leftarrow}$ when $t : \text{TV} \wedge$ $\exists t_s(t_s : \text{TV} \wedge t_s@slf \wedge t + \delta \leq t_s) \wedge$ $oth : \text{P} \wedge$ $key : \text{K} \wedge$ $\varphi.$ $\text{Out}_{\text{Eve}}\, t.1$
$\text{WMF}(init, srv, resp, x_i, x_s, x_r, \delta) \stackrel{\text{def}}{=} init.x_i[\, \text{WMF}_{\text{INIT}}(init, srv, resp, \delta)\,] \,\|\|\|$ $srv.x_s[\, \text{WMF}_{\text{SERV}}(srv, \delta)\,] \,\|\|\|$ $resp.x_r[\, \text{WMF}_{\text{RESP}}(resp, srv, \delta)\,]$		

Table 11. Initialisation trace for WMF

$\mathfrak{h}_{init} := \epsilon \cdot \mathsf{N}(\mathrm{Trent}, x_{\mathrm{Trent}}, k_{(\mathrm{Alice,Trent})}, ((\mathrm{Trent}, \mathrm{Alice}), (-\infty, \infty))) \cdot$
$\quad \mathsf{N}(\mathrm{Trent}, x_{\mathrm{Trent}}, k_{(\mathrm{Bob,Trent})}, ((\mathrm{Trent}, \mathrm{Bob}), (-\infty, \infty))) \cdot$
$\quad \mathsf{sO}(\mathrm{Trent}, x_{\mathrm{Trent}}, k_{(\mathrm{Alice,Trent})}, \mathrm{Alice}) \cdot \mathsf{sI}(\mathrm{Alice}, x_{\mathrm{Alice}}, k_{(\mathrm{Alice,Trent})}, \mathrm{Trent}) \cdot$
$\quad \mathsf{sO}(\mathrm{Trent}, x_{\mathrm{Trent}}, k_{(\mathrm{Bob,Trent})}, \mathrm{Bob}) \cdot \mathsf{sI}(\mathrm{Bob}, x_{\mathrm{Bob}}, k_{(\mathrm{Bob,Trent})}, \mathrm{Trent}) \cdot$
$\quad \mathsf{S}(\mathrm{Eve}, \blacksquare, 0) \cdot \mathsf{S}(\mathrm{Alice}, x_{\mathrm{Alice}}, 0) \cdot \mathsf{S}(\mathrm{Bob}, x_{\mathrm{Bob}}, 0) \cdot \mathsf{S}(\mathrm{Trent}, x_{\mathrm{Trent}}, 0)$

Table 12. Attack set-up for WMF

$\mathrm{Alice}.x_{\mathrm{Alice}}[\ \mathrm{WMF}_{\mathrm{INIT}}(\mathrm{Alice}, \mathrm{Trent}, \mathrm{Bob}, \delta)\ ] \mid\mid\mid$
$\mathrm{Bob}.x_{\mathrm{Bob}}[\ \mathrm{WMF}_{\mathrm{RESP}}(\mathrm{Bob}, \mathrm{Trent}, \delta)\ ] \mid\mid\mid$
$\mathrm{Trent}.x_{\mathrm{Trent}}[\ \mathrm{WMF}_{\mathrm{SERV}}(\mathrm{Trent}, \delta)\ ] \mid\mid\mid$
$\mathrm{Trent}.x'_{\mathrm{Trent}}[\ \mathrm{WMF}_{\mathrm{SERV}}(\mathrm{Trent}, \delta)\ ] \mid\mid\mid$
$\mathrm{Trent}.x''_{\mathrm{Trent}}[\ \mathrm{WMF}_{\mathrm{SERV}}(\mathrm{Trent}, \delta)\ ]$

We now reconstruct the impersonation attack on WMF (cf. Table 9) in tC^3. The attack involves adversarial replay and impersonation across three different sessions. The corresponding attack set-up in tC^3 is shown in Table 12. This set-up can, via process reduction, produce the family of traces that is generated by instantiating the parameters t_1, t_2, and t_3 of the history template shown in Table 13 — for clarity, without interception events (cf. Rule OUT and IN in Table 6). The only possible time values for the parameters t_1, t_2, and t_3 in this history template are those mentioned in the set-events of the adversary. For the implementation, we may have $t_1 = \delta$, $t_2 = 2\delta$, and $t_3 = 3\delta$, where t_3 is observed by the adversary in clear in the last event. However, the specification cannot accept a stale key, i.e., a key older than 2δ. Hence, the specification cannot generate a history that conforms to the above template, in particular a history such that the respondent outputs 3δ as her last action. Thus the implementation and the specification are not equivalent from the point of view of the adversary, so the specification is not met.

Table 13. History template for WMF

$\mathfrak{h} := \mathfrak{h}_{init} \cdot \mathsf{N}(\mathrm{Alice}, x_{\mathrm{Alice}}, k_{(\mathrm{Alice,Bob})}, ((\mathrm{Alice}, \mathrm{Bob}), (-\infty, 2\delta))) \cdot$
$\quad \mathsf{O}(\mathrm{Alice}, x_{\mathrm{Alice}}, \mathrm{Alice}, \mathrm{Trent}) \cdot$
$\quad \mathsf{O}(\mathrm{Alice}, x_{\mathrm{Alice}}, \{((0, \mathrm{Bob}), k_{(\mathrm{Alice,Bob})})\}_{k_{(\mathrm{Alice,Trent})}}, \mathrm{Trent}) \cdot \mathsf{S}(\mathrm{Eve}, \blacksquare, \delta) \cdot$
$\quad \mathsf{I}(\mathrm{Trent}, x_{\mathrm{Trent}}, \mathrm{Alice}) \cdot \mathsf{I}(\mathrm{Trent}, x_{\mathrm{Trent}}, \{((0, \mathrm{Bob}), k_{(\mathrm{Alice,Bob})})\}_{k_{(\mathrm{Alice,Trent})}}) \cdot$
$\quad \mathsf{O}(\mathrm{Trent}, x_{\mathrm{Trent}}, \{((t_1, \mathrm{Alice}), k_{(\mathrm{Alice,Bob})})\}_{k_{(\mathrm{Bob,Trent})}}, \mathrm{Bob}) \cdot \mathsf{S}(\mathrm{Eve}, \blacksquare, 2\delta) \cdot$
$\quad \mathsf{I}(\mathrm{Trent}, x'_{\mathrm{Trent}}, \mathrm{Bob}) \cdot \mathsf{I}(\mathrm{Trent}, x'_{\mathrm{Trent}}, \{((t_1, \mathrm{Alice}), k_{(\mathrm{Alice,Bob})})\}_{k_{(\mathrm{Bob,Trent})}}) \cdot$
$\quad \mathsf{O}(\mathrm{Trent}, x'_{\mathrm{Trent}}, \{((t_2, \mathrm{Bob}), k_{(\mathrm{Alice,Bob})})\}_{k_{(\mathrm{Alice,Trent})}}, \mathrm{Alice}) \cdot \mathsf{S}(\mathrm{Eve}, \blacksquare, 3\delta) \cdot$
$\quad \mathsf{I}(\mathrm{Trent}, x''_{\mathrm{Trent}}, \mathrm{Alice}) \cdot \mathsf{I}(\mathrm{Trent}, x''_{\mathrm{Trent}}, \{((t_2, \mathrm{Bob}), k_{(\mathrm{Alice,Bob})})\}_{k_{(\mathrm{Alice,Trent})}}) \cdot$
$\quad \mathsf{O}(\mathrm{Trent}, x''_{\mathrm{Trent}}, \{((t_3, \mathrm{Alice}), k_{(\mathrm{Alice,Bob})})\}_{k_{(\mathrm{Bob,Trent})}}, \mathrm{Bob}) \cdot$
$\quad \mathsf{I}(\mathrm{Bob}, x_{\mathrm{Bob}}, \{((t_3, \mathrm{Alice}), k_{(\mathrm{Alice,Bob})})\}_{k_{(\mathrm{Bob,Trent})}}) \cdot \mathsf{O}(\mathrm{Bob}, x_{\mathrm{Bob}}, t_3, \mathrm{Eve})$

4   Conclusion

We have demonstrated that adding (dense-valued) real-time to an untimed formalism for the model-based specification and verification of cryptographic protocols can be *simple*, when properly conceived. Essentially, only two additional axioms (and no modified axioms/rules!) are needed in the operational semantics of our Calculus of Cryptographic Communication. Moreover, the extension of the untimed calculus to the calculus with real-time is *backwards-compatible* in the sense that the untimed fragment of the process syntax is — thanks to sorts, tags, and the abstract message — a subset (up to tags) of the timed process syntax; and that the process equivalence of the calculus can — thanks to protocol histories — handle both timed and untimed process terms. Another advantage of our process equivalence is that it has a common definitional basis with the epistemic modality (cf. property-based specification) of our co-designed logic CPL. We believe that the simplicity and backwards-compatibility of our extension is the result of a well-designed core calculus, and of a simple generalisation of the adversary. Notably, the adversary's scheduling power is generalised from the control of the (relative) temporal *order* (logical time) of protocol events in the network (space) to the control of their absolute scheduling *time* (real time).

Our calculus provides all the necessary ingredients for realistic, timed cryptographic protocols, i.e., rational-number valued time, time stamps, timed keys, and potentially drifting local clocks. We conjecture that count-down and count-up timers are encodable, and checkable on process input. We are planning to extend our calculus with *probabilistic polynomial* time.

References

1. Schneider, S.: Concurrent and Real-Time Systems. Wiley, Chichester (1999)
2. Evans, N., Schneider, S.: Analysing time-dependent security properties in CSP using PVS. In: Proceedings of the European Symposium on Research in Computer Security (2000)
3. Gorrieri, R., Martinelli, F.: A simple framework for real-time cryptographic protocol analysis with compositional proof rules. Science of Computer Programming 50(1–3) (2004)
4. Haack, C., Jeffrey, A.: Timed Spi-calculus with types for secrecy and authenticity. In: Abadi, M., de Alfaro, L. (eds.) CONCUR 2005. LNCS, vol. 3653, Springer, Heidelberg (2005)
5. Bozga, L., Ene, C., Lakhnech, Y.: A symbolic decision procedure for cryptographic protocols with time stamps. The Journal of Logic and Algebraic Programming 65 (2005)
6. Gong, L.: A security risk of depending on synchronized clocks. ACM SIGOPS Operating Systems Review 26(1) (1992)
7. Lamport, L.: Real time is really simple. Technical Report MSR-TR-2005-30, Microsoft Research (2005)
8. Borgström, J., Kramer, S., Nestmann, U.: Calculus of Cryptographic Communication. In: Proceedings of the LICS-Affiliated Workshop on Foundations of Computer Security and Automated Reasoning for Security Protocol Analysis (2006)
9. Kramer, S.: Logical concepts in cryptography. Cryptology ePrint Archive, Report 2006/262 (2006), http://eprint.iacr.org/
10. Kramer, S.: Timed Cryptographic Protocol Logic presented at the Nordic Workshop on Programming Theory (2006)

11. Haack, C., Jeffrey, A.: Pattern-matching Spi-calculus. In: Proceedings of the Workshop on Formal Aspects in Security and Trust (2004)
12. Paulson, L.C.: The inductive approach to verifying cryptographic protocols. Journal of Computer Security 6(1) (1998)
13. Abadi, M., Rogaway, P.: Reconciling two views of cryptography (the computational soundness of formal encryption). Journal of Cryptology 15(2) (2002)
14. Fagin, R., Halpern, J.Y., Moses, Y., Vardi, M.Y.: Reasoning about Knowledge. MIT Press, Cambridge (1995)

A Semantic Paradigm for Component-Based Specification Integrating a Notion of Security Risk

Gyrd Brændeland[1,2,*] and Ketil Stølen[1,2]

[1] Department of Informatics, University of Oslo, Norway
[2] SINTEF, Norway
gyb@sintef.uio.no

Abstract. We propose a semantic paradigm for component-based specification supporting the documentation of security risk behaviour. By security risk, we mean behaviour that constitutes a risk with regard to ICT security aspects, such as confidentiality, integrity and availability. The purpose of this work is to investigate the nature of security risk in the setting of component-based system development. A better understanding of security risk at the level of components facilitates the prediction of risks related to introducing a new component into a system. The semantic paradigm provides a first step towards integrating security risk analysis into the system development process.

Keywords: component, formal specification, risk analysis, security.

1 Introduction

The flexibility of component-oriented software systems enabled by component technologies such as Sun's Enterprise Java Beans (EJB), Microsoft's .NET or the Open Source Gateway initiative (OSGi) gives rise to new types of security concerns. In particular the question of how a system owner can know whether to trust a new component to be deployed into a system. A solution to this problem requires integrating the process of security risk analysis in the early stages of component-based system development. The purpose of security risk analysis is to decide upon the necessary level of asset protection against security risks, such as a confidentiality or integrity breach. Unfortunately, the processes of system development and security risk analysis are often carried out independently with little mutual interaction. The result is expensive redesigns and unsatisfactory security solutions. To facilitate a tighter integration we need a better understanding of security risk at the level of components. But knowing the security risks of a single component is not enough, since two components can affect the risk level of each other. An example is the known buffer overflow vulnerability of previous versions of the media player Winamp, that may allow an unauthenticated attacker using a crafted file to execute arbitrary code on a vulnerable system. By default Internet Explorer opens affected files without prompting the user [20]. Hence, the probability of a successful attack is much higher if a user

---

* Corresponding author.

T. Dimitrakos et al. (Eds.): FAST 2006, LNCS 4691, pp. 31–46, 2007.

utilises both Internet Explorer and Winamp, than only one of them. As this example illustrates we need a strategy for predicting system level risks that may be caused by introducing a new component. A better understanding of security risk at the level of components is a prerequisite for compositional security level estimation. Such understanding also provides the basis for trust management, because as argued by Jøsang and Presti [12] there is a close dependency between trust and risk. The contributions of this paper is a novel semantic paradigm for component-based specification explaining

- basic components with provided and required interfaces;
- the composition of components into composite components;
- unpredictability which is often required to characterise confidentiality properties (secure information flow);
- the notion of security risk as known from asset-oriented security risk analysis.

This paper is divided into ten sections. In Sections 2 and 3 we explain our notions of security risk analysis and component. In Section 4 we introduce the basic vocabulary of the semantic model. In Sections 5 to 7 we define the semantic paradigm for component-based specifications. In Section 8 we describe how security risk analysis concepts relate to the component model and how they are represented in the semantics. In Section 9 we attempt to place our work in relation to ongoing research within related areas and finally, in Section 10, we summarise our findings.

2   Asset-Oriented Security Risk Analysis

By security risk analysis we mean risk analysis applied to the domain of information and communication technology (ICT) security. For convenience we often use *security analysis* as a short term for *security risk analysis*. ICT security includes all aspects related to defining, achieving and maintaining confidentiality, integrity, availability, non-repudiation, accountability, authenticity and reliability of ICT [11].

Hogganvik and Stølen [7] have provided a conceptual model for security analysis based on a conceptual model originally developed in the CORAS project [3]. The CORAS risk management process is based on the the "Code of practise for information security management" (ISO/IEC 17799:2000) [9] and the Australian/New Zealand standard "Risk Management" (AS/NZS 4360:2004) [22].

With some adjustments the model is expressed as a class diagram in UML 2.0 [18], see Figure 1. The associations between the elements have cardinalities specifying the number of instances of one element that can be related to one instance of the other. The hollow diamond symbolises aggregation and the filled composition. Elements connected with an aggregation can also be part of other aggregations, while composite elements only exist within the specified composition.

We explain Figure 1 as follows: *Stakeholders* are those people and organisations who may affect, be affected by, or perceive themselves to be affected by, a decision or activity or risk [22]. The CORAS security analysis process is

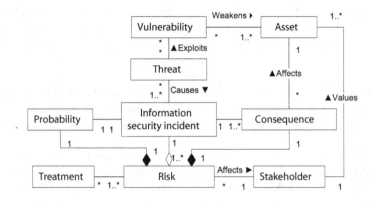

Fig. 1. CORAS conceptual model of security analysis terms

asset-oriented. An *asset* is something to which a stakeholder directly assigns value and, hence, for which the stakeholder requires protection [23][1]. CORAS links assets uniquely to their stakeholders. A *vulnerability* is a weakness of an asset or group of assets that can be exploited by one or more threats [11]. A *threat* is a potential cause of an incident that may result in harm to a system or organisation [11]. An *information security incident* refers to any unexpected or unwanted event that might cause a compromise of business activities or information security, such as malfunction of software or hardware and access violations [11]. A *risk* is the combination of the *probability* of an event and its *consequence* [10]. Conceptually, as illustrated in Figure 1, a risk consist of an information security incident, the probability of its happening and its consequence. *Probability* is the extent to which an *event* will occur [10]. *Consequence* is the outcome of an event expressed qualitatively or quantitatively, being a loss, injury or disadvantage. There may be a range of possible outcomes associated with an event [23]. This implies that an information security incident may lead to the reduction in value of several assets. Hence, an information security incident may be part of several risks. *Risk treatment* is the process of selection and implementation of measures to modify risks [10].

3   The Component Model

There exist various definitions of what a software component is. The classic definition by Szyperski [24] provides a basic notion of a component that is widely adopted in later definitions: "A software component is a unit of composition with contractually specified interfaces and explicit context dependencies only. A software component can be deployed independently and is subject to composition by third parties."

---

[1] The Australian handbook [23] uses the term *organisation* instead of the broader term stakeholder. For simplicity of the conceptual model we prefer the broader term stakeholder which includes organisation.

Lau and Wang [15] criticise Szyperski's definition for not relating the component concept to a component model. Lau and Wang emphasise the importance of a component model as a provider of an underlying semantic framework, defining:

- the *syntax* of components, i.e., how they are constructed and represented;
- the *semantics* of components, i.e. what components are meant to be;
- the *composition* of components, i.e. how they are composed or assembled.

Lau and Wang present a taxonomy of current component models, comparing their similarities and differences with regard to these three criteria. They compare the component models facilities for composition both in the design phase and the deployment phase. Our approach focuses on the specification of components. Hence, composition takes place in the design phase.

According to Cheesman and Daniels [2] the main motivation for using a component-oriented approach is to make dependencies explicit, in order to facilitate management of component systems and independent deployment of components. Since the client of a component is not necessarily the same as the deployer of the component, they distinguish between two types of contracts corresponding to these two roles: usage and realisation contracts. This distinction motivates the separation of specifications into interfaces and components. Our conceptual model of a component, shown in Figure 2, is inspired by the definitions given in [2].

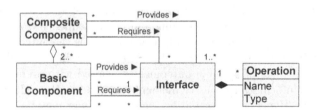

Fig. 2. Conceptual model of a component

We explain the conceptual component model as follows: An *interface* is a contract with a client, describing a set of behaviours provided by a component object. It defines a list of operations that the interface provides, their signatures and semantics. A *component* is a contract with the realiser. It describes provided interfaces and component dependencies in terms of required interfaces. By required interface we mean the calls the component needs to make, in order to implement the operations described in the provided interfaces. We distinguish between basic components and composite components. A basic component provides only one interface. We obtain components with more than one provided interface by the composition of basic components. Composite components can also be combined to obtain new composite components.

4   The Semantic Model of STAIRS

We build our semantic paradigm on top of the trace semantics of STAIRS [6,5]. STAIRS is an approach to the compositional development of UML 2.0 interactions. For a thorough account of the STAIRS semantics, see Haugen et al. [6,5].

The most common interaction diagram is the sequence diagram, which shows a set of messages arranged in time sequence [18]. A sequence diagram typically captures the behaviour of a single scenario. A sequence diagram describes one or more positive (i.e. valid) and/or negative (i.e. invalid) behaviours.

The sequence diagram in Figure 3 specifies a scenario in which the client lifeline sends the message displayAcc to the bank lifeline, which then sends the message check with argument *pin* to the environment. When the bank lifeline receives the message ok it sends the message acc to the client lifeline.

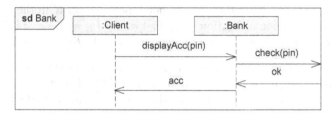

Fig. 3. Example interaction

Formally STAIRS uses denotational trace semantics in order to explain the meaning of a single interaction. A trace is a sequence of events, representing a system run. There are two kinds of events: sending and reception of a message, where a message is a triple (s, re, tr) consisting of a signal s, a transmitter lifeline tr and a receiver lifeline re. We let $\mathcal{E}$ denote the set of all events.

The set of traces described by a diagram like the one in Figure 3 are all positive sequences consisting of events such that the transmit event is ordered before the corresponding receive event, and events on the same lifeline are ordered from the top downwards. Shortening each message to the first letter of each signal, we thus get that Figure 3 specifies the trace $\langle !d, ?d, !c, ?o, !a, ?a \rangle$ where ! denotes transmission and ? reception of the message.

Formally we let $\mathcal{H}$ denote the set of all well-formed traces. A trace is well-formed if, for each message, the send event is ordered before the corresponding receive event. An *interaction obligation* (p_i, n_i) is a classification of all of the traces in $\mathcal{H}$ into three categories: the positive traces p_i, representing desired and acceptable behaviour, the negative traces n_i, representing undesired or unacceptable behaviour, and the inconclusive traces $\mathcal{H} \setminus (p_i \cup n_i)$. The inconclusive traces are a result of the incompleteness of interactions, representing traces that are not described as positive or negative by the current interaction.

The reason we operate with inconclusive traces is that sequence diagrams normally gives a partial description of a system behaviour. It is also possible to specify complete behaviour. Then every trace is either positive or negative.

5   Semantics of Basic Components

In this section we describe how basic components can be described semantically using STAIRS. Our semantic paradigm is independent of the concrete syntactic representation of specifications. In this paper we use sequence diagrams based on the semantic mapping defined in STAIRS, as they are simple to understand and well suited to exemplify parts of a component behaviour. We could have defined similar mappings for other specification languages.

A basic component has a unique identifier. In STAIRS this identifier is represented by a lifeline. As explained in Section 3 the provided interface of a basic component corresponds to the method calls it can receive and the required interface corresponds to the method calls the component needs to make to other component interfaces, in order to implement the operations described in the provided interface.

The denotation $[\![\, K \,]\!]$ of a basic component specification K in the STAIRS semantics is an interaction obligation (P_K, N_K) where P_K and N_K are the positive and negative traces over some set of component events E_K, respectively.

Example 1. The sequence diagram in Figure 4 specifies a scenario where a login lifeline receives the message login with arguments *id* and *pwd*. The login lifeline then sends the message authenticate to the environment. STAIRS uses the alt operator to describe that a system can include alternative behaviours. There are three alternatives: Firstly, when a user attempts to login she can either succeed or fail. If she fails there are two alternatives, of which only one is legal: When the login lifeline receives the reply fail it should reply with fail.

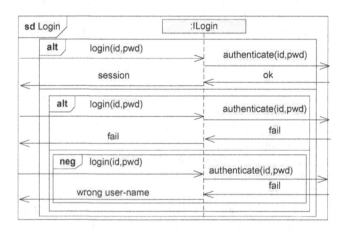

Fig. 4. Specifying component dependencies

We specify that the component should never return simply the message wrong user-name, by placing the event of returning this message within a neg construct in the sequence diagram. That is because we do not wish to reveal information that can be useful for a potential impostor, if a login attempt fails. The sequence diagram in Figure 4 specifies an interaction obligation (P, N) where $P = \{\langle ?l, !a, ?o, !s \rangle, \langle ?l, !a, ?f, !f \rangle\}$ and $N = \{\langle ?l, !a, ?f, !w \rangle\}$ when shortening each message to the first letter of each signal.   □

We define an interface and its denotation as an abstraction over a basic component. An interface describes the view of the user, who does not need to know how the login operation is implemented. We obtain the provided interface of a basic component by filtering away the interactions on the required interface. Hence, a provided interface corresponds to a basic component, if the component has no required interface.

6   Semantics of Composite Components

As described in Section 5 we distinguish between basic and composite components. A basic component provides only one interface. We obtain components with more than one interface by the composition of basic components. Composite components can also be combined to obtain new composite components.

In order to define composition we need the functions ⓢ for filtering of sequences, and ⓣ for filtering of pairs of sequences, defined by Haugen et al. [6,5]. The filtering function ⓢ is used to filter away elements. By B ⓢ a we denote the sequence obtained from the sequence a by removing all elements in a that are not in the set of elements B. For example, we have that

$$\{1, 3\} \text{ⓢ} \langle 1, 1, 2, 1, 3, 2 \rangle = \langle 1, 1, 1, 3 \rangle$$

The filtering function ⓣ may be understood as a generalisation of ⓢ. The function ⓣ filters pairs of sequences with respect to pairs of elements in the same way as ⓢ filters sequences with respect to elements. For any set of pairs of elements P and pair of sequences t, by P ⓣ t we denote the pair of sequences obtained from t by

- truncating the longest sequence in t at the length of the shortest sequence in t if the two sequences are of unequal length;
- for each $j \in [1, \ldots, k]$, where k is the length of the shortest sequence in t, selecting or deleting the two elements at index j in the two sequences, depending on whether the pair of these elements is in the set P.

For example, we have that

$$(1, f), (1, g) \text{ⓣ}(\langle 1, 1, 2, 1, 2 \rangle, \langle f, f, f, g, g \rangle) = (\langle 1, 1, 1 \rangle, \langle f, f, g \rangle)$$

Parallel execution of trace sets is defined as:

$$s_1 \otimes s_2 \stackrel{\text{def}}{=} \{h \in \mathcal{H} \mid \exists p \in \{1, 2\}^\infty : \pi_2((\{1\} \times \mathcal{E} \text{ⓣ}(p, h))) \in s_1 \wedge$$
$$\pi_2((\{2\} \times \mathcal{E} \text{ⓣ}(p, h))) \in s_2\}$$

In this definition, we make use of an oracle, the infinite sequence p, to resolve the non-determinism in the interleaving. It determines the order in which events from traces in s_1 and s_2 are sequenced. π_2 is a projection operator returning the second element of a pair.

Given two components K_1 and K_2 with distinct component identifiers (lifelines). By $K_1 \otimes K_2$ we denote their composition. Semantically, composition is defined as follows:

$$[\![\, K_1 \otimes K_2 \,]\!] = [\![\, K_1 \,]\!] \otimes [\![\, K_2 \,]\!]$$

where for all interaction obligations $(p_1, n_1), (p_2, n_2)$ we define

$$(p_1, n_1) \otimes (p_2, n_2) \overset{\text{def}}{=} (p_1 \otimes p_2, (n_1 \otimes p_2) \cup (n_1 \otimes n_2) \cup (p_1 \otimes n_2))$$

Note how any trace involving a negative trace will remain negative in the resulting interaction obligation.

We also introduce a hiding operator δ that hides all behaviour of a component which is internal with regard to a set of lifelines L. Formally

$$[\![\, \delta L : K \,]\!] \overset{\text{def}}{=} (\delta L : \pi_1.[\![\, K \,]\!], \delta L : \pi_2.[\![\, K \,]\!])$$

where for a set of traces H and a trace h

$$\delta L : H \overset{\text{def}}{=} \{\delta L : h \mid h \in H\}$$

$$\delta L : h \overset{\text{def}}{=} \{e \in \mathcal{E} \mid re.e \notin L \vee tr.e \notin L\} \circledS h$$

where the functions $tr.e$ and $re.e$ yields the transmitter and receiver of an event. Finally we define composition with hiding of local interaction as:

$$K_1 \oplus K_2 \overset{\text{def}}{=} \delta(ll.[\![\, K_1 \,]\!] \cup ll.[\![\, K_2 \,]\!]) : K_1 \otimes K_2$$

where the function ll yields the set of lifelines of an interaction obligation.

7   Generalising the Semantics to Support Unpredictability

As explained by Zakinthinos and Lee [26], the purpose of a confidentiality property is to prevent low level users from being able to make deductions about the events of the high level users. A confidentiality property will often typically require nondeterministic behaviour (unpredictability) to achieve this. Unpredictability in the form of non-determinism is known to be problematic in relation to specifications because non-determinism is also often used to represent underspecification and when underspecification is refined away during system development we may easily also reduce the required unpredictability and thereby reduce security. For this reason, STAIRS (as explained carefully by Seehusen and Stølen [21]) distinguishes between mandatory and potential choice. Mandatory choice is used to capture unpredictability while potential choice captures underspecification. One of the main concerns in STAIRS is the ability to distinguish between traces that an implementation *may* exhibit (e.g. due to underspecification), and traces that it *must* exhibit (e.g. due to unpredictability). Semantically, this distinction is captured by stating that the semantics of an interaction d is a *set* of interaction obligations $[\![\ d\ ]\!] = \{(p_1, n_1), \ldots, (p_m, n_m)\}$. Intuitively, the traces allowed by an interaction obligation (i.e. its positive and inconclusive traces) represent potential alternatives, where being able to produce only one of these traces is sufficient for an implementation. On the other hand, the different interaction obligations represent mandatory alternatives, each obligation specifying traces where at least one must be possible for any correct implementation of the specification.

We adapt the definition of a basic component to allow mandatory behaviour alternatives as follows: The denotation $[\![\ K\ ]\!]$ of a basic component is a set of interaction obligations over some set of events E_K. We also lift the definition of composition to handle unpredictability by point-wise composition of interaction obligations

$$[\![\ K_1 \otimes K_2\ ]\!] \overset{\text{def}}{=} \{o_1 \otimes o_2 \mid o_1 \in [\![\ K_1\ ]\!] \wedge o_2 \in [\![\ K_2\ ]\!]\}$$

The δ operator is overloaded to sets of interaction obligations:

$$[\![\ \delta L : K\ ]\!] \overset{\text{def}}{=} \{[\![\ \delta L : o\ ]\!] \mid o \in [\![\ K\ ]\!]\}$$

and composition with hiding is defined as before.

8   Relating Security Risk to the Semantic Paradigm

Having introduced the underlying semantic component paradigm and formalised unpredictability, the next step is to relate this paradigm to the main notions of security analysis and generalise the paradigm to the extent this is necessary. The purpose of extending the component model with security analysis concepts is to be able to specify security risks and document security analysis results of components. This facilitates integration of security analysis into the early stages of component-based system development. Security analysis documentation provides information about the risk level of the component with regard to its assets, i.e., the probability of behaviour leading to reduction of asset values. At this point we do not concern ourselves with *how* to obtain such security analysis results. We refer to [1] for an evaluation of an integrated process, applying the semantic paradigm. In the following we focus on how security analysis concepts can be understood in a component-setting and how they can be represented formally. In Sections 8.1– 8.4 we explain how the security analysis concepts of Figure 1 may be understood in a component setting. In Section 8.5 we formalise the required extensions of the semantic paradigm.

8.1   Representing Stakeholders and Threats

We represent *stakeholders* as lifelines, since the stakeholders of a component can be understood as entities interacting with it via its interfaces. We also represent *threats* as lifelines. A threat can be external (e.g. hackers or viruses) or internal (e.g. system failures). An internal threat of a component is a sub-component, represented by a lifeline or a set of lifelines. An external threat may initiate a threat scenario by calling an operation of one of the component's external interfaces.

8.2   Representing Assets

For each of its stakeholders a component holds a (possibly empty) set of assets. An asset is a physical or conceptual entity of value for a stakeholder. There are different strategies we can choose for representing assets, their initial values and the change in asset values over time: Represent assets (1) as variables and add an operator for assignment; (2) as data using extensions to STAIRS introduced by Runde et al. [19] or (3) as lifelines indicating the change in asset value through the reception of special messages. We have chosen the latter because it keeps our semantics simpler (we do not have to add new concepts) and provides the same extent of expressive power as the other alternatives. Formally an asset is a triple (a, c, V) of an asset lifeline a, a basic component lifeline c and an initial value V. In a trace we represent the reduction of asset value by a special kind of message called reduce, which takes as argument the amount by which the asset value should be reduced. The value of an asset at a given point in time is computed by looking at its initial value and all occurrences of reduce, with the asset as receiver, up to that point in the trace. Events on the lifeline of an asset can only be receptions of reduce messages. The value of an asset can not go below zero.

8.3   Representing Vulnerabilities

As pointed out by Verdon and McGraw [25] vulnerabilities can be divided into two basic categories: flaws, which are design level problems, and bugs, which are implementation level problems. When conducting security analysis during the early stages of system development, the vulnerabilities that can be detected are of the former type. I.e., a vulnerability is a weakness in the component specification, allowing interactions that can be exploited by threats to cause harm to assets.

8.4   Representing Incidents and Risks

As explained in Section 2 an information security incident is an unexpected or unwanted event that might compromise information security. In a component setting we can represent security incidents in the same manner as we represent normal behaviour; by sets of traces. A risk is measured in terms of the probability and consequence of an information security incident. Hence, in order to represent risks we need to be able to represent the probability of a set of traces constituting an information security incident and its consequence.

Inspired by Refsdal et al. [17] in our semantic model we represent this set of traces by a so called *risk obligation*. A risk obligation is a generalisation of an interaction obligation. Formally a risk obligation is a triple (o, Q, A) of an interaction obligation o, a set of probabilities Q and a set of assets A. The probability of the risk is an element of Q. We operate with a set of probabilities instead of a single probability to allow the probability to range freely within an interval.

Example 2. Figure 5 illustrates how we can specify a risk in accordance with the extensions to the semantic paradigm, described above. As most dynamic web applications, the login component pass data on to a subsystem. This may be an SQL data base or a component interacting with a database. If the system is not protected against SQL injection an attacker can modify or add queries that are sent to a database by crafting input to the web application. The attack example is from Sverre H. Huseby's [8] book on web-server security.

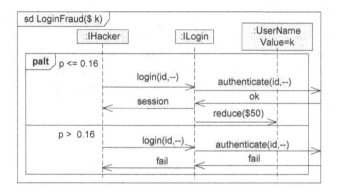

Fig. 5. Login without password using SQL injection

The sequence diagram in Figure 5 shows the interactions of a hacker using a modified query to attempt an SQL injection and the login lifeline receiving the query. Instead of a password the hacker writes a double hyphen (--). Unless the system is programmed to handle such metacharacters in a secure manner, this has the effect that the test for a matching password is inactivated allowing the hacker to login with only a user name. We have assigned the asset UserName to the basic component ILogin. As the sequence diagram illustrates an example run, we assume the initial asset value has been set elsewhere and parameterise the specification with the asset value k of type $. If the SQL attack is successful the asset value is reduced with $50.

We specify the risk as a probabilistic choice between the scenario where the attack is successful and the scenario where it fails. Probabilistic STAIRS [17] uses the palt construct to specify probabilistic alternatives, as illustrated in Figure 5.

In order to estimate the probability of a successful login using SQL injection, we must know both the probability of an attack (threat probability) and the probability of the success of an attack (degree of vulnerability), given that an attack is attempted. We assume that an attack has been estimated to have a 0.2 probability. The probability that the attack will be successful is determined from looking at the system's existing vulnerabilities, such as lack of control mechanisms. In the example there is not specified any protection mechanisms against attempt at SQL injection. The probability of success given an attack is therefore estimated as high: 0.8. The alternative to the risk is that the modified query is rejected, and hence the asset value is not reduced. The consequence of the risk is the loss of $50 in asset value. We multiply the probability of an attack with the probability of its success to obtain the total probability of the risk. Hence, the probability of a successful false login is $0.2 * 0.8 = 0.16$.   □

8.5   Generalising the Paradigm to Support Security Risk

Above we have outlined the relation between security risks as described in Figure 1 and our semantic paradigm. We now go on to adapt the semantic paradigm to capture this understanding formally.

In order to allow assignment of probabilities to trace sets, we represent basic components by sets of risk obligations instead of sets of interaction obligations. Moreover, contrary to earlier a basic component may now have more than one lifeline, namely the lifeline of the component itself and one additional lifeline for each of its assets. Hence, the denotation $[\![\,K\,]\!]$ of a basic component K is a set of risk obligations. Composition of components is defined point-wise as previously, i.e.:

$$[\![\,K_1 \otimes K_2\,]\!] \stackrel{\text{def}}{=} \{r_1 \otimes r_2 \mid r_1 \in [\![\,K_1\,]\!] \wedge r_2 \in [\![\,K_2\,]\!]\}$$

Composition of risk obligations is defined as follows

$$(o_1, Q_1, A_1) \otimes (o_1, Q_1, A_2) \stackrel{\text{def}}{=} (o_1 \otimes o_2, Q_1 * Q_2, A_1 \cup A_2)$$

where

$$Q_1 * Q_2 \stackrel{\text{def}}{=} \{q_1 * q_2 \mid q_1 \in Q_1 \wedge q_2 \in Q_2\}$$

and $*$ is the multiplication operator. The use of the $\otimes$-operator requires that K_1 and K_2 are described independently as components. In STAIRS the $\otimes$ operator corresponds to parallel composition ($\|$) (which is the same as $\succsim$ since K_1 and K_2 have disjoint lifelines). The scenario described in Figure 5 involves the palt construct, which imposes a global constraint on the interactions between the hacker and the login lifelines. Calculating the semantics of the overall scenario involves the use of several additional operators. See [6,5] for further details.

We also update the hiding operator δ to ensure that external assets are not hidden. An asset is external if it is associated with the interfaces of a basic component that has externally visible behaviour. We define the function A_{Ext} to yield the external assets with regard to a set of assets A, a set of basic component lifelines L and an interaction obligation o:

$$A_{\text{Ext}}(A, L, o) \stackrel{\text{def}}{=} \{a \in \mathcal{A} \mid \pi_2.a \in ll.\delta L : o\}$$

Given a component K and a set of basic component lifelines L, at the component level hiding is defined as the pointwise application of the hiding operator to each risk obligation:

$$[\![\, \delta L : K \,]\!] \stackrel{\text{def}}{=} \{\delta L : r \mid r \in [\![\, K \,]\!]\}$$

where hiding at the level of risk obligation is defined as:

$$\delta L : (o, Q, A) \stackrel{\text{def}}{=} (\delta(L \setminus A_{\text{Ext}}(A, L, o)) : o, Q, A_{\text{Ext}}(A, L, o))$$

Composition with hiding is defined as before.

9 Related Work

Fenton and Neil [4] addresses the problem of predicting risks related to introducing a new component into a system, by applying Bayesian networks to analyse failure probabilities of components. They combine quantitative and qualitative evidence concerning the reliability of a component and use Bayesian networks to calculate the overall failure probability. Although Fenton and Neil address the same problem as we do, the focus is different. At this point we do not concern ourselves with how the security analysis results are obtained. Rather than focusing on the process we look at how the results of security analysis can be represented at the component level to facilitate composition of security analysis results in a development process.

There are a number of proposals to integrate security requirements into the requirements specification, such as for example in SecureUML [16] and in UMLsec [13]. SecureUML is a method for modelling access control policies and their integration into model-driven software development. SecureUML is based on role-based access control and models security requirements for well-behaved applications in predictable environments. UMLsec is an extension to UML that enables the modelling of security-related features such as confidentiality and access control. These approaches have no particular focus on component-based specification. One approach that has a particular focus on component security is the security characterisation framework proposed by Khan and Han [14] to characterise and certify the security properties of components as a basis for deriving system-level risks during the deployment phase. These methods focus on specifying security properties of systems which is orthogonal to what we do. They include no notion of risk or probability. Rather than specifying security properties of systems, we focus on representing risks, i.e., we integrate the documentation of the probability that unwanted behaviour may occur into component specifications.

10 Conclusion

We have provided a semantic paradigm for component-based specifications explaining: basic components with provided and required interfaces; the composition of components into composite components and unpredictability which is

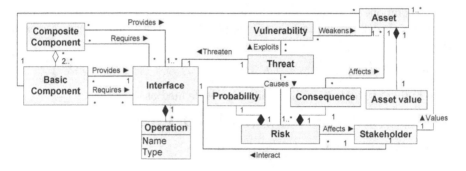

Fig. 6. Integrated conceptual model of a component risk specification

often required to characterise confidentiality properties. Furthermore we have extended the semantic paradigm with the notion of security risk as known from asset-oriented security analysis. Figure 6 summarises the relations between the conceptual component model and security assessment concepts: A component holds a set of assets that has value for its stakeholders. We limit the notion of a stakeholder to that of a component client or supplier interacting with it through its interfaces. We represent threats as lifelines that may interact with a component through its interface. There is a one-to-one association between an interface on the one hand and stakeholder and threat on the other, as a component interface can interact with one stakeholder or threat at a time. A vulnerability is represented implicitly as an interaction that may be exploited by a threat to cause harm to a components assets. Instead of representing the two concepts of information security incident and risk, we represent only the concept of a risk as a probabilistic interaction leading to the reduction of an asset value. In the extended component model we associate a threat directly with a risk, as someone or something that may initiate a risk.

The formal representation of security analysis results at the component-level allows us to specify security risks and document security analysis results of components. This is a step towards integration of security analysis into the system development process. Component-based security analysis can be conducted on the basis of requirement specification in parallel with conventional analysis. If new components are accompanied by security risk analysis, we do not need to carry out a security analysis from scratch each time a system is upgraded with new components, but can apply rules for composition to update the security risk analysis.

Acknowledgements

The research on which this paper reports has been funded by the Research Council of Norway via the two research projects COMA 160317 (Component-oriented model-based security analysis) and SECURIS (152839/220).

References

1. Brændeland, G., Stølen, K.: Using model-based security analysis in component-oriented system development. A case-based evaluation. In: Proceedings of the second Workshop on Quality of Protection (QoP'06) (to appear, 2006)

2. Cheesman, J., Daniels, J.: UML Components. A simple process for specifying component-based software. Component software series. Addison-Wesley, Reading (2001)

3. den Braber, F., Dimitrakos, T., Gran, B.A., Lund, M.S., Stølen, K., Aagedal, J.Ø.: UML and the Unified Process, chapter The CORAS methodology: model-based risk management using UML and UP, pp. 332–357. IRM Press (2003)

4. Fenton, N., Neil, M.: Combining evidence in risk analysis using bayesian networks. Agena White Paper W0704/01 (2004)

5. Haugen, Ø., Husa, K.E., Runde, R.K., Stølen, K.: Why timed sequence diagrams require three-event semantics. Technical Report 309, University of Oslo, Department of Informatics (2004)

6. Haugen, Ø., Stølen, K.: STAIRS – steps to analyze interactions with refinement semantics. In: Stevens, P., Whittle, J., Booch, G. (eds.) UML 2003 LNCS, vol. 2863, pp. 388–402. Springer, Heidelberg (2003)

7. Hogganvik, I., Stølen, K.: On the comprehension of security risk scenarios. In: 13th International Workshop on Program Comprehension (IWPC 2005), pp. 115–124. IEEE Computer Society, Los Alamitos (2005)

8. Huseby, S.H.: Innocent code. A security wake-up call for web programmers. Wiley, Chichester (2004)

9. ISO/IEC.: Information technology – Code of practice for information security management. ISO/IEC 17799:2000

10. ISO/IEC.: Risk management – Vocabulary – Guidelines for use in standards, ISO/IEC Guide 73:2002 (2002)

11. ISO/IEC.: Information Technology – Security techniques – Management of information and communications technology security – Part 1: Concepts and models for information and communications technology security management, ISO/IEC 13335-1:2004 (2004)

12. Jøsang, A., Presti, S.L.: Analysing the relationship between risk and trust. In: Jensen, C., Poslad, S., Dimitrakos, T. (eds.) iTrust 2004. LNCS, vol. 2995, pp. 135–145. Springer, Heidelberg (2004)

13. Jürjens, J. (ed.): Secure systems develoment with UML. Springer, Heidelberg (2005)

14. Khan, K.M., Han, J.: A process framework for characterising security properties of component-based software systems. In: Australian Software Engineering Conference, pp. 358–367. IEEE Computer Society, Los Alamitos (2004)

15. Lau, K.-K., Wang, Z.: A taxonomy of software component models. In: Proc. 31st Euromicro Conference, pp. 88–95. IEEE Computer Society Press, Los Alamitos (2005)

16. Lodderstedt, T., Basin, D.A., Doser, J.: SecureUML: A UML-based modeling language for model-driven security. In: Jézéquel, J.-M., Hussmann, H., Cook, S. (eds.) UML 2002 - The Unified Modeling Language. Model Engineering, Concepts, and Tools. LNCS, vol. 2460, pp. 426–441. Springer, Heidelberg (2002)

17. Refsdal, A., Runde, R.K., Stølen, K.: Underspecification, inherent nondeterminism and probability in sequence diagrams. In: Gorrieri, R., Wehrheim, H. (eds.) FMOODS 2006. LNCS, vol. 4037, pp. 138–155. Springer, Heidelberg (2006)

18. Rumbaugh, J., Jacobsen, I., Booch, G.: The unified modeling language reference manual. Addison-Wesley, Reading (2005)
19. Runde, R.K., Haugen, Ø., Stølen, K.: Refining UML interactions with underspecification and nondeterminism. Nordic Journal of Computing (2005)
20. Winamp skin file arbitrary code execution vulnerability. Secunia Advisory: SA12381. Secunia (2006)
21. Seehusen, F., Stølen, K.: Information flow property preserving transformation of uml interaction diagrams. In: 11th ACM Symposium on Access Control Models and Technologies (SACMAT 2006), pp. 150–159. ACM, New York (2006)
22. Standards Australia: Standards New Zealand. Australian/New Zealand Standard. Risk Management, AS/NZS 4360:2004 (2004)
23. Standards Australia: Standards New Zealand. Information security risk management guidelines, HB 231:2004 (2004)
24. Szyperski, C., Pfister, C.: Workshop on component-oriented programming. In: Mülhauser, M. (ed.) Special Issues in Object-Oriented Programming – ECOOP'96 Workshop Reader, dpunkt Verlag, pp. 127–130 (1997)
25. Verdon, D., McGraw, G.: Risk analysis in software design. IEEE Security & Privacy 2(4), 79–84 (2004)
26. Zakinthinos, A., Lee, E.S.: A general theory of security properties. In: IEEE Symposium on Security and Privacy, pp. 94–102. IEEE Computer Society, Los Alamitos (1997)

Game-Based Criterion Partition Applied to Computational Soundness of Adaptive Security

M. Daubignard, R. Janvier, Y. Lakhnech, and L. Mazaré

VERIMAG, 2, av. de Vignates, 38610 Gières - France
{marion.daubignard,romain.janvier,yassine.lakhnech,
laurent.mazare}@imag.fr

Abstract. The composition of security definitions is a subtle issue. As most security protocols use a combination of security primitives, it is important to have general results that allow to combine such definitions. We present here a general result of composition for security criteria (i.e. security requirements). This result can be applied to deduce security of a criterion from security of one of its sub-criterion and an indistinguishability criterion. To illustrate our result, we introduce joint security for asymmetric and symmetric cryptography and prove that it is equivalent to classical security assumptions for both the asymmetric and symmetric encryption schemes. Using this, we give a modular proof of computational soundness of symbolic encryption. This result holds in the case of an adaptive adversary which can use both asymmetric and symmetric encryption.

Keywords: Provable Security, Security Games, Probabilistic Encryption, Computational Soundness of Formal Methods.

1 Introduction

Provable security consists in stating the expected security properties in a formally defined adversarial model and providing a mathematical proof that the properties are satisfied by the designed system/protocol. Micali and Goldwasser are probably the first to put forward the idea that security can be proved in a formally defined model under well-believed rigorously defined complexity-assumptions [GM84]. Although provable security has by now become a very active research field there is a lack of a general "proof theory" for cryptographic systems. As underlined by V. Shoup in [Sho04], security proofs often *become so messy, complicated, and subtle as to be nearly impossible to understand.* Ideally there should be a verification theory for cryptographic systems in the same way as there are verification theories for "usual" sequential and concurrent systems (cf. [Cou90, MP92]).

As security proofs are mostly *proofs by reduction* a promising approach seems to be one that is based on transforming the system to be verified into a system that obviously satisfies the required properties. Sequences of games have

T. Dimitrakos et al. (Eds.): FAST 2006, LNCS 4691, pp. 47–64, 2007.

been recently proposed as a tool for taming the complexity of security proofs [Sho04, BR04] and first implementations of tools that assisted in deriving such sequences have been developed [Bla06]. In particular, three types of transitions between games are proposed. One of the most powerful transitions is based on *indistinguishability*. Informally, to bound the probability of an event E_i in game i and the probability of event E_{i+1} in game $i+1$, one shows that there is a *distinguisher algorithm* D that interpolates between Game i and Game $i+1$, such that given an element from distribution P_i, for $i = 1, 2$, D outputs 1 with probability $Pr[E_i]$. Hence, $Pr[E_i] - Pr[E_{i+1}] = Pr[D(x) \rightarrow 1|x \in P_1] - Pr[D(x) \rightarrow 1|x \in P_2]$, and hence, the indistinguishability assumption implies that $Pr[E_i] - Pr[E_{i+1}]$ is negligible.

In this paper we prove a theorem that provides a powerful instance of the indistinguishability-based transition technique. This theorem can be used for compositional verification of cryptographic libraries as it allows one to reduce a security criterion into simpler ones. A typical use is to allow the comparison of a criterion that involves a set of oracles (which can for example all use the same challenge bit b) with a criterion that only involves a subset of the oracles. As a simple application of this result, we can for instance prove the equivalence of semantic security of one key and semantic security in the multi-party setting [BBM00]. The advantage of applying our theorem in that case is that the proof is done without having to design adversaries, the only thing to do is to provide a partition of the criterion.

Moreover we believe that our main result is helpful when proving computational soundness of symbolic analysis for cryptographic protocols. This recent trend in bridging the gap that separates the computational and symbolic views of protocols has been initiated by Abadi and Rogaway [AR00]. In this paper, they prove that symbolic equivalence of messages implies computational indistinguishability provided that the cryptographic primitives are secure. This result has then been adapted for protocols where the adversary is an eavesdropper and has a passive behavior and the only allowed cryptographic primitive is symmetric encryption [AJ01].

Various extensions of [AR00, AJ01] have been presented recently by adding new cryptographic primitives [BCK05] or by removing the passive adversary hypothesis. There are different ways to consider non-passive adversaries, this can be done by using the simulatability approach [BPW03], by proving trace properties on protocols [MW04, CW05, JLM05]. Another possibility is to consider an adaptive adversary as introduced by Micciancio and Panjwani [MP05]. In this context, the adversary issues a sequence of adaptively chosen equivalent pairs of messages (m_0^1, m_1^1) to (m_0^q, m_1^q). After query (m_0^i, m_1^i) the adversary receives a bit-string that instantiates either m_0^i or m_1^i and it has to tell which is the case. The main improvement with respect to the result of Abadi and Rogaway [AR00] is that the adversary has an adaptive behavior: it can first send a query (m_0^1, m_1^1) then using the result determine a new query and submit it. However Micciancio and Panjwani only consider symmetric encryption. In order to illustrate how our main result can be used in such situations, we prove a similar result when considering both asymmetric and symmetric encryption. Besides by using our partition theorem, the proof we give is modular and hence easier to extend to more cryptographic primitives than the original one. For that purpose, we introduce new security criteria which define *pattern semantic security* and prove that these criteria are equivalent to classical semantic security requirements. The main interest of these criteria is to easily allow encryption of secret keys (either symmetric or private keys).

Organization. In section 2 after recalling some basic definitions, we introduce security criteria and some examples of cryptography-related criteria. A powerful way of composing security criteria is introduced and proved in section 3: the criterion partition theorem. Section 4 shows how to use this result soundly. To illustrate this we prove that some composition of asymmetric and symmetric encryption schemes can be directly stated secure by using the partition theorem. Using this last result, section 5 proves computational soundness of symbolic equivalence for an adaptive adversary using both asymmetric and symmetric encryption schemes. Eventually, section 6 draws some concluding remarks.

2 Preliminaries

2.1 Cryptographic Schemes

We first recall classical definitions for cryptographic schemes in the computational setting. In this setting, messages are bit-strings and a security parameter η is used to characterize the strength of the different schemes, for example η can denote the length of the keys used to perform an encryption.

An *asymmetric encryption scheme* $\mathcal{AE} = (\mathcal{KG}, \mathcal{E}, \mathcal{D})$ is defined by three algorithms. The key generation algorithm $\mathcal{KG}$ is a randomized function which given a security parameter η outputs a pair of keys (pk, sk), where pk is a public key and sk the associated secret key. The encryption algorithm $\mathcal{E}$ is also a randomized function which given a message and a public key outputs the encryption of the message by the public key. Finally the decryption algorithm $\mathcal{D}$ takes as input a cipher-text and a secret key and outputs the corresponding plain-text, i.e. $\mathcal{D}(\mathcal{E}(m, pk), sk) = m$, if key pair (pk, sk) has been generated by $\mathcal{KG}$. The execution time of the three algorithms is assumed to be polynomially bounded by η.

A *symmetric encryption scheme* $\mathcal{SE} = (\mathcal{KG}, \mathcal{E}, \mathcal{D})$ is also defined by three algorithms. The key generation algorithm $\mathcal{KG}$ is a randomized function which given a security parameter η outputs a key k. The encryption algorithm $\mathcal{E}$ is also a randomized function which given a message and a key outputs the encryption of the message by this key. Finally the decryption algorithm $\mathcal{D}$ takes as input a cipher-text and a key and outputs the corresponding plain-text, i.e. $\mathcal{D}(\mathcal{E}(m, k), k) = m$. The execution time of the three algorithms is also assumed polynomially bounded by η.

A function $g : \mathbb{R} \to \mathbb{R}$ is *negligible*, if it is ultimately bounded by x^{-c}, for each positive $c \in \mathbb{N}$, i.e. for all $c > 0$ there exists N_c such that $|g(x)| < x^{-c}$, for all $x > N_c$.

2.2   Turing Machines with Oracles

Adversaries are polynomial-time random Turing machines (PRTM) with oracles. Oracles are also implemented using PRTMs. In order to detail the oracles an adversary can query, the definition of an adversary $\mathcal{A}$ is for example:

Adversary $\mathcal{A}/\mathcal{O}_1, \mathcal{O}_2$:
    Code of $\mathcal{A}$ e.g: $s \leftarrow \mathcal{O}_1(x)$

Where the code of $\mathcal{A}$ can call two oracles using names $\mathcal{O}_1$ and $\mathcal{O}_2$. When executing this adversary $\mathcal{A}$, we use the notation $\mathcal{A}/\mathcal{B}_1, \mathcal{B}_2$ where $\mathcal{B}_1$ and $\mathcal{B}_2$ are two PRTMs to denote that names $\mathcal{O}_1$ and $\mathcal{O}_2$ are respectively implemented with oracles $\mathcal{B}_1$ and $\mathcal{B}_2$.

We use the standard λ-notation to concisely describe PRTMs obtained from others by fixing some arguments. For instance, let G be a PRTM that has two inputs. Then, we write $\lambda s.G(s, \theta)$ to describe the machine that is obtained from G by fixing the second argument to the value θ. Thus, $\mathcal{A}/\lambda s.G(s, \theta)$ denotes the machine $\mathcal{A}$ that may query an oracle obtained from G by instantiating its second argument by θ. The argument θ of G is defined in the context of $\mathcal{A}$ and may not be known by $\mathcal{A}$. So typically, $\mathcal{A}$ may be trying to compute some information on θ through successive queries.

Moreover, adversaries are often used as sub-routines in other adversaries. Consider the following description of a randomized algorithm with oracles. Here adversary $\mathcal{A}'$ uses $\mathcal{A}$ as a sub-routine. Moreover, $\mathcal{A}'$ may query oracle $\mathcal{O}_1$. On its turn $\mathcal{A}$ may query the same oracle $\mathcal{O}_1$ and additionally the oracle $\lambda s.F_2(s, \theta_2)$. The latter is obtained from F_2 by fixing the second argument to θ_2 which is generated by $\mathcal{A}'$.

Adversary $\mathcal{A}'/\mathcal{O}_1$:
    $\theta_2 \leftarrow ...$
    $s \leftarrow \mathcal{A}/\mathcal{O}_1,$
        $\lambda s.F_2(s, \theta_2)$

2.3   Games and Criteria

A security criterion is defined as a game involving an adversary (represented by a PRTM). The game proceeds as follows. First some parameters θ are generated randomly using a PRTM Θ. The adversary is executed and can query an oracle F which depends on θ. At the end, the adversary has to answer a bit-string whose correctness is checked by an algorithm V which also uses θ (e.g. θ includes a bit b and the adversary has to output the value of b). Thus, a criterion is given by a triple consisting of three randomized algorithms:

- Θ is a PRTM that randomly generates some challenge θ.
- F is a PRTM that takes as arguments a bit-string s and a challenge θ and outputs a new bit-string. F represents the oracles that an adversary can call to solve its challenge.
- V is a PRTM that takes as arguments a bit-string s and a challenge θ and outputs either true or false. It represents the verification made on the result computed by the adversary. The answer true (resp. false) means that the adversary solved (resp. did not solve) the challenge.

As an example let us consider an asymmetric encryption scheme $(\mathcal{KG}, \mathcal{E}, \mathcal{D})$. Semantic security against chosen plain-text attacks (IND-CPA) can be represented using a security criterion $(\Theta; F; V)$ defined as follows: Θ randomly samples the challenge bit b and generates a key pair (pk, sk) using $\mathcal{KG}$; F represents the public key oracle (this oracle returns pk) and the left-right encryption oracle (given bs_0 and bs_1 this oracle returns $\mathcal{E}(bs_b, pk)$); and V checks whether the returned bit equals b.

Note that Θ can generate several parameters and F can represent several oracles. Thus, it is possible to define criteria with multiples Θ and F. For example, a criterion with two challenge generators Θ_1 and Θ_2, two oracles F_1 and F_2 and a verifier V is denoted by $(\Theta_1, \Theta_2; F_1, F_2; V)$.

Let $\gamma = (\Theta; F; V)$. The advantage of a PRTM $\mathcal{A}$ against γ is defined as the probability that $\mathcal{A}$ has to win its game minus the probability that an adversary can get without accessing oracle F.

$$\mathbf{Adv}_{\mathcal{A}}^{\gamma}(\eta) = 2\left(Pr[\mathbf{G}_{\mathcal{A}}^{\gamma}(\eta) = true] - PrRand^{\gamma}(\eta)\right)$$

where $\mathbf{G}_{\mathcal{A}}^{\gamma}(\eta)$ is the Turing machine defined by:

Game $\mathbf{G}_{\mathcal{A}}^{\gamma}(\eta)$:
 $\theta \leftarrow \Theta(\eta)$
 $d \leftarrow \mathcal{A}(\eta)/\lambda s.F(s, \theta)$
 return $V(d, \theta)$

and $PrRand^{\gamma}(\eta)$ is the best probability to solve the challenge that an adversary can have without using oracle F. Formally, let γ' be the criterion $(\Theta; \epsilon; V)$ then $PrRand^{\gamma}(\eta)$ is defined by:

$$PrRand^{\gamma}(\eta) = \max_{\mathcal{A}}\left(Pr[\mathbf{G}_{\mathcal{A}}^{\gamma'}(\eta) = true]\right)$$

where $\mathcal{A}$ ranges over any possible PRTM. For example when considering a criterion $\gamma = (\Theta; F; V)$ where a challenge bit b is generated in Θ and V checks that the adversary guessed the value of b, then $PrRand^{\gamma}(\eta)$ equals $1/2$, in particular this is the case for IND-CPA.

3 The Criterion Partition Theorem

Consider a criterion $\gamma = (\Theta_1, \Theta_2; F_1, F_2; V_1)$, composed of two challenge generators Θ_i, their related oracles F_i, and a verifier V_1. Assume that F_1 and V_1

do not depend on θ_2 (which is the part generated by Θ_2). Because of these assumptions, $\gamma_1 = (\Theta_1; F_1; V_1)$ is a valid criterion. We are going to relate the advantages against γ and γ_1. To do so, let us consider the game $\mathbf{G}_{\mathcal{A}}^{\gamma}(\eta)$ played by an adversary $\mathcal{A}$ against γ:

Game $\mathbf{G}_{\mathcal{A}}^{\gamma}(\eta)$:
$$\theta_1 \leftarrow \Theta_1(\eta)$$
$$\theta_2 \leftarrow \Theta_2(\eta)$$
$$s \leftarrow \mathcal{A}/\lambda s.F_1(s,\theta_1),$$
$$\lambda s.F_2(s,\theta_1,\theta_2)$$
$$\textbf{return } V_1(s,\theta_1)$$

We define an adversary $\mathcal{A}'$ against γ_1 which tries to act like $\mathcal{A}$. However, $\mathcal{A}'$ does not have access to its challenge θ_1 and hence it generates a new challenge θ_1' (using Θ_1) and uses it to answer queries made by $\mathcal{A}$ to F_2.

Adversary $\mathcal{A}'/\mathcal{O}_1$:
$$\theta_1' \leftarrow \Theta_1(\eta)$$
$$\theta_2 \leftarrow \Theta_2(\eta)$$
$$s \leftarrow \mathcal{A}/\mathcal{O}_1,$$
$$\lambda s.F_2(s,\theta_1',\theta_2)$$
$$\textbf{return } s$$

The game involving $\mathcal{A}'$ against γ_1, $\mathbf{G}_{\mathcal{A}'}^{\gamma_1}(\eta)$, is given by:

Game $\mathbf{G}_{\mathcal{A}'}^{\gamma_1}(\eta)$:
$$\theta_1 \leftarrow \Theta_1(\eta)$$
$$\theta_1' \leftarrow \Theta_1(\eta)$$
$$\theta_2 \leftarrow \Theta_2(\eta)$$
$$s \leftarrow \mathcal{A}/\lambda s.F_1(s,\theta_1),$$
$$\lambda s.F_2(s,\theta_1',\theta_2)$$
$$\textbf{return } V_1(s,\theta_1)$$

Our aim is to establish a bound on

$$|Pr[\mathbf{G}_{\mathcal{A}}^{\gamma}(\eta) = true] - Pr[\mathbf{G}_{\mathcal{A}'}^{\gamma_1}(\eta) = true]|$$

To do so, we construct an adversary $\mathcal{B}$ that tries to distinguish game $\mathbf{G}_{\mathcal{A}}^{\gamma}(\eta)$ from game $\mathbf{G}_{\mathcal{A}'}^{\gamma_1}(\eta)$, i.e. $\mathcal{B}$ tries to distinguish the case where $\mathcal{A}$ uses correlated oracles (i.e. the same θ_1 is used by F_1 and F_2) from the case where $\mathcal{A}$ uses decorrelated oracles (i.e. θ_1 is used by F_1 and a different θ_1' is used by F_2), figure 1 gives the intuition of how $\mathcal{B}$ works: $\mathcal{B}$ either simulates $\mathcal{A}$ with correlated oracles in the upper part of the figure or $\mathcal{A}$ with decorrelated oracles. Finally, $\mathcal{B}$ uses the answer of $\mathcal{A}$ in order to win its challenge. We introduce a new indistinguishability criterion γ_2 that uses a challenge bit b, in this criterion the adversary has to guess the value of bit b. Our objective is to build a distinguisher $\mathcal{B}$ such that the following equations hold:

$$Pr[\mathbf{G}_{\mathcal{B}}^{\gamma_2} = true \mid b = 1] = Pr[\mathbf{G}_{\mathcal{A}}^{\gamma}(\eta) = true] \tag{1}$$

$$Pr[\mathbf{G}_{\mathcal{B}}^{\gamma_2} = false \mid b = 0] = Pr[\mathbf{G}_{\mathcal{A}'}^{\gamma_1}(\eta) = true] \tag{2}$$

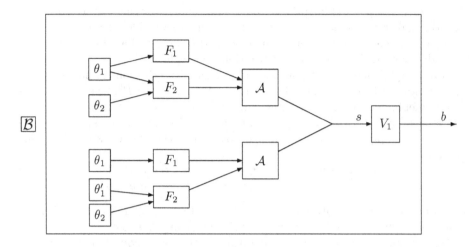

Fig. 1. Correlated and Decorrelated Oracles

Indeed, using these equations we will be able to derive the following bound:

$$|Pr[\mathbf{G}_{\mathcal{A}}^{\gamma}(\eta) = true] - Pr[\mathbf{G}_{\mathcal{A}'}^{\gamma_1}(\eta) = true]| = \mathbf{Adv}_{\mathcal{B}}^{\gamma_2}(\eta)$$

3.1   Construction of the Distinguisher

In the following, we give a methodology that tells us how to build the indistinguishability criterion γ_2 and the adversary $\mathcal{B}$. To do so, we need an assumption on the form of the second oracle F_2 from γ. This assumption is stated through the following hypothesis.

Hypothesis 1. *There exist three probabilistic random functions f, g and f' such that oracle F_2's implementation consists of two parts: $\lambda s.f(g(s, \theta_1), \theta_2)$ and $\lambda s.f'(s, \theta_2)$. The first part depends on both θ_1 and θ_2 whereas the second depends only on θ_2.*

The idea when introducing two parts for oracle F_2 is to separate the oracles contained in F_2 that really depend on both θ_1 and θ_2 (these oracles are placed in $f(g(...))$) from the oracles that do not depend on θ_1 (placed in f'). Let us illustrate this on the IND-CPA criterion with two keys: there are one left-right encryption oracle and one public key oracle for each key. Θ_1 generates the challenge bit b and the first key pair (pk_1, sk_1), Θ_2 generates the other key pair (pk_2, sk_2). Oracle F_2 contains the left-right oracle related to pk_2 and the public key oracle that reveals pk_2. Hence f' is used to store the public key oracle whereas the left-right oracle has the form $\lambda s.f(g(s, \theta_1), \theta_2)$ where f performs an encryption using key pk_2 from θ_2 and $g((s_0, s_1), \theta_1)$ returns s_b according to the value of challenge bit b from θ_1. It is possible to split the oracles differently but this would not lead to interesting sub-criteria. In general it is always possible to perform a splitting that satisfies the previous hypothesis (for example,

f' is empty and $g(s, \theta_1)$ outputs both s and θ_1), however this can lead to some criteria against which adversaries may have a non-negligible advantage. In that situation the partition theorem cannot be used to obtain that the advantage of any adversary against the original criterion γ is negligible.

Adversary $\mathcal{B}$ plays against an indistinguishability criterion. It has access to two oracles: $\hat{\mathcal{O}}_1$ is implemented by the left-right oracle $f \circ LR^b$, where LR^b takes as argument a pair and returns either the first or the second element according to the value of bit b, i.e. $LR^b(x_0, x_1) = x_b$. Hence, we have $f \circ LR^b(s_0, s_1) = f(s_b, \theta_2)$ and $\hat{\mathcal{O}}_2$ is simply implemented by f'. Notice now that we have the following equations:

$$f \circ LR^b(g(s, \theta'_1), g(s, \theta_1)) = F_2(s, \theta_1, \theta_2), \text{ if } b = 1$$
$$f \circ LR^b(g(s, \theta'_1), g(s, \theta_1)) = F_2(s, \theta'_1, \theta_2), \text{ if } b = 0$$

More formally, our γ_2 criterion is given by $\gamma_2 = (b, \Theta_2; f \circ LR^b, f'; v_b)$, where v_b just checks whether the bit returned by the adversary equals b.

We are now ready to give a distinguisher $\mathcal{B}$ such that equations (1) and (2) hold:

Adversary $\mathcal{B}/\hat{\mathcal{O}}_1, \hat{\mathcal{O}}_2$:
> $\theta_1 \leftarrow \Theta_1(\eta)$
> $\theta'_1 \leftarrow \Theta_1(\eta)$
> $s \leftarrow \mathcal{A}/\lambda s.F_1(s, \theta_1),$ // oracle F_1
> $\lambda s.\hat{\mathcal{O}}_1(g(s, \theta'_1), g(s, \theta_1)),$ // part f of oracle F_2
> $\hat{\mathcal{O}}_2$ // part f' of oracle F_2
> $\hat{b} \leftarrow V_1(s, \theta_1)$
> **return** $\hat{b}$

Recall that $\mathcal{A}$ may query two oracles: F_1 and F_2 while $\mathcal{B}$ may query the left-right oracle $f \circ LR^b$ and f'. Therefore, $\mathcal{B}$ uses Θ_1 to generate θ_1 and θ'_1. It is important to notice that θ_1 and θ'_1 are generated independently. Then, $\mathcal{B}$ uses $\mathcal{A}$ as a sub-routine using $\lambda s.F_1(s, \theta)$ for $\mathcal{A}$'s first oracle, and the pair of functions $\lambda s.\hat{\mathcal{O}}_1(g(s, \theta'_1), g(s, \theta_1))$ and f' for F_2.

The game corresponding to $\mathcal{B}$ playing against γ_2 can now be detailed:

Game $\mathbf{G}_{\mathcal{B}}^{\gamma_2}(\eta)$:
> $b \leftarrow \{0, 1\}$
> $\theta_2 \leftarrow \Theta_2(\eta)$
> $\hat{b} \leftarrow \mathcal{B}/\lambda s.f(LR^b(s), \theta_2),$
> $\lambda s.f'(s, \theta_2)$
> **return** $v_b(\hat{b})$

3.2   Comparing the Games

Let us now check equations (1) and (2). To do so, we first consider that b equals 1. Then game $\mathbf{G}_{\mathcal{B}}^{\gamma_2}$ can be detailed by introducing the definition of $\mathcal{B}$ within the game:

Game $\mathbf{G}_{\mathcal{B}}^{\gamma_2}(\eta)|b=1$:

$\quad \theta_2 \leftarrow \Theta_2(\eta)$

$\quad \theta_1 \leftarrow \Theta_1(\eta)$

$\quad \theta_1' \leftarrow \Theta_1(\eta)$

$\quad s \leftarrow \mathcal{A}/\lambda s.F_1(s,\theta_1)$

$\quad\quad\quad \lambda s.f(g(s,\theta_1),\theta_2),$

$\quad\quad\quad \lambda s.f'(s,\theta_2)$

$\quad \hat{b} \leftarrow V_1(s,\theta_1)$

$\quad$ **return** $\hat{b}=1$

After the hypothesis we made about the decomposition of oracle F_2, and when detailing $\mathcal{B}$, this game can be rewritten as follows, and rigorously compared to the game played by adversary $\mathcal{A}$ against criterion γ:

Game $\mathbf{G}_{\mathcal{B}}^{\gamma_2}(\eta)|b=1$:

$\quad \theta_1 \leftarrow \Theta_1(\eta)$

$\quad \theta_1' \leftarrow \Theta_1(\eta)$

$\quad \theta_2 \leftarrow \Theta_2(\eta)$

$\quad s \leftarrow \mathcal{A}/\lambda s.F_1(s,\theta_1),$

$\quad\quad\quad \lambda s.F_2(s,\theta_1,\theta_2)$

$\quad \hat{b} \leftarrow V_1(s,\theta_1)$

$\quad$ **return** $\hat{b}=1$

Game $\mathbf{G}_{\mathcal{A}}^{\gamma}(\eta)$:

$\quad \theta_1 \leftarrow \Theta_1(\eta)$

$\quad \theta_2 \leftarrow \Theta_2(\eta)$

$\quad s \leftarrow \mathcal{A}/\lambda s.F_1(s,\theta_1),$

$\quad\quad\quad \lambda s.F_2(s,\theta_1,\theta_2)$

$\quad$ **return** $V_1(s,\theta_1)$

Therefore these two games are equivalent and so equation (1) holds:

$$Pr[\mathbf{G}_{\mathcal{B}}^{\gamma_2} = true \mid b = 1] = Pr[\mathbf{G}_{\mathcal{A}}^{\gamma}(\eta) = true]$$

We now detail the game played by adversary $\mathcal{B}$ against γ_2 when the challenge bit b is 0. This game is compared to the game played by $\mathcal{A}'$ against γ_1.

Game $\mathbf{G}_{\mathcal{B}}^{\gamma_2}(\eta)|b=0$:

$\quad \theta_2 \leftarrow \Theta_2(\eta)$

$\quad \theta_1 \leftarrow \Theta_1(\eta)$

$\quad \theta_1' \leftarrow \Theta_1(\eta)$

$\quad s \leftarrow \mathcal{A}/\lambda s.F_1(s,\theta_1),$

$\quad\quad\quad \lambda s.F_2(s,\theta_1',\theta_2)$

$\quad \hat{b} \leftarrow V_1(s,\theta_1)$

$\quad$ **return** $\hat{b}=0$

Game $\mathbf{G}_{\mathcal{A}'}^{\gamma_1}(\eta)$:

$\quad \theta_1 \leftarrow \Theta_1(\eta)$

$\quad \theta_1' \leftarrow \Theta_1(\eta)$

$\quad \theta_2 \leftarrow \Theta_2(\eta)$

$\quad s \leftarrow \mathcal{A}/\lambda s.F_1(s,\theta_1),$

$\quad\quad\quad \lambda s.F_2(s,\theta_1',\theta_2)$

$\quad$ **return** $V_1(s,\theta_1)$

It is easy to see that these two games can be compared: adversary $\mathcal{B}$ wins anytime $\mathcal{A}'$ loses, and thus:

$$Pr[\mathbf{G}_{\mathcal{A}'}^{\gamma_1}(\eta) = false] = Pr[\mathbf{G}_{\mathcal{B}}^{\gamma_2}(\eta) = true | b = 0]$$

We can therefore evaluate our distinguisher's advantage. For that purpose let us first notice that as γ_2 consists in guessing the value of a random bit b, $PrRand^{\gamma_2}$ equals $1/2$. Furthermore γ and γ_1 have the same verifier V_1, hence $PrRand^{\gamma}$ is equal to $PrRand^{\gamma_1}$.

$$\mathbf{Adv}_{\mathcal{B}}^{\gamma_2}(\eta) = 2\big(Pr[\mathbf{G}_{\mathcal{B}}^{\gamma_2}(\eta) = true] - PrRand^{\gamma_2}\big)$$
$$= 2Pr[\mathbf{G}_{\mathcal{B}}^{\gamma_2}(\eta) = true|b = 1]Pr[b = 1] +$$
$$\quad 2Pr[\mathbf{G}_{\mathcal{B}}^{\gamma_2}(\eta) = true|b = 0]Pr[b = 0] - 1$$
$$= Pr[\mathbf{G}_{\mathcal{A}}^{\gamma}(\eta) = true] + Pr[\mathbf{G}_{\mathcal{A}'}^{\gamma_1}(\eta) = false] - 1$$
$$= Pr[\mathbf{G}_{\mathcal{A}}^{\gamma}(\eta) = true] - Pr[\mathbf{G}_{\mathcal{A}'}^{\gamma_1}(\eta) = true]$$
$$= Pr[\mathbf{G}_{\mathcal{A}}^{\gamma}(\eta) = true] - PrRand^{\gamma}$$
$$\quad + PrRand^{\gamma_1} - Pr[\mathbf{G}_{\mathcal{A}'}^{\gamma_1}(\eta) = true]$$
$$= \frac{1}{2}\mathbf{Adv}_{\mathcal{A}}^{\gamma}(\eta) - \frac{1}{2}\mathbf{Adv}_{\mathcal{A}'}^{\gamma_1}(\eta)$$

Given an adversary $\mathcal{A}$ against γ, we were able to build an adversary $\mathcal{A}'$ against γ_1 and an adversary $\mathcal{B}$ against γ_2 such that:

$$\forall \eta, \mathbf{Adv}_{\mathcal{A}}^{\gamma}(\eta) = 2\mathbf{Adv}_{\mathcal{B}}^{\gamma_2}(\eta) + \mathbf{Adv}_{\mathcal{A}'}^{\gamma_1}(\eta)$$

This is summed up in the following theorem which is our core result.

Theorem 1 (Criterion Partition). *Let γ be the criterion $(\Theta_1, \Theta_2; F_1, F_2; V_1)$ where:*

1. *V_1 and F_1 only depend on the challenge generated by Θ_1, denoted by θ_1.*
2. *There exist some PRTMs f, f' and g such that F_2 is constituted of two parts: $\lambda s.f(g(s, \theta_1), \theta_2)$ and $\lambda s.f'(s, \theta_2)$*

Then, for any adversary $\mathcal{A}$ against criterion γ, there exist two adversaries $\mathcal{B}$ and $\mathcal{A}'$, such that:
$$\forall \eta, \boldsymbol{Adv}_{\mathcal{A}}^{\gamma}(\eta) = 2\boldsymbol{Adv}_{\mathcal{B}}^{\gamma_2}(\eta) + \boldsymbol{Adv}_{\mathcal{A}'}^{\gamma_1}(\eta)$$

where $\gamma_2 = (\Theta_2, b; f \circ LR^b, f'; v_b)$ is an indistinguishability criterion and $\gamma_1 = (\Theta_1; F_1; V_1)$.

This theorem can be used to prove that the advantage of any adversary against a criterion γ is negligible. For that purpose, one has to provide a partition of γ such that the advantage of any adversary against γ_1 or γ_2 is negligible. Then we get that for an adversary $\mathcal{A}$ against γ, the advantage of $\mathcal{A}$ can be bounded by the advantage of an adversary against γ_1 and the advantage of an adversary against γ_2. The advantage of these two new adversaries are negligible and so the advantage of $\mathcal{A}$ is also negligible.

4   Mixing Asymmetric and Symmetric Encryption

4.1   Cryptographic Game: N-PAT-IND-CCA

We introduce a security criterion that turns out to be useful for protocols where secret keys are exchanged. This criterion is an extension of semantic security against chosen cipher-text attacks (IND-CCA). In the classical N-IND-CCA criterion (see [BBM00] about N-IND-CCA and its reduction to IND-CCA), a random bit b is sampled. For each key, the adversary has access to a left-right oracle (the adversary submits a pair of bit-strings bs_0, bs_1 and receives the encoding of bs_b) and a decryption oracle (that does not work on the outputs of the left-right oracle). The adversary has to guess the value of b. Criterion IND-CPA is the same as IND-CCA except that the adversary does not have access to the decryption oracle.

Since it has no information concerning secret keys, the adversary cannot get the encryption of a challenge secret key under a challenge public key. Therefore, we introduce the N-PAT-IND-CCA criterion where the adversary can obtain the encryption of messages containing challenge secret keys, even if it does not know their values. For that purpose, the adversary is allowed to give pattern terms to the left-right oracles.

Pattern terms are terms where new atomic constants have been added: pattern variables. These variables represent the different challenge secret keys and are denoted by $[i]$ (this asks the oracle to replace the pattern variable by the value of sk_i). Variables can be used as atomic messages (data pattern) or at a key position (key pattern). When a left-right oracle is given a pattern term, it replaces patterns by values of corresponding keys and encodes the so-obtained message.

More formally, patterns are given by the following grammar where bs is a bit-string and i is an integer. In the definition of pattern terms, we use two binary operators: concatenation and encryption. Concatenation of patterns pat_0 and pat_1 is written (pat_0, pat_1). Encryption of pat with key bs is denoted by $\{pat\}_{bs}$. Similarly, when the key is a challenge key, it is represented by a pattern variable $[i]$.

$$pat ::= (pat, pat) \mid \{pat\}_{bs} \mid \{pat\}_{[i]}$$
$$\mid bs \mid [i]$$

The computation (evaluation) made by the oracle is easily defined recursively in a context θ associating bit-string values to the different keys. Its result is a bit-string and it uses the encryption algorithm $\mathcal{E}$ and the concatenation denoted by "." in the computational setting.

$$v(bs, \theta) = bs$$
$$v([i], \theta) = \theta(sk_i)$$
$$v((p_1, p_2), \theta) = v(p_1, \theta) \cdot v(p_2, \theta)$$

$$v(\{p\}_{bs}, \theta) = \mathcal{E}(v(p, \theta), bs)$$
$$v(\{p\}_{[i]}, \theta) = \mathcal{E}(v(p, \theta), \theta(pk_i))$$

There is yet a restriction. Keys are ordered and a pattern $[j]$ can only be encrypted under pk_i if $i < j$ to avoid key cycles. This restriction is well-known in cryptography and widely accepted [AR00]. When the left-right pattern encryption oracle related to key i is given two pattern terms pat_0 and pat_1, it tests that none contains a pattern $[j]$ with $j \leq i$. If this happens, it outputs an error message, else it produces the encryption of the message corresponding to pat_b, $v(pat_b, \theta)$, using public key pk_i. To win, the adversary has to guess the value of secret bit b. In fact our acyclicity hypothesis only occurs on secret keys: when considering pattern $\{\{p\}_{[j]}\}_{[j]}$, the public key oracle related to key j can be called and returns bit-string bs, then pattern $\{\{p\}_{bs}\}_{[j]}$ can be used to get the awaited result. We do not detail restrictions on the length of arguments submitted to the left-right oracle, an interesting discussion on that point appears in [AR00]. The most simple restriction is to ask that both submitted patterns can only be evaluated (using v) to bit-strings of equal length.

Henceforth, let $\mathcal{AE} = (\mathcal{KG}, \mathcal{E}, \mathcal{D})$ be an asymmetric encryption scheme. Then, criterion N-PAT-IND-CCA is given by $\gamma_N = (\Theta; F; V)$, where Θ randomly generates N pairs of keys (pk_1, sk_1) to (pk_N, sk_N) using $\mathcal{KG}$ and a bit b; V verifies whether the adversary gave the right value for bit b; and F gives access to three oracles for each i between 1 and N: a left-right encryption oracle that takes as argument a pair of patterns (pat_0, pat_1) and outputs pat_b completed with the secret keys ($v(pat_b, \theta)$) and encoded using pk_i; a decryption oracle that decodes any message that was not produced by the former encryption oracle; and an oracle that simply makes the public key pk_i available.

Then, $\mathcal{AE}$ is said N-PAT-IND-CCA iff for any adversary $\mathcal{A}$, $\mathbf{Adv}_{\mathcal{A}}^{\gamma_N}(\eta)$ is negligible. Note that N-PAT-IND-CCA with $N = 1$ corresponds to IND-CCA.

Proposition 1. *Let N be an integer. If an asymmetric encryption scheme $\mathcal{AE}$ is IND-CCA, then $\mathcal{AE}$ is N-PAT-IND-CCA.*

Proof. We want to establish first that an IND-CCA asymmetric encryption scheme is an N-PAT-IND-CCA secure one. We use the criterion reduction theorem on N-PAT-IND-CCA (denoted by δ_N). We now consider $\delta_N = (\Theta_1, \Theta_2; F_1, F_2; V_1)$, where the criterion partition has been performed the following way:

- Θ_1 randomly generates the bit b and $N - 1$ pairs of matching public and secret keys (pk_2, sk_2) to (pk_N, sk_N) using $\mathcal{KG}$.
- Θ_2 randomly generates the first key pair (pk_1, sk_1).
- F_1 contains the oracles related to θ_1; hence as neither pk_1 nor sk_1 can be asked to this oracle (because of acyclicity), F_1 does not depend on θ_2.
- F_2 contains the oracles related to key pair (pk_1, sk_1), it uses θ_1 for the bit b and the different keys needed to fill in patterns.
- V_1 compares the output to b, and therefore only depends on θ_1.

This splitting complies with the first hypothesis of theorem 1. Let us then check whether the second hypothesis holds. The decryption and public key oracles included in F_2 only depend on θ_2, we place them in f'. We let the encryption oracle be $\lambda s.f(g(s, \theta_1), \theta_2)$ where $g((pat_0, pat_1), \theta_1) = v(pat_b, \theta_1)$ plays the role of a left-right oracle, b being the challenge bit included in θ_1, composed with the valuation function v that completes patterns, and $f(bs, \theta_2) = \mathcal{E}(bs, pk_1)$ is the original encryption oracle.

The theorem can now be applied. It thus follows that for any adversary $\mathcal{A}$ against criterion δ_N, there exist two adversaries $\mathcal{B}$ and $\mathcal{A}'$, such that:

$$\forall \eta, \mathbf{Adv}_{\mathcal{A}}^{\delta_N}(\eta) = 2\mathbf{Adv}_{\mathcal{B}}^{\gamma_2}(\eta) + \mathbf{Adv}_{\mathcal{A}'}^{\gamma_1}(\eta)$$

where $\gamma_2 = (\Theta_2, b; f \circ LR^b, f'; v_b)$ is IND-CCA and $\gamma_1 = (\Theta_1; F_1; V_1)$ is criterion δ_{N-1}.

Hence if we suppose that the asymmetric encryption scheme $\mathcal{AE}$ is IND-CCA and $N - 1$-PAT-IND-CCA, then the advantages of $\mathcal{A}'$ and $\mathcal{B}$ are negligible, so the advantage of $\mathcal{A}$ is also negligible and $\mathcal{AE}$ is N-PAT-IND-CCA. Moreover, as 0-PAT-IND-CCA consists in guessing a challenge bit without access to any oracle, any adversary's advantage against it is thus null, which obviously implies that any encryption scheme is 0-PAT-IND-CCA. Using a quick recursion, it now appears clearly that if an asymmetric encryption scheme is IND-CCA, it is also N-PAT-IND-CCA for any integer N.

In this proof, we bound the advantage against N-PAT-IND-CCA by $2N$ times the advantage against IND-CCA. This bound is not contradictory with the one proposed by [BBM00] as the number of queries to each oracle is unbounded in our model.

4.2   Cryptographic Game: N-PAT-SYM-CPA

In this section, we introduce a new criterion describing safety of a symmetric encryption scheme. This definition is an extension of semantic security against chosen plain-text attacks. The main difference with the N-PAT-IND-CCA criterion is that there are no public key oracles and no decryption oracles. Hence the left-right encryption oracles are similar to those presented in the previous section and the adversary still has to guess the value of the challenge bit b. The hypothesis related to acyclicity of keys still holds: k_i can only appear encoded by k_j if $i > j$.

The N-PAT-SYM-CPA criterion is $\gamma_N = (\Theta, F, V)$ where Θ generates N symmetric keys and a bit b; F gives access to one oracle for each key: a left-right encryption oracle that takes as argument a pair of patterns (pat_0, pat_1) and outputs pat_b completed with the secret keys $(v(pat_b, \theta))$ and encoded by k_i. Finally, V returns true when the adversary returns bit b.

Let γ_N be a criterion including the oracles detailed above. A symmetric encryption scheme $\mathcal{SE}$ is said N-PAT-SYM-CPA iff for any adversary $\mathcal{A}$, the advantage of $\mathcal{A}$ against γ_N, $\mathbf{Adv}_{\mathcal{SE}, \mathcal{A}}^{\gamma_N}(\eta)$, is negligible in η.

Using the criterion partition theorem, it is possible to reduce criterion N-PAT-SYM-CPA to criterion SYM-CPA. This can be done by using the same partition as for criterion N-PAT-IND-CCA.

Proposition 2. *Let N be an integer. If a symmetric encryption scheme $\mathcal{SE}$ is SYM-CPA, then $\mathcal{SE}$ is N-PAT-SYM-CPA.*

4.3   Cryptographic Games: N-PAS-CCA and N-PAS-CPA

These criteria combine both precedent ones. N asymmetric and symmetric keys are generated along with a single challenge bit b. The adversary can access oracles it was granted in both previous criteria (left-right encryption, public key and decryption for the asymmetric scheme in N-PAS-CCA) and has to deduce the value of the challenge bit b. The acyclicity condition still holds on both primitives. However, we authorize patterns using symmetric keys when accessing left-right oracles from the asymmetric part. Hence symmetric encryption and symmetric keys can be used under asymmetric encryption but the converse is forbidden. The pattern definition has to be extended so that the adversary can ask for both asymmetric and symmetric encryptions and asymmetric and symmetric keys.

Let γ_N be the criterion including the oracles detailed above. A cryptographic library $(\mathcal{AE}, \mathcal{SE})$ is said N-PAS-CCA iff for any adversary $\mathcal{A}$ the advantage of $\mathcal{A}$, $\mathbf{Adv}_{\mathcal{AE}, \mathcal{SE}, \mathcal{A}}^{\gamma_N}(\eta)$, is negligible. The challenge bit b is common to asymmetric and symmetric encryption, thus it is non trivial to prove that IND-CCA and SYM-CPA imply N-PAS-CCA. However using our partition theorem, it is possible to prove this implication.

Proposition 3. *Let N be an integer. If an asymmetric encryption scheme $\mathcal{AE}$ is IND-CCA and a symmetric encryption scheme $\mathcal{SE}$ is SYM-CPA, then the cryptographic library $(\mathcal{AE}, \mathcal{SE})$ is N-PAS-CCA.*

This can easily be adapted to prove variants of this property, for example let us consider the IND-CPA criterion for the symmetric encryption scheme (the adversary only has access to the left-right oracle and has to guess the challenge bit) and the N-PAS-CPA criterion for a cryptographic library (the adversary has access to public keys for the asymmetric encryption scheme, to left-right oracles using patterns such that asymmetric secret keys cannot be asked to symmetric encryption oracles).

Proposition 4. *Let N be an integer. If an asymmetric encryption scheme $\mathcal{AE}$ is IND-CPA and a symmetric encryption scheme $\mathcal{SE}$ is SYM-CPA, then the cryptographic library $(\mathcal{AE}, \mathcal{SE})$ is N-PAS-CPA.*

5   Computational Soundness of Adaptive Security

In this section, we prove computational soundness of symbolic equivalence for messages that use both asymmetric and symmetric encryption in the case of an adaptive adversary. This model has been introduced in [MP05]. Roughly, speaking it corresponds to the case of a passive adversary that however can adaptively chose symbolic terms and ask for their computational evaluation whereas in the passive case [AR00], the adversary is confronted with two fixed symbolic terms. The practical significance of this model is discussed in [MP05]. Our result is an extension of the soundness result from [MP05], moreover we propose a more modular approach which does not use any hybrid argument but is based on proposition 4. Another improvement is that we allow the adversary to reuse computational values within symbolic terms, constants in messages can be used to represent any bit-string. To simplify things up, we do not consider polynomial sequences of messages as in [MP05] but rather bounded sequences of messages. In fact, to cope with the polynomial case, we need to extend theorem 1 in order to handle a polynomial number of challenges. This extension is presented in [Maz06].

5.1   A Symbolic Treatment of Cryptography

Let **SymKeys**,**PKeys**,**SKeys** and **Const** be four disjoint sets of symbols representing *symmetric keys*, *public keys*, *secret keys* and *constants*. Let **Atoms** be the union of the previous sets. We assume the existence of a bijection $[]^{-1}$ from **PKeys** to **SKeys** that associates to each public key the corresponding secret key. The inverse of this function is also denoted $[]^{-1}$. The set **Msg** of messages is defined by the following grammar.

$$\mathbf{Msg} ::= \mathbf{SymKeys} \mid \mathbf{Const} \mid (\mathbf{Msg}, \mathbf{Msg}) \mid \{\mathbf{Msg}\}^s_{\mathbf{SymKeys}} \mid \{\mathbf{Msg}\}^a_{\mathbf{PKeys}}$$

Elements of **SymKeys** can be thought of as randomly sampled keys, elements of **Const** as bit-strings. Term (m, n) represents the pairing of message m and n, $\{m\}^s_k$ represents the symmetric encryption of m using key k and $\{m\}^a_{pk}$ represents the asymmetric encryption of m using public key pk. In the sequel, when presenting examples, we use symbols 0 and 1. These are to be understood as elements of **Const** which computational interpretations are respectively bit-strings 0 and 1.

Next we define when a message $m \in \mathbf{Msg}$ can be deduced from a set of messages $E \subseteq \mathbf{Msg}$ (written $E \vdash m$) by a passive eavesdropper. The deduction relation $\vdash$ is defined by the standard Dolev-Yao inference system [DY83] and is given by the following rules:

$$\frac{m \in E}{E \vdash m} \qquad \frac{E \vdash (m_1, m_2)}{E \vdash m_1} \qquad \frac{E \vdash (m_1, m_2)}{E \vdash m_2} \qquad \frac{E \vdash m_1 \quad E \vdash m_2}{E \vdash (m_1, m_2)}$$

$$\frac{E \vdash m \quad E \vdash k}{E \vdash \{m\}^s_k} \qquad \frac{E \vdash \{m\}^s_k \quad E \vdash k}{E \vdash m} \qquad \frac{E \vdash m \quad E \vdash pk}{E \vdash \{m\}^a_{pk}} \qquad \frac{E \vdash \{m\}^a_{pk} \quad E \vdash pk^{-1}}{E \vdash m}$$

The information revealed by a symbolic expression can be characterized using *patterns* [AR00, MP05]. For a message $m \in \mathbf{Msg}$ its pattern is defined by the following inductive rules:

$$
\begin{aligned}
pattern\big((m_1, m_2)\big) &= \big(pattern(m_1), pattern(m_2)\big) && \\
pattern\big(\{m'\}^s_k\big) &= \{pattern(m')\}^s_k && \text{if } m \vdash k \\
pattern\big(\{m'\}^s_k\big) &= \{\Box\}^s_k && \text{if } m \not\vdash k \\
pattern\big(\{m'\}^a_{pk}\big) &= \{pattern(m')\}^a_{pk} && \text{if } m \vdash pk^{-1} \\
pattern\big(\{m'\}^a_{pk}\big) &= \{\Box\}^a_{pk} && \text{if } m \not\vdash pk^{-1} \\
pattern(m') &= m' && \text{if } m' \in \mathbf{Atoms}
\end{aligned}
$$

The symbol $\Box$ represents a cipher-text that the adversary cannot decrypt. As $\Box$ does not store any information on the length or structure of the corresponding plain-text, we assume that the encryption schemes used here do not reveal plain-text lengths (see [AR00] for details). Two messages are said to be *equivalent* if they have the same pattern: $m \equiv n$ if and only if $pattern(m) = pattern(n)$. Two messages are *equivalent up to renaming* if they are equivalent up to some renaming of keys: $m \cong n$ if there exists a renaming σ of keys from n such that $m \equiv n\sigma$.

Example 1. Let us illustrate this equivalence notion. We have that:

– $\{0\}_k^s \cong \{1\}_k^s$ encryptions with different plain-text cannot be distinguished if the key is not deducible.
– $(\{0\}_k^s, \{k\}_{pk}^a, pk^{-1}) \not\cong (\{1\}_k^s, \{k\}_{pk}^a, pk^{-1})$ but it is not the case if the key can be deduced.

5.2   Computational Soundness

This model is parameterized by an asymmetric encryption scheme $\mathcal{AE} = (\mathcal{KG}^a, \mathcal{E}^a, \mathcal{D}^a)$ and a symmetric encryption scheme $\mathcal{SE} = (\mathcal{KG}^s, \mathcal{E}^s, \mathcal{D}^s)$. Computational semantics are given by a concretization function $concr$ which can be derived from the v function that was introduced previously. This algorithm uses a computational substitution θ which stores bit-string values for keys. Constants from **Const** represents bit-strings so the concretization of c from **Const** is c itself.

$$concr((m_1, m_2), \theta) = concr(m_1, \theta) \cdot concr(m_2, \theta)$$
$$concr(\{m\}_{pk}^a, \theta) = \mathcal{E}^a(concr(m, \theta), \theta(pk))$$
$$concr(\{m\}_k^s, \theta) = \mathcal{E}^s(concr(m, \theta), \theta(k))$$

$$concr(k, \theta) = \theta(k)$$
$$concr(c, \theta) = c$$

Thus the computational distribution generated by a message can be obtained by randomly sampling the necessary keys and using the $concr$ function.

We consider a model where the adversary can see the computational version of a bounded sequence of adaptively chosen messages. Let α be a bound on the sequence length. The adaptive experiment proceeds as follows: the adversary has access to one oracle which takes as argument a pair of messages (m_0, m_1) and either outputs a concretization of m_0 (oracle $\mathcal{O}_0$) or a concretization of m_1 (oracle $\mathcal{O}_1$). These oracles work by randomly sampling the necessary keys then using the $concr$ function on either m_0 or on m_1. Finally, the adversary has to tell against which oracle it is playing, $\mathcal{O}_0$ or $\mathcal{O}_1$. The advantage of $\mathcal{A}$ is defined by:

$$\mathbf{Adv}_{\mathcal{AE}, \mathcal{SE}, \mathcal{A}}^{adpt}(\eta) = Pr[\mathcal{A}/\mathcal{O}_1 = 1] - Pr[\mathcal{A}/\mathcal{O}_0 = 1]$$

Moreover there are restrictions on the sequence of messages submitted by the adversary (m_0^1, m_1^1) to (m_0^q, m_1^q). Such a sequence is said to be *legal* if:

1. Messages $(m_0^1, ..., m_0^q)$ and $(m_1^1, ..., m_1^q)$ are equivalent up to renaming.
2. Messages $(m_0^1, ..., m_0^q)$ and $(m_1^1, ..., m_1^q)$ contain no encryption cycles, moreover secret keys cannot be sent under symmetric encryptions.
3. The lengths of $(m_0^1, ..., m_0^q)$ and $(m_1^1, ..., m_1^q)$ are lower than α.

Proposition 5. *If $\mathcal{AE}$ is an IND-CPA secure encryption scheme and $\mathcal{SE}$ is a SYM-CPA secure encryption scheme, then the advantage of any legal adversary $\mathcal{A}$, $\mathbf{Adv}_{\mathcal{AE}, \mathcal{SE}, \mathcal{A}}^{adpt}(\eta)$, is a negligible function in η.*

This result can be used to model secure multicast as presented in [MP05].

6   Conclusion

This paper contributes to the development of a proof theory for cryptographic systems by providing a theorem that allows to decompose the proof of correctness of a security criterion to the correctness of a sub-criterion and an indistinsguishability criterion. We apply this decomposition result to prove that given secure asymmetric and symmetric encryption schemes we can combine them to obtain a secure cryptographic library.

This security result can be used to easily prove computational soundness of formal methods. This has been illustrated in the case of the adaptive setting for asymmetric and symmetric encryption.

In future works, we intend to develop this computational soundness result to the case of security protocols in general against an active adversary. We believe that our partition theorem will also be useful in this situation, in particular by giving simpler and more modular proofs of soundness.

References

[AJ01]   Abadi, M., Jürjens, J.: Formal eavesdropping and its computational interpretation. In: Kobayashi, N., Pierce, B.C. (eds.) TACS 2001. LNCS, vol. 2215, pp. 82–94. Springer, Heidelberg (2001)

[AR00]   Abadi, M., Rogaway, P.: Reconciling two views of cryptography (the computational soundness of formal encryption). In: IFIP International Conference on Theoretical Computer Science (IFIP TCS2000), Sendai, Japan, Springer, Berlin (2000)

[BBM00]   Bellare, M., Boldyreva, A., Micali, S.: Public-key encryption in a multi-user setting: Security proofs and improvements. In: Preneel, B. (ed.) EURO-CRYPT 2000. LNCS, vol. 1807, pp. 259–274. Springer, Heidelberg (2000)

[BCK05]   Baudet, M., Cortier, V., Kremer, S.: Computationally sound implementations of equational theories against passive adversaries. In: Caires, L., Italiano, G.F., Monteiro, L., Palamidessi, C., Yung, M. (eds.) ICALP 2005. LNCS, vol. 3580, Springer, Heidelberg (2005)

[Bla06]   Blanchet, B.: A computationally sound mechanized prover for security protocols. In: IEEE Symposium on Security and Privacy, Oakland, California (May 2006)

[BPW03]   Backes, M., Pfitzmann, B., Waidner, M.: A composable cryptographic library with nested operations. In: Proceedings of the 10th ACM conference on Computer and communication security, pp. 220–230 (2003)

[BR04]   Bellare, M., Rogaway, P.: The game-playing technique. Cryptology ePrint Archive, Report 2004/331 (2004), http://eprint.iacr.org/

[Cou90]   Cousot, P.: Methods and Logics for Proving Programs. In: Handbook of Theoretical Computer Science, vol. B: Formal Methods and Semantics, pp. 841–994. Elsevier Science Publishers B.V, Amsterdam (1990)

[CW05]   Cortier, V., Warinschi, B.: Computationally sound, automated proofs for security protocols. In: Sagiv, M. (ed.) ESOP 2005. LNCS, vol. 3444, Springer, Heidelberg (2005)

[DY83]   Dolev, D., Yao, A.C.: On the security of public key protocols. IEEE Transactions on Information Theory 29(2), 198–208 (1983)

[GM84]   Goldwasser, S., Micali, S.: Probabilistic encryption. Journal of Computer and System Sciences 28(2), 270–299 (1984)

[JLM05]   Janvier, R., Lakhnech, Y., Mazaré, L.: Completing the picture: Soundness of formal encryption in the presence of active adversaries. In: Sagiv, M. (ed.) ESOP 2005. LNCS, vol. 3444, Springer, Heidelberg (2005)

[Maz06]   Mazaré, L.: Computational Soundness of Symbolic Models for Cryptographic Protocols. PhD thesis, INPG, Grenoble (October 2006) (to appear)

[MP92]   Manna, Z., Pnueli, A.: The temporal logic of reactive and concurrent systems. Springer, Heidelberg (1992)

[MP05]   Micciancio, D., Panjwani, S.: Adaptive security of symbolic encryption. In: Kilian, J. (ed.) TCC 2005. LNCS, vol. 3378, pp. 169–187. Springer, Heidelberg (2005)

[MW04]   Micciancio, D., Warinschi, B.: Soundness of formal encryption in the presence of active adversaries. In: Proceedings of the Theory of Cryptography Conference, pp. 133–151. Springer, Heidelberg (2004)

[Sho04]   Shoup, V.: Sequences of games: a tool for taming complexity in security proofs (2004)

Measuring Anonymity with Relative Entropy

Yuxin Deng[1,2], Jun Pang[3], and Peng Wu[4]

[1] The University of New South Wales
School of Computer Science and Engineering, 2052 Sydney, Australia
yuxind@cse.unsw.edu.au
[2] Shanghai Jiaotong University
Department of Computer Science and Engineering, 200240 Shanghai, China
[3] Carl von Ossietzky Universität Oldenburg
Department für Informatik, 26111 Oldenburg, Germany
jun.pang@informatik.uni-oldenburg.de
[4] INRIA Futurs and LIX, École Polytechnique
Rue de Saclay, 91128 Palaiseau, France
wu@lix.polytechnique.fr

Abstract. Anonymity is the property of maintaining secret the identity of users performing a certain action. Anonymity protocols often use random mechanisms which can be described probabilistically. In this paper, we propose a probabilistic process calculus to describe protocols for ensuring anonymity, and we use the notion of relative entropy from information theory to measure the degree of anonymity these protocols can guarantee. Furthermore, we prove that the operators in the probabilistic process calculus are non-expansive, with respect to this measuring method. We illustrate our approach by using the example of the Dining Cryptographers Problem.

1 Introduction

With the growth and commercialisation of the Internet, users become more and more concerned about their anonymity and privacy in the digital world. Anonymity is the property of keeping secret the identity of the user who has performed a certain action. The need for anonymity may arise in a wide range of situations, from votings and donations to postings on electronic forums. Anonymity protocols often use random mechanisms. Typical examples are the Dining Cryptographers [5], Crowds [22], Onion Routing [27], SG-MIX [16], and many others.

Quantifying the degree of anonymity a protocol can guarantee is a line of active research. Various notions, like anonymity set and information theoretic metric, have been investigated in the literature [5,22,2,25,9,6]. (See detailed discussions in Section 5.) In particular, [25,9] used the notion of *entropy* from information theory as a measure for anonymity. It takes into account the probability distribution of the users performing certain actions, where the probabilities are assigned by an attacker after observing the system. However, it does not take into account the attacker's knowledge about the users before running a protocol.

T. Dimitrakos et al. (Eds.): FAST 2006, LNCS 4691, pp. 65–79, 2007.

In this paper we propose to use *relative entropy* as a general extension of the aforementioned approaches. Our method quantifies the amount of probabilistic information revealed by the protocol, i.e. how much information an attacker can obtain after observing the outcomes of the protocol, together with the information he has before the protocol running. For a protocol that contains both non-deterministic and probabilistic behaviours, we extend this measuring method to deal with two sets of probability distributions by using Hausdorff distance (see Definition 4).

Nowadays, the need for applying formal methods to security protocols has been widely recognised. To our knowledge, there have been several attempts to develop a formal framework for specifying and reasoning about anonymity properties. Schneider and Sidiropoulos [23] studied anonymity in CSP [14], but they only considered non-deterministic behaviour. Bhargava and Palamidessi [3] proposed a notion of probabilistic anonymity with careful distinction between non-deterministic and probabilistic behaviours and used a probabilistic π-calculus as a specification language. This work was extended by Deng, Palamidessi and Pang in [6], where a weak notion of probabilistic anonymity was defined to capture the amount of probabilistic information that may be revealed by a protocol. Other researchers define their notions of anonymity in terms of epistemic logic [13,12] and "function views" [15].

In this paper, we follow the approach based on process calculi. Specifically, we propose a probabilistic extension of CCS [19], in the style of [1], to describe protocols for ensuring anonymity. It allows us to specify both non-deterministic and probabilistic behaviours. The operational semantics of a process is defined in terms of a probabilistic automaton [24]. Our formal characterisation of anonymity is then based on permutations over the traces of a probabilistic automaton. Inspired by [7,8], we prove that except for the parallel composition all operators in our probabilistic CCS are non-expansive, with respect to the measuring method using relative entropy, which allows us to estimate the degree of anonymity of a complex system from its components, rather than analyse the system as a whole. We illustrate our ideas by using the example of the Dining Cryptographers Problem (DCP), in which a number of cryptographers cooperate to ensure that the occurrence of a certain action is visible, while the user who has performed it remains anonymous.

We summarise our main contributions of this work as follows:

- We propose to use relative entropy for measuring the degree of anonymity a protocol can guarantee. It is an extension of the results in [25,9].
- We define a probabilistic CCS for specifying protocols, and prove the non-expansiveness of some operators.
- We show how to use our framework to reason about the degree of anonymity of protocols by the example of the Dining Cryptographers Problem.

Plan of the paper. In next section we recall some basic notations which are used throughout the paper. In Section 3, we use relative entropy to measure anonymity, and we present the non-expansiveness proof for the operators in a probabilistic CCS. In Section 4, we apply our framework to the Dining Cryptographers Problem. In Section 5, we compare our approach with some related work. Finally, we conclude the paper by discussing our future work in Section 6.

2   Preliminaries

In this section, we present some basic definitions from probability theory, the notion of probabilistic automata, and a probabilistic CCS.

2.1   Probability Measure

Let Ω be a set. A *σ-field* over Ω is a collection $\mathcal{F}$ of subsets of Ω containing $\emptyset$ and closed under complements and countable unions. A *probability measure* on a σ-field $\mathcal{F}$ is a function $\eta : \mathcal{F} \to [0,1]$ such that $\eta(\Omega) = 1$ and, for each family $\{Z_i\}_{i \in \mathbb{N}}$ of pairwise disjoint elements of $\mathcal{F}$, $\eta(\bigcup_{i \in \mathbb{N}} Z_i) = \sum_{i \in \mathbb{N}} \eta(Z_i)$. A *discrete probability measure* over Ω is a probability measure whose σ-field is the powerset of Ω. A *discrete probability distribution* is a function $\eta : \Omega \to [0,1]$ such that $\sum_{s \in \Omega} \eta(s) = 1$. The *support* of η is defined to be the set $supp(\eta) = \{s \in \Omega \mid \eta(s) \neq 0\}$. We denote by $\mathcal{D}(\Omega)$ the set of probability distributions over Ω.

2.2   Probabilistic Automata

We give a brief review of the formalism *probabilistic automata* [24].

Definition 1. *A* probabilistic automaton *is a tuple* $M = (S, s_0, E, H, \to)$ *where*

- S *is a set of* states,
- s_0 *is the* start state,
- E *is a set of* external *actions,*
- H *is a set of* internal (hidden) *actions,*
- $\to \subseteq S \times (E \cup H) \times \mathcal{D}(S)$ *is a* transition relation.

We often write $s \xrightarrow{a} \eta$ for $(s, a, \eta) \in \to$. Informally, a probabilistic automaton is like an ordinary automaton except that a labelled transition leads to a probability distribution over a set of states instead of a single state. We will use probabilistic automata to give operational semantics for the probabilistic CCS that will be introduced in next section.

A *path* π of M is a (finite or infinite) sequence of the form $s_0 a_1 \eta_1 s_1 a_2 \eta_2 s_2 ...$ such that

1. each s_i (resp. a_i, η_i) denotes a state (resp. action, distribution over states);
2. s_0 is the initial state;
3. if π is finite, then it ends with a state;
4. $s_i \xrightarrow{a_{i+1}} \eta_{i+1}$ and $s_{i+1} \in supp(\eta_{i+1})$, for each non-final i.

The set of all paths of M is denoted $Path(M)$, while the set of finite paths is denoted $Path^*(M)$. The last state of a finite path π is written $last(\pi)$. A path π is *maximal* if either it is infinite or it is a finite path without any outgoing transitions from $last(\pi)$.

A *scheduler* σ of M is a partial function of type $Path^*(M) \rightarrow (E \cup H) \times \mathcal{D}(S)$ such that (i) for each path π that is not maximal $\sigma(\pi)$ is defined, (ii) $\sigma(\pi) = (a, \eta)$ implies $last(\pi) \xrightarrow{a} \eta$. A scheduler σ of M induces a discrete probability measure on the σ-field generated by cones of paths as follows. If π is a finite path, then the *cone* generated by π is the set of paths $C_\pi = \{\pi' \in Path(M) \mid \pi \preceq \pi'\}$, where $\preceq$ denotes the prefix ordering on sequences. The measure ϵ of a cone C_π is defined by

$$
\epsilon(C_\pi) = \begin{cases} 1 & \text{if } \pi = s_0 \\ \epsilon(C_{\pi'}) \cdot \eta(s') & \text{if } \pi = \pi' a \eta s' \text{ and } \sigma(\pi') = (a, \eta) \\ 0 & \text{otherwise.} \end{cases}
$$

The measure ϵ is called a *probabilistic execution* of M.

The *trace* of a path π of an automaton M, written $tr(\pi)$, is the sequence obtained by restricting π to the set of external actions of M. A trace is *maximal* if it is so obtained from a maximal path. The cone of a finite trace γ is defined by $C_\gamma = \{\gamma' \in E^\omega \mid \gamma \preceq \gamma'\}$. Given a probabilistic execution ϵ, the *trace distribution* of ϵ, $td(\epsilon)$, is the measure on the σ-field generated by cones of traces defined by

$$
td(\epsilon)(C_\gamma) = \sum_{tr(\pi) = \gamma} \epsilon(C_\pi).
$$

If there are only countably many maximal traces in a probabilistic automaton (which is the case in many applications including all examples in this paper), a trace distribution corresponds to a discrete probability distribution on the maximal traces of a fully probabilistic automaton resulted from resolving all non-determinism of the probabilistic automaton. We denote the set of trace distributions of probabilistic executions of a probabilistic automaton M by $tds(M)$.

2.3   Probabilistic CCS

In this section we give a probabilistic extension of Milner's CCS [19] which is based on the calculus of [1] that allows for non-deterministic and probabilistic choice. We assume a countable set of variables, $Var = \{X, Y, ...\}$, and a countable set of atomic actions, $\mathcal{A} = \{a, b, ...\}$. Given a special action τ not in $\mathcal{A}$, we let $u, v, ...$ range over the set of *actions*, $Act = \mathcal{A} \cup \overline{\mathcal{A}} \cup \{\tau\}$. The class of expressions $\mathcal{E}$ is defined by the following syntax:

$$
E ::= \mathbf{0} \mid \sum_{i \in I} u_{p_i}.E_i \mid E1 \boxplus E_2 \mid E_1 \mid E_2 \mid E \setminus A \mid f[E] \mid X \mid \mu_X E
$$

where $A \subseteq \mathcal{A}$, $f : Act \rightarrow Act$ is a renaming function, I is a nonempty countable indexing set and $\{p_i\}_{i \in I}$ a family of probabilities such that $\sum_{i \in I} p_i = 1$. For finite indexing set $I = \{i_1, ..., i_n\}$ we also write $u_{p_{i_1}}.E_{p_{i_1}} + ... + u_{p_{i_n}}.E_{p_{i_n}}$ instead of $\sum_{i \in I} u_{p_i}.E_i$. The construction $E_1 \boxplus E_2$ stands for *non-deterministic choice*, which is denoted by $+$ in CCS. We use $|$ to denote the usual *parallel composition*. The *restriction* and *renaming* operators are as in CCS: $E \setminus A$ behaves like E as long as E does not perform an action $a \in A$; $f[E]$ behaves like E where each action $a \in Act$ is replaced by $f(a)$. We let variables range over process expressions. The notation μ_X stands for a recursion which binds the variable X. We use $fv(E)$ for the set of free variables (i.e., not bound by any μ_X) in E. As usual we identify expressions which differ only by a change of bound variables.

We use $P, Q, ...$ to range over $\mathcal{P}r$, the set of expressions without free variables, called *processes*. The operational semantics of a process P is defined as a probabilistic automaton whose states are the processes reachable from P and the transition relation is defined by the rules in Figure 1, where $P \xrightarrow{u} \eta$ describes a transition that, by performing an action u, leaves from P and leads to a distribution η over $\mathcal{P}r$.

The presence of both probabilistic and non-deterministic choice in the probabilistic CCS allows us to specify systems that have both probabilistic and non-deterministic behaviour. Given a process P, we denote by $pa(P)$ the probabilistic automaton that represents the operational semantics of P via the rules in Figure 1. If there is no occurrence of non-deterministic choice in P, the automaton $pa(P)$ is fully probabilistic. In this case $tds(pa(P))$ is a singleton set of trace distribution.

1. $\sum_{i \in I} u_{p_i}.P_i \xrightarrow{u} \eta$ where $\eta(P) = \sum\{p_i \mid i \in I, P_i = P\}$
2. $P_1 \boxplus P_2 \xrightarrow{u} \eta$ if $P_1 \xrightarrow{u} \eta$ or $P_2 \xrightarrow{u} \eta$
3. $P_1 \mid P_2 \xrightarrow{u} \eta$ if one the following four conditions is satisfied:

   (a) $P_1 \xrightarrow{u} \eta_1$ and $\eta(P) = \begin{cases} \eta_1(P_1') & \text{if } P = P_1' \mid P_2 \\ 0 & \text{otherwise} \end{cases}$

   (b) $P_2 \xrightarrow{u} \eta_2$ and $\eta(P) = \begin{cases} \eta_2(P_2') & \text{if } P = P_1 \mid P_2' \\ 0 & \text{otherwise} \end{cases}$

   (c) $u = \tau$ and there exists $a \in \mathcal{A}$ with $P_1 \xrightarrow{a} \eta_1$ and $P_2 \xrightarrow{\bar{a}} \eta_2$ such that

   $$\eta(P) = \begin{cases} \eta_1(P_1') \cdot \eta_2(P_2') & \text{if } P = P_1' \mid P_2' \\ 0 & \text{otherwise} \end{cases}$$

   (d) the symmetric case of (c)

4. $P \setminus A \xrightarrow{u} \eta$ if $u \notin A \cup \bar{A}$, $P \xrightarrow{u} \eta_1$, and $\eta(P) = \begin{cases} \eta_1(P') & \text{if } P = P' \setminus A \\ 0 & \text{otherwise} \end{cases}$

5. $f[P] \xrightarrow{u} \eta$ if $P \xrightarrow{v} \eta_1$, $f(v) = u$ and $\eta(P) = \begin{cases} \eta_1(P') & \text{if } P = f[P'] \\ 0 & \text{otherwise} \end{cases}$

6. $\mu_X E \xrightarrow{u} \eta$ if $E\{\mu_X E/X\} \xrightarrow{u} \eta$

Fig. 1. Operational semantics for Probabilistic CCS

3 Measuring Anonymity

3.1 Relative Entropy

We make a convention $0 \log \infty = 0$.

Definition 2 (Relative entropy [17]). *Let θ, θ' be two discrete probability distributions on a set S. The relative entropy of θ w.r.t. θ' is defined by*

$$D(\theta, \theta') = \sum_{s \in S} \theta(s) \cdot \log \frac{\theta(s)}{\theta'(s)}.$$

In the sequel, whenever we write $D(\theta, \theta')$, it is implicitly assumed that the domains of θ and θ' are the same, i.e., $dom(\theta) = dom(\theta')$.

In general, we have $D(\theta, \theta') \neq D(\theta', \theta)$, so relative entropy is not a true metric. But it satisfies many important mathematical properties, e.g. it is always nonnegative, and equals zero only if $\theta = \theta'$. It plays an important role in quantum information theory, as well as statistical mechanics.

We now present a few properties of relative entropy.

Proposition 3. *Relative entropy D has the following properties:*

1. *(Nonnegativity) $D(\eta, \eta') \geq 0$, with $D(\eta, \eta') = 0$ if and only if $\eta = \eta'$;*
2. *(Possibility of extension) $D(\eta_1, \eta_2) = D(\eta'_1, \eta'_2)$ where $dom(\eta'_1) = dom(\eta) \cup \{s\}$ and $\eta'_1(s) = 0$, similarly for η'_2 w.r.t. η_2;*
3. *(Additivity) $D(\eta_1 \times \eta_2, \eta'_1 \times \eta'_2) = D(\eta_1, \eta'_1) + D(\eta_2, \eta'_2)$, where $(\eta_1 \times \eta_2)(s_1, s_2)$ is defined as $\eta_1(s_1) \cdot \eta_2(s_2)$;*
4. *(Joint convexity) For $0 \leq r \leq 1$, we have*

$$D(r\eta_1 + (1-r)\eta_2, r\eta'_1 + (1-r)\eta'_2) \leq rD(\eta_1, \eta'_1) + (1-r)D(\eta_2, \eta'_2).$$

5. *(Strong additivity) Let $dom(\eta_1) = dom(\eta'_1) = S \cup \{s\}$, $dom(\eta_2) = dom(\eta'_2) = S \cup \{s_1, s_2\}$ with $\eta_1(s) = \eta_2(s_1) + \eta_2(s_2)$ and $\eta'_1(s) = \eta'_2(s_1) + \eta'_2(s_2)$. Then it holds that $D(\eta_1, \eta'_1) \leq D(\eta_2, \eta'_2)$.*

Proof. Similar properties for Tsallis relative entropy have been proved in [11]; their proofs can be adapted for relative entropy. □

We extend D to sets of distributions by using Hausdorff distance.

Definition 4. *Given two sets of discrete probability distributions $\Theta = \{\theta_i\}_{i \in I}$ and $\Theta' = \{\rho_j\}_{j \in J}$, the relative entropy of Θ w.r.t. Θ' is defined by*

$$D(\Theta, \Theta') = \sup_{i \in I} \inf_{j \in J} D(\theta_i, \rho_j)$$

where $\inf \emptyset = \infty$ and $\sup \emptyset = 0$.

3.2 Anonymity Systems

The concept of anonymity is relative to a certain set of anonymous actions, which we denote by A. Note that the actions in A normally depend on the identity of users, and thus are not visible to the observer. However, for the purpose of defining and verifying anonymity we model the elements of A as visible outcomes of the system. We write F_A for the set of all renaming functions that are permutations on A and identity elsewhere.

The idea of measuring anonymity is to consider a fully probabilistic automaton (resp. a probabilistic automaton) M as a trace distribution (resp. a set of trace distributions) $tds(M)$, and then apply the distance defined in Definition 2 (resp. Definition 4). The interpretation of a probabilistic automaton as a set of trace distributions is given in Section 2.2. Usually we find it convenient to describe a system as a process in the probabilistic CCS. To measure the distance between two processes, we just view a process P as its corresponding automaton $pa(P)$ and simply write $D(P,Q)$ for the distance between the set of trace distributions represented by $tds(pa(P))$ and that represented by $tds(pa(Q))$.

Definition 5 (α-anonymity[1]). *Given $\alpha \in [0,1]$, a process P is α-anonymous on a set of actions A if*

$$\forall f \in F_A : D(P,\ f[P]) \leq \alpha$$

In the particular case $\alpha = 0$, we say P is strongly anonymous *or P provides* strong anonymity.

In [23] Schneider and Sidiropoulos consider a process as a set of traces, thus P is strongly anonymous if $f[P]$, the process after the permutation of anonymous actions, represents the same set of traces as that of P. The non-determinism plays a crucial role in their formalism. A system is anonymous if the set of the possible outcomes is saturated with respect to the intended anonymous users, i.e. if one such user can cause a certain observable trace in one possible computation, then there must be alternative computations in which each other anonymous user can give rise to the same observable trace (modulo the identity of the anonymous users). In our case, P is strongly anonymous if P and $f[P]$ represent the same set of trace distributions. Thus, we extend their definition to the probabilistic setting in a natural way. We define $D_A(P)$ as $max\{D(P, f[P]) \mid f \in F_A\}$. Thus, P is α-anonymous if and only if $D_A(P) \leq \alpha$.

Proposition 6 (Non-expansiveness). *All the operators of the probabilistic CCS except for parallel composition are non-expansive.*

1. $D_A(\sum_{i \in I} u_{p_i}.P_i) \leq \sum_{i \in I} p_i D_A(P_i)$ *if $u \notin A$;*
2. $D_A(P_1 \boxplus P_2) \leq max\{D_A(P_1), D_A(P_2)\};$

---

[1] The notion of α-anonymity already appeared in [6] to describe weak probabilistic anonymity, but the measuring method used here is different and no explicit notion of schedulers is considered.

3. $D_A(P \setminus B) \leq D_A(P)$ if $A \cap B = \emptyset$;
4. $D_A(f[P]) \leq D_A(P)$ if $f(a) = a$ for all $a \in A$;
5. $D_A(\mu_X E) = D_A(E\{\mu_X E/X\})$.

Proof. We sketch the proof for each clause.

1. Given any $f \in F_A$, we show that for each $\eta \in tds(pa(\sum_{i \in I} u_{p_i}.P_i))$ there exists some $\eta' \in tds(pa(\sum_{i \in I} u_{p_i}.f[P_i]))$ such that $D(\eta, \eta') \leq \sum_{i \in I} p_i D_A(P_i)$. Note that η is determined by a scheduler σ. Restricting σ to $pa(P_i)$, for each $i \in I$, we have a scheduler σ_i that resolves all non-deterministic choices in P_i, resulting in a trace distribution $\eta_i \in tds(pa(P_i))$. It is easy to see that

$$\eta(C_u) = 1 \quad \text{and} \quad \eta(C_{u\gamma}) = \sum_{i \in I} p_i \cdot \eta_i(C_\gamma)$$

for any trace γ. Observe that, as a graph, $pa(\sum_{i \in I} u_{p_i}.f[P_i])$ is isomorphic to $pa(\sum_{i \in I} u_{p_i}.P_i)$. Hence there is a scheduler σ' of $\sum_{i \in I} u_{p_i}.f[P_i]$ that resolves all non-deterministic choices in the same way as σ does for $\sum_{i \in I} u_{p_i}.P_i$. It follows that each scheduler σ_i also has a counterpart σ'_i that is a scheduler of $f[P_i]$, for each $i \in I$. Each σ'_i determines a trace distribution $\eta'_i \in tds(pa(f[P_i]))$ satisfying

$$\eta'(C_u) = 1 \quad \text{and} \quad \eta'(C_{u\gamma}) = \sum_{i \in I} p_i \cdot \eta'_i(C_\gamma).$$

for some $\eta' \in tds(pa(\sum_{i \in I} u_{p_i}.f[P_i]))$. Therefore, it holds that

$$D(\eta, \eta') = D(\sum_{i \in I} p_i \eta_i, \sum_{i \in I} p_i \eta'_i) \leq \sum_{i \in I} p_i D(\eta_i, \eta'_i) \leq \sum_{i \in I} p_i D_A(P_i).$$

The first inequality above is justified by the joint convexity property of relative entropy given in Proposition 3.

2. Given any $f \in F_A$, we let $\Theta = tds(pa(P_1 \boxplus P_2))$ and $\Theta' = tds(pa(f[P_1] \boxplus f[P_2]))$. Each $\eta \in \Theta$ is determined by a scheduler σ. We consider the interesting case in which σ chooses an outgoing transition from P_i, for $i = 1, 2$. It follows from the isomorphism between $pa(P_1 \boxplus P_2)$ and $pa(f[P_1] \boxplus f[P_2])$ that σ has a counterpart σ' which chooses an outgoing transition from $f[P_i]$, and which determines a trace distribution $\eta' \in \Theta'$ satisfying

$$D(\eta, \eta') \leq D_A(P_i) \leq max\{D_A(P_1), D_A(P_2)\}.$$

3. Note that $pa(P \setminus B)$ is the same as $pa(P)$ except that all transitions labelled with actions in B are blocked. If $\eta_1 \in tds(pa(P \setminus B))$, there is some $\eta_2 \in tds(pa(P))$ such that all probabilities assigned by η_2 to maximal traces of the form $\gamma a \gamma'$ with $a \in B$ are now assigned by η_1 to γ. Similar relation holds between the peer trace distribution $\eta'_1 \in tds(pa(f[P] \setminus B))$ of η_1 and the peer trace distribution $\eta'_2 \in tds(pa(f[P]))$ of η_2, for any $f \in F_A$. By the strong additivity property given in Proposition 3, we derive that

$$D(\eta_1, \eta'_1) \leq D(\eta_2, \eta'_2) \leq D_A(P).$$

4. If f is an injective renaming function, i.e., $a \neq b$ implies $f(a) \neq f(b)$, then it is immediate that $D_A(f[P]) = D_A(P)$. Otherwise, two different actions may be renamed into the same one. As a result, two different maximal traces in P may become the same in $f[P]$. We can then appeal to the strong additivity property of relative entropy to infer that $D_A(f[P]) \leq D_A(P)$.

5. The result follows from the fact that $\mu_X E$ and $E\{\mu_X E / X\}$ have the same transition graph.   □

The above proposition shows a nice property of our approach using relative entropy to measure anonymity. The non-expansiveness of the operators in the probabilistic CCS allows us to estimate the degree of anonymity of a complex system from its components, rather than analyse the system as a whole.

Remark 7. Unfortunately, the parallel composition operator is expansive. For example, let $A = \{b, c\}$, $P = a_{\frac{1}{3}}.b + a_{\frac{2}{3}}.c$ and $Q = \bar{a}_{\frac{1}{3}}.b + \bar{a}_{\frac{2}{3}}.c$. We have

$$D_A(P) = D_A(Q) = \frac{1}{3} \log \frac{\frac{1}{3}}{\frac{2}{3}} + \frac{2}{3} \log \frac{\frac{2}{3}}{\frac{1}{3}} = \frac{1}{3}.$$

However, $(P \mid Q) \setminus a = \tau_{\frac{1}{9}}.(b \mid b) + \tau_{\frac{2}{9}}.(b \mid c) + \tau_{\frac{2}{9}}.(c \mid b) + \tau_{\frac{4}{9}}.(c \mid c)$ and

$$D_A((P \mid Q) \setminus a) = \frac{1}{9} \log \frac{\frac{1}{9}}{\frac{4}{9}} + \frac{2}{9} \log \frac{\frac{2}{9}}{\frac{2}{9}} + \frac{2}{9} \log \frac{\frac{2}{9}}{\frac{2}{9}} + \frac{4}{9} \log \frac{\frac{4}{9}}{\frac{1}{9}} = \frac{2}{3}.$$

It follows from Proposition 6 that $D_A(P \mid Q) \geq D_A((P \mid Q) \setminus a) = \frac{2}{3}$.

3.3   Small Examples

We present some toy examples to show the basic ideas of our approach.

Example 8. Consider a communication system that provides anonymous email with 2 potential senders, a mix network and a recipient. The attacker wants to find out which sender sent an email to the recipient. By means of traffic analysis, the attacker obtains a communication system described by the process P.

$$P = \tau_p.sender(0).email.receive.\mathbf{0} + \tau_{1-p}.sender(1).email.receive.\mathbf{0}$$

The senders require anonymity, i.e., anonymity is required for the set $A = \{sender(0), sender(1)\}$. In this case, F_A is a singleton set $\{f\}$ with $f[P]$ taking the form:

$$f[P] = \tau_{1-p}.sender(0).email.receive.\mathbf{0} + \tau_p.sender(1).email.receive.\mathbf{0}$$

It is easy to see that $D_A(P) = p \log \frac{p}{1-p} + (1 - p) \log \frac{1-p}{p}$. If $p = \frac{1}{2}$, the attacker cannot distinguish the two senders, and indeed the system provides strong anonymity. If $p \to 0$ or $p \to 1$, we have $D_A(P) = +\infty$, which means that the system does not ensure any anonymity of the senders.

Example 9. Now suppose the actual system in Example 8 has a built-in non-determinism and behaves in a way described by the process Q.

$$Q = (\tau_{\frac{1}{3}}.sender(0).email.receive.\mathbf{0} + \tau_{\frac{2}{3}} sender(1).email.receive.\mathbf{0}) \boxplus$$
$$(\tau_{\frac{2}{3}}.sender(0).email.receive.\mathbf{0} + \tau_{\frac{1}{3}}.sender(1).email.receive.\mathbf{0})$$

We observe that $f[Q] = Q$ for $f \in F_A$, thus $D_A(Q) = 0$ and the system provides strong anonymity.

4   The Dining Cryptographers

The general Dining Cryptographers Problem [5] is described as follows: A number of cryptographers sitting around a table are having dinner. The representative of their organisation (master) may or may not pay the bill of the dinner. If he does not, then he will select exactly one cryptographer and order him to pay the bill. The master will tell secretly each cryptographer whether he has to pay or not. The cryptographers would like to reveal whether the bill is paid by the master or by one of them, but without knowing who among them, if any, is paying. In this paper we consider a DCP with three cryptographers connected by a ring. It is not difficult to extend it to the general case.

A possible solution to this problem, as described in [5], is to associate a coin to every two neighbouring cryptographers. The result of each coin-tossing is only visible to the adjacent cryptographers. Each cryptographer examines the two adjacent coins: If he is not paying, he announces "agree" if the results are the same, and "disagree" otherwise. If he is paying, he says the opposite. If the number of "disagree" is even, then the master is paying. Otherwise, one of the cryptographers is paying.

4.1   Fully Probabilistic Users

We consider the case in which the master probabilistically select one cryptographer to pay. We formalise the DCP as a process in the probabilistic CCS, as illustrated in Figure 2[2], where Π is the parallel composition. We use $\oplus$ (resp. $\ominus$) to represent the sum (resp. the subtraction) modulo 3. Messages p and n are the instructions sent by the master, requiring each cryptographer to pay or not to pay, respectively. The set of anonymous actions is $A = \{pay(i) \mid i = 0, 1, 2\}$. The restriction operator $\backslash$ over the action sequences $\overrightarrow{c}$ and $\overrightarrow{m}$ enforces these actions into internal communications. The traces of $\mathcal{DCP}$ are in the form of $pay(i)xyz$ with $i \in \{0, 1, 2\}$ and $x, y, z \in \{a, d\}$ (a for "agree" and d for "disagree"). F_A contains two elements, one renames $pay(i)$ according to the permutation $f_1 = \{0 \mapsto 1, 1 \mapsto 2, 2 \mapsto 0\}$ and the other $f_2 = \{0 \mapsto 2, 1 \mapsto 0, 2 \mapsto 1\}$.

We assume that all the coins are uniform. With a probabilistic master, $tds(pa(\mathcal{DCP}))$ contains only one trace distribution. Each maximal trace of $\mathcal{DCP}$ can only contain one of the following sequences: ddd, aad, ada, and daa.

---

[2] For the sake of brevity, we formalise the DCP in a value-passing version of the probabilistic CCS, which can be encoded into the probabilistic CCS in the standard way [19]; incorporating the "if-then-else" construct is also straightforward.

$$Master = \sum_{i=0}^{2} \tau_{p_i} . \overline{m}_i(p). \overline{m}_{i\oplus 1}(n). \overline{m}_{i\oplus 2}(n). \mathbf{0}$$
$$Coin_i = \tau_{p_h} . Head_i + \tau_{p_t} . Tail_i$$
$$Head_i = \overline{c}_{i,i}(head). \overline{c}_{i\ominus 1,i}(head). \mathbf{0}$$
$$Tail_i = \overline{c}_{i,i}(tail). \overline{c}_{i\ominus 1,i}(tail). \mathbf{0}$$
$$Crypt_i = m_i(x). c_{i,i}(y). c_{i,i\oplus 1}(z).$$
$$\text{if } x = p \text{ then } \overline{pay}_i.$$
$$\text{if } y = z \text{ then } \overline{out}_i(disagree) \text{ else } \overline{out}_i(agree)$$
$$\text{else if } y = z \text{ then } \overline{out}_i(agree) \text{ else } \overline{out}_i(disagree)$$
$$DCP = (Master \mid (\Pi_{i=0}^{2} Crypt_i \mid \Pi_{i=0}^{2} Coin_i) \setminus \overrightarrow{c}) \setminus \overrightarrow{m}$$

Fig. 2. Specification of the DCP in the probabilistic CCS

Fair coins. With fair coins, if the master assigns the initial probabilities $p_0 = \frac{1}{3}$, $p_1 = \frac{1}{3}$ and $p_2 = \frac{1}{3}$, i.e., each cryptographer has an equal chance to pay, then it is easy to see that $f_1[DCP] = DCP$ and $f_2[DCP] = DCP$. Therefore, $D_A(DCP) = 0$ and the DCP provides strong anonymity.

If the master assigns the initial probabilities $p_0 = \frac{1}{2}$, $p_1 = \frac{1}{3}$ and $p_2 = \frac{1}{6}$. The probabilities of traces with *ddd*, *aad*, *ada*, and *daa* are all $\frac{1}{4}$. By the definition of D, we can check that

$$D(DCP, f_1[DCP]) = 0.431 \quad \text{and} \quad D(DCP, f_2[DCP]) = 0.362$$

Hence, the degree of anonymity of such DCP is 0.431.

Table 1. A trace distribution (with biased coins: $p_h = \frac{2}{5}$)

	$crypt_0$ pays $(i = 0)$	$crypt_1$ pays $(i = 1)$	$crypt_2$ pays $(i = 2)$
$p(pay(i)ddd)$	0.120	0.080	0.040
$p(pay(i)aad)$	0.120	0.080	0.047
$p(pay(i)ada)$	0.120	0.093	0.040
$p(pay(i)daa)$	0.140	0.080	0.040

Biased coins. We assume the coins are biased, e.g. $p_h = \frac{2}{5}$. We also consider the case that $p_0 = \frac{1}{2}$, $p_1 = \frac{1}{3}$ and $p_2 = \frac{1}{6}$. Then the probabilities of traces can be calculated as in Table 1. We have

$$D(DCP, f_1[DCP]) = 0.209 \quad \text{and} \quad D(DCP, f_2[DCP]) = 0.878$$

Hence, the degree of anonymity of such DCP is 0.878, which is greater than 0.431. Therefore, the biased coins leak more information to the attacker than fair coins. If $p_h \rightarrow 1.0$, then $D(DCP, f_1[DCP]) = D(DCP, f_2[DCP]) = +\infty$. Hence, the degree of anonymity of such DCP is $+\infty$, in such case the DCP does not provide any anonymity.

Table 2. Three trace distributions (with biased coins: $p_h = \frac{2}{5}$)

	$crypt_0$ pays ($i = 0$)	$crypt_1$ pays ($i = 1$)	$crypt_2$ pays ($i = 2$)
$p(pay(i)ddd)$	0.24	0.24	0.24
$p(pay(i)aad)$	0.24	0.24	0.28
$p(pay(i)ada)$	0.24	0.28	0.24
$p(pay(i)daa)$	0.28	0.24	0.24

4.2 Non-deterministic Users

We now consider the case in which the master non-deterministically choose a cryptographer to pay, i.e., the master is of the form

$$Master = \overline{m}_0(p).\ \overline{m}_1(n).\ \overline{m}_2(n).\ \mathbf{0}\ \boxplus\ \overline{m}_0(n).\ \overline{m}_1(p).\ \overline{m}_2(n).\ \mathbf{0}\ \boxplus$$
$$\overline{m}_0(n).\ \overline{m}_1(n).\ \overline{m}_2(p).\ \mathbf{0}$$

Fair coins. With fair coins, it is easy to see that $f_1[\mathcal{DCP}] = \mathcal{DCP}$ and $f_2[\mathcal{DCP}] = \mathcal{DCP}$, i.e., $tds(pa(f_1[\mathcal{DCP}]))$ and $tds(pa(f_2[\mathcal{DCP}]))$ represent the same set of trace distributions as $tds(pa(\mathcal{DCP}))$. Therefore, $D_A(\mathcal{DCP}) = 0$ and the DCP provides strong anonymity.

Biased coins. We assume the coins are biased, e.g. $p_h = \frac{2}{5}$. Then $tds(pa(\mathcal{DCP}))$ contains the three trace distributions shown in the last three columns of Table 2. It can then be checked that

$$D(\mathcal{DCP}, f_1[\mathcal{DCP}]) = D(\mathcal{DCP}, f_2[\mathcal{DCP}]) = 0.009$$

Hence, the degree of anonymity of such DCP is 0.009

Remark 10. The master of a DCP models the *a priori* knowledge of the attacker. In the particular case that the master is purely non-deterministic, the attacker has no *a priori* knowledge of the users. The attacker simply assumes that there is a uniform probability distribution among the users, we then get an ideal situation of anonymity similar to that considered in [9].

5   Related Work

In his seminal paper, Chaum [5] used the size of an anonymity set to indicate the degree of anonymity provided by a DC network. An anonymity set is defined as the set of participants who could have sent a particular message as observed by the attacker. Berthold *et al.* [2] defined the degree of anonymity as $\ln(N)$, where N is the number of users of the protocols. Both [5] and [2] only deal with non-deterministic cases, and do not consider the probabilistic information of the users the attacker can gain by observing the system.

Reiter and Rubin [22] defined the degree of anonymity as $1 - p$, where p is the probability assigned to a particular user by the attacker. Halpern and O'Neill have proposed in [13] several notions of probabilistic anonymity. Their basic notion is formulated as a requirement on the knowledge of the attacker about the probability of the user. They have given both strong and weak version of this notion, proposing a formal interpretation of the three levels of the hierarchy proposed in [22]. Deng, Palamidessi and Pang [6] proposed a weak notion of probabilistic anonymity as an extension of [3] to measure the leaked information, which can be used by an attacker to infer the likeliness that the action has been performed by a certain user. Thus, the degree of anonymity is formalised as an factor by which the probability the attacker attributes to a user as the performer of the anonymous action has increased, after observing the system. All these methods focus on the probability of the users. Thus, they do not give any information on how distinguishable the user is within the anonymity set.

Serjantov and Danezis [25] and Claudia *et al.* [9] independently proposed an information theoretic metric based on the idea of measuring probability distributions. They used entropy to define the quality of anonymity and to compare different anonymity systems. Compared to [9], [25] does not normalise the degree in order to get a value relative to the anonymity level of the ideal system for the same number of users. Both [25] and [9] take into account the probabilities of the users performing certain actions which are assigned by an attacker after observing the system. However, they do not take into account the *a priori* information that the attacker might have. The attacker simply assumes a uniform distribution among the users before observation. Our method uses relative entropy, and it quantifies the amount of probabilistic information revealed by the protocol, i.e. how much information an attacker can achieve after observing the outcomes of the protocol, together with the information he has before the protocol running. Furthermore, we extend the measuring method to two sets of probability distributions using Hausdorff distance for protocols containing both non-deterministic and probabilistic behaviours.

Moskowitz *et al.* [20] proposed to use a related notion of mutual information to measure the capacity of covert channels. They have applied it to the analysis of a wide range of Mix-networks [21]. Recently, Chatzikokolakis, Palamidessi and Panangaden [4] developed a framework in which anonymity protocols can be interpreted as noisy channels. They also used it to express various notions of anonymity. Our work is still different from them in the sense that we use relative entropy instead of mutual information, and we focus on the non-expansiveness of the operators of the probabilistic CCS, which potentially allows for compositional analysis.

6   Conclusion and Future Work

In this paper, we have proposed to use relative entropy as a distance of two discrete probability distributions to measure anonymity for protocols which can be interpreted as a fully probabilistic automaton. This definition has been extended for two sets of probability distributions to also capture the non-deterministic aspect of these protocols. We have proved that based on this measuring method, most of the operators in the probabilistic CCS are non-expansive. We have demonstrated our approach by using the example of the Dining Cryptographers Problem.

Model checking anonymity protocols in the logic of knowledge was considered in [28]. It would also be interesting to investigate the problem in a probabilistic setting. The probabilistic model checker PRISM [18] was used to find novel attacks on Crowds [26], and to analyse cascase networks [10]. We intend to integrate our method with PRISM to build an automatic tool to assist the calculation of the degree of anonymity as defined in the paper. We also plan to apply our approach to more complex and real protocols to justify its usefulness.

Acknowledgments. We are very grateful to Kostas Chatzikokolakis, Catuscia Palamidessi, and Prakash Panangaden. From discussions with them we learnt more about relative entropy, which helped us to improve the paper a lot.

References

1. Baier, C., Kwiatkowaska, M.Z.: Domain equations for probabilistic processes. Mathematical Structures in Computer Science 10(6), 665–717 (2004)
2. Berthold, O., Pfiztmann, A., Standtke, R.: The disavantages of free mix routes and how to overcome them. In: Federrath, H. (ed.) Designing Privacy Enhancing Technologies. LNCS, vol. 2009, pp. 30–45. Springer, Heidelberg (2001)
3. Bhargava, M., Palamidessi, C.: Probabilistic anonymity. In: Abadi, M., de Alfaro, L. (eds.) CONCUR 2005. LNCS, vol. 3653, pp. 171–185. Springer, Heidelberg (2005)
4. Chatzikokolakis, K., Palamidessi, C., Panangaden, P.: Anonymity protocols as noisy channels. In: Proc. 2nd Symposium on Trustworthy Global Computing. LNCS, Springer, Heidelberg (2006) (to appear)
5. Chaum, D.: The dining cryptographers problem: Unconditional sender and recipient untraceability. Journal of Cryptology 1, 65–75 (1988)
6. Deng, Y., Palamidessi, C., Pang, J.: Weak probabilistic anonymity. In: Proc. 3rd Workshop on Security Issues in Concurrency, ENTCS (2006) (to appear)
7. Desharnais, J., Jagadeesan, R., Gupta, V., Panangaden, P.: The metric analogue of weak bisimulation for probabilistic processes. In: Proc. 17th IEEE Symposium on Logic in Computer Science, pp. 413–422. IEEE Computer Society, Los Alamitos (2002)
8. Desharnais, J., Jagadeesan, R., Gupta, V., Panangaden, P.: Metrics for labelled Markov processes. Theoretical Computer Science 318(3), 323–354 (2004)
9. Díaz, C., Seys, S., Claessens, J., Preneel, B.: Towards measuring anonymity. In: Dingledine, R., Syverson, P.F. (eds.) PET 2002. LNCS, vol. 2482, pp. 54–68. Springer, Heidelberg (2003)
10. Dingledine, R., Shmatikov, V., Syverson, P.F.: Synchronous batching: From cascades to free routes. In: Martin, D., Serjantov, A. (eds.) PET 2004. LNCS, vol. 3424, pp. 186–206. Springer, Heidelberg (2005)
11. Furuichi, S., Yanagi, K., Kuriyama, K.: Fundamental properties of Tsallis relative entropy. Journal of Mathematical Physics 45(12), 4868–4877 (2004)
12. Garcia, F.D., Hasuo, I., Pieters, W., van Rossum, P.: Provable anonymity. In: Proc.3rd ACM Workshop on Formal Methods in Security Engineering, pp. 63–72. ACM Press, New York (2005)

13. Halpern, J.Y., O'Neill, K.R.: Anonymity and information hiding in multiagent systems. In: Proc. 16th IEEE Computer Security Foundations Workshop. IEEE Computer Society, Los Alamitos (2003)
14. Hoare, C.A.R.: Communicating Sequential Processes. Prentice Hall, Englewood Cliffs (1985)
15. Hughes, D., Shmatikov, V.: Information hiding, anonymity and privacy: a modular approach. Journal of Computer Security 12(1), 3–36 (2004)
16. Kesdogan, D., Egner, J.: Stop-and-go MIXes: Providing probabilistic anonymity in an open system. In: Aucsmith, D. (ed.) IH 1998. LNCS, vol. 1525, pp. 83–98. Springer, Heidelberg (1998)
17. Kullback, S., Leibler, R.A.: On information and sufficiency. Annals of Mathematical Statistics 22(1), 79–86 (1951)
18. Kwiatkowska, M., Norman, G., Parker, D.: PRISM: Probabilistic symbolic model checker. In: Field, T., Harrison, P.G., Bradley, J., Harder, U. (eds.) TOOLS 2002. LNCS, vol. 2324, pp. 200–204. Springer, Heidelberg (2002)
19. Milner, R.: Communication and Concurrency. Prentice-Hall, Englewood Cliffs (1989)
20. Moskowitz, I.S., Newman, R.E., Crepeau, D.P., Miller, A.R.: Covert channels and anonymizing networks. In: Proceedings of 2nd ACM Workshop on Privacy in the Electronic Society, pp. 79–88. ACM Press, New York (2003)
21. Newman, R.E., Nalla, V.R., Moskowitz, I.S.: Anonymity and covert channels in simple timed mix-firewalls. In: Martin, D., Serjantov, A. (eds.) PET 2004. LNCS, vol. 3424, pp. 1–16. Springer, Heidelberg (2005)
22. Reiter, M.K., Rubin, A.D.: Crowds: Anonymity for Web transactions. ACM Transactions on Information and System Security 1(1), 66–92 (1998)
23. Schneider, S., Sidiropoulos, A.: CSP and anonymity. In: Martella, G., Kurth, H., Montolivo, E., Bertino, E. (eds.) Computer Security - ESORICS 96. LNCS, vol. 1146, pp. 198–218. Springer, Heidelberg (1996)
24. Segala, R.: Modeling and Verification of Randomized Distributed Real-Time Systems. PhD thesis, MIT, Deptartment of EECS (1995)
25. Serjantov, A., Danezis, G.: Towards an information theoretic metric for anonymity. In: Dingledine, R., Syverson, P.F. (eds.) PET 2002. LNCS, vol. 2482, pp. 41–53. Springer, Heidelberg (2003)
26. Shmatikov, V.: Probabilistic model checking of an anonymity system. Journal of Computer Security 12(3/4), 355–377 (2004)
27. Syverson, P.F., Goldschlag, D.M., Reed, M.G.: Anonymous connections and onion routing. In: Proc. 18th IEEE Symposium on Security and Privacy, pp. 44–54. IEEE Computer Society Press, Los Alamitos (1997)
28. van der Meyden, R., Su, K.: Symbolic model checking the knowledge of the dining cryptographers. In: Proc. 17th IEEE Computer Security Foundations Workshop, pp. 280–291. IEEE Computer Society Press, Los Alamitos (2004)

Formalizing and Analyzing Sender Invariance*

Paul Hankes Drielsma, Sebastian Mödersheim, Luca Viganò, and David Basin

Information Security Group, Dep. of Computer Science, ETH Zurich, Switzerland
{drielsma,moedersheim,vigano,basin}@inf.ethz.ch
www.infsec.ethz.ch/~{drielsma,moedersheim,vigano,basin}

Abstract. In many network applications and services, agents that share
no secure channel in advance may still wish to communicate securely
with each other. In such settings, one often settles for achieving security
goals weaker than authentication, such as sender invariance. Informally,
sender invariance means that all messages that seem to come from the
same source actually do, where the source can perhaps only be identified
by a pseudonym. This implies, in particular, that the relevant parts of
messages cannot be modified by an intruder.

In this paper, we provide the first formal definition of sender invariance as well as a stronger security goal that we call strong sender invariance. We show that both kinds of sender invariance are closely related
to, and entailed by, weak authentication, the primary difference being
that sender invariance is designed for the context where agents can only
be identified pseudonymously. In addition to clarifying how sender invariance and authentication are related, this result shows how a broad
class of automated tools can be used for the analysis of sender invariance protocols. As a case study, we describe the analysis of two sender
invariance protocols using the OFMC back-end of the AVISPA Tool.

1   Introduction

The establishment of a secure channel between communicating parties requires a
pre-existing relationship between them. Examples of such relationships include
shared passwords and transitive relationships, for instance where the parties
exchange public-key certificates issued by a trusted certification authority. Common to these types of relationships is the prerequisite that some data is available
in order to bootstrap the secure channel. This data may have been exchanged in
advance, or it might be produced on the fly by a reliable source like a certification
authority.

In many network applications and services, however, agents that share no
such bootstrap data in advance may still wish to communicate securely with
each other. Indeed, they might have no prior relationship whatsoever, not even

---

* This work was partially supported by the National Competence Center in Research
on Mobile Information and Communication Systems (NCCR-MICS), a center supported by the Swiss National Science Foundation under grant number 5005-67322,
and by the Zurich Information Security Center. It represents the views of the authors.

T. Dimitrakos et al. (Eds.): FAST 2006, LNCS 4691, pp. 80–95, 2007.

a transitive one. In such situations, classical authentication (e.g. via public keys) is impossible. To remedy this problem, one would have to define a process by which bootstrap data is established and distributed, but in many settings this is too expensive or cumbersome, as one must require that every participant must somehow "register" before using a service. For a small coffee shop offering its customers a wireless hotspot, such a registration process could detract from one of its main selling points: convenience.

In settings where no bootstrap data is available, a weaker security goal is still achievable, namely *sender invariance*. Informally, sender invariance means that all messages that seem to come from the same source actually do, where the source can perhaps only be identified by a pseudonym. This implies, in particular, that the messages cannot be modified by an intruder, at least not their relevant parts. Moreover, one may want to ensure the secrecy of the communicated data between the participants.

Sender invariance arises in a variety of situations, both wired and wireless. Consider, for instance, any of the many free web-based e-mail services available online. In general, users register for an online e-mail service via an informal process whereby a new username and password are established. At no point does a formal authentication process take place involving, for example, photo identification or a physical signature. This process is acceptable, as an email address can be seen as a pseudonym that is not necessarily linkable with its owner's true identity. This, however, has ramifications concerning how one should describe the login process, as there is no reliable means of linking the established username with the identity of the user. If one considers the login process and ignores registration, simply assuming that credentials have been exchanged sometime in the past, then the user login process can be called authentication. However, in light of this informal registration process, the login process should more accurately be described as ensuring sender invariance: that is, the user with pseudonym *John Doe* is the same user who originally opened the account registered as *John Doe*, although the e-mail provider does not know his proper identity.

Such online services, whose users can be logged in based only on credentials which are not linkable to their actual identities, are already prevalent. As networks move towards increased mobility and ad-hoc connections, situations in which reliable pre-shared cryptographic credentials are limited or unavailable will arise with increasing frequency. Understanding what security goals can be achieved in such situations is important for the design of next-generation network protocols. In this paper, we aim to further this understanding by examining sender invariance in detail.

Contributions: Our first contribution is a formal definition of sender invariance and a stronger, related security goal which we call *strong sender invariance*. We also show that (strong) sender invariance is closely related to weak authentication, the primary difference being that sender invariance assumes that agents can only be identified pseudonymously. Based on this, we show that the three security goals constitute a hierarchy. Furthermore, we show how a broad class of automated analysis tools can be used to analyze sender invariance protocols. We also describe the analysis of two protocols using the On-the-Fly Model Checker OFMC [7], one of the back-ends of the AVISPA Tool for security protocol analysis [3].

Related Work: Our work focuses on the formal definition security goals and the relationships between them. Gollmann [14] considered authentication in detail, and Lowe [16] subsequently defined a hierarchy of authentication goals which apply in settings where relationships between agents have been established in advance. In §2.5, we similarly define a hierarchy that relates the two forms of sender invariance and weak authentication. Our focus, however, is on settings in which the kinds of relationships that one would normally require to bootstrap a secure channel are not available.

Our motivation to examine settings where agents know each other perhaps only via pseudonyms was inspired by current trends in protocol development, in particular the work of the Internet Engineering Task Force on Mobile IPv6 [15]. In [17], for instance, the authors identify sender invariance as a goal that should be ensured by the IPv6 SEcure Neighbor Discovery protocol (SEND [2]) in ad hoc networks.[1] In SEND, this is achieved via a mechanism for providing sender invariance called Cryptographically Generated Addresses (CGA [4]). In this paper, we consider a similar idea, the Purpose-Built Keys Framework [10].

Organization: In §2, we define and discuss sender invariance and strong sender invariance. In §3, we present a case study based on the Purpose-Built Keys Framework that illustrates the formal analysis of sender invariance with the OFMC tool. In §4, we discuss settings in which agents share some bootstrap data, but not enough to achieve mutual authentication. In §5, we summarize our results and discuss future work.

2   Sender Invariance

Designers of modern security protocols face a challenge. On the one hand, protocols need to be designed with ever-increasing mobility in mind. On the other hand, this very mobility means that designers should also make few assumptions about the amount of information shared, in advance, among protocol participants; indeed, one must often assume that participants share no a priori relationships at all. Yet authentication protocols tend to rely on just such pre-shared information, such as a public key or a shared password. Indeed, in [9], Boyd argues that in the absence of authenticated shared information, no secure channels can be established.

Sender invariance protocols are based on the idea that, in many situations, one party of a protocol does not need to be authenticated in the classical sense,

---

[1] Note that the authors do not actually call the goal sender invariance, but merely describe the intuition: "nodes ensure that they are talking to the same nodes (as before)" [17, §3.3].

but rather could pick a pseudonym and be identified by that pseudonym thereafter. The protocols ensure that an intruder cannot "take over" somebody else's pseudonym, i.e. generate messages that appear to originate from the owner of the pseudonym, or read messages that are sent to the owner of the pseudonym.

A variety of mechanisms can be used to realize sender invariance. Perhaps the most common one, and the one used in our running example PBK, is as follows. An agent creates an asymmetric key pair, publishes the public key, and uses a hash value of the public key as a pseudonym. Clearly, the intruder can generate his own pseudonym, but he cannot sign or decrypt messages with the private key associated with somebody else's pseudonym. The remarkable thing about these mechanisms is thus that we get—out of nothing—variants of authentic channels that only differ from the classical ones by the fact that one end point is identified by a pseudonym.

The goals that are considered for sender invariance protocols are thus similar to classical authentication and secrecy goals, but with the twist that one side is identified by a pseudonym rather than a real name. By *sender invariance*, we informally mean that all messages come from the same source that is identified by a pseudonym:

> A two-party protocol P guarantees the responder role *sender invariance with respect to the initiator role* iff the following holds: whenever an agent b in the responder role receives a message that appears to have been sent by an agent with pseudonym id, then this message originates from the same agent playing the initiator role as all previous messages that appeared to come from pseudonym id.

Note that sender invariance differs in several respects from privacy (for instance, the privacy properties defined in [1]). Privacy means to protect the identities of the communicating agents from being observable (to an outstanding party or even to each other); for sender invariance, the protection of identities is not an issue (and agents may expose their identities, even if they cannot prove them). Sender invariance is rather the best we can achieve when identification/authentication is not possible.

The relation of this goal with classical authentication will be discussed shortly. We note that one may similarly develop a concept of *receiver invariance* as an analogue of secrecy goals in this pseudonym-based communication; we do not, however, consider this further in this paper.

2.1 Purpose-Built Keys

As a running example, we introduce a protocol based on the Purpose-Built Keys Framework (PBK [10]), a mechanism for achieving sender invariance. PBK uses freshly generated, temporary, asymmetric key pairs. A user's pseudonym is simply a hash of the temporary public key, the so-called PBID. In an initialization phase, the sender agent transmits his purpose-built public key. If this exchange is not tampered with, then the sender can sign subsequent messages, thus assuring the receiver that the source of the messages has not changed.

$$1. \ A \rightarrow B : PBK_A$$

$$\dots\dots\dots\dots\dots\dots\dots\dots\dots\dots\dots\dots\dots$$

$$2. \ A \rightarrow B : \{Msg\}_{PBK_A{}^{-1}}.H(PBK_A)$$
$$3. \ B \rightarrow A : N_B.H(PBK_A)$$
$$4. \ A \rightarrow B : \{N_B\}_{PBK_A{}^{-1}}.H(PBK_A)$$

Protocol 1. An example PBK protocol

We note that denial of service attacks are possible, in the sense that the intruder can drop messages from an honest initiator. We do not consider such attacks here, however, as they do not constitute violations of sender invariance.

Example. Protocol 1 is an example protocol which uses PBK to ensure sender invariance between an initiator A and a responder B. Upon starting the protocol, A generates her purpose-built key pair PBK_A and $PBK_A{}^{-1}$. She sends the former to B in message 1. The dotted line separates the initialization phase from the rest of the protocol. In message 2, A sends some payload Msg to B signed with her PBK. Messages 3 and 4 perform a challenge-response exchange in order to prove to B that the party purporting to possess $PBK_A{}^{-1}$ is indeed active and the signed messages are not simply being replayed. We assume that A and B might want to exchange multiple payload messages with the pseudonym $H(PBK_A)$, so messages 2 through 4 might be repeated arbitrarily often.

The running example of Protocol 1 will serve as a basis for the discussions below, where we describe our model and define sender invariance formally.

2.2   Formalizing Sender Invariance

The informal definition given above is meant to provide the intuition behind the goal of sender invariance: namely, that a sequence of messages that apparently all originate from the same sender truly do. Note that we do not assume that the agent playing the responder role knows the real identity of the initiator with whom he communicates; this property should hold even if the receiver knows the sender only via some pseudonym. It is this intuition that we strive to capture in our formal definition of sender invariance below.

To formulate sender invariance independently of which particular formalism or tool is adopted for modeling and analysis, we define requirements for protocol models (summarized in Fig. 1), that are sufficient to formalize sender invariance. We assume that there exists a set Msg of all *messages*, which we represent as free terms with the standard perfect cryptography assumption. Let Agent $\subseteq$ Msg denote the set of all possible *agent identifiers*, including both real names and a set ID $\subseteq$ Agent of *pseudonyms*. We also assume that there exists a set of *honest agent identifiers*, which we denote HAgent $\subseteq$ Agent, and a set of *honest pseudonyms*, which is H_ID = ID $\cap$ HAgent. As notation, we will use upper case $A, B, \dots$ to denote role names and lower case $a, b, \dots$ for agent names.

E	Set of events
AE ⊇ {*witness, request*}	Auxiliary events, with AE ⊆ E
Msg	Set of all possible messages
Agent ⊆ Msg	Agent identifiers, both names and pseudonyms
HAgent ⊆ Agent	Honest agent identifiers
ID ⊆ Agent	Pseudonyms
H_ID = ID ∩ HAgent	Pseudonyms belonging to honest agents
Vars	Set of protocol variable identifiers

Fig. 1. Notation

We follow the standard Dolev-Yao model [13] of an active intruder who controls the network but cannot break cryptography: the intruder can intercept messages and analyze them if he possesses the respective keys for decryption, and he can generate messages from his knowledge and send them under any party's name.

The protocol models must also provide some means to reason about the way that an agent interprets particular concrete messages. In Protocol 1, for instance, the responder B might want to ensure that a concrete value he receives and interprets as A's payload message Msg was indeed intended by A as a payload message and not, for instance, as a response to the challenge N_B. To this end, we require the existence of a set Vars of identifiers for the *variables of the protocol*. The elements of Vars are logical identifiers indicating how an agent interprets a given value. The definition of the set itself is protocol specific. For instance, for Protocol 1, the set Vars = $\{PBK_A, Msg, N_B\}$ would be appropriate.

We assume that protocol models have behaviors that can be expressed as *linearly ordered traces of events* from a fixed event set E. Traces contain events from a set AE of *auxiliary events* that express information about an honest agent's assumptions or intentions when executing a protocol. These events provide a language over which we then define the goals of the protocol.[2] We assume that the intruder can neither generate events from AE nor modify those AE events generated by honest agents. By convention, we call the events in AE *witness* and *request*. For $a, b \in$ Agent, $v \in$ Vars, and $m \in$ Msg,

- *witness*(a, b, v, m) expresses that initiator a intends to execute the protocol with responder b and wishes to use value m as the protocol variable v; and
- *request*(b, a, v, m) expresses that responder b accepts the value m and now relies on the guarantee that agent a exists and agrees with him on this value for protocol variable v.

Consider an honest initiator a who wishes to execute a protocol with a responder b. For all $v \in$ Vars that are of interest (where the definition of interest

---

[2] This approach to formalizing protocol goals is standard. It is adopted, for instance, in the AVISPA Tool [3,7], and it is analogous to other approaches like that of [16], where goals are formulated in terms of "status signals" exchanged on special channels to which the intruder has no access.

will depend strongly on the goals of the protocol in question), a will generate an event $witness(a, b, v, m)$ upon setting a value m for v, and each honest responder will generate an event $request(b, a, v, m')$ after reaching an accepting state in which he has assigned the value m' to v. Following [3,7], we define protocol goals below as conditions on traces that specify how $witness$ and $request$ events must correspond with one another.

Example. In Protocol 1, one can define the variables of interest to be those which the responder wants to be sure originated from the pseudonym $H(PBK_A)$: namely, Msg and the signed N_B. Honest agents will, as mentioned, generate auxiliary events for each of these variables of interest, but we consider only Msg in this example. We assume that agent a with PBK pbk_a wishes to execute Protocol 1 with agent b, and that a wishes to transmit the payload message 17. Furthermore, for the sake of example, we ignore possible manipulations by the intruder and assume that messages are transmitted without modification.

Upon sending message 1, a generates the event $witness(H(pbk_a), b, Msg, 17)$, expressing that, under her pseudonym, she intends to send to b the value 17, interpreting it as protocol variable Msg. The responder accepts the protocol run only after receiving message 4, which confirms recentness. After receiving message 4, b will generate the event $request(b, H(pbk_a), Msg, 17)$, indicating that he accepts the value 17, believes that it originates from the agent associated with pseudonym $H(pbk_a)$, and interprets it as the protocol variable Msg.

We now formally define the security goal of sender invariance as the following temporal property of traces of events over the set E, where $\square$ and $\diamondsuit$ denote the linear time temporal operators "always in the future" and "sometime in the past", respectively:

$$\text{SI:} \quad \forall b \in \mathsf{HAgent}.\forall id \in \mathsf{H\_ID}.\forall m \in \mathsf{Msg}.\forall v \in \mathsf{Vars}.$$
$$\square(request(b, id, v, m) \rightarrow \exists v' \in \mathsf{Vars}.\diamondsuit\, witness(id, b, v', m))$$

We assume, in this definition, that the initiator knows the real name of the responder b, but we do not require that b knows the real name of the initiator. This definition expresses that every honest agent b is guaranteed that, if $id \in \mathsf{H\_ID}$, then there exists an honest agent who sent all the values m that b believes originated from pseudonym id. Recall that only honest agents generate the auxiliary events in AE, therefore the presence of a $witness$ event implies that it was generated by an honest agent. Moreover, for each incoming message m that b associates with the protocol variable v in the $request$, there exists some protocol variable v' that expresses how the honest owner of pseudonym id intended to send the value m. This implies that the values m have not been modified in transit, but the sender and receiver may have assigned different interpretations to the transmitted values.

2.3   Strong Sender Invariance

A stronger goal results when the interpretations must agree. We define *strong sender invariance*, a modification of sender invariance, by requiring that the sender and the receiver agree on the interpretation of each message. We formalize this as follows:

$$\text{STRONGSI:} \quad \forall b \in \mathsf{HAgent}.\forall id \in \mathsf{H\_ID}.\forall m \in \mathsf{Msg}.\forall v \in \mathsf{Vars}.$$
$$\Box(request(b, id, v, m) \rightarrow \Diamond\, witness(id, b, v, m))$$

Strong sender invariance, as the name implies, provides a stronger guarantee than sender invariance itself (we will show this formally in §2.5). Specifically, it requires that all values m received by b apparently from an honest pseudonym id indeed originated from the same honest agent. Moreover, for each m, the protocol variable v with which b associates m must be the same as the v for which the value was intended by the sender id; that is, v is the same in both auxiliary events. As before, this implies that the value was not modified in transit, but we now additionally require that the interpretations agree. In the extreme case, that the protocol-specific set of "interesting" protocol variables includes *all* protocol variables, this implies that the exact messages sent by the initiator arrive, without tampering, at the responder.

2.4   Discussion

The informal notion that the source of a communication does not change suffers from ambiguities that one must resolve when defining sender invariance formally. Perhaps most importantly, one must define to what extent sender invariance implies message integrity.

Conservatively, one can define sender invariance in such a way that any message modification violates sender invariance. This would be akin to the notion of matching conversations, defined in [8]. Such a definition is quite restrictive and of limited practical use, particularly in ad-hoc settings with potentially no relationships among protocol participants.

Instead, we opt for a finer-grained definition in which integrity must be guaranteed only for relevant parts of the exchanged messages, where "relevant" can be defined in a protocol-specific way. The case described above is then a special case of this more general approach in which all parts of the protocol messages are considered relevant. In order to pursue this fine-grained approach, we formalize sender invariance over the auxiliary trace events *witness* and *request* rather than, for instance, over the communication events themselves.

The auxiliary events *witness* and *request* confer a further benefit; namely, they contain all the information one needs to formalize authentication itself. This facilitates a direct comparison of the two forms of sender invariance with authentication, discussed in the next subsection.

Finally, we note that alternate definitions of (strong) sender invariance are also possible and may be appropriate for certain settings. In our definition, we assume a setting in which the owner of pseudonym id knows the identity of the agent b with whom he wants to communicate. This assumption is appropriate for one of our larger case-study protocols, Mobile IPv6 [15]. One could, however, envision protocols in which the recipient is unimportant, or indeed known via a pseudonym. For such protocols, one might define sender invariance as follows (and strong sender invariance analogously):

$$\text{SI}':\ \forall b \in \mathsf{HAgent}.\forall id \in \mathsf{H\_ID}.\forall m \in \mathsf{Msg}.\forall v \in \mathsf{Vars}.\exists b' \in \mathsf{Agent}.$$
$$\Box(request(b, id, v, m) \rightarrow \exists v' \in \mathsf{Vars}.\Diamond\, witness(id, b', v', m))\ .$$

For the rest of the paper, however, we will focus on our original definition SI.

2.5   Relating Sender Invariance and Authentication

We now examine the relationship between sender invariance, strong sender invariance, and authentication. We first recall the informal definition of weak authentication (adapted from [16], where it is termed non-injective agreement):

> A protocol guarantees *weak authentication* to a responder B on a set of protocol variables V iff whenever B completes a run of the protocol, apparently with initiator A, then A has previously been executing the protocol as initiator, apparently with responder B, and the two agents agree on the data values corresponding to all the variables in V.

In our model, we equate the responder's completion of a protocol run with his arrival in an accepting state. Since we assume that responders issue *request* events only after reaching an accepting state, we can formally define weak authentication as follows:

$$\text{WAUTH:}\ \forall b \in \mathsf{HAgent}.\forall a \in \mathsf{HAgent}.\forall m \in \mathsf{Msg}.\forall v \in \mathsf{Vars}.$$
$$\Box(request(b, a, v, m) \rightarrow \Diamond\, witness(a, b, v, m))$$

Observe that strong sender invariance differs from weak authentication only in the inclusion of the pseudonym $id \in \mathsf{H\_ID}$ rather than an actual agent identifier $b \in \mathsf{HAgent}$, which may be either a pseudonym or a real name. Thus, strong sender invariance is the direct analogue to weak authentication for the pseudonymous setting, and we have that WAUTH implies STRONGSI. The converse, however, does not hold, as expressed as Proposition 1.

Proposition 1. Weak authentication is a strictly stronger security goal than strong sender invariance.

Proof. We first show that every trace that satisfies weak authentication also satisfies strong sender invariance; thus, if all traces induced by a protocol satisfy weak authentication, then they also satisfy strong sender invariance. To that end, consider an arbitrary trace that satisfies weak authentication and any event on this trace of the form $request(b, id, v, m)$, for arbitrary $b \in \mathsf{HAgent}$, $id \in \mathsf{H\_ID}$, $v \in \mathsf{Vars}$ and $m \in \mathsf{Msg}$. We have to show that this event is preceded by the event $witness(id, b, v, m)$. This follows directly, since $\mathsf{H\_ID} \subseteq \mathsf{HAgent}$, and weak authentication demands that any event $request(b, a, v, m)$—where now $a \in \mathsf{HAgent}$—is preceded by $witness(a, b, v, m)$. Note that if $a \notin \mathsf{H\_ID}$ for all initiators $a \in \mathsf{HAgent}$ for which request terms are generated, then sender invariance holds trivially. Since we have not assumed any specific property about b, id, v, and m, or where in the trace the *request* event occurs, every $request(b, id, v, m)$ is preceded by $witness(id, b, v, m)$.

To see that weak authentication is strictly stronger than strong sender invariance, consider a trace with the event $request(b, a, v, m)$ with $a \in \mathsf{HAgent} \setminus \mathsf{H\_ID}$, and no other *witness* or *request* events. This trace trivially satisfies strong sender invariance (as $a \notin \mathsf{H\_ID}$) but not weak authentication. This example is a bit contrived, but we give a more realistic example (Protocol 2) in §3.1.   □

We now examine the relationship between the two types of sender invariance itself.

Proposition 2. Strong sender invariance is a strictly stronger security goal than sender invariance.

Proof. As before, we show that strong sender invariance is at least as strong as sender invariance by showing that any trace satisfying the stronger form also satisfies the weaker one. Consider an arbitrary trace that satisfies strong sender invariance, and consider any event of the form $request(b, id, v, m)$ in the trace, again for arbitrary values b, id, v, and m of the respective types. We have to show that this event is preceded on the trace by the event $witness(b, id, v', m)$ for some $v' \in \mathsf{Vars}$. This holds for $v = v'$, since the trace satisfies strong sender invariance, which requires that $witness(id, b, v, m)$ must precede said *request* event. As we have not assumed anything about the arguments of the *request* event and its position in the trace, this holds for all such *request* events, which shows that sender invariance holds of the trace.

A trivial example to show that sender invariance does not imply strong sender invariance is a trace that contains $request(b, id, v, m)$, preceded by $witness(id, b, v', m)$ for arbitrary constants b, id, v, v', and m, where $v \neq v'$, and such that the trace contains no other *witness* and *request* events. This satisfies sender invariance, but not strong sender invariance. Another example is Protocol 1, which will be discussed in the following section.   □

It follows from these propositions that there is a hierarchy of security goals in which weak authentication is strongest, followed by strong sender invariance, and finally sender invariance itself. Specifically, we have seen that strong sender invariance is precisely weak authentication in which pseudonyms are used in place of true agent names. We can observe the same of sender invariance, modulo the fact that the agreement of protocol variables is also ignored. As we will discuss in the next section, this result also illustrates the potential to take existing tools for the automated analysis of authentication protocols and directly use them for the analysis of (strong) sender invariance as well.

3 Analyzing Sender Invariance

We now show how to apply automated tools to analyze (strong) sender invariance protocols. We illustrate this with a case study: the formal analysis of two protocols that use the Purpose-Built Keys Framework.

Classically, the model checking problem $M \vDash \varphi$ verifies whether a model M of a system fulfills a specification of the goal φ. We have analyzed our case-study protocols using the On-the-Fly Model Checker OFMC [5,6,7], a state-of-the art tool for protocol analysis. OFMC is one of the back-ends of the AVISPA Tool, in which protocols are specified using the *High-Level Protocol Specification Language HLPSL* [3,11].[3] Protocol models built using this specification language capture the requirements for formalizing sender invariance that we identified in Fig. 1. OFMC allows the modeler to specify φ, where goals are specified negatively as attack states. Thus, for the analyses described in the coming sections, we were able to translate the formulas STRONGSI and SI into HLPSL directly.

Note that while OFMC allows for user-defined goals, some model checkers for security protocols consider a fixed, built-in set of goals φ tailored to the application domain: in general, authentication and secrecy. In the previous section, however, we showed that both forms of sender invariance can be seen as a generalization of weak authentication. Based on this, we can identify the following additional requirements on protocol models for use with such fixed-goal model checkers. If

- one can construct protocol specifications in which authentication is performed on pseudonyms,
- honest pseudonyms can be distinguished in the model from those belonging to the intruder, and
- in the case of SI, agreement on protocol variables can be ignored,

then model checkers that are tailored to check WAUTH can be employed, out of the box, to also check STRONGSI and SI.

3.1 Case Study: Purpose-Built Keys

Analyzing Protocol 1. We return to Protocol 1, introduced in §2.1. We constructed a formal model of the Protocol 1 in HLPSL and analyzed it in a scenario with a bounded number of protocol sessions. For brevity, we omit the HLPSL specification itself and describe only the aspects most important for the analysis.

In our model of the protocol, honest agents generate new PBKs freshly for each session, and these are added to the set H_ID upon generation. HLPSL

---

[3] The HLPSL is an expressive, modular, role-based, formal language that allows for the specification of control flow patterns, data structures, complex security properties, as well as different cryptographic operators and their algebraic properties. The AVISPA Tool automatically translates a user-defined security problem into an equivalent specification written in the rewrite-based formalism *IF* (for *Intermediate Format*). An IF specification describes an infinite-state transition system amenable to formal analysis: this specification is input to OFMC and the other back-ends of the AVISPA Tool, which implement a variety of techniques to search the corresponding infinite-state transition system for states that represent attacks on the intended properties of the protocol.

1. $A \to i : PBK_A$
2. $A \to i : \{Msg_A\}_{PBK_A{}^{-1}}.H(PBK_A)$
3. $i \to A : Msg_I.H(PBK_A)$
4. $A \to i : \{Msg_I\}_{PBK_A{}^{-1}}.H(PBK_A)$
1'. $i \to B : PBK_A$
2'. $i \to B : \{Msg_I\}_{PBK_A{}^{-1}}.H(PBK_A)$

Fig. 2. An attack on Protocol 1 that violates STRONGSI

supports the modeling of sets, and using this we maintain a single, global H_ID. The intruder, who is active and has full Dolev-Yao [13] control over the network as described, may also generate fresh PBKs (and may apply the function H to generate valid pseudonyms), but he may not add them to H_ID. He may, however, replay any of the keys in that set. We assume that the responder wants sender invariance guarantees on the contents of every message after the initialization phase. Thus, the set Vars = $\{Msg, N_B\}$, and in the model the responder issues two *request* facts after receiving message 4. In turn, the initiator role issues *witness* facts upon sending messages 2 and 4.

OFMC employs a number of symbolic techniques to perform falsification (by finding an attack on the input protocol) and bounded verification, i.e. verification for a finite number of protocol sessions. In our analysis scenario, we assumed four concurrent protocol sessions (four instances each of the initiator and responder roles). In OFMC, these sessions are specified symbolically, so we need not specify concretely which agent plays which role. Rather, the identities of the agents participating in each session are given simply as variables, and OFMC searches symbolically through all possible assignments of these variables. Our first analysis used SI, sender invariance, as the goal of the protocol. As our analysis found no attacks, this amounts to bounded verification of all possible analysis scenarios consisting of four protocol sessions. This shows that PBK is indeed a strong mechanism for providing sender invariance.

Strong Sender Invariance. We also analyzed Protocol 1 against the goal of strong sender invariance. Recall that, by design, sender invariance ignores the interpretation that agents assign to messages, which we express via the protocol variables in set Vars. Thus, protocols guaranteeing sender invariance may well suffer from vulnerabilities in which an intruder succeeds in causing a confusion between the interpretation assigned to a message by the sender and that assigned by the receiver. Indeed, our analysis found an attack on strong sender invariance, shown in Fig. 2.

In this execution, the intruder intercepts the purpose-built key PBK_A and wishes to pass himself off to B as someone who possesses the associated private key. To this end, after receiving A's second message, he replies with the challenge Msg_I, the payload message he actually wants to send to B. A replies in good faith, signing the challenge with $PBK_A{}^{-1}$. In a second session, i then claims PBK_A as his own purpose-built key and sends the signed payload message

$$1. \ A \to B : PBK_A$$

. . . .

$$2. \ A \to B : \{tag_1.Msg\}_{PBK_A{}^{-1}}.H(PBK_A)$$
$$3. \ B \to A : N_B.H(PBK_A)$$
$$4. \ A \to B : \{tag_2.N_B\}_{PBK_A{}^{-1}}.H(PBK_A)$$

Protocol 2. A refined PBK-Based protocol

$\{Msg_I\}_{PBK_A{}^{-1}}$. Recall that we assume that messages 2 through 4 may be repeated multiple times to transmit payload data over the lifetime of a pseudonym, therefore the intruder can even perform the challenge-response exchange with B as soon as A sends another payload message.

This attack represents a confusion of the protocol variables assigned to message 4 by A and message 2' by B. Although A did indeed once send the message $\{Msg_I\}_{PBK_A{}^{-1}}.H(PBK_A)$, she sent it interpreting it as message 4 of the protocol and thus assigned $N_B = Msg_I$, whereas B interprets it as message 2 upon receipt, assigning $Msg = Msg_I$. Thus, this attack violates the goal of strong sender invariance, but not sender invariance itself. As discussed in §2.5, Protocol 1 illustrates that SI is strictly weaker than STRONGSI.

Analyzing Protocol 2. Protocol 2 shows an alternative example of a protocol that uses the PBK framework. It is identical to Protocol 1 save for the fact that so-called tags have been added to messages 2 and 4. The tags tag_1 and tag_2 are intended as identifiers for the signed messages that signify the purpose of the signature. They avoid, for instance, that B or an intruder can bring A to sign arbitrary data without indicating what the signature is intended for.

We used OFMC to analyze Protocol 2 in the same setting as used in our analysis of Protocol 1. The *witness* and *request* facts generated contain protocol variables indicating the interpretation assigned by the agents, $m2$ and $m4$ for messages 2 and 4, respectively. As specified in the formula STRONGSI, matching *request* and *witness* events must agree on this interpretation. Our analysis results show that, for scenarios consisting of four protocol sessions, Protocol 2 is safe from attacks on strong sender invariance. From Proposition 2, we can conclude that Protocol 2 is thus safe from attacks on sender invariance as well.

4   Varying Amounts of Pre-shared Information

Sender invariance appears to be an appealing security goal that is appropriate for settings such as those that arise in mobile networks where users do not know one another in advance. Naturally, situations arise that fall between the case in which two agents involved in a protocol run initially share cryptographically authenticated information and the other extreme case in which they share nothing. Perhaps the most prevalent example of this arises in E-commerce situations in which the selling party presents a public-key certificate signed by a well-known

1. $A \rightarrow B : PBK_A$

. . . .

2. $A \rightarrow B : \{tag_1.\{K\}_{PK_B}\}_{PBK_A{}^{-1}}.H(PBK_A)$
3. $B \rightarrow A : \{N_B.B\}_K.H(PBK_A)$
4. $A \rightarrow B : \{N_B.H(PBK_A)\}_K.H(PBK_A)$

Protocol 3. A PBK-Based protocol in which A knows B's public key in advance

certification authority, while the buyer's credentials comprise, at most, a username and password set up via an informal registration procedure.

In cases like these, where the amount of information shared between protocol participants is greater, we can achieve accordingly stronger security goals. We illustrate this with a brief example: Protocol 3 is another protocol that employs the PBK framework. Unlike in the previous ones, however, we assume that the initiator A knows the public key PK_B of the responder B in advance. After A sends her PBK, she generates a new session key K for use between A and B. She encrypts this key with PK_B and signs it, together with a tag indicating the purpose of the signature. B responds, encrypting a nonce N_B together with his name using the new key K. A responds to the challenge and returns the nonce N_B together with her pseudonym $H(PBK_A)$ (twice, once encrypted and once in plaintext).

In discussing the previous protocols, we focused on role B's guarantee of (strong) sender invariance with respect to role A. The agent playing role A, however, could say little or nothing about the security of her communication with B. As in Protocol 2, B is ensured sender invariance with respect to role A. Here, however, A is able to leverage the fact that she knows B's public key to send a new session key K secretly. Messages 3 and 4 serve to ensure recentness and key confirmation to both parties. Subsequent communication secured with the key K should then enjoy the following security properties:

- secrecy of the communication,
- responder B should be guaranteed sender invariance with respect to role A, and
- initiator A should be guaranteed authenticity of the communication from B (as only B should have been able to decrypt K).

This simple example shows how a pre-existing relationship, even a unilateral one, enables significantly greater security. A more prominent example of this is found in the use of SSL/TLS [12] in E-commerce. Most E-commerce applications employ server certificates for servers to authenticate themselves to clients, but forgo the use of client certificates. Hence, this situation is analogous to the one just described: the client is guaranteed the authenticity of the server, but—at least on the transport layer—the server can only refer to the client via a pseudonym.

Overall, as mobile and ad-hoc networks gain ground, we expect to see an increase in situations in which some measure of information, though perhaps not as much as is assumed by traditional authentication protocols, is initially shared. It is therefore important to precisely understand what security goals are achievable in the different settings.

5 Conclusion

Sender invariance is a variant of authentication, with the difference that the identity of a sender is not known to the receiver, but rather the sender is identified by a pseudonym. The key point is that sender invariance can be achieved out of nothing, i.e. even when the agents have no previous security relationship (like shared keys, public keys, or a relationship via a trusted third party) and therefore classical authentication cannot be achieved.

In this paper, we have formalized two forms of sender invariance as variants of classical authentication, and showed that these goals form a hierarchy in the sense that one goal is strictly stronger than the other, with classical authentication being the strongest.

This relationship with classical authentication has allowed us to formalize sender invariance goals for an existing protocol analysis system, the OFMC back-end of the AVISPA Tool. As a case study, we have analyzed protocols using the Purpose-Built Keys Framework (PBK [10]), showing that a naïve protocol implementation has vulnerabilities but still provides a weak form of sender invariance, while an improved implementation with tags provides strong sender invariance.

Our current work includes further investigations into sender invariance protocols. We have recently completed a formal analysis of the secure neighbor discovery protocol of Mobile IPv6 [2] and will report on our findings in an upcoming paper. Moreover, we plan to examine a further generalization of the view on sender invariance and, conversely, investigate "receiver invariance", i.e. the property that only the party that sent the first message (and who created the respective pseudonym) can read the messages directed to him. Receiver invariance can then be the counterpart of classical secrecy goals in the realm of sender invariance protocols.

References

1. Abadi, M.: Private Authentication. In: Dingledine, R., Syverson, P.F. (eds.) PET 2002. LNCS, vol. 2482, pp. 27–40. Springer, Heidelberg (2003)
2. Arkko, J., Kempf, J., Zill, B., Nikander, P.: RFC3971 – SEcure Neighbor Discovery (SEND) (March 2005)
3. Armando, A., Basin, D., Boichut, Y., Chevalier, Y., Compagna, L., Cuellar, J., Hankes Drielsma, P., Heàm, P.C., Mantovani, J., Moedersheim, S., von Oheimb, D., Rusinowitch, M., Santiago, J., Turuani, M., Viganò, L., Vigneron, L.: The AVISPA Tool for the Automated Validation of Internet Security Protocols and Applications. In: Etessami, K., Rajamani, S.K. (eds.) CAV 2005. LNCS, vol. 3576, pp. 281–285. Springer, Heidelberg (2005), http://www.avispa-project.org

4. Aura, T.: RFC3972 – Cryptographically Generated Addresses (CGA) (March 2005)
5. Basin, D., Mödersheim, S., Viganò, L.: Constraint Differentiation: A New Reduction Technique for Constraint-Based Analysis of Security Protocols. In: CCS'03. Proceedings of CCS'03, pp. 335–344. ACM Press, New York (2003)
6. Basin, D., Mödersheim, S., Viganò, L.: Algebraic intruder deductions. In: Sutcliffe, G., Voronkov, A. (eds.) LPAR 2005. LNCS (LNAI), vol. 3835, pp. 549–564. Springer, Heidelberg (2005)
7. Basin, D., Mödersheim, S., Viganò, L.: OFMC: A Symbolic Model-Checker for Security Protocols. International Journal of Information Security 4(3), 181–208 (2005)
8. Bellare, M., Rogaway, P.: Entity authentication and key distribution. In: Stinson, D.R. (ed.) CRYPTO 1993. LNCS, vol. 773, pp. 232–249. Springer, Heidelberg (1994)
9. Boyd, C.: Security architectures using formal methods. IEEE Journal on Selected Areas in Communications 11(5), 694–701 (1993)
10. Bradner, S., Mankin, A., Schiller, J.I.: A framework for purpose built keys (PBK), Work in Progress (Internet Draft) (June 2003)
11. Chevalier, Y., Compagna, L., Cuellar, J., Hankes Drielsma, P., Mantovani, J., Mödersheim, S., Vigneron, L.: A High Level Protocol Specification Language for Industrial Security-Sensitive Protocols. In: Proceedings of SAPS'04, pp. 193–205. Austrian Computer Society (2004)
12. Dierks, T., Allen, C.: RFC2246 – The TLS Protocol Version 1 (January 1999)
13. Dolev, D., Yao, A.: On the Security of Public-Key Protocols. IEEE Transactions on Information Theory 2(29) (1983)
14. Gollmann, D.: What do we mean by Entity Authentication. In: Proceedings of the 1996 IEEE Symposium on Security and Privacy, pp. 46–54. IEEE Computer Society Press, Los Alamitos (1996)
15. Johnson, D., Perkins, C., Arkko, J.: RFC3775 – Mobility Support in IPv6 (June 2004)
16. Lowe, G.: A hierarchy of authentication specifications. In: Proceedings of CSFW'97, pp. 31–43. IEEE Computer Society Press, Los Alamitos (1997)
17. Nikander, P., Kempf, J., Nordmark, E.: RFC3756 – IPv6 Neighbor Discovery (ND) Trust Models and Threats (May 2004)

From Simulations to Theorems: A Position Paper on Research in the Field of Computational Trust
(Extended Abstract)*

Karl Krukow and Mogens Nielsen

BRICS**
University of Aarhus,
Denmark
{krukow, mn}@brics.dk

Abstract. Since the millennium, a quickly increasing number of research papers in the field of "computational trust and reputation" have appeared in the Computer Science literature. However, it remains hard to compare and evaluate the respective merits of proposed systems. We argue that rigorous use of formal probabilistic models enables the clear specification of the assumptions and objectives of systems, which is necessary for comparisons. To exemplify such probabilistic modeling, we present a simple probabilistic trust model in which the system assumptions as well as its objectives are clearly specified. We show how to compute (in this model) the so-called predictive probability: The probability that the next interaction with a specific principal will have a specific outcome. We sketch preliminary ideas and first theorems indicating how the use of probabilistic models could enable us to quantitatively compare proposed systems in various different environments.

1 Introduction

What are the fundamental models in the field of computational trust?

While this question is highly relevant for researches in the field of computational trust and reputation, in fact, it is hard to identify one model (or even a few) *accepted widely* by the community. One common classification of proposals is into "probabilistic" and "non-probabilistic" systems [1,2,3]. The non-probabilistic systems may be further classified into various different types (e.g., social networks and cognitive); in contrast, the probabilistic systems usually have a common objective and structure: Probabilistic systems *(i)* assume a particular (probabilistic) model for principal behavior; and *(ii)* propose algorithms for approximating

---

* Full Paper will be published in a special collection dedicated to Gordon Plotkin (to appear). Available online: http://www.brics.dk/~krukow

** BRICS: Basic Research in Computer Science (www.brics.dk), funded by the Danish National Research Foundation.

T. Dimitrakos et al. (Eds.): FAST 2006, LNCS 4691, pp. 96–111, 2007.

the behavior of principals (i.e., prediction in the model). In systems based on such models, the trust information about a principal is information about its past behavior. Probabilistic systems usually do not classify this information as 'good,' 'bad,' 'trustworthy' or 'untrustworthy;' rather, such systems attempt to approximate the probability of various outcomes in a potential next interaction, given the past behavior. The probabilistic systems, known as "game-theoretical" in the terminology of Sabater and Sierra [2], are based on the view on trust of Gambetta: "(...) trust (or, symmetrically, distrust) is a particular level of the subjective probability with which an agent assesses that another agent or group of agents will perform a particular action, both *before* he can monitor such action (or independently of his capacity ever to be able to monitor it) *and* in a context in which it affects *his* own action" [4].

The contributions of this paper relate only to this, i.e., the probabilistic or *predictive* view on trust. We restrict ourselves to this approach for two primary reasons: *(i)* It is founded on well-understood mathematical theory and models (i.e., probability theory);[1] and *(ii)* the assumptions and objectives of systems are *precise*. Lack of formal models leads to in-clarity about the exact objectives of proposed systems; as Samuel Karlin was quoted to have said in a tribute lecture to honor R.A. Ficher: "The purpose of models is not to fit the data but to sharpen the questions." We need to sharpen *our* questions. Our position is that for *any* approach to computational trust, probabilistic or not, it should be possible to: *(i)* Specify precisely the assumptions about the intended environments for the proposed system, i.e., in which applications does the system do well? *(ii)* Specify precisely the objective of the system, i.e., exactly what does the system compute?

The purpose of this paper is to highlight some of the advantages of formal probabilistic models. We show how formal probabilistic models enable systems that satisfy our two mentioned criteria of foundation and precision. Further, we sketch ideas towards a theoretically well-founded technique for comparing probabilistic systems in various different environments.

Outline. To illustrate probabilistic models, we develop a probabilistic extension of the event structure framework [6], used previously in the SECURE project [7] to model outcomes of interactions. The probabilistic event structure model generalizes previous probabilistic models from binary outcomes, e.g., each interaction is either 'good' or 'bad,' to multiple structured outcomes (technically, we obtain probabilities on the configurations of finite confusion-free event structures).[2] This is developed in Section 2 and Section 3.

To further illustrate the benefits of probabilistic models, we present preliminary ideas towards solving one open problem in computational trust research: Comparison of algorithms for probabilistic trust computation. We develop a measure which 'scores' a probabilistic algorithm in a given probabilistic model

---

[1] We follow the Bayesian approach to probability theory, as advocated by Jaynes [5].

[2] For those familiar with Bayesian analysis, we generalize models with beta priors to multiple structured outcomes where the prior pdfs are products of Dirichlet distributions.

of principal behavior. The measure is *parametric in the model* in the sense that for *any* probabilistic model, λ, the 'score' quantitatively measures how well a given algorithm approximates the true principal behavior in λ. Algorithms can then be compared by comparing their scores in various models. This work is presented in Section 4.

2   Probabilistic Event Structures

We have previously proposed to use event structures to model outcomes of principal interactions in distributed systems [6]; the model was used in the SECURE project [8,7] to formalize the notions of outcomes and observations. However, we did not present a formal probabilistic model of principal behavior; hence, although we showed how to compute "trust values" which could be interpreted as probabilities of outcomes, there was no probabilistic model to justify the computation. In the next two sections, we augment the event structure framework with a probabilistic model which generalizes the model used in systems based on the beta distribution [9,10,11,12]. We show how to compute the probabilities of outcomes given a history of observations. This could be valuable in its own right; however, we would like to emphasize that our primary reason is to *illustrate an example* of a formal probabilistic model which enables "sharp" questions; the heart of this paper is really Section 4. The system proposed in Sections 2 and 3 is well-founded on probability theory and it generalizes many existing systems; however, it not yet practical: There are many issues it does not handle, e.g., dynamic principal behavior-change, lying reputation sources, multiple contexts, etc. We believe that the probabilistic models must be properly understood before we can deal with such issues in a theoretically well-founded manner. For further examples of probabilistic systems we refer to Aberer and Despotovic [1], and to most of the systems based on Bayesian analysis with beta prior distributions [9,10,11,12].

Observations and interaction outcomes. Agents in a distributed system obtain information by observing events which are typically generated by the reception or sending of messages. The structure of these message exchanges are given in the form of protocols known to both parties before interaction begins. By *behavioral observations*, we mean observations that the parties can make about specific runs of such protocols. These include information about the contents of messages, diversion from protocols, failure to receive a message within a certain time-frame, etc.

We will use the event-structure framework that we have proposed previously for modeling observations and outcomes in the SECURE project [6,7]. The framework is suitable for our purpose as it provides a *generic* model for observations that is independent of any specific programming language. In the framework, the information that an agent has about the behavior of another agent p, is information about a number of (possibly active) protocol-runs with p, represented as a sequence of *sets of events*, $x_1 x_2 \cdots x_n$, where event-set x_i represents information about the ith initiated protocol-instance. Note that, as opposed to many existing systems, we are not *rating* the behavior of principals, but instead, we *record* the actual behavior, i.e., which events occurred in the interaction.

Event structures. We briefly recapture the basic definitions (for more details and examples, we refer to Nielsen and Krukow [6] and Krukow et al. [13,3]). An *event structure* is a triple $(E, \leq, \#)$ consisting of a set E of *events* which are partially ordered by $\leq$, the *necessity relation* (or causality relation), and $\#$ is a binary, symmetric, irreflexive relation $\# \subset E \times E$, called the *conflict relation*. The relations satisfy

$$[e] \stackrel{(\text{def})}{=} \{e' \in E \mid e' \leq e\} \text{ is finite; and}$$

$$\text{if } e \# e' \text{ and } e' \leq e'' \text{ then } e \# e''$$

for all $e, e', e'' \in E$. We say that two events are *independent* if they are not in either of the two relations.

The two basic relations on event structures have an intuitive meaning in our set up. An event may *exclude* the possibility of the occurrence of a number of other events; this is what the conflict relation models. The necessity relation is also natural: Some events are *only possible* when others have already occurred. Finally, if two events are in neither of the relations, they are said to be independent.

The event structure models the set of events that can occur in a protocol; however, due to the relations on event structures, not all sets of events can occur in a particular run. The notion of configurations formalizes this: A set of events $x \subseteq E$ is a *configuration* (of *ES*) if it satisfies the following two properties: Conflict free, i.e., for any $e, e' \in x : e \# e'$; Causally closed, i.e., for any $e \in x, e' \in E : e' \leq e \Rightarrow e' \in x$. Write $\mathcal{C}_{ES}$ for the set of configurations of *ES*. Note that the set of all maximal configurations defines a set of mutually exclusive and exhaustive outcomes of an interaction.

Histories. A finite configuration models information regarding *a single* interaction, i.e., a single run of a protocol. In general, the information that one principal possesses about another will consist of information about *several* protocol runs; the information about each individual run being represented by a configuration in the corresponding event structure. The concept of a (local) interaction history models this. An *interaction history* in *ES* is a finite ordered sequence of configurations, $h = x_1 x_2 \cdots x_n \in \mathcal{C}_{ES}^*$. The entries x_i (for $1 \leq i \leq n$) are called the *sessions* (of h).

Remarks. While the order of sessions is recorded (histories are *sequences*), in contrast, the order of *independent* events within *a single session* is not. Hence independence of events is a *choice of abstraction* one may make when designing an event-structure model (because one is not interested in the particular order of events, or because the exact recording of the order of events is not feasible).

However, note that this is not a limitation of event structures: In a scenario where this order of events is relevant (and observable), one can always use a "serialized" event structure in which this order of occurrences is recorded. A serialization of events consists of splitting the events in question into different events depending on the order of occurrence.

2.1   Confusion-Free Event Structures

We consider a special type of event structures, the *confusion free* event structures with independence, for which it is especially simple to adjoin probabilities [14]. Consider the following event structure ($\sim$ represents conflict, and $\rightarrow$ represents causality).

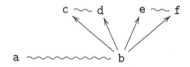

The events c and e are *independent*; as are c and f; d and e; and finally, d and f. However, in terms of the relations of event structures, *independent* simply means that both events can occur in the same configuration and in any order. Later we shall consider a probabilistic model where *independence* means also *probabilistic independence*. To do this we first introduce a notion of *cells* and *immediate conflict* [14]. In the following $ES = (E, \leq, \#)$ is a fixed event structure.

Write $[e)$ for $[e] \setminus \{e\}$, and say that events $e, e' \in E$ are in *immediate conflict*, writing $e \#_\mu e'$, if $e \# e'$ and both $[e) \cup [e']$ and $[e] \cup [e')$ are configurations. It is easy to see that a conflict $e \# e'$ is immediate if-and-only-if there exists a configuration x where both e and e' are enabled (i.e., can occur in x). For example the conflict $a \# b$ is immediate, whereas $a \# c$ is not.

A *partial cell* is a non-empty set of events $c \subseteq E$ such that $e, e' \in c$ implies $e \#_\mu e'$ and $[e) = [e')$. A maximal partial cell is called a *cell*. There are three cells in the above event structure: $\{a, b\}, \{c, d\}$ and $\{e, f\}$. Cells represent choices; in probabilistic event structures, *probabilistic choices*. A *confusion free* event structure is an event structure where (the reflexive closure of) immediate conflict is an equivalence relation and *within cells* (i.e., that $e \#_\mu e'$ implies $[e) = [e')$). We suspect that most event structures for simple interaction protocols are confusion free.

In confusion-free event structures, if an event e of a cell c is enabled at configuration x, then all events $e' \in c$ are also enabled at x. If the event structure is also finite, a maximal configuration (i.e., an outcome of an interaction) is obtained by starting with the empty configuration and then repeating the following: Let C be the set of cells that are enabled in the current configuration. If C is empty then stop: The current configuration is maximal; otherwise, non-deterministically select a cell $c \in C$, and then non-deterministically select, or probabilistically sample, an event $e \in c$; finally, update the current configuration by adding e.

The following notion of cell-valuation formalizes probabilistic sampling in cells.

Definition 1 (Cell valuation, Varacca et al. [14]). *When $f : X \to [0, +\infty]$ is a function, for every $Y \subseteq X$, we define $f[Y] = \sum_{y \in Y} f(y)$. A cell valuation on a confusion free event structure $ES = (E, \leq, \#)$ is a function $p : E \to [0,1]$ such that for every cell c, we have $p[c] = 1$.*

If cell choices are probabilistic, say given by a cell-valuation p, and if we assume independence between cells, then one can obtain the probability of any configuration x (i.e., any outcome) as the product of the probabilities of each event in x given p.

3   A Probabilistic Framework

We will be concerned with adjoining probabilities to the configurations of a finite confusion-free event structure ES. As mentioned in the previous section, we can do this by finding a cell valuation $p : E \to [0, 1]$, or, equivalently, for each cell c, a function $p_c : c \to [0, 1]$ with $p_c[c] = 1$. The functions p_c should be derived from the past experience obtained from interacting with an entity in ES. In the following paragraph, we state the assumptions about the behavior of entities in our model. We then proceed to *(i)* find abstractions that preserve sufficient information under the model; and *(ii)* derive equations for the predictive probabilities, i.e., answering "what is the probability of outcome x in the next interaction with entity q (in the model)?"

The model. Let us consider a finite and confusion-free event structure ES. Let us write $C(ES)$ for the set of cells (which are then the equivalences classes of immediate conflict). Write $C(ES) = \{c_1, c_2, \ldots, c_k\}$, and let $N_i = |c_i|$ for each i. Let us make the following assumptions about principal behavior, and write $\lambda_{\mathcal{D}ES}$ for the assumptions of this model:

> Each principal's behavior is so that there are fixed parameters such that at each interaction we have, *independently of anything we know about other interactions*, the probability $\theta_{c,e}$ for event e at cell c.

Each θ_{c_i} for $c_i \in C(ES)$ is a vector of size N_i such that $\sum_{e \in c_i} \theta_{c_i,e} = 1$. Hence, the collection $\theta = (\theta_c \mid c \in C(ES))$ defines a cell valuation on ES. For each configuration $x \in \mathcal{C}_{ES}$ the probability of obtaining x in any run of ES with a principal parametrized by θ is

$$P(x \mid \theta\lambda_{\mathcal{D}ES}) = \prod_{e \in x} \theta_e \tag{1}$$

where θ_e is defined by $\theta_{c,e}$ where c is the unique cell with $e \in c$.

The goal of our probabilistic framework is to estimate the parameters θ given a prior distribution and data regarding past interactions. In the $\lambda_{\mathcal{D}ES}$ model,

we need only estimate the parameters of each cell c, i.e., θ_c, to obtain a probability distribution on configurations (Equation 1). Furthermore, it follows from
λ_{DES} that given a sequence $h = x_1 x_2 \cdots x_n \in C^*_{ES}$ of observed data (about a
fixed principal), we need only keep track of event counts of h to estimate the
parameters of each θ_c (e.g., according to λ_{DES}, the order of sessions does not
matter). This means that an event count, i.e., a function $\mathbf{X} : E \to \mathbb{N}$, is sufficient
information to estimate θ_c for each cell c.

To estimate the parameters θ, we shall use Bayesian analysis. Hence, we need
prior distributions. It turns out that the family of Dirichlet distributions are a
family of conjugate prior distributions to the family of multinomial trials. A family F of distributions is a *conjugate prior for a likelihood function L* if whenever
the prior distribution belongs to F then also the posterior distribution belongs
to F. The use of conjugate priors represents a computational convenience common for Bayesian analysis: The distributions always maintain the same algebraic
form (i.e., that of family F). As we shall see, the uniform distribution belongs
to the Dirichlet family; this means that the prior, if desired, can be chosen not
to bias any event over another.

Since each sampling from a cell is a multinomial trial (according to λ_{DES}), we
use Dirichlet distributions as our prior distributions. Specifically, a prior Dirichlet
distribution is assigned to each cell c of ES. Event counts are then used to update
the Dirichlet at each cell. Hence, at any time we have, for each cell c, a Dirichlet
distribution f_c on the parameters θ_c of the events of that cell; we show that the
probability of an outcome $x \subseteq E$ is then the product of certain expectations of
these distributions. We explain the Dirichlet distributions in the following.

3.1   The Dirichlet Distribution

The Dirichlet family $\mathcal{D}$ of order K, where $2 \le K \in \mathbb{N}$, is a parametrized collection of continuous probability density functions defined on $[0,1]^K$. There are K
parameters of positive reals, $\alpha = (\alpha_i)_{i=1}^K$, that select a specific Dirichlet distribution from the family. For a variable $\theta \in [0,1]^K$, the pdf $\mathcal{D}(\theta \mid \alpha)$ is given by
the following:

$$\mathcal{D}(\theta \mid \alpha) = \frac{\Gamma(\sum_i \alpha_i)}{\prod_i \Gamma(\alpha_i)} \prod_i \theta_i^{\alpha_i - 1}$$

(where Γ is the Gamma function, $\Gamma(z) = \int_0^\infty dt\, t^{z-1} e^{-t}$, for $z > 0$). Define
$[\alpha] = \sum_j \alpha_j$; the expected value and variance of each parameter θ_i are given by

$$\mathbf{E}_{\mathcal{D}(\theta|\alpha)}(\theta_i) = \frac{\alpha_i}{[\alpha]}, \qquad \sigma^2_{\mathcal{D}(\theta|\alpha)}(\theta_i) = \frac{\alpha_i([\alpha] - \alpha_i)}{[\alpha]^2([\alpha] + 1)}$$

A conjugate prior. Consider sequences of independent experiments with K'ary
outcomes ($K \in \mathbb{N}$), each yielding outcome i with some fixed probability θ_i; let us
call such experiments multinomial trials (in our framework, such experiments will
correspond to probabilistic event-choices at a cell). Let $\lambda_{\mathcal{D}}$ denote background
information encoding this. Let X_i, for $i = 1, 2, \ldots, n$, represent the ith trial, i.e.,

$X_i = j$ is the statement that the ith trial has outcome $j \in \{1, 2, \ldots, K\}$. Let $\mathbf{X}$ be a conjunction of n statements, $(Z_i)_{i=1}^{n}$, of the form:

$$Z_i \equiv (X_i = j_i), \qquad \text{where each } j_i \in \{1, \ldots, K\}.$$

Suppose there are m_j statements of the form $X_i = j$, and let $\theta = (\theta_i)_{i=1}^{K}$. Then, by definition of multinomial trials, we have the following likelihood:

$$P(\mathbf{X} \mid \theta \lambda_{\mathcal{D}}) = \prod_{i=1}^{n} P(Z_i \mid \theta \lambda_{\mathcal{D}}) = \prod_{i=1}^{K} \theta_i^{m_i}.$$

The Dirichlet distributions constitute a family of conjugate prior distributions for this likelihood. In other words, if the prior distribution on θ, say $g(\theta \mid \lambda_{\mathcal{D}})$, is a Dirichlet $\mathcal{D}(\theta \mid \alpha)$, for $\alpha = (\alpha_i)_{i=1}^{K}$, then the posterior given data $\mathbf{X}$ (obtained via Bayes' Theorem), $g(\theta \mid \mathbf{X}\lambda_{\mathcal{D}})$, is also Dirichlet. In the language equations:

$$g(\theta \mid \mathbf{X}\lambda_{\mathcal{D}}) = g(\theta \mid \lambda_{\mathcal{D}}) \frac{P(\mathbf{X} \mid \theta \lambda_{\mathcal{D}})}{P(\mathbf{X} \mid \lambda_{\mathcal{D}})}.$$

In fact, it is not hard to show that $g(\theta \mid \mathbf{X}\lambda_{\mathcal{D}}) = \mathcal{D}(\theta \mid \alpha_1 + m_1, \ldots, \alpha_K + m_K)$.

Note, choosing $\alpha_i = 1$ (for all i) in the prior gives the uniform prior distribution.

The predictive probability ($\lambda_{\mathcal{D}}$). Now, let $Z_{n+1} \equiv (X_{n+1} = i)$, then one can interpret $P(Z_{n+1} \mid \mathbf{X}\lambda_{\mathcal{D}})$ as a predictive probability: Given no direct knowledge of θ, but only past evidence ($\mathbf{X}$) and the model ($\lambda_{\mathcal{D}}$), then $P(Z_{n+1} \mid \mathbf{X}\lambda_{\mathcal{D}})$ is the probability that the next trial will result in a type i outcome. It is easy to show that:

$$P(Z_{n+1} \mid \mathbf{X}\lambda_{\mathcal{D}}) = \mathbf{E}_{g(\theta \mid \mathbf{X}\lambda_{\mathcal{D}})}(\theta_i) = \frac{\alpha_i + m_i}{[\alpha] + n}$$

(since $g(\theta \mid \mathbf{X}\lambda_{\mathcal{D}})$ is $\mathcal{D}(\theta \mid (\alpha_1 + m_1, \alpha_2 + m_2, \ldots, \alpha_K + m_K))$ and $\sum_i m_i = n$).

To summarize, in the Dirichlet model, $\lambda_{\mathcal{D}}$, one can compute the probability of outcome i in the next multinomial trial as the expectation of the ith parameter of the Dirichlet pdf $g(\theta \mid \mathbf{X}\lambda_{\mathcal{D}})$ which results via Bayesian updating given history $\mathbf{X}$.

3.2 Dirichlets on Cells

Let us return to our probabilistic model. For each cell $c \in C(ES)$ we will associate a prior distribution on the parameters θ_c determining the behavior of a fixed principal for the events of c. As we interact, we obtain data about these parameters, and the distribution on each cell is updated via Bayes' Theorem. Each cell $c \in C(ES)$ presents a choice between the mutually exclusive and exhaustive events of c, and by the assumptions of $\lambda_{\mathcal{D}ES}$ a sequence of such choices from c is a sequence multinomial trials. We use Dirichlet priors on each cell so that the posterior distributions are also Dirichlets. At any time, we obtain the predictive probability of the next interaction resulting in a particular configuration by multiplying the expectations (according to the current cell distributions) of the parameters for each event in the configuration.

Let us be precise: Let $f_c(\theta_c \mid \lambda_{\mathcal{D}ES})$ denote the prior distribution on the parameters for each cell $c \in C(ES)$ (when interacting with a fixed principal). Let α_c be a vector of positive real numbers of size $N_c = |c|$; we take,

$$f_c(\theta_c \mid \lambda_{\mathcal{D}ES}) = \mathcal{D}(\theta_c \mid \alpha_c) = \frac{\Gamma(\sum_{i=1}^{N_c} \alpha_{c,i})}{\prod_{i=1}^{N_c} \Gamma(\alpha_{c,i})} \prod_{i=1}^{N_c} \theta_{c,i}^{\alpha_{c,i}-1}$$

For example, taking $\alpha_{c,j} = 1$ (for all j) gives the uniform distribution. Let $\mathbf{X} : E \to \mathbb{N}$ be an event count modeling data about past runs with a specific principal. Let $\mathbf{X}_c = \mathbf{X}_{|c}$ (i.e., the restriction of $\mathbf{X}$ to cell c), then the posterior pdf is given by the following: Assume that $c = \{e_1, e_2, \ldots, e_{N_c}\}$ then,

$$\begin{aligned} f_c(\theta_c \mid \mathbf{X}\lambda_{\mathcal{D}ES}) &= \frac{\Gamma(\sum_{i=1}^{N_c} \alpha_{c,i} + \mathbf{X}(e_i))}{\prod_{i=1}^{N_c} \Gamma(\alpha_{c,i} + \mathbf{X}(e_i))} \prod_{i=1}^{N_c} \theta_{c,i}^{\alpha_{c,i}+\mathbf{X}(e_i)-1} \\ &= \mathcal{D}(\theta_c \mid \alpha_c + \mathbf{X}_c) \end{aligned}$$

Hence, each event count $\mathbf{X} : E \to \mathbb{N}$ can be used to do Bayesian updating of the distribution at each cell.

The predictive probability ($\lambda_{\mathcal{D}ES}$). By Bayesian updating, we obtain a Dirichlet distribution for each cell c of ES. Let $\mathbf{X}$ be an event count corresponding to n previously observed configurations, and let Z be the proposition that "the $(n+1)$'st interaction results in outcome i" (where $1 \le i \le M$ and M is the number of maximal configurations in ES). Let x_i be the i'th maximal configuration, and for $e \in x_i$ let $c(e)$ denote the unique cell c with $e \in c$. The predictive probability is the product of the expectations of each of the cell parameters.

$$P(Z \mid \mathbf{X}\lambda_{\mathcal{D}ES}) = \prod_{e \in x_i} \mathbf{E}_{f_{c(e)}(\theta_{c(e)} \mid \mathbf{X}\lambda_{\mathcal{D}ES})}(\theta_{c(e),e}) = \prod_{e \in x_i} \frac{\alpha_{c(e),e} + \mathbf{X}(e)}{[\alpha_{c(e)}] + \mathbf{X}[c(e)]}$$

3.3   Summary

We have presented a probabilistic model $\lambda_{\mathcal{D}ES}$ based on probabilistic confusion-free event structures. The model generalizes previous work on probabilistic models using binary outcomes and beta priors. In our model, given a past history with a principal we need only remember the event counts of the past, i.e., a function $\mathbf{X} : E \to \mathbb{N}$. Given such an event count, there is a unique probability of any particular configuration occurring as the next interaction. We have derived equations for this probability and it is easily computed in real systems.

For example, suppose we have the following event count, $\mathbf{X}$.

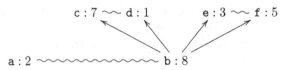

With the following prior pdfs for the cells:

$$f_{ab}((\theta_a, \theta_b) \mid \lambda_{DES}) = \mathcal{D}((\theta_a, \theta_b) \mid (1, 1)),$$
$$f_{cd}((\theta_c, \theta_d) \mid \lambda_{DES}) = \mathcal{D}((\theta_c, \theta_d) \mid (1, 1)) \text{ and}$$
$$f_{ef}((\theta_e, \theta_f) \mid \lambda_{DES}) = \mathcal{D}((\theta_e, \theta_f) \mid (1, 1));$$

this count gives rise to three updated Dirichlets

$$f_{ab}((\theta_a, \theta_b) \mid \mathbf{X}\lambda_{DES}) = \mathcal{D}((\theta_a, \theta_b) \mid (1 + 2, 1 + 8)),$$
$$f_{cd}((\theta_c, \theta_d) \mid \mathbf{X}\lambda_{DES}) = \mathcal{D}((\theta_c, \theta_d) \mid (1 + 7, 1 + 1)) \text{ and}$$
$$f_{ef}((\theta_e, \theta_f) \mid \mathbf{X}\lambda_{DES}) = \mathcal{D}((\theta_e, \theta_f) \mid (1 + 3, 1 + 5)).$$

As an example, the probability of configuration $\{b, c\}$ is

$$P(\{b, c\} \mid \mathbf{X}\lambda_{DES}) = \frac{9}{12} \times \frac{8}{10} = \frac{3}{5}.$$

4   Advantages of Probabilistic Models: A Preliminary Idea

While the purpose of models may not be to fit the data but to sharpen the questions, good models must do both! Our probabilistic models must be more realistic. For example, the beta model of principal behavior (which we consider to be state-of-the-art) assumes that for each principal p there is a single fixed parameter θ_p so at each interaction, *independently of anything else we know*, there is probability θ_p for a 'good' outcome and probability $1 - \theta_p$ for a 'bad' outcome. For *some* applications, one might argue that this is unrealistic, e.g.: *(i)* The parameter θ_p is fixed, independent of time, i.e., no dynamic behavior; and *(ii)* principal p's behavior when interacting with us is likely to depend on our behavior when interacting with p; let us call this property 'recursive behavior.' (Note, the same issues are present in the Dirichlet model λ_D and the Dirichlet-Event-Structure model λ_{DES} that we propose). Some beta-based reputation systems attempt to deal with the first problem by introducing so-called "forgetting factors;" essentially this amounts to choosing a number $0 \leq \delta \leq 1$, and then each time the parameters (α, β) of the pdf for θ_p are updated, they are also scaled with δ, e.g., when observing a single 'good' interaction, (α, β) become $(\alpha\delta + 1, \beta\delta)$. In effect, this performs a form of exponential "decay" on the parameters. The idea is that information about old interactions should weigh less than information about new ones; however, this represent a departure from the probabilistic beta model, where all interactions "weigh the same." Since a new model is *not* introduced, i.e., to formalize this preference towards newer information, it is not clear what the exact benefits of forgetting factors are, e.g., why exponential decay as opposed to linear? As far as we know, no-one has considered the 'recursive behavior' problem before.

The notion of context is also relevant for computational trust models, as have been recognized by many. Given a single-context model, one can obtain a multi-context model by instantiating the single-context model in each context. However, as Sierra and Sabater [2] argue, this is too naive: The goal of a true multi-context model is not just to *model* multiple contexts, but to provide the basis for transferring information from one context to another related context. To our knowledge, there are no techniques that deal with this problem within the field of trust and reputation.

Finally, we believe (as do Sierra and Sabater [2]) that our field is lacking a way of comparing the qualities of the many proposed trust-based systems. Sierra and Sabater propose that our field develop "(...) test-beds and frameworks to evaluate and compare the models under a set of representative and common conditions" [2]. We agree with Sierra and Sabater (note that "a set of representative and common conditions" could be a formal probabilistic model).

In the following, we sketch ideas towards solving this last problem: We develop what one might call "a theoretical test-bed" for comparing systems for probabilistic trust computation.

4.1   Towards Comparing Probabilistic Trust-Based Systems

We shall propose a generic measure to "score" specific probabilistic trust-based systems in a particular environment (i.e., "a set of representative and common conditions"). The score, which is based on the so-called Kullback-Leibler divergence, is a measure of how well an algorithm approximates the "true" probabilistic behavior of principals.

Consider a probabilistic model of principal behavior, say λ. We consider only the behavior of a single fixed principal p, and we consider only algorithms that attempt to solve the following problem: Suppose we are given an interaction history $\mathbf{X} = [(x_1, t_1), (x_2, t_2), \ldots, (x_n, t_n)]$ obtained by interacting n times with principal p, observing outcome x_i at time t_i. Suppose also that there are m possible outcomes $(y_1, \ldots, y_m)$ for each interaction. The goal of a probabilistic trust-based algorithm, say $\mathcal{A}$, is to approximate a distribution on the outcomes $(y_1, \ldots, y_m)$ given this history $\mathbf{X}$. That is, $\mathcal{A}$ satisfies:

$$\mathcal{A}(y_i \mid \mathbf{X}) \in [0, 1] \text{ (for all } i), \qquad \sum_{i=1}^{m} \mathcal{A}(y_i \mid \mathbf{X}) = 1.$$

We assume that the probabilistic model, λ, defines the following probabilities: $P(y_i \mid \mathbf{X}\lambda)$, i.e., the probability of "y_i in the next interaction given a past history of $\mathbf{X}$" and $P(\mathbf{X} \mid \lambda)$, i.e., the "a priori probability of observing sequence $\mathbf{X}$ in the model."[3]

Now, $(P(y_i \mid \mathbf{X}\lambda) \mid i = 1, 2, \ldots, m)$ defines the true distribution on outcomes for the next interaction (according to the model); in contrast, $(\mathcal{A}(y_i \mid \mathbf{X}) \mid i = 1, 2, \ldots, m)$ attempts to approximate this distribution. The Kullback-Leibler

---

[3] In a way, this model takes into account also the 'recursive behavior' problem: The probabilities $P(y_i \mid \mathbf{X}\lambda)$ and $P(y_i \mid \lambda)$ are distinguished. We have not yet given this further thoughts.

divergence [15], which is closely related to Shannon entropy, is a measure of the distance from a true distribution to an approximation of that distribution. The Kullback-Leibler divergence from distribution $\hat{p} = (p_1, p_2, \ldots, p_m)$ to distribution $\hat{q} = (q_1, q_2, \ldots, q_m)$ on a finite set of m outcomes, is given by

$$\mathrm{D_{KL}}(\hat{p} \| \hat{q}) = \sum_{i=1}^{m} p_i \log_2(\frac{p_i}{q_i})$$

(any log-base could be used). The Kullback-Leibler divergence is almost a distance (in the mathematical sense), but the symmetry property fails. That is $\mathrm{D_{KL}}$ satisfies $\mathrm{D_{KL}}(\hat{p} \| \hat{q}) \geq 0$ and $\mathrm{D_{KL}}(\hat{p} \| \hat{q}) = 0$ only if $\hat{p} = \hat{q}$. The asymmetry comes from considering one distribution as "true" and the other as approximating.

For each n let $\mathbf{O}^n$ denote the set of interaction histories of length n. Let us define, for each n, the *n'th expected Kullback-Leibler divergence from λ to $\mathcal{A}$*:

$$\mathrm{D_{KL}^n}(\lambda \| \mathcal{A}) \stackrel{\mathrm{(def)}}{=} \sum_{\mathbf{X} \in \mathbf{O}^n} P(\mathbf{X} \mid \lambda) \mathrm{D_{KL}}(P(\cdot \mid \mathbf{X}\lambda) \| \mathcal{A}(\cdot \mid \mathbf{X})),$$

that is,

$$\mathrm{D_{KL}^n}(\lambda \| \mathcal{A}) = \sum_{\mathbf{X} \in \mathbf{O}^n} P(\mathbf{X} \mid \lambda)(\sum_{i=1}^{m} P(y_i \mid \mathbf{X}\lambda) \log_2(\frac{P(y_i \mid \mathbf{X}\lambda)}{\mathcal{A}(y_i \mid \mathbf{X})})).$$

Note that, for each input sequence $\mathbf{X} \in \mathbf{O}^n$ to the algorithm, we evaluate its performance as $\mathrm{D_{KL}}(P(\cdot \mid \mathbf{X}\lambda) \| \mathcal{A}(\cdot \mid \mathbf{X}))$; however, we accept that some algorithms may perform poorly on very unlikely training sequences, $\mathbf{X}$. Hence, we weigh the penalty on input $\mathbf{X}$, i.e., $\mathrm{D_{KL}}(P(\cdot \mid \mathbf{X}\lambda) \| \mathcal{A}(\cdot \mid \mathbf{X}))$, with the intrinsic probability of sequence $\mathbf{X}$; that is, we compute the *expected* Kullback-Leibler divergence.

The Kullback-Leibler divergence is a well-established measure in statistic; however, to our knowledge, the measure $\mathrm{D_{KL}^n}$ on probabilistic algorithms is new. Due to the relation to Shannon's Information Theory, one can interpret $\mathrm{D_{KL}^n}(\lambda \| \mathcal{A})$ quantitatively as the expected number of bits of information one would gain if one would know the true distribution instead of $\mathcal{A}$'s approximation on n-length training sequences.

An example. For an example of our measure, we compare the beta-based algorithm of Mui et al. [10] with the maximum-likelihood algorithm of Aberer and Despotovic [16]. We can compare these because they both deploy the same fundamental assumptions:

> *Assume* that the behavior of each principal is so that there is a fixed parameter such that at each interaction we have, *independently of anything we know about other interactions*, the probability θ for a 'success' and therefore probability $1 - \theta$ for 'failure.'

This gives us the *beta model*, $\lambda_{\mathbf{B}}$. Let s stand for 'success' and f stand for 'failure,' and let $\mathbf{X} \in \{s, f\}^n$ for some $n > 0$.

We have the following likelihood for any $\mathbf{X} \in \{s, f\}^n$:

$$P(\mathbf{X} \mid \lambda_{\mathbf{B}}\theta) = \theta^{N_s(\mathbf{X})}(1 - \theta)^{N_f(\mathbf{X})}$$

(where $N_x(\mathbf{X})$ denotes the number of x occurrences in $\mathbf{X}$).

Let $\mathcal{A}$ denote the algorithm of Mui et al., and let $\mathcal{B}$ denote the algorithm of Aberer and Despotovic. Then,

$$\mathcal{A}(s \mid \mathbf{X}) = \frac{N_s(\mathbf{X}) + 1}{n + 2} \text{ and } \mathcal{A}(f \mid \mathbf{X}) = \frac{N_f(\mathbf{X}) + 1}{n + 2},$$

and it is easy to show that

$$\mathcal{B}(s \mid \mathbf{X}) = \frac{N_s(\mathbf{X})}{n} \text{ and } \mathcal{B}(f \mid \mathbf{X}) = \frac{N_f(\mathbf{X})}{n}.$$

For each choice of $\theta \in [0, 1]$, and each choice of training-sequence length, we can compare the two algorithms by computing and comparing $D_{\mathrm{KL}}^n(\lambda_{\mathbf{B}}\theta \parallel \mathcal{A})$ and $D_{\mathrm{KL}}^n(\lambda_{\mathbf{B}}\theta \parallel \mathcal{B})$. For example:

Theorem 1. *If $\theta = 0$ or $\theta = 1$ then the algorithm $\mathcal{B}$ of Aberer and Despotovic [16] computes a better approximation of principal behavior than the algorithm $\mathcal{A}$ of Mui et al. [10]. In fact, $\mathcal{B}$ always computes the exact probability of success on any possible training sequence.*

Proof. Assume that $\theta = 0$, and let $n > 0$. The only sequence of length n which has non-zero probability is f^n, and we have $\mathcal{B}(f \mid f^n) = 1$; in contrast, $\mathcal{A}(f \mid f^n) = \frac{n+1}{n+2}$, and $\mathcal{A}(s \mid f^n) = \frac{1}{n+2}$). Since $P(s \mid f^n \lambda_{\mathbf{B}}\theta) = \theta = 0 = \mathcal{B}(s \mid f^n)$ and $P(f \mid f^n \lambda_{\mathbf{B}}\theta) = 1 - \theta = 1 = \mathcal{B}(f \mid f^n)$, we have

$$D_{\mathrm{KL}}^n(\lambda_{\mathbf{B}}\theta \parallel \mathcal{B}) = 0.$$

Since $D_{\mathrm{KL}}^n(\lambda_{\mathbf{B}}\theta \parallel \mathcal{A}) > 0$ we are done (the argument for $\theta = 1$ is similar).   □

Now let us compare $\mathcal{A}$ and $\mathcal{B}$ with $0 < \theta < 1$. Since $\mathcal{B}$ assigns probability 0 to s on input f^k (for all $k \geq 1$) which results in $D_{\mathrm{KL}}^n(\lambda \parallel \mathcal{B}) = \infty$, then according to our measure D_{KL}^n, algorithm $\mathcal{A}$ is always better than $\mathcal{B}$. However, this results from a property of the Kullback-Leibler measure: Given two distribution $\hat{p} = (p_1, \ldots, p_n)$ and $\hat{q} = (q_1, \ldots, q_n)$, if one of the "real" probabilities, p_i is non-zero and the corresponding "approximating" probability q_i is zero, then $D_{\mathrm{KL}}(\hat{p} \parallel \hat{q}) = \infty$. To obtain a stronger and more informative result, we shall consider a continuum of algorithms, denoted $\mathcal{A}_\epsilon$ for a real number $0 < \epsilon < 1$, defined as

$$\mathcal{A}_\epsilon(s \mid \mathbf{X}) = \frac{N_s(\mathbf{X}) + \epsilon}{n + 2\epsilon} \text{ and } \mathcal{A}_\epsilon(f \mid \mathbf{X}) = \frac{N_f(\mathbf{X}) + \epsilon}{n + 2\epsilon}.$$

One can think of $\mathcal{A}_\epsilon$ as approximating $\mathcal{B}(= \mathcal{A}_0)$ for small epsilon.

We have the following theorem which compares $\mathcal{A}_\epsilon$ and the algorithm of Mui et al., $\mathcal{A}$, in a continuum of different environments.

Theorem 2. *Let $\lambda_{\mathbf{B}}$ be the beta model with parameter $\theta \in [\frac{1}{2} - \frac{1}{\sqrt{12}}, \frac{1}{2} + \frac{1}{\sqrt{12}}]$. For any $n \geq 0$ we have*

$$D^n_{\mathrm{KL}}(\lambda_{\mathbf{B}}\theta \parallel \mathcal{A}) < D^n_{\mathrm{KL}}(\lambda_{\mathbf{B}}\theta \parallel \mathcal{A}_\epsilon),$$

for all $\epsilon \in (0,1)$.

Proof. See the full paper, to appear soon. □

What does this mean? Another way to put it is that if θ is in the interval $[.215, .785]$ (approximately), then *independently* of training-sequence length (n), then the algorithm of Mui et al. is better (on average) than *any* algorithm $\mathcal{A}_\epsilon$ (for $0 < \epsilon < 1$). To our knowledge, this is the first *theorem* which compares two algorithms for trust computation: All previous comparisons have been via computer simulations. In fact, it is not so much the concrete comparison of algorithms $\mathcal{A}$ and $\mathcal{B}$ that interests us; rather, our message is that using probabilistic models enables the *possibility* of such theoretical comparisons. Notice that without formal probabilistic models we would be unable to even *state* precisely such theorems.

5 Conclusion

Our "position" on computational trust research is that any proposed system should be able to answer two fundamental questions precisely: What are the assumptions about the intended environments for the system? And, what is the objective of the system? An advantage of formal probabilistic models is that they enable rigorous answers to these questions. To illustrate this point, we have presented an example of a formal probabilistic model, $\lambda_{\mathcal{DES}}$. There are other examples: The beta model specifies the assumption of the computational trust model of Jøsang et al. [9], and under these assumptions their algorithm computes the probability of a principal well-behaving in the next interaction.

There are further benefits of formal probabilistic models: As we have illustrated, it is possible to compare two algorithms, say $\mathcal{X}$ and $\mathcal{Y}$, under the same type of principal behavior, say model λ, by examining which algorithm best approximates the true principal behavior (as specified by λ). For example, we propose to compute and compare:

$$D^n_{\mathrm{KL}}(\lambda \parallel \mathcal{X}) \text{ and } D^n_{\mathrm{KL}}(\lambda \parallel \mathcal{Y}).$$

Note, no simulations of algorithms $\mathcal{X}$ and $\mathcal{Y}$ are necessary; the numbers give a theoretical justification, e.g., stating that "in environment λ, on the average, algorithm $\mathcal{X}$ outperforms algorithm $\mathcal{Y}$ on training sequences of length n." If one can further show that this holds for all n, or for all n greater than some number, this gives a way of saying that $\mathcal{X}$ is better than $\mathcal{Y}$. Another type of property one might desire is the following: Suppose $\mathcal{X}$ satisfies for each $\epsilon > 0$ there exists an

$N > 0$ so that for all $n \geq N$ we have $D_{KL}^n(\lambda \parallel \mathcal{X}) < \epsilon$. This means that given a long enough training sequence, algorithm $\mathcal{X}$ approximates the true principal behavior to an arbitrary precision.

We have further results which will be published in the full paper. We consider $\mathcal{A}_\epsilon$ for *all* epsilon, not just $[0,1]$. We show that for each choice of θ there is an optimal ϵ_θ for which $\mathcal{A}_{\epsilon_\theta}$ is best among algorithms $\mathcal{A}_\epsilon$. Recall that the results of Section 4 were all based on the simple beta model, λ_B. We illustrate how our measure is parametric by considering a probabilistic model of dynamic principal behavior based on Hidden Markov Models. We show how one can use our measure "out-of-the-box" to compare algorithms working in this model.

Acknowledgments. We thank the anonymous reviewers for pointing to several places where clarification of our position and intention was necessary.

References

1. Despotovic, Z., Aberer, K.: P2P reputation management: Probabilistic estimation vs. social networks. Computer Networks 50(4), 485–500 (2006)
2. Sabater, J., Sierra, C.: Review on computational trust and reputation models. Artificial Intelligence Review 24(1), 33–60 (2005)
3. Krukow, K.: Towards a Theory of Trust for the Global Ubiquitous Computer. PhD thesis, University of Aarhus, Denmark (2006) available online (submitted) http://www.brics.dk/~krukow
4. Gambetta, D.: Can we trust trust? In Gambetta, D. (ed.) Trust: Making and Breaking Cooperative Relations. University of Oxford, Department of Sociology, pp. 213–237. ch. 13. Electronic edition (2000) http://www.sociology.ox.ac.uk/papers/gambetta213-237.pdf
5. Jaynes, E.T.: Probability Theory: The Logic of Science. In: The Edinburgh Building, Cambridge, CB2 2RU, United Kingdom, Cambridge University Press, Cambridge (2003)
6. Nielsen, M., Krukow, K.: On the formal modelling of trust in reputation-based systems. In: Karhumäki, J., Maurer, H., Păun, G., Rozenberg, G. (eds.) Theory Is Forever: Essays Dedicated to Arto Salomaa on the Occasion of His 70th Birthday LNCS, vol. 3113, pp. 192–204. Springer, Heidelberg (2004)
7. Cahill, V., Seigneur, J.M.: The SECURE website (2004) http://secure.dsg.cs.tcd.ie
8. Cahill, V., Gray, E., et al.: Using trust for secure collaboration in uncertain environments. IEEE Pervasive Computing 2(3), 52–61 (2003)
9. Jøsang, A., Ismail, R.: The beta reputation system. In: Proceedings from the 15th Bled Conference on Electronic Commerce, Bled. (2002)
10. Mui, L., Mohtashemi, M., Halberstadt, A.: A computational model of trust and reputation (for ebusinesses). In: HICSS'02. Proceedings from 5th Annual Hawaii International Conference on System Sciences, p. 188. IEEE, Orlando, Florida, USA (2002)
11. Buchegger, S., Le Boudec, J.Y.: A Robust Reputation System for Peer-to-Peer and Mobile Ad-hoc Networks. In: P2PEcon 2004 (2004)

12. Teacy, W.T.L., Patel, J., Jennings, N.R., Luck, M.: Coping with inaccurate reputation sources: experimental analysis of a probabilistic trust model. In: AAMAS '05. Proceedings of the fourth international joint conference on Autonomous agents and multiagent systems, New York, NY, USA, pp. 997–1004. ACM Press, New York, NY, USA (2005)
13. Krukow, K., Nielsen, M., Sassone, V.: A logical framework for reputation systems. (2006) Submitted. Available online `www.brics.dk/~krukow`
14. Varacca, D., Völzer, H., Winskel, G.: Probabilistic event structures and domains. In: Gardner, P., Yoshida, N. (eds.) CONCUR 2004. LNCS, vol. 3170, pp. 481–496. Springer, Heidelberg (2004)
15. Kullback, S., Leibler, R.A.: On information and sufficiency. Annals of Mathematical Statistics 22(1), 79–86 (1951)
16. Despotovic, Z., Aberer, K.: A probabilistic approach to predict peers' performance in P2P networks. In: Klusch, M., Ossowski, S., Kashyap, V., Unland, R. (eds.) CIA 2004. LNCS (LNAI), vol. 3191, pp. 62–76. Springer, Heidelberg (2004)

A Tool for the Synthesis of Controller Programs*

Ilaria Matteucci

Istituto di Informatica e Telematica - C.N.R., Pisa, Italy
Dipartimento di Scienze Matematiche ed Informatiche, Università degli Studi di Siena
Ilaria.Matteucci@iit.cnr.it

Abstract. In previous works we have developed a theory based on formal methods for enforcing security properties by defining process algebra *controller operators*. In this paper we continue our line of research, by describing a tool developed for synthesizing a model for a given security property that is also a *control program* for a given controller operator. The tool implements the partial model checking technique and the satisfiability procedure for a modal μ-calculus formula.

1 Overview

In the last few years the amount of information and sensible data that circulate on the net has been growing up. This is one of important reasons that have contribute to increase research on the definition of formal methods for the analysis and the verification of *secure systems*, that are systems that satisfy some security properties that specify acceptable executions of programs. The interest in this topic is mainly due to the practical relevance of these systems and moreover to preliminary encouraging results achieved by the application of formal methods to security properties analysis.

More recently there also has been interest on developing techniques to study how to enforce *security policy* (e.g., see [3,4,5,11,12,17]).

In [12,13,14] we have given a methodology, based on known techniques in concurrency and process logics theory, for automatically enforcing a desired security property. In particular, we have shown how to secure a system S with a possible un-specified component X, through the usage of a controller operator $Y \triangleright X$, where Y is a *controller program* that prevents X to express a behavior that, in cooperation with S, could make the overall system violate a security property ϕ.

In this paper we continue our line of research by showing the implementation of a tool that is effectively able to generate a controller program Y starting from a system S and ϕ.

The tool is made up of two main parts, the first one is the *MuDiv* tool developed by Nielsen and Andersen, that implements the partial model checking function for process algebra operators (see [1,2]). It takes in input a system S and a formula of equational μ-calculus, ϕ, and calculate $\phi' = \phi_{//s}$ that is the partial evaluation of ϕ w.r.t. the system

---

* Work partially supported by CNR project "Trusted e-services for dynamic coalitions" and by EU-funded project "Software Engineering for Service-Oriented Overlay Computers"(SENSORIA) and by EU-funded project "Secure Software and Services for Mobile Systems "(S3MS).

T. Dimitrakos et al. (Eds.): FAST 2006, LNCS 4691, pp. 112–126, 2007.

S. The second part is developed in O'caml 3.09 (see [9]) and implements a satisfiability procedure in order to generate a model for ϕ' that is also a controller program for a given controller operator. In particular, it implements the satisfiability procedure developed by Walukiewicz in [19] for a modal μ-calculus formula. It takes in input ϕ', that is the output of the *MuDiv* tool, and, by exploiting the satisfiability procedure, generates a model for it that is also a controller program for chosen controller operator. It is important to note that, in order to generate a control program for a controller operator that models a security automaton (see [4,5]), we have to apply a relabeling function. Hence we have implemented relabeling functions, one for each kind of security automata.

The satisfiability procedure is given for a modal μ-calculus formula while the *MuDiv* tool works on equational μ-calculus formulae. Hence we have developed a translation function that permits to translate an equational μ-calculus formula into a modal μ-calculus one.

This paper is organized as follows. Section 2 recalls basic theory about process algebras, modal logic and the partial model checking technique. Section 3 briefly explains our theory for the synthesis of process algebra controller operators able to enforce security properties. Section 4 describes our synthesis tool and Section 5 presents an example of application. Eventually, Section 6 concludes the paper.

2   Background

2.1   *CCS* Process Algebra

CCS of Milner (see [15]) is a language for describing concurrent systems. Here, we present a formulation of Milner's *CCS* in the *Generalized Structured Operational Semantics (GSOS)* (see [6]) format[1].

Let $\mathcal{L}$ be a finite set of actions, $\bar{\mathcal{L}} = \{\bar{a} \mid a \in \mathcal{L}\}$ be the set of complementary actions where $\bar{}$ is a bijection with $\bar{\bar{a}} = a$, Act be $\mathcal{L} \cup \bar{\mathcal{L}} \cup \{\tau\}$, where τ is a special action that denotes an internal action.

The syntax of CCS is the following:

$$E ::= \mathbf{0} \mid A \mid a.E \mid E_1 + E_2 \mid E_1 \| E_2 \mid E\backslash L \mid E[f]$$

where $L \subseteq Act$. To give a formulation of CCS dealing with $GSOS$, we define the function $arity \geq 0$ as follows: $arity(\mathbf{0}) = 0$, $\|$ and $+$ are binary operators and the other ones are unary operators.

We will often use some common syntactic simplifications, e.g., omission of trailing $\mathbf{0}$'s as well as omission of brackets on restriction on a single action. $Der(E)$ denotes the set of derivatives of a (closed) term E, i.e. the set of process that can be reached through the transition relation.

The operational semantics of CCS closed terms is given by means of the $GSOS$ system in Table 1 and it is described by a *labeled transition system*, LTS for short. An LTS, is a structure of the form $(\mathcal{E}, \mathcal{T})$ where $\mathcal{E}$ is the set of terms and $\mathcal{T}$ is a ternary

---

[1] We decide to omit the description of $GSOS$ framework that can be found in [6]. The reader is expected to be familiar with the SOS notation used for operational semantics.

Table 1. *GSOS* system for CCS

Prefixing:

$$a.x \xrightarrow{a} x$$

Choice:

$$\frac{x \xrightarrow{a} x'}{x + y \xrightarrow{a} x'} \qquad \frac{y \xrightarrow{a} y'}{x + y \xrightarrow{a} y'}$$

Parallel:

$$\frac{x \xrightarrow{a} x'}{x\|y \xrightarrow{a} x'\|y} \qquad \frac{y \xrightarrow{a} y'}{x\|y \xrightarrow{a} x\|y'} \qquad \frac{x \xrightarrow{l} x' \quad y \xrightarrow{\bar{l}} y'}{x\|y \xrightarrow{\tau} x'\|y'}$$

Restriction:

$$\frac{x \xrightarrow{a} x'}{x \backslash L \xrightarrow{a} x'\backslash L} \quad a \notin L$$

Relabeling:

$$\frac{x \xrightarrow{a} x'}{x[f] \xrightarrow{f(a)} x'[f]}$$

---

relation $T \subseteq (\mathcal{E} \times Act \times \mathcal{E})$, known as a *transition relation*. The transition relation is defined by structural induction as the least relation generated by the set of $GSOS$ rules of Table 1. CCS operators have the following informal meaning:

- **0** is a process that does nothing;
- $a.E$ (*prefix*) is a process that can perform an a action and then behaves as E;
- $E_1 + E_2$ (*choice*) represents the nondeterministic choice between the two processes E_1 and E_2;
- $E_1 \| E_2$ (*parallel*) is the parallel composition of two processes that can proceed in an asynchronous way, synchronizing on complementary actions, represented by an internal action τ, to perform a communication;
- $E \backslash L$ (*restriction*) is the process E when actions in $L \cup \bar{L}$ are prevented;
- $E[f]$ (*relabeling*) is the process E when names of actions are changed according to the function $f : Act \rightarrow Act$.

2.2 Behavioral Equivalences

Several behavioral relations are defined to compare the behavior of processes. Here we recall the definition of *weak simulation* and *weak bisimulation*.

First of all we give the notion of *observational relations* as follows: $E \xRightarrow{\tau} E'$ (or $E \Rightarrow E'$) if $E \xrightarrow{\tau}{}^* E'$ (where $\xrightarrow{\tau}{}^*$ is the reflexive and transitive closure of the $\xrightarrow{\tau}$ relation); for $a \neq \tau$, $E \xRightarrow{a} E'$ if $E \xRightarrow{\tau}\xrightarrow{a}\xRightarrow{\tau} E'$.[2]

The *weak bisimulation* relation (see [16]) permits to abstract to some extent from the internal behavior of the systems, represented by the invisible τ actions.

---

[2] Note that it is a short notation for $E \xRightarrow{\tau} E_\tau \xrightarrow{a} E'_\tau \xRightarrow{\tau} E'$ where E_τ and E'_τ denote intermediate states that is not important for this framework.

Table 2. Modal μ-calculus

$$[T]_\rho = S$$
$$[F]_\rho = \emptyset$$
$$[X]_\rho = \rho(X)$$
$$[\neg A]_\rho = S \setminus [A]_\rho$$
$$[A_1 \wedge A_2]_\rho = [A_1]_\rho \cap [A_2]_\rho$$
$$[A_1 \vee A_2]_\rho = [A_1]_\rho \cup [A_2]_\rho$$
$$[\langle a \rangle A]_\rho = \{s | \exists s' : s \xrightarrow{a} s' \text{ and } s' \in [A]_\rho\}$$
$$[[a]A]_\rho = \{s | \forall s' : s \xrightarrow{a} s' \text{ implies } s' \in [A]_\rho\}$$
$$[\mu X.A]_\rho = \bigcap \{S' | [A]_{\rho[S'/X]} \subseteq S'\}$$
$$[\nu X.A]_\rho = \bigcup \{S' | S' \subseteq [A]_{\rho[S'/X]}\}$$

Definition 1. *Let $(\mathcal{E}, \mathcal{T})$ be an* LTS *of concurrent processes, and let $\mathcal{R}$ be a binary relation over $\mathcal{E}$. Then $\mathcal{R}$ is called* weak simulation, *denoted by $\preceq$, over $(\mathcal{E}, \mathcal{T})$ if and only if, whenever $(E, F) \in \mathcal{R}$ we have:*

$$\text{if } E \xrightarrow{a} E' \text{ then there exists } F' \text{ s.t. } F \xRightarrow{a} F' \text{ and } (E', F') \in \mathcal{R},$$

A weak bisimulation *is a relation $\mathcal{R}$ s.t. both $\mathcal{R}$ and $\mathcal{R}^{-1}$ are weak simulations. We represent with $\approx$ the union of all the weak bisimulations.*

2.3 Modal Logic: Two Variants of μ-Calculus

Modal μ-calculus is a process logic well suited for specification and verification of systems whose behavior is naturally described by using state changes by means of actions. It permits to express a lot of interesting properties like *safety* ("nothing bad happens") and *liveness* ("something good happens") properties, and it allows us to express equivalence conditions over *LTS*.

Let a be in *Act*, X be a variable ranging over a set of variables *Var*. Modal μ-calculus formulae are generated by the following grammar:

$$A ::= X \mid T \mid F \mid \neg A \mid A_1 \wedge A_2 \mid A_1 \vee A_2 \mid \langle a \rangle A \mid [a]A \mid \mu X.A \mid \nu X.A$$

where the meaning of $\langle a \rangle A$ is "it is possible to do an a-action to a state where A holds" and the meaning of $[a]A$ is "for all a-actions that are performed then A holds". We consider the usual definitions of bound and free variables. The interpretation of $\mu X.\alpha(X)$ ($\nu X.\alpha(X)$) is the least (greatest) fixpoint of this function.

Formally, given an *LTS*, let S be the set of states of it, the semantics of a formula A is a subset $[A]_\rho$ of S, as defined in Table 2, where ρ is a function (called environment) from free variables of A to subsets of S. The environment $\rho[S'/X](Y)$ is equal to $\rho(Y)$ if $Y \neq X$, otherwise $\rho[S'/X](X) = S'$. The denotational semantics is given in Table 2.

Equational μ-calculus is a variant of μ-calculus that is very suitable for *partial model checking*, that is described later (see [1,2]).

In equational μ-calculus recursion operators are replaced by fixpoint equations. This permits to recursively define properties of a given system. Hence the grammar is the same given before in which $\mu X.A$ and $\nu X.A$ are replaced by the following fixpoint equations:

$$D ::= X =_\nu AD \mid X =_\mu AD \mid \epsilon$$

$X =_\nu A$ is a maximal fixpoint equation, where A is an assertion (i.e. a simple modal formula without recursion operator), and $X =_\mu A$ is a minimal fixpoint equation. Roughly, the semantics $[\![D]\!]$ of the list of equations D is the solution of the system of equations corresponding to D. According to this notation, $[\![D]\!](X)$ is the value of the variable X, and $E \models D \downarrow X$ can be used as a short notation for $E \in [\![D]\!](X)$. The formal semantics of equational μ-calculus is the same as the one given in Table 2 in which the semantics of recursion operators is replaced by the semantics of fixed point equations. As a matter of fact, let $\sqcup$ be the symbol that represents union of disjoint environments. Let ρ be the environment and σ be in $\{\mu, \nu\}$, then $\sigma U.f(U)$ represents the σ fixpoint of the function f in one variable U.

$$[\![\epsilon]\!]_\rho = [] \quad [\![X =_\sigma AD']\!]_\rho = [\![D']\!]_{(\rho \sqcup [U'/X])} \sqcup [U'/X]$$

where $U' = \sigma U.[\![A]\!]'_{(\rho \sqcup [U/X] \sqcup \rho'(U))}$ and $\rho'(U) = [\![D']\!]_{(\rho \sqcup [U/X])}$.

It informally says that the solution to $(X =_\sigma A)D$ is the σ fixpoint solution U' of $[\![A]\!]$ where the solution to the rest of the lists of equations D is used as environment.

For both of these logics the following theorem holds.

Theorem 1 ([18]). *Given a formula ϕ it is possible to decide in exponential time in the length of ϕ if there exists a model of ϕ and it is also possible to give an example of such model.*

2.4 Partial Model Checking

Partial model checking is a technique that relies upon compositional methods for proving properties of concurrent system. It has been firstly introduced by Andersen (see [1,2]). The intuitive idea underlying partial evaluation is the following: proving that $(P\|Q)$ satisfies an equational μ-calculus formula ϕ is equivalent to proving that Q satisfies a modified formula $\phi' = \phi_{//P}$, where $//_P$ is the *partial evaluation function* for the operators of parallel composition. In Table 3 we give the definition of the partial evaluation function for the CCS parallel and relabeling operators. Andersen proves the following lemma:

Lemma 1 ([2]). *Given a process $P\|Q$ and a formula ϕ we have: $P\|Q \models \phi$ iff $Q \models \phi_{//P}$.*

A lemma similar to the previous one holds for all CCS operators (see [1,2]). It is worth noticing that partial model checking function may be automatically derived from the semantics rules used to define a language semantics. Thus, the proposed technique is very flexible.

Table 3. Partial evaluation function for parallel operator and relabeling operator

---

Parallel:
$(D \downarrow X)//t = (D//t) \downarrow X_t$ $\epsilon//t = \epsilon$
$(X =_\sigma AD)//t = ((X_s =_\sigma A//s)_{s \in Der(E)})(D)//t$ $X//t = X_t$
$[a]A//s = [a](A\!/\!s) \wedge \bigwedge_{s \xrightarrow{a} s'} A//s'$, if $a \neq \tau$ $A_1 \wedge A_2//s = (A_1//s) \wedge (A_2//s)$
$\langle a \rangle A//s = \langle a \rangle (A//s) \vee \bigvee_{s \xrightarrow{a} s'} A//s'$, if $a \neq \tau$ $A_1 \vee A_2//s = (A_1//s) \vee (A_2//s)$
$[\tau]A//s = [\tau](A\!/\!s) \wedge \bigwedge_{s \xrightarrow{\tau} s'} A//s' \wedge \bigwedge_{s \xrightarrow{a} s'} [\bar{a}](A //s')$
$\langle \tau \rangle A//s = \langle \tau \rangle (A//s) \vee \bigvee_{s \xrightarrow{\tau} s'} A//s' \vee \bigvee_{s \xrightarrow{a} s'} \langle \bar{a} \rangle (A//_{s'})$ $\mathbf{T}//s = \mathbf{T}$ $\mathbf{F}//s = \mathbf{F}$
Relabeling:
$X//[f] = X$
$(X =_\sigma AD)//[f] = (X =_\sigma A//[f](D)//[f])$
$\langle a \rangle A//[f] = \bigvee_{b:f(b)=a} \langle b \rangle (A//[f])$
$[a]A//[f] = \bigwedge_{b:f(b)=a} [b](A//[f])$ $A_1 \wedge A_2//[f] = (A_1//[f]) \wedge (A_2//[f])$
$A_1 \vee A_2//[f] = (A_1//[f]) \vee (A_2//[f])$ $\mathbf{T}//[f] = \mathbf{T}$ $\mathbf{F}//[f] = \mathbf{F}$

---

3 Controllers Synthesis Theory

Starting from works of Schneider ([17]) and Ligatti & al. ([4,5]), in [12,13,14] we have defined process algebra operators, called *controller operators*. We denote them by $Y \triangleright X$, where X is an unspecified component (target) and Y is a *controller program*. The controller program is the process that controls X in order to guarantee that a given security property is satisfied. Moreover we are able to automatically synthesize a controller program for a controller operator.

In this section we recall our theory, then, in the next one, we will describe the tool based on it.

Let S be a system and let X be the target that works in parallel with S, $S\|X$. We want to guarantee that, given a security property ϕ, the system $S\|X$ satisfies it. Hence we use controller operator in such way the specification of the system becomes:

$$\exists Y \quad \forall X \quad \text{s.t.} \quad S\|(Y \triangleright X) \models \phi \tag{1}$$

By partially evaluating ϕ w.r.t. S by the usage of *partial model checking* the Formula (1) is reduced as follows:

$$\exists Y \quad \forall X \quad Y \triangleright X \models \phi' \tag{2}$$

where $\phi' = \phi_{//s}$.

In [12,13] we have dealt with security automata (*truncation, suppression, insertion, edit*) defined in [4,5] by modeling them by process algebra controller operators $Y \triangleright_K X$, where $K \in \{T, S, I, E\}$.[3] We have proved that for every $K \in \{T, S, I, E\}$ $Y \triangleright_K X \preceq Y[f_K]$ holds, where f_K is a relabeling function depending on K. In particular, f_T is the identity function on Act^4 and

$$f_S(a) = \begin{cases} \tau & \text{if } a = -a \\ a & \text{othw} \end{cases} \quad f_I(a) = \begin{cases} \tau & \text{if } a = +a \\ a & \text{othw} \end{cases} \quad f_E(a) = \begin{cases} \tau & \text{if } a \in \{+a, -a\} \\ a & \text{othw} \end{cases}$$

---

[3] T stays for *Truncation*, S for *Suppression*, I for *Insertion* and E for *Edit*.

[4] Here the set *Act* must be consider enriched by control actions.

According to [4,5], these operators are applied in order to enforce safety properties. For this class of formulae it is possible to prove that if E and F are two processes, such that $F \preceq E$ then $E \models \phi \Rightarrow F \models \phi$. Hence, in order to satisfy the Formula (2) it is sufficient to prove the following one:

$$\exists Y \quad Y \models \phi'' \tag{3}$$

where $\phi'' = \phi'_{//[f_K]}$ (see Table 3). In this case we obtain a satisfiability problem in μ-calculus, that can be solved by Theorem 1.

Other controller operators able to enforce not only safety properties but also *information flow properties*[5] can be defined (see [14]).

In this case we prove that if a controller operator $Y \rhd^* X$ satisfy the following assumption:

$$\text{For every } X \text{ and } Y \quad Y \rhd^* X \approx Y.$$

Then the Formula (2) becomes:

$$\exists Y \quad Y \models \phi' \tag{4}$$

Also in this case we obtain a satisfiability problem in μ-calculus that can be solved by Theorem 1. Hence, by exploiting satisfiability procedure for μ-calculus we are able to synthesize appropriate controller program for a given controller operator.

3.1 Examples of Controller Operators

Here we give the semantics of some controller operators.

Controller operators for Safety properties

Truncation $Y \rhd_T X$

$$\frac{E \xrightarrow{\alpha} E' \; F \xrightarrow{a} F'}{E \rhd_T F \xrightarrow{a} E' \rhd_T F'}$$

If F and E perform the same action a, then $E \rhd_T F$ performs it, otherwise the system halts.

Suppression $Y \rhd_S X$

$$\frac{E \xrightarrow{a} E' \; F \xrightarrow{a} F'}{E \rhd_S F \xrightarrow{a} E' \rhd_S F'} \qquad \frac{E \xrightarrow{a} \quad E \xrightarrow{-a} E' \; F \xrightarrow{a} F'}{E \rhd_S F \xrightarrow{\tau} E' \rhd_S F'}$$

where ^-a is a control action not in Act (so it does not admit a complementary action). If F and E perform the same action a then also $E \rhd_S F$ performs it. On the contrary, if F performs an action a that E does not perform, and E performs ^-a then $E \rhd_S F$ *suppresses* the action a by performing τ, i.e. a becomes not visible from external observation.

---

[5] To describe this property, we can consider two users, *High* and *Low* interacting with the same computer system. We wonder if there is any flow of information from *High* to *Low*. We can find several formal definitions in the literature, e.g. [7,10], for concurrent processes.

Insertion $Y \rhd_I X$

$$\frac{E \xrightarrow{a} E'' \quad F \xrightarrow{a} F'}{E \rhd_I F \xrightarrow{a} E' \rhd_I F'} \qquad \frac{E \not\xrightarrow{a} E'' \quad E \xrightarrow{+a.b} E' \quad F \xrightarrow{a} F'}{E \rhd_I F \xrightarrow{b} E' \rhd_I F}_6$$

where ^+a is an action not in Act. If F and E perform an action a then also $E \rhd_I F$ performs it. If F performs an action a that E does not perform and E performs ^+a followed by b, then the whole system performs b.

Edit $Y \rhd_E X$

$$\frac{E \xrightarrow{a} E' \quad F \xrightarrow{a} F'}{E \rhd_E F \xrightarrow{a} E' \rhd_E F'} \qquad \frac{E \not\xrightarrow{a} \quad E \xrightarrow{-a} E' \quad F \xrightarrow{a} F'}{E \rhd_E F \xrightarrow{\tau} E' \rhd_E F'} \qquad \frac{E \not\xrightarrow{a} E'' \quad E \xrightarrow{+a.b} E' \quad F \xrightarrow{a} F'}{E \rhd_E F \xrightarrow{b} E' \rhd_E F}$$

This operator combines the power of the previous two ones. Hence it is able to suppress and insert actions.

Controller operators for Information flow properties. We define the controller operator $\rhd'$ by the following rules.

$$\frac{E \xrightarrow{a} E' \quad F \xrightarrow{a} F'}{E \rhd' F \xrightarrow{a} E' \rhd' F'} \; a \neq \tau \qquad \frac{E \xrightarrow{a} E'}{E \rhd' F \xrightarrow{a} E' \rhd' F} \qquad \frac{F \xrightarrow{\tau} F'}{E \rhd' F \xrightarrow{\tau} E \rhd' F'}$$

This operator forces the system to perform always the right action also if we do not know what action the target is going to perform.

Another controller operator, $\rhd''$, can be defined as follows.

$$\frac{E \xrightarrow{a} E' \quad F \xrightarrow{a} F'}{E \rhd'' F \xrightarrow{a} E' \rhd'' F'} \; a \neq \tau \qquad \frac{E \xrightarrow{a} E' \quad F \not\xrightarrow{a} F'}{E \rhd'' F \xrightarrow{a} E' \rhd'' F} \qquad \frac{F \xrightarrow{\tau} F'}{E \rhd'' F \xrightarrow{\tau} E \rhd'' F'}$$

If E and F perform the same action a then the whole system performs it. On the contrary, the whole system performs the action performed by E. The τ action can be always performed by both of the processes.

4 Controller Synthesis Tool

In order to solve the satisfiability problem described by the Formula (3) and Formula (4), we have developed a tool that, given a system S and a formula ϕ, generates a process Y. This process is a model for ϕ', the formula obtained by the partial evaluation of ϕ by S. Moreover, such Y guarantees that $S \| (Y \rhd X)$ satisfies ϕ whatever X is. As a matter of fact, according to the synthesis theory presented before, the tool is made up of two main parts: the first part implements the partial model checking function; the second one implements the satisfiability procedure developed by Walukiewicz in [19] and generates a process Y for each controller operator we want to apply in order to enforce the property ϕ.

---

6 This means $E \xrightarrow{+a} E_a \xrightarrow{b} E'$. However we consider $^+a.b$ as a single action, i.e. the state E_a is hide.

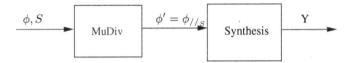

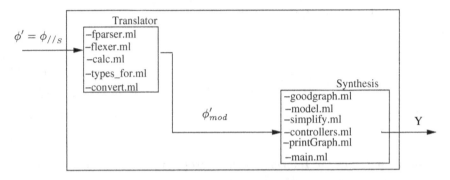

a) The architecture of the whole tool

b) A zoom of the Synthesis module

Fig. 1. Architecture of the tool

4.1 Architecture of the Tool

The tool is composed by several parts. We can divide them in two main modules. In Figure 1 there is a graphical representation of the architecture of the whole tool. The Figure 1.a) represents the whole tool by showing the two main modules, the *MuDiv* module and the *Synthesis* module. The *MuDiv* tool implements the partial model checking function. It has been developed in C++ by J.B. Nielsen and H.R. Andersen. The *MuDiv* takes in input a process S described by an LTS and an equational μ-calculus formula ϕ and returns an equational μ-calculus formula $\phi' = \phi_{//s}$. The *Synthesis* module is developed in O'caml 3.09 (see [9]) and it is described better in Figure 1.b).

The Figure 1.b) shows the *Synthesis* module in more detail. It is composed by several functions as we can see in the figure. Roughly, it is able to build a model for a given modal μ-calculus formula by exploiting the satisfiability procedure developed by Walukiewicz in [19]. In order to describe this module we can see that it consists of two submodules: the *Translator* and the *Synthesis*.

The *Translator*. manages the formula ϕ, output of the *MuDiv* tool and input of our tool, by translating it from an equational to a modal μ-calculus formula. It consists in four functions: `fparser.ml` and `flexer.ml` that permit to read the *MuDiv* output file and analyze it as input sequence in order to determine its grammatical structure with respect to our grammar. The function `calc.ml` calls `flexer.ml` and `fparser.ml` on a specified file. In this way we obtain an equational μ-calculus formula ϕ' according to the type that we have defined in `type_for.ml`. The last function, `convert.ml`, translates the equational μ-calculus formula ϕ' in the modal one

Table 4. System of rules

$$
\text{(and)} \; \frac{\varphi_1 \wedge \varphi_2, \Gamma \vdash_{\mathcal{D}}}{\varphi_1, \varphi_2, \Gamma \vdash_{\mathcal{D}}} \quad \text{(or)} \; \frac{\varphi_1 \vee \varphi_2, \Gamma \vdash_{\mathcal{D}}}{\varphi_1, \Gamma \vdash_{\mathcal{D}} \quad \varphi_2, \Gamma \vdash_{\mathcal{D}}}
$$

$$
\text{(cons)} \; \frac{U, \Gamma \vdash_{\mathcal{D}}}{\varphi U, \Gamma \vdash_{\mathcal{D}}} \; \text{whenever } (U = \sigma X.\varphi(X)) \in \mathcal{D}
$$

$$
(\mu) \; \frac{\mu X.\varphi(X), \Gamma \vdash_{\mathcal{D}}}{U, \Gamma \vdash_{\mathcal{D}}} \; \text{whenever } (U = \mu X.\varphi(X)) \in \mathcal{D}
$$

$$
(\nu) \; \frac{\nu X.\varphi(X), \Gamma \vdash_{\mathcal{D}}}{U, \Gamma \vdash_{\mathcal{D}}} \; \text{whenever } (U = \nu X.\varphi(X)) \in \mathcal{D}
$$

$$
\text{(all } \langle\rangle) \; \frac{\Gamma \vdash_{\mathcal{D}}}{\{\varphi_1, \{\varphi_2 : [\alpha]\varphi_2 \in \Gamma\} \vdash_{\mathcal{D}} \quad : \langle \alpha \rangle \varphi_1 \in \Gamma\}}
$$

ϕ'_{mod}. This translation is necessary because the Walukiewicz's satisfiability procedure was developed for modal μ-calculus formulae instead the partial model checking was developed for equational μ-calculus ones[7].

The *Synthesis*: An implementation of Walukiewicz satisfiability procedure. Let *definition list* be a finite sequence of equations: $\mathcal{D} = ((U_1 = \sigma_1 X.\alpha_1(X)), \cdots, (U_n = \sigma_n X.\alpha_n(X))$ where $U_1, \cdots, U_n$ are new constant symbols and $\sigma_i X.\alpha_i(X)$ is a formula such that all definition constants appearing in α_i are among $U_1, \cdots, U_{i-1}$. Let *tableau sequent* be a pair $(\Gamma, \mathcal{D})$ where $\mathcal{D}$ is a definition list and Γ is a finite set of formulae such that the only constants that occur in them are those from $\mathcal{D}$. Let *tableau axiom* be a sequent $\Gamma \vdash_{\mathcal{D}}$ such that some formula and its negation occurs in Γ, a *tableau* is built using the system of rules $\mathcal{S}$ presented in Table 4.

Definition 2. *Given a positive guarded formula ϕ, a tableau for ϕ is any labeled tree $\langle K, L \rangle$, where K is a tree and L a labeling function, such that*

1. *the root of K is labeled with $\phi \vdash_{\mathcal{D}}$ where $\mathcal{D}$ is the definition list of ϕ;*
2. *if $L(n)$ is a tableau axiom then n is a leaf of K;*
3. *if $L(n)$ is not an axiom then the sons of n in K are created and labeled according to the rules of the system $\mathcal{S}$.*

Walukiewicz has proven that it is possible to extract from tableau either a refutation or a model for a modal μ-calculus formula. In order to do this he has defined two different systems of rules, $\mathcal{S}_{mod}$ and $\mathcal{S}_{ref}$. The system $\mathcal{S}_{mod}$ is obtained from $\mathcal{S}$ by replacing the rule *(or)* by two rules (or_{left}) and (or_{right}) defined in the obvious way; the system $\mathcal{S}_{ref}$ is obtained from $\mathcal{S}$ by replacing the rule $(all\langle\rangle)$ by the rule

$$
(\langle\rangle) \quad \frac{\langle a \rangle \alpha, \Gamma \vdash_{\mathcal{D}}}{\alpha, \{\beta : [a]\beta \in \Gamma\} \vdash_{\mathcal{D}}}
$$

---

[7] As a matter of fact, the equational μ-calculus is close for partial model checking. This means that applying the partial model checking function to an equational μ-calculus formula we pbtain an equational μ-calculus formula.

with the same restrictions on formulae in Γ as in the case of $(all\langle\rangle)$ rule, i.e. each formula in Γ is a propositional constant, a variable, or a formula of the form $\langle b\rangle\varphi$ or $[b]\varphi$ for some action b and a formula α. A *quasi-model* of ϕ is defined in a similar way to tableau, except the system $\mathcal{S}_{mod}$ is used instead of $\mathcal{S}$ and we impose the additional requirement that no leaf is labeled by a tableau axiom. A *quasi-refutation* of ϕ is defined in a similar way to tableau, except the system $\mathcal{S}_{ref}$ is used instead of $\mathcal{S}$ and we impose the additional requirement that every leaf is labeled by a tableau axiom.

Let $\mathcal{P} = (v_1, v_2, \cdots)$ be a path in the tree K. A *trace* Tr on the path $\mathcal{P}$ is any sequence of formulas $\{\varphi_i\}_{i\in I}$ such that $\varphi_i \in L(v_i)$ and φ_{i+1} is either φ_i, if formula φ_i was not reduced by the rule applied in v_i, or otherwise φ_{i+1} is one of the formulae obtained by applying the rule to φ_i. A constant U *regenerates* on the trace Tr if for some i, $\alpha_i = U$ and $\alpha_{i+1} = \varphi(U)$ where $(U = \sigma X.\varphi(X)) \in \mathcal{D}$. The trace Tr is called a ν-*trace* iff it is finite and does not end with a tableau axiom, or if the oldest constant in the definition list $\mathcal{D}$ which is regenerated infinitely often on Tr is a ν-constant. Otherwise the trace is called a μ-*trace*.

Definition 3. *A quasi model* $\mathcal{PM}$ *is called* pre-model *iff any trace on any path of* $\mathcal{PM}$ *is a ν-trace* .

A quasi-refutation of ϕ is called a refutation *of ϕ iff on every path of there exists a μ-trace.*

We represent a tableau as a graph. Hence we define the type graph as a list of triple $(n, a, n) \in GNode \times Act \times GNode$ where $GNode$ is the set of graph nodes. Each node of the graph represents a state $L(n)$ of the tableau. Each node is characterized by the set of formulae that it satisfies.

We build the pre-model by exploiting the system of rules $\mathcal{S}_{mod}$ in model.ml. First of all we check if conditions for the pre-model given in the Definition 3 are satisfied by using the function goodgraph.ml. This function takes in input a graph and gives back the boolean value TRUE if pre-model conditions are respected, FALSE otherwise. The function model.ml takes as input a pair in $GNode \times Graph$ and, in a recursive way, builds the graph that is the pre-model for ϕ. At the beginning we give in input a node labeled by ϕ and Empty_Graph, that represents the empty graph. Then, in a recursive way, we build the pre-model by checking, at each step, that the pre-model condition is satisfied, by using goodgraph.ml.

According to the Walukiewicz theory, from the pre-model it is possible to find a model for ϕ as follow.

Definition 4. *Given a pre-model* $\mathcal{PM}$, *the* canonical structure *for* $\mathcal{PM}$ *is a structure* $\mathcal{M} = \langle S^{\mathcal{M}}, R^{\mathcal{M}}, \rho^{\mathcal{M}}\rangle$ *such that*

1. $S^{\mathcal{M}}$ *is the set of all nodes of* $\mathcal{PM}$ *which are either leaves or to which* $(all\langle\rangle)$ *rule was applied. For any node n of* $\mathcal{PM}$ *we will denote by s_n the closest descendant of n belonging to* $S^{\mathcal{M}}$.
2. $(s, s') \in R^{\mathcal{M}}(a)$ *iff there is a son n of s with $s_n = s'$, such that $L(n)$ was obtained from $L(s)$ by reducing a formula of the form $\langle a\rangle\varphi$.*
3. $\rho^{\mathcal{M}}(p) = \{s : p \text{ occurs in the sequent } L(s)\}$.

Through the application of the function simplify.ml we are able to find the canonical structure from the pre-model generated by model.ml. In this way we have obtained a model for ϕ'_{mod}. This is a controller program for controller operators that do not require a relabeling function, e.g. $Y \rhd_T X$.

As we can seen in Figure 1.b) there are other functions in the *Synthesis* module. The controllers.ml implements relabeling functions f_K, one for each controller operators described in Section 3.1. The function printGraph.ml permits to print the graph as a sequence of nodes labeled by a list of formulae, connected by arrows labeled by an action. The last function is the main.ml that calls all the other functions and permits to create the executable file (.exe).

5 A Cases Study

In order to explain better how the tool works, we present an example in which a system must satisfy a safety property. We generate a controller program for each of the four controllers defined in Section 3.1.

Let S be a system. We suppose that all users that work on S have to satisfy the following rule:

You cannot open a new file while another file is open.

It can be formalized by an equation system $\mathcal{D}$ as follows:

$$X =_\nu [\tau]X \wedge [\text{open}]Y$$
$$Y =_\nu [\tau]Y \wedge [\text{close}]X \wedge [\text{open}]F$$

5.1 Truncation

We halt the system if the user try to open a file while another is already open. In this case we generate a controller program Y for $Y \rhd_T X$ and we obtain:

$$Y = \text{open.close.}Y$$

Y is a model for $\mathcal{D}$.

In order to show how it works as controller program for $Y \rhd_T X$ we suppose to have a possible user X that tries to open two different files. Hence $X = \text{open.open.0}$. Applying $Y \rhd_T X$ we obtain:

$$Y \rhd_T X = \text{open.close.}Y \rhd_T \text{open.open.0} \overset{\text{open}}{\longrightarrow} \text{close.}Y \rhd_T \text{open.0}$$

Since Y and X are going to perform a different action, i.e. Y is going to perform close while X is going to perform open, the whole system halts.

5.2 Suppression

We suppose to decide to suppress any possible open action that can violate the property $\mathcal{D}$. In this case we generate a controller program Y for the controller $Y \rhd_S X$. We obtain:

$$Y = {}^{-}\text{open.}Y + \text{open.}Y'$$
$$Y' = {}^{-}\text{open.}Y' + \text{close.}Y$$

Let we suppose to be in the same scenario described for the previous operator. Let X be a user that tries to open two different files. Hence $X = \text{open.open.0}$. Applying $Y \triangleright_S X$ we obtain:

$$Y \triangleright_S X = {}^-\text{open}.Y + \text{open}.Y' \triangleright_S \text{open.open.0}$$
$$\xrightarrow{\text{open}} {}^-\text{open}.Y' + \text{close}.Y \triangleright_S \text{open.0} \xrightarrow{\tau} Y' \triangleright_S 0$$

The whole system halts again because, even if a wrong action is suppressed, this controllers cannot introduce right actions.

5.3   Insertion

We decide to implement a controller program Y for the controller $Y \triangleright_I X$. We obtain:

$$Y = {}^+\text{open.close.open}.Y + \text{open}.Y'$$
$$Y' = {}^+\text{open.close.open}.Y' + \text{close}.Y$$

We consider X that tries to open two different files. Hence $X = \text{open.open.0}$. We obtain:

$$Y \triangleright_I X = {}^+\text{open.close.open}.Y + \text{open}.Y' \triangleright_I \text{open.open.0}$$
$$\xrightarrow{\text{open}} {}^+\text{open.close.open}.Y' + \text{close}.Y \triangleright_I \text{open.0} \xrightarrow{\text{close}} \text{open}.Y' \triangleright_I \text{open.0}$$
$$\xrightarrow{\text{open}} Y' \triangleright_I 0$$

We can note the Y permits X to perform the first action open. Then it checks that X is going to perform another open by the action ${}^+\text{open}$. Hence Y insert an action close. After this action it permits X to perform the action open. Since X does not perform any another actions the whole system halts.

5.4   Edit

We consider to apply the controller operator $Y \triangleright_E X$. The controller program that we generate is the following:

$$Y = {}^-\text{open}.Y + {}^+\text{open.close.open}.Y + \text{open}.Y' \quad {}_8$$
$$Y' = {}^-\text{open}.Y' + {}^+\text{open.close.open}.Y' + \text{close}.Y$$

We suppose again that $X = \text{open.open.0}$. We have:

$$Y \triangleright_E X =$$
$${}^-\text{open}.Y + {}^+\text{open.close.open}.Y + \text{open}.Y' \triangleright_E \text{open.open.0}$$
$$\xrightarrow{\text{open}} {}^-\text{open}.Y' + {}^+\text{open.close.open}.Y' + \text{close}.Y \triangleright_E \text{open.0}$$
$$\xrightarrow{\text{close}} \text{open}.Y' \triangleright_E \text{open.0} \xrightarrow{\text{open}} Y' \triangleright_E 0$$

Also in this case, after the first action open, Y checks if X is going to perform another open by the action ${}^+\text{open}$ and then it inserts the action close in order to satisfy the property $\mathcal{D}$. Then it permit to perform another open action.

---

[8] In order to obtain a deterministic process we say that, when the target is going to perform a wrong action we apply the third rule before the second one.

6 Conclusion and Future Work

In this paper we have described a tool for the synthesis of a controller program based on Walukiewicz's satisfiability procedure as well as on the partial model checking technique. In particular, starting from a system S and a formula ϕ that describes a security property, the tool generates a process that, by monitoring a possible un-trusted component, guarantees that a system $S\|X$ satisfies ϕ whatever X is.

This tool is made up of several parts. Starting from the *MuDiv* tool, developed to calculate the partial model checking function, we create a module that implements the satisfiability procedure of Walukiewicz for modal μ-calculus formula. As we have already said (Theorem 1), this procedure is exponential in the size of the formula. There are some classes of μ-calculus formulae for which the satisfiability procedure is not exponential, e.g. *universal disjunctive formulae* (see [8]).

Some optimizations can be done in order to obtain manageable formulae from the *MuDiv* tool.

We plan to extend this approach to GRID systems and also we would like to extend our work to systems with several un-trusted components.

Acknowledgement. We thank the anonymous referees of FAST06 for valuable comments that helped us to improve this paper.

References

1. Andersen, H.R.: Verification of Temporal Properties of Concurrent Systems. PhD thesis, Department of Computer Science, Aarhus University, Denmark (1993)
2. Andersen, H.R.: Partial model checking. In: LICS '95. In: Proceedings of the 10th Annual IEEE Symposium on Logic in Computer Science, p. 398. IEEE Computer Society Press, Los Alamitos (1995)
3. Bartoletti, M., Degano, P., Ferrari, G.: Policy framings for access control. In: Proceedings of the 2005 workshop on Issues in the theory of security, pp. 5 – 11, Long Beach, California (2005)
4. Bauer, L., Ligatti, J., Walker, D.: More enforceable security policies. In: Cervesato, I. (ed.) Foundations of Computer Security. proceedings of the FLoC'02 workshop on Foundations of Computer Security, Copenhagen, Denmark, 25–26 July 2002, pp. 95–104. DIKU Technical Report (2002)
5. Bauer, L., Ligatti, J., Walker, D.: Edit automata: Enforcement mechanisms for run-time security policies. International Journal of Information Security. 4(1–2) (2005)
6. Bloom, B., Istrail, S., Meyer, A.R.: Bisimulation can't be traced. J.ACM 42(1) (1995)
7. Focardi, R., Gorrieri, R.: A classification of security properties. Journal of Computer Security 3(1), 5–33 (1997)
8. Janin, D., Walukiewicz, I.: Automata for the μ-calculus and related results. In: Hájek, P., Wiedermann, J. (eds.) MFCS 1995. LNCS, vol. 969, Springer, Heidelberg (1995)
9. Leroy, X., Doligez, D., Garrigue, J., Rémy, D., Vouillon, J.: The objective caml systemrelease 3.09 (2004)
10. Lowe, G.: Semantic models for information flow. Theor. Comput. Sci. 315(1), 209–256 (2004), doi:10.1016/j.tcs.2003.11.019

11. Martinelli, F., Matteucci, I.: Partial model checking, process algebra operators and satisfiability procedures for (automatically) enforcing security properties. In: Presented at the International Workshop on Foundations of Computer Security (FCS05) (2005)
12. Martinelli, F., Matteucci, I.: Modeling security automata with process algebras and related results. In: Informal proceedings Presented at the 6th International Workshop on Issues in the Theory of Security (WITS '06) (March 2006)
13. Martinelli, F., Matteucci, I.: Through modeling to synthesis of security automata. In: Proceedings of ENTCS STM06 (2006)
14. Matteucci, I.: Automated synthesis of enforcing mechanisms for security properties in a timed setting. In: Proceedings of ENTCS ICS'06 (2006)
15. Milner, R.: Synthesis of communicating behaviour. In: Proceedings of 7th MFCS, Poland (1978)
16. Milner, R.: Communicating and mobile systems: the π-calculus. Cambridge University Press, Cambridge (1999)
17. Schneider, F.B.: Enforceable security policies. ACM Transactions on Information and System Security 3(1), 30–50 (2000)
18. Street, R.S., Emerson, E.A.: An automata theoretic procedure for the propositional μ-calculus. Information and Computation 81(3), 249–264 (1989)
19. Walukiewicz, I.: A Complete Deductive System for the μ-Calculus. PhD thesis, Institute of Informatics, Warsaw University (June 1993)

Where Can an Insider Attack?

Christian W. Probst[1], René Rydhof Hansen[2], and Flemming Nielson[1]

[1] Informatics and Mathematical Modelling, Technical University of Denmark*
{probst,nielson}@imm.dtu.dk
[2] Department of Computer Science, University of Copenhagen
rrhansen@diku.dk

Abstract. By definition an insider has better access, is more trusted, and has better information about internal procedures, high-value targets, and potential weak spots in the security, than an outsider. Consequently, an insider attack has the potential to cause significant, even catastrophic, damage to the targeted organisation. While the problem is well recognised in the security community as well as in law-enforcement and intelligence communities, the main resort still is to audit log files *after the fact*. There has been little research into developing models, automated tools, and techniques for analysing and solving (parts of) the problem. In this paper we first develop a formal model of systems, that can describe real-world scenarios. These high-level models are then mapped to acKlaim, a process algebra with support for access control, that is used to study and analyse properties of the modelled systems. Our analysis of processes identifies which actions may be performed by whom, at which locations, accessing which data. This allows to compute a superset of audit results—before an incident occurs.

1 Introduction

One of the toughest and most insidious problems in information security, and indeed in security in general, is that of protecting against attacks from an insider. By definition, an insider has better access, is more trusted, and has better information about internal procedures, high-value targets, and potential weak spots in the security. Consequently, an insider attack has the potential to cause significant, even catastrophic, damage to the targeted IT-infrastructure. The problem is well recognised in the security community as well as in law-enforcement and intelligence communities, cf. [1,13,6]. In spite of this there has been relatively little focused research into developing models, automated tools, and techniques for analysing and solving (parts of) the problem. The main measure taken still is to audit log files *after* an insider incident has occurred [13].

In this paper we develop a model that allows to define a notion of insider attacks and thereby enables to study systems and analyse the potential consequences of such an attack. Formal modelling and analysis is increasingly important in a modern computing environment with widely distributed systems,

* Part of this work has been supported by the EU research project #016004, *Software Engineering for Service-Oriented Overlay Computers*.

computing grids, and service-oriented architectures, where the line between insider and outsider is more blurred than ever.

With this in mind we have developed a formal model in two parts: an abstract high-level system model based on graphs and a process calculus, called *acKlaim*, providing a formal semantics for the abstract model. As the name suggests, the acKlaim calculus belongs to the Klaim family of process calculi [9] that are all designed around the tuple-space paradigm, making them ideally suited for modelling distributed systems like the interact/cooperate and service-oriented architectures. Specifically, acKlaim is an extension of the μKlaim calculus with access-control primitives. In addition to this formal model we also show how techniques from static program analysis can be applied to automatically compute a sound estimate, i.e., an over-approximation, of the potential consequences of an insider attack. This result has two immediate applications—on the one hand it can be used in designing access controls and assigning security clearances in such a way as to minimise the damage an insider can do. On the other hand, it can direct the auditing process after an insider attack has occurred, by identifying *before* the incident which events should be monitored. The important contribution is to separate the actual threat and attack from reachability. Once we have identified, which places an insider can reach, we can easily put existing models and formalisms on top of our model.

The rest of the paper is structured as follows. In the remainder of this section the terms *insider* and *insider threat* are defined. Section 2 introduces our abstract system model and an example system, and Section 3 defines acKlaim, the process calculus we use to analyse these systems. The analysis itself is introduced in Section 4, followed by a discussion of related work (Section 5). Section 6 concludes our paper and gives an outlook and future work.

1.1   The Insider Problem

Recently, the insider problem has attracted interest by both researchers and intelligence agencies [13,14]. However, most of the work is on detecting insider attacks, modelling the threat itself, and assessing the threat. This section gives an overview of existing work.

Bishop [1] introduces different definitions of the insider threat found in literature. The RAND report [13] defines the problem as "*malevolent actions by an already trusted person with access to sensitive information and information systems*", and the insider is defined as "*someone with access, privilege, or knowledge of information systems and services*". Bishop also cites Patzakis [12] to define the insider as "*anyone operating inside the security perimeter*", thereby contrasting it from *outside* attacks like denial-of-service attacks, which originate from outside the perimeter. Bishop then moves on to define the terms *insider* and *insider threat*:

Definition 1. *(Insider, Insider threat). An* insider *with respect to rules R is a user who may take an action that would violate some set of rules R in the security policy, were the user not trusted. The insider is trusted to take the action only*

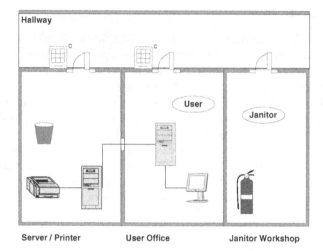

Fig. 1. The example system used to illustrate our approach. The user can use the network connection to print some potentially confidential data in the server/printer room. Depending on the configuration on the cipher locks, the janitor might or might not be able to pick up that print out.

when appropriate, as determined by the insider's discretion. The insider threat is the threat that an insider may abuse his discretion by taking actions that would violate the security policy when such actions are not warranted.

Obviously, these definitions are expressive in that they connect actors in a system and their actions to the rules of the security policy. On the other hand, they are rather vague, since in a given system it is usually hard to identify vulnerabilities that might occur based on an insider taking unwarranted actions. In the rest of the paper we will use Bishop's definitions to analyse abstractions of real systems for potential attacks by insiders. To do so, in the next section we define the abstract model of systems, actors, data, and policies.

2 Modelling Systems

This section introduces our abstract model of systems, which we will analyse in Section 4 to identify potential insider threats. Our system model is at a level that is high enough to allow easy modelling of real-world systems. The system model naturally maps to an abstraction using the process calculus acKlaim (Section 3). Here it is essential that our model is detailed enough to allow expressive analysis results. The abstraction is based on a system consisting of locations and actors. While locations are static, actors can move around in the system. To support these movements, locations can be connected by directed edges, which define freedoms of movements of actors. This section first motivates the choice of our abstraction by an example, and thereafter formally defines the elements.

2.1   Example System

In Figure 1 we show our running example system inspired by [1]. It models part of an environment with physical locations (a server/printer room with a waste-basket, a user office, and a janitor's workshop connected through a hallway), and network locations (two computers connected by a network, and a printer connected to one of them). The access to the server/printer room and the user office is restricted by a cipher lock, and additional by use of a physical master key. The actors in this system are a user and a janitor.

Following Bishop's argumentation, the janitor might pose an insider threat to this system, since he is able to access the server room and pick up printouts from the printer or the wastebasket. We assume a security policy, which allows the janitor access to the server room only in case of fire. Modelling these *soft* constraints is part of ongoing and future work.

2.2   System Definition

We start with defining the notion of an *infrastructure*, which consists of a set of *locations* and *connections*:

Definition 2. *(Infrastructure, Locations, Connections). An* infrastructure *is a directed graph* $(\mathsf{Loc}, \mathsf{Con})$*, where* Loc *is a set of nodes representing* locations*, and* $\mathsf{Con} \subseteq \mathsf{Loc} \times \mathsf{Loc}$ *is a set of directed* connections *between locations.* $n_d \in \mathsf{Loc}$ *is reachable from* $n_s \in \mathsf{Loc}$*, if there is a path* $\pi = n_0, n_1, n_2, \cdots, n_k$*, with* $k \leq 1$*,* $n_0 = n_s$*,* $n_k = n_d$*, and* $\forall 0 \leq i \leq k - 1 : n_i \in \mathsf{Loc} \wedge (n_i, n_{i+1}) \in \mathsf{Con}$*.*

Next, we define *actors*, which can move in systems by following edges between nodes, and *data*, which actors can produce, pickup, or read. In the example setting, actors would be the user, the janitor, or processes on the computers, whereas data for example would be a printout generated by a program. Usually, actors can only move in a certain domain. In the example system, the user and the janitor can move in the physical locations, but they can only access, e.g., the printer and the waste basket to take items out of them. This is modelled by nodes falling in different domains.

Definition 3. *(Actors, Domains). Let* $\mathcal{I} = (\mathsf{Loc}, \mathsf{Con})$ *be an infrastructure,* Actors *be a set. An actor* $\alpha \in \mathsf{Actors}$ *is an entity that can move in* $\mathcal{I}$*. Let* Dom *be a set of unique domain identifiers. Then* $\mathcal{D} : \mathsf{Loc} \rightarrow \mathsf{Dom}$ *defines the domain* d *for a node* n*, and* $\mathcal{D}^{-1}$ *defines all the nodes that are in a domain.*

Definition 4. *(Data). Let* $\mathcal{I} = (\mathsf{Loc}, \mathsf{Con})$ *be an infrastructure,* Data *be a set of data items, and* $\alpha \in \mathsf{Actors}$ *an actor. A data item* $d \in \mathsf{Data}$ *represents data available in the system. Data can be stored at both locations and actors, and* $\mathcal{K} : (\mathsf{Actors} \cup \mathsf{Loc}) \rightarrow \mathcal{P}(\mathsf{Data})$ *maps an actor or a location to the set of data stored at it.*

Finally, we need to model how actors can obtain the right to access locations and data, and how these can decide whether to allow or to deny the access.

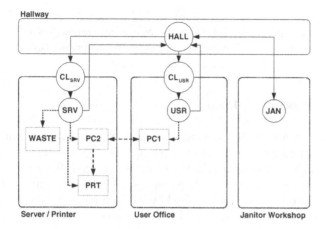

Fig. 2. Abstraction for the example system from Figure 1. The different kinds of arrows indicate how connections can be accessed. The solid lines, e.g., are accessible by actors modelling persons, the dashed lines by processes executing on the network. The dotted lines are special in that they express possible actions of actors.

We associate actors with a set of *capabilities*, and locations and data with a set of *restrictions*. Both restrictions and capabilities can be used to restrain the mobility of actors, by requiring, e.g., a certain key to enter a location, or allowing access only for certain actors or from certain locations. In the example, the code stored in the cipher locks is a restriction, and an actor's knowledge of that code is a capability. Similarly, data items can have access restrictions based on the security classification of the user or based on encryption.

Definition 5. *(Capabilities and Restrictions). Let* $\mathcal{I} = (\mathsf{Loc}, \mathsf{Con})$ *be an infrastructure,* Actors *be a set of actors, and* Data *be a set of data items.* Cap *is a set of* capabilities *and* Res *is a set of restrictions. For each restriction* $r \in \mathsf{Res}$, *the checker* $\Phi_r : \mathsf{Cap} \to \{\mathtt{true}, \mathtt{false}\}$ *checks whether the capability matches the restriction or not.* $\mathcal{C} : \mathsf{Actors} \to \mathcal{P}(\mathsf{Cap})$ *maps each actor to a set of capabilities, and* $\mathcal{R} : (\mathsf{Loc} \cup \mathsf{Data}) \to \mathcal{P}(\mathsf{Res})$ *maps each location and data item to a set of restrictions.*

Figure 2 shows the modelling for the example system from Figure 1. Locations are the rooms and cipher locks (circles), and the computers, the printer, and the wastebasket (squares). The different kinds of arrows indicate how connections can be accessed. The solid lines, e.g., are accessible by actors modelling persons, the dashed lines by processes executing on the network. The dotted lines are special in that they express possible *actions* of actors. An actor at the server location, e.g., can access the wastebasket. Finally, we combine the above elements to a system:

Definition 6. *(System). Let* $\mathcal{I} = (\mathsf{Loc}, \mathsf{Con})$ *be an infrastructure,* Actors *a set of actors in* $\mathcal{I}$, Data *a set of data items,* Cap *a set of capabilities,* Res *a set* *of restrictions,* $\mathcal{C}$: Actors $\rightarrow \mathcal{P}(\mathsf{Cap})$ *and* $\mathcal{R}$: $(\mathsf{Loc} \cup \mathsf{Data}) \rightarrow \mathcal{P}(\mathsf{Res})$ *maps from actors and location and data, respectively, to capabilities and restrictions, respectively, and for each restriction* r, *let* Φ_r : $\mathsf{Cap} \rightarrow \{\mathsf{true}, \mathsf{false}\}$ *be a checker. Then we call* $\mathcal{S} = \langle \mathcal{I}, \mathsf{Actors}, \mathsf{Data}, \mathcal{C}, \mathcal{R}, \Phi \rangle$ *a system.*

3   The acKlaim Calculus

In this section we present the process calculus that provides the formal underpinning for the system model presented in the previous section. The calculus, called *acKlaim*, belongs to the Klaim family of process calculi [9]; it is a variation of the μKlaim calculus enhanced with access control primitives and equipped with a *reference monitor semantics* (inspired by [8]) that ensures compliance with the system's access policy. The main additions are access policies (Section 3.1), the tagging of processes with names and keys (Section 3.2), and the addition of a reference monitor in the semantics (Figure 7). In addition to providing a convenient and well-understood formal framework, the use of a process calculus also enables us to apply a range of tools and techniques originally developed in a programming language context. In particular it facilitates the use of *static analyses* to compute a sound approximation of the consequences of an insider attack.

3.1   Access Policies

We start by defining the *access policies* that are enforced by the reference monitor. Access policies come in three varieties: access can be granted based on the location it is coming from, based on the actor that is performing the access, or based on the knowledge of the secret, e.g., a key in (a)symmetric encryption. In the above system model, these are modelled by capabilities and restrictions.

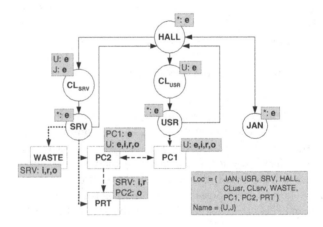

Fig. 3. The abstracted example system from Figure 2, extended with policy annotations. There are two actors, janitor J and user U, who, e.g., have different access rights to the user office and the server room.

$$\pi \subseteq \mathsf{AccMode} = \{\mathbf{i}, \mathbf{r}, \mathbf{o}, \mathbf{e}, \mathbf{n}\}$$
$$\kappa \subseteq \mathsf{Keys} = \{unique\ key\ identifiers\}$$
$$\delta \in \mathsf{Policy} = (\mathsf{Loc} \cup \mathsf{Name} \cup \mathsf{Keys} \cup \{\star\}) \rightarrow \mathcal{P}(\mathsf{AccMode})$$

The access modes $\mathbf{i}, \mathbf{r}, \mathbf{o}, \mathbf{e}, \mathbf{n}$ correspond to *destructively read a tuple, non-destructively read a tuple, output a tuple, remote evaluation,* and *create new location* respectively. These modes reflect the underlying reference monitor semantics and are explained in detail below. The special element $\star$ allows to specify a set of access modes that are allowed by default. The separation of *locations* and *names* is artificial in that both sets simply contain unique identifiers. They are separated to stress the distinction between locations as part of the infrastructure and actors that are moving around in the infrastructure.

The elements of the domain **Keys** are keys used, e.g., for symmetric or asymmetric encryption. We assume that each key uniquely maps to the method used to check it (a checker Φ_r).

Intuitively, every *locality* in the system defines an access policy that specifies how other localities and actors are allowed to access and interact with it. This approach affords fine-grained control for individual localities over both *who* is allowed access and *how*. Semantically the access control model is formalised by a *reference monitor* embedded in the operational semantics for the calculus. The reference monitor verifies that every access to a locality is in accordance with that locality's access policy.

We use the function *grant* to decide whether an actor n at location l knowing keys κ should be allowed to perform an action a on the location l' (Figure 4).

Additionally, access policies can be defined for every *data item*. In this case, only the subset $\{\mathbf{i}, \mathbf{r}\}$ of access modes can be used for name- or location based specification, as well as keys specifying how the data item has been encrypted.

$$\text{grant} : \mathsf{Names} \times \mathsf{Loc} \times \mathsf{Keys} \times \mathsf{AccMode} \times \mathsf{Loc} \rightarrow \{\texttt{true}, \texttt{false}\}$$

$$\text{grant}(n, l, \kappa, a, l') = \begin{cases} \texttt{true} & \text{if } a \in \delta_{l'}(n) \vee a \in \delta_{l'}(l) \vee \exists k \in \kappa : a \in \delta_{l'}(k) \\ \texttt{false} & \text{otherwise} \end{cases}$$

$$\frac{l = t}{\langle \mathcal{I}, n, \kappa \rangle \succ (l, t)} \qquad \frac{\exists (l, l') \in \mathsf{Con} : \text{grant}(n, l, \kappa, \mathbf{e}, l') \wedge \langle \mathcal{I}, n, \kappa \rangle \succ (l', t)}{\langle \mathcal{I}, n, \kappa \rangle \succ (l, t)}$$

$$\frac{\text{grant}(n, l, \kappa, a, t) \wedge \langle \mathcal{I}, n, \kappa \rangle \succ (l, t)}{\langle \mathcal{I}, n, \kappa \rangle \rightsquigarrow (l, t, a)}$$

Fig. 4. Function *grant* (upper part) checks whether an actor n at location l knowing keys κ should be allowed to perform an action a on the location l' based on the location it is at, its name, or a key it knows. The judgement $\succ$ (lower part) decides whether an actor n at location s can reach location t based on the edges present in the infrastructure $\mathcal{I}$, by testing $\langle \mathcal{I}, n, \kappa \rangle \succ (s, t)$. Finally, the judgement $\rightsquigarrow$ uses *grant* and judgement $\succ$ to test whether n is allowed to execute action a at location t.

$$\ell ::= l \qquad \text{locality}$$
$$| \quad u \qquad \text{locality variable}$$

$$N ::= l ::^\delta [P]^{\langle n,\kappa \rangle} \qquad \text{single node}$$
$$| \quad l ::^\delta \langle et \rangle \qquad \text{located tuple}$$
$$| \quad N_1 \| N_2 \qquad \text{net composition}$$

$$P ::= \mathbf{nil} \qquad \text{null process}$$
$$| \quad a.P \qquad \text{action prefixing}$$
$$| \quad P_1 | P_2 \quad \text{parallel composition}$$
$$| \quad A \qquad \text{process invocation}$$

$$a ::= \mathbf{out}\,(t)\,@\ell \qquad \text{output}$$
$$| \quad \mathbf{in}\,(T)\,@\ell \qquad \text{input}$$
$$| \quad \mathbf{read}\,(T)\,@\ell \qquad \text{read}$$
$$| \quad \mathbf{eval}\,(P)\,@\ell \qquad \text{migration}$$
$$| \quad \mathbf{newloc}(u^\pi : \delta) \quad \text{creation}$$

Fig. 5. Syntax of nets, processes, and actions

$$T ::= F \mid F,T \qquad \text{templates}$$
$$F ::= f \mid !x \mid !u \quad \text{template fields}$$
$$t ::= f \mid f,t \qquad \text{tuples}$$
$$f ::= e \mid l \mid u \qquad \text{tuple fields}$$

$$et ::= ef \mid ef, et \quad \text{evaluated tuple}$$
$$ef ::= V \mid l \qquad \text{evaluated tuple field}$$
$$e ::= V \mid x \mid \ldots \quad \text{expressions}$$

Fig. 6. Syntax for tuples and templates

3.2 Syntax and Semantics

The Klaim family of calculi, including acKlaim, are motivated by and designed around the *tuple space* paradigm in which a system consists of a set of distributed nodes that interact and communicate through shared tuple spaces by reading and writing tuples. Remote evaluation of processes is used to model mobility.

The acKlaim calculus, like other members of the Klaim family, consists of three layers: nets, processes, and actions. Nets give the overall structure where tuple spaces and processes are located; processes execute by performing actions. The syntax is shown in Figure 5 and Figure 6. The main difference to standard Klaim calculi is, that processes are annotated with a name, in order to model actors moving in a system, and a set of keys to model the capabilities they have.

The semantics for acKlaim (Figure 7) is specified as a small step operational semantics and follows the semantics of μKlaim quite closely. A process is either comprised of subprocesses composed in parallel, an action (or a sequence of actions) to be executed, the nil-process, i.e., the process that does nothing, or it can be a recursive invocation through a place-holder variable explicitly defined by equation. The **out** action outputs a tuple to the specified tuple space; the **in** and **read** actions read a tuple from the specified tuple space in a destructive/non-destructive manner, respectively. When reading from a tuple space, using either the **in** or the **read** action, only tuples that match the input template (see Figure 6) are read. This pattern matching is formalised in Figure 8. The **eval** action implements remote process evaluation, and the **newloc** action creates a new location, subject to a specified access policy. While locations representing physical

$$\frac{[\![t]\!] = et \qquad \boxed{\langle \mathcal{I}, n, \kappa \rangle \rightsquigarrow (l, l', \mathbf{o})}}{l ::^{\delta} [\mathbf{out}\,(t)\,@l'.P]^{\langle n, \kappa \rangle} \parallel l' ::^{\delta'} [P']^{\langle n', \kappa' \rangle} \;\succ\!\!\longrightarrow_{\mathcal{I}}}{l ::^{\delta} [P]^{\langle n, \kappa \rangle} \parallel l' ::^{\delta'} [P']^{\langle n', \kappa' \rangle} \parallel l' ::^{\delta'} \langle et \rangle}$$

$$\frac{\mathrm{match}([\![T]\!], et) = \sigma \qquad \boxed{\langle \mathcal{I}, n, \kappa \rangle \rightsquigarrow (l, l', \mathbf{i})}}{l ::^{\delta} [\mathbf{in}\,(T)\,@l'.P]^{\langle n, \kappa \rangle} \parallel l' ::^{\delta'} \langle et \rangle \;\succ\!\!\longrightarrow_{\mathcal{I}} l ::^{\delta} [P\sigma]^{\langle n, \kappa \rangle} \parallel l' ::^{\delta'} \mathbf{nil}}$$

$$\frac{\mathrm{match}([\![T]\!], et) = \sigma \qquad \boxed{\langle \mathcal{I}, n, \kappa \rangle \rightsquigarrow (l, l', \mathbf{r})}}{l ::^{\delta} [\mathbf{read}\,(T)\,@l'.P]^{\langle n, \kappa \rangle} \parallel l' ::^{\delta'} \langle et \rangle \;\succ\!\!\longrightarrow_{\mathcal{I}} l ::^{\delta} [P\sigma]^{\langle n, \kappa \rangle} \parallel l' ::^{\delta'} \langle et \rangle}$$

$$\frac{\boxed{\langle \mathcal{I}, n, \kappa \rangle \rightsquigarrow (l, l', \mathbf{e})}}{l ::^{\delta} [\mathbf{eval}\,(Q)\,@l'.P]^{\langle n, \kappa \rangle} \parallel l' ::^{\delta'} [P']^{\langle n', \kappa' \rangle} \;\succ\!\!\longrightarrow_{\mathcal{I}}}{l ::^{\delta} [P]^{\langle n, \kappa \rangle} \parallel l' ::^{\delta'} [Q]^{\langle n, \kappa \rangle} \parallel l' ::^{\delta'} [P']^{\langle n', \kappa' \rangle}}$$

$$\frac{l' \notin L \qquad \lfloor l' \rfloor = \lfloor u \rfloor}{L \vdash l ::^{\delta} [\mathbf{newloc}(u^{\pi} : \delta').P]^{\langle n, \kappa \rangle} \;\succ\!\!\longrightarrow_{\mathcal{I}}}{L \cup \{l'\} \vdash l ::^{\delta[l' \mapsto \pi]} [P[l'/u]]^{\langle n, \kappa \rangle} \parallel l' ::^{\delta'[l'/u]} [\mathbf{nil}]^{\langle n, \kappa \rangle}}$$

$$\frac{L \vdash N_1 \;\succ\!\!\longrightarrow_{\mathcal{I}} L' \vdash N_1'}{L \vdash N_1 \parallel N_2 \;\succ\!\!\longrightarrow_{\mathcal{I}} L' \vdash N_1' \parallel N_2} \qquad \frac{N \equiv N_1 \qquad L \vdash N_1 \;\succ\!\!\longrightarrow_{\mathcal{I}} L' \vdash N_2 \qquad N_2 \equiv N'}{L \vdash N \;\succ\!\!\longrightarrow_{\mathcal{I}} L' \vdash N'}$$

Fig. 7. Operational semantics for acKlaim. The semantics is annotated with the spatial structure $\mathcal{I}$ of the underlying physical system. We omit the structure wherever it is clear from context or is not needed. The boxes contain the reference monitor functionality, that uses the structure $\mathcal{I}$ to verify that an intended action is allowable.

structures usually would be static in our system view, **newloc** can be used to model, e.g., the spawning of processes in computer systems. Note that the semantic rule for the **newloc** action is restricted through the use of *canonical names*; these give a convenient way for the control flow analysis (cf. Section 4) to handle the potentially infinite number of localities arising from unbounded use of **newloc**. These will be explained in detail in Section 4. As is common for process calculi, the operational semantics is defined with respect to a built-in structural congruence on nets and processes. This simplifies presentation and reasoning about processes. The congruence is shown in Figure 9.

In addition to the features of the standard semantics of μKlaim, we add the *spatial* structure of the system to the semantics of acKlaim. This structure is used to limit how access to other locations is granted. The system component $\mathcal{S}$ is, among others, represented by a graph $\mathcal{I}$ as specified in Definition 6. The reference monitor passes $\mathcal{I}$ to the judgement $\rightsquigarrow$ (Figure 4) to check whether there is a path from the current location of a process and the target location of the action. The reference monitor is formalised as additional premises of the reduction rules, shown as boxes in Figure 7.

$$\text{match}(V, V) = \epsilon \qquad \text{match}(!x, V) = [V/x] \qquad \text{match}(l, l) = \epsilon \qquad \text{match}(!u, l') = [l'/u]$$

$$\frac{\text{match}(F, ef) = \sigma_1 \qquad \text{match}(T, et) = \sigma_2}{\text{match}((F, T), (ef, et)) = \sigma_1 \circ \sigma_2}$$

Fig. 8. Semantics for template matching

$$
\begin{aligned}
&N_1 \parallel N_2 \equiv N_2 \parallel N_1 && (N_1 \parallel N_2) \parallel N_3 \equiv N_1 \parallel (N_2 \parallel N_3) \\
&l ::^\delta [P]^{\langle n, \kappa \rangle} \equiv l ::^\delta [(P \mid \mathbf{nil})]^{\langle n, \kappa \rangle} \\
&l ::^\delta [A]^{\langle n, \kappa \rangle} \equiv l ::^\delta [P]^{\langle n, \kappa \rangle} && \text{if } A \triangleq P \\
&l ::^\delta [(P_1 \mid P_2)]^{\langle n, \kappa \rangle} \equiv l ::^\delta [P_1]^{\langle n, \kappa \rangle} \parallel l ::^\delta [P_2]^{\langle n, \kappa \rangle}
\end{aligned}
$$

Fig. 9. Structural congruence on nets and processes

3.3   The Example Revisited

We now use acKlaim to model the system as specified in Figure 3, resulting in the acKlaim program in Figure 10. The system property we are most interested in is the spatial structure of the system, therefore most locations run either the **nil** process or have an empty tuple space, if their location does not allow any actor to execute processes at them. The user's office and the janitor's workshop contain process variables, that can be used to plug in and analyse arbitrary processes for these actors.

4   Analysing the System Abstraction

In this section we describe several analyses that we perform on the infrastructure underlying a system as well as on possible actors in the system. The first analysis (Section 4.1) determines, which locations in a system an actor with name n and keys κ can reach from location l—either directly or by performing an action on them. With respect to an insider threat this allows to determine which locations an insider can reach and which data he can potentially access.

$$
\begin{aligned}
&\text{HALL} ::^{\langle * \mapsto e \rangle} \mathbf{nil} && \parallel \text{USR} ::^{\langle * \mapsto e \rangle} U && \parallel \text{JAN} ::^{\langle * \mapsto e \rangle} J \parallel \\
&\text{CL}_{\text{USR}} ::^{\langle U \mapsto e \rangle} \mathbf{nil} && \parallel \text{PC1} ::^{\langle U \mapsto e, i, r, o \rangle} \mathbf{nil} \parallel \\
&\text{CL}_{\text{SRV}} ::^{\langle U \mapsto e, J \mapsto e \rangle} \mathbf{nil} && \parallel \text{SRV} ::^{\langle * \mapsto e \rangle} \mathbf{nil} && \parallel \text{WASTE} ::^{\langle \text{SRV} \mapsto i, o, r \rangle} \langle \rangle \parallel \\
&\text{PC2} ::^{\langle \text{PC1} \mapsto e, U \mapsto e, i, r, o \rangle} \mathbf{nil} && \parallel \text{PRT} ::^{\langle \text{SRV} \mapsto i, r, \text{PC2} \mapsto o \rangle} \langle \rangle
\end{aligned}
$$

Fig. 10. The example system translated into acKlaim. The two process variables J and U can be instantiated to hold actual process definitions. The system property we are most interested in is the spatial structure of the system, therefore most locations run either the **nil** process or have an empty tuple space, if their location does not allow any actor to execute processes at them.

This analysis can be compared to a before-the-fact system analysis to identify possible vulnerabilities and actions that an audit should check for.

The second analysis (Section 4.2) is a control-flow analysis of actors in a system. It determines, which locations a specific process may reach, which actions it may execute, and which data it may read. This can be compared to an after-the-fact audit of log files.

4.1 Attack Points

In identifying potential insider attacks in a system, it is important to understand, which locations in the system an insider can actually reach. This reachability problem comes in two variations—first we analyse the system *locally* for a specific actor located at a specific location. Then, we put this information together to identify all system-wide locations in the system that an actor possibly can reach. Finally, the result of the reachability analyses can be used in computing which data an actor may access on system locations, by evaluating which actions he can execute from the locations he can reach.

Given that this analysis is very similar to a reachability analysis, we only sketch how it works. Figure 11 shows the pseudo code specification for both reachability analyses and the global data analysis, parametrised in the system structure, the name n of the actor, and the set of keys κ that the actor knows.

For the example system from Figure 3, the analysis finds out, that the actor with name J and an empty set of keys can reach the location SRV and can therefore execute the **read** action on both the waste basket and the printer,

---

checkloc : $\mathsf{Names} \times \mathsf{Loc} \times \mathsf{Keys} \times (\mathsf{Con} \times \mathsf{Loc}) \to \mathcal{P}(\mathsf{Loc})$
$\quad$ for all $(l, l') \in \mathsf{Con}$
$\quad\quad$ if $\langle \mathcal{I}, n, \kappa \rangle \succ (l, l') \vee \mathrm{grant}(n, l, \kappa, \mathbf{e}, l')$
$\quad\quad\quad$ return $\{l'\} \cup \mathrm{checkloc}(n, l', \kappa, \mathcal{I})$

---

checksys : $\mathsf{Names} \times \mathsf{Keys} \times (\mathsf{Con} \times \mathsf{Loc}) \to \mathcal{P}(\mathsf{Loc})$
$\quad$ checksys$(n, \kappa, \mathcal{I}) = \bigcup_{l \in \mathsf{Loc}} \mathrm{checkloc}(n, l, \kappa, \mathcal{I})$

---

checkdata : $\mathsf{Names} \times \mathsf{Keys} \times (\mathsf{Con} \times \mathsf{Loc}) \to \mathcal{P}(\mathsf{AccMode} \times \mathsf{Loc})$
$\quad$ checkdata$(n, \kappa, \mathcal{I}) = \bigcup_{l \in \mathrm{checkloc}(n, l, \kappa, \mathcal{I})} \{(a, l) | \exists a \in \mathsf{AccMode}, (l, l') \in \mathsf{Con} :$
$\quad\quad\quad\quad\quad\quad\quad\quad\quad\quad \mathrm{grant}(n, l, \kappa, a, l')\}$

Fig. 11. Analysing a given system for attack points. The local analysis (upper part) takes a name n, a location l and a key set κ, and returns the set of all locations that n could possibly reach using κ. The system-wide analysis (middle part) puts these together to obtain the global view, by executing the local analysis on all locations in the system. Finally, the data analysis uses the system-wide analysis to compute at which locations the actor may invoke which actions, allowing to identify which data he may possibly access. A local data-analysis similar to the upper part is defined analogous.

possibly accessing confidential data printed or trashed. While this is obvious for the simplistic example system, those properties are usually not easily spotted in complex systems.

4.2   Control-Flow Analysis

While the reachability analysis defined in the previous section is easily computed and verified, it also is highly imprecise in that it does not take into account the actual actions executed in an attack. As described before, the reachability analysis can be used in identifying vulnerable locations that might have to be put under special scrutiny.

In this section we specify a static *control flow analysis* for the acKlaim calculus. The control flow analysis computes a conservative approximation of all the possible flows into and out of all the tuple spaces in the system. The analysis is specified in the Flow Logic framework [10], which is a specification-oriented framework that allows "rapid development" of analyses. An analysis is specified through a number of *judgements* that each determine whether or not a particular analysis estimate correctly describes all configurations that are reachable from the initial state. Concretely we define three judgements: for nets, processes, and actions respectively. The definitions are shown in Figure 12.

Information is collected by the analysis in two components: $\hat{T}$ and $\hat{\sigma}$. The former records for every tuple space (an over-approximation of) the set of tuples possibly located in that tuple space at any point in time. The latter component tracks the possible values that variables may be bound to during execution, i.e., this component acts as an abstract environment.

$$
\begin{array}{lll}
(\hat{T}, \hat{\sigma}, \mathcal{I}) \models_{\mathrm{N}} l ::^{\delta} [P]^{\langle n, \kappa \rangle} & \text{iff} & (\hat{T}, \hat{\sigma}, \mathcal{I}) \models_{\mathrm{P}}^{\lfloor l \rfloor, n, \kappa} P \\[4pt]
(\hat{T}, \hat{\sigma}, \mathcal{I}) \models_{\mathrm{N}} l ::^{\delta} \langle et \rangle & \text{iff} & \langle et \rangle \in \hat{T}(\lfloor l \rfloor) \\[4pt]
(\hat{T}, \hat{\sigma}, \mathcal{I}) \models_{\mathrm{N}} N_1 \parallel N_2 & \text{iff} & (\hat{T}, \hat{\sigma}, \mathcal{I}) \models_{\mathrm{N}} N_1 \wedge (\hat{T}, \hat{\sigma}, \mathcal{I}) \models_{\mathrm{N}} N_2 \\[10pt]
(\hat{T}, \hat{\sigma}, \mathcal{I}) \models_{\mathrm{P}}^{l, n, \kappa} \mathbf{nil} & \text{iff} & \textit{true} \\[4pt]
(\hat{T}, \hat{\sigma}, \mathcal{I}) \models_{\mathrm{P}}^{l, n, \kappa} P_1 \mid P_2 & \text{iff} & (\hat{T}, \hat{\sigma}, \mathcal{I}) \models_{\mathrm{P}}^{l, n, \kappa} P_1 \wedge (\hat{T}, \hat{\sigma}, \mathcal{I}) \models_{\mathrm{P}}^{l, n, \kappa} P_2 \\[4pt]
(\hat{T}, \hat{\sigma}, \mathcal{I}) \models_{\mathrm{P}}^{l, n, \kappa} A & \text{iff} & (\hat{T}, \hat{\sigma}, \mathcal{I}) \models_{\mathrm{P}}^{l, n, \kappa} P \quad \text{if } A \stackrel{\triangle}{=} P \\[4pt]
(\hat{T}, \hat{\sigma}, \mathcal{I}) \models_{\mathrm{P}}^{l, n, \kappa} a.P & \text{iff} & (\hat{T}, \hat{\sigma}, \mathcal{I}) \models_{\mathrm{A}}^{l, n, \kappa} a \wedge (\hat{T}, \hat{\sigma}, \mathcal{I}) \models_{\mathrm{P}}^{l, n, \kappa} P \\[10pt]
(\hat{T}, \hat{\sigma}, \mathcal{I}) \models_{\mathrm{A}}^{l, n, \kappa} \mathbf{out}\,(t)\,@\ell' & \text{iff} & \forall \hat{l} \in \hat{\sigma}(\ell'): (\langle \mathcal{I}, n, \kappa \rangle \rightsquigarrow (l, \hat{l}, \mathbf{o}) \Rightarrow \hat{\sigma}\llbracket t \rrbracket \subseteq \hat{T}(\hat{l})) \\[4pt]
(\hat{T}, \hat{\sigma}, \mathcal{I}) \models_{\mathrm{A}}^{l, n, \kappa} \mathbf{in}\,(T)\,@\ell' & \text{iff} & \forall \hat{l} \in \hat{\sigma}(\ell'): (\langle \mathcal{I}, n, \kappa \rangle \rightsquigarrow (l, \hat{l}, \mathbf{i}) \Rightarrow \\
& & \qquad\qquad \hat{\sigma} \models_1 T : \hat{T}(\hat{l}) \triangleright \hat{W}_{\bullet}) \\[4pt]
(\hat{T}, \hat{\sigma}, \mathcal{I}) \models_{\mathrm{A}}^{l, n, \kappa} \mathbf{read}\,(T)\,@\ell' & \text{iff} & \forall \hat{l} \in \hat{\sigma}(\ell'): (\langle \mathcal{I}, n, \kappa \rangle \rightsquigarrow (l, \hat{l}, \mathbf{r}) \Rightarrow \\
& & \qquad\qquad \hat{\sigma} \models_1 T : \hat{T}(\hat{l}) \triangleright \hat{W}_{\bullet}) \\[4pt]
(\hat{T}, \hat{\sigma}, \mathcal{I}) \models_{\mathrm{A}}^{l, n, \kappa} \mathbf{eval}\,(Q)\,@\ell' & \text{iff} & \forall \hat{l} \in \hat{\sigma}(\ell'): (\langle \mathcal{I}, n, \kappa \rangle \rightsquigarrow (l, \hat{l}, \mathbf{e}) \Rightarrow \\
& & \qquad\qquad (\hat{T}, \hat{\sigma}, \mathcal{I}) \models_{\mathrm{P}}^{\hat{l}, n, \kappa} Q) \\[4pt]
(\hat{T}, \hat{\sigma}, \mathcal{I}) \models_{\mathrm{A}}^{l, n, \kappa} \mathbf{newloc}(u^{\pi} : \delta) & \text{iff} & \{\lfloor u \rfloor\} \subseteq \hat{\sigma}(\lfloor u \rfloor)
\end{array}
$$

Fig. 12. Flow Logic specification for control flow analysis of acKlaim

$$\hat{\sigma} \models_i \epsilon : \hat{V_\circ} \triangleright \hat{V_\bullet} \qquad \text{iff} \quad \{\hat{et} \in \hat{V_\circ} |\, |\hat{et}| = i\} \sqsubseteq \hat{V_\bullet}$$
$$\hat{\sigma} \models_i V, T : \hat{V_\circ} \triangleright \hat{W_\bullet} \qquad \text{iff} \quad \hat{\sigma} \models_{i+1} T : \hat{V_\bullet} \triangleright \hat{W_\bullet} \wedge \{\hat{et} \in \hat{V_\circ} |\, \pi_i(\hat{et}) = V\} \sqsubseteq \hat{V_\bullet}$$
$$\hat{\sigma} \models_i l, T : \hat{V_\circ} \triangleright \hat{W_\bullet} \qquad \text{iff} \quad \hat{\sigma} \models_{i+1} T : \hat{V_\bullet} \triangleright \hat{W_\bullet} \wedge \{\hat{et} \in \hat{V_\circ} |\, \pi_i(\hat{et}) = V\} \sqsubseteq \hat{V_\bullet}$$
$$\hat{\sigma} \models_i x, T : \hat{V_\circ} \triangleright \hat{W_\bullet} \qquad \text{iff} \quad \hat{\sigma} \models_{i+1} T : \hat{V_\bullet} \triangleright \hat{W_\bullet} \wedge \{\hat{et} \in \hat{V_\circ} |\, \pi_i(\hat{et}) \in \hat{\sigma}(x)\} \sqsubseteq \hat{V_\bullet}$$
$$\hat{\sigma} \models_i u, T : \hat{V_\circ} \triangleright \hat{W_\bullet} \qquad \text{iff} \quad \hat{\sigma} \models_{i+1} T : \hat{V_\bullet} \triangleright \hat{W_\bullet} \wedge \{\hat{et} \in \hat{V_\circ} |\, \pi_i(\hat{et}) \in \hat{\sigma}(u)\} \sqsubseteq \hat{V_\bullet}$$
$$\hat{\sigma} \models_i !x, T : \hat{V_\circ} \triangleright \hat{W_\bullet} \qquad \text{iff} \quad \hat{\sigma} \models_{i+1} T : \hat{V_\bullet} \triangleright \hat{W_\bullet} \wedge \hat{V_\circ} \sqsubseteq \hat{V_\bullet} \wedge \pi_i(\hat{W_\bullet}) \sqsubseteq \hat{\sigma}(x)$$
$$\hat{\sigma} \models_i !u, T : \hat{V_\circ} \triangleright \hat{W_\bullet} \qquad \text{iff} \quad \hat{\sigma} \models_{i+1} T : \hat{V_\bullet} \triangleright \hat{W_\bullet} \wedge \hat{V_\circ} \sqsubseteq \hat{V_\bullet} \wedge \pi_i(\hat{W_\bullet}) \sqsubseteq \hat{\sigma}(u)$$

Fig. 13. Flow Logic specification for pattern match analysis

We briefly mention a technical issue before continuing with specification of the analysis: the handling of dynamic creation of locations. In order to avoid having the analysis keep track of a potentially infinite number of locations we define and use so-called *canonical names* that divides all concrete location names and location variables into equivalence classes in such a way that all (new) location names generated at the same program point belong to the same equivalence class and thus share the same canonical name. The canonical name (equivalence class) of a location or location variable, ℓ, is written $\lfloor \ell \rfloor$. In the interest of legibility we use a *unique representative* for each equivalence class and thereby dispense with the $\lfloor \cdot \rfloor$ notation whenever possible. We avoid possible inconsistencies in the security policy for two locations with the same canonical names we only consider policies that are *compatible* with the choice of canonical names; a policy is compatible if and only if $\lfloor \ell_1 \rfloor = \lfloor \ell_2 \rfloor \Rightarrow \delta(\ell_1) = \delta(\ell_2)$. This implies that the policy assigns the exact same set of capabilities to all locations with the same canonical name. Throughout this paper we assume that policies are compatible with the chosen canonical names.

A separate Flow Logic specification, shown in Figure 13, is developed in order to track the pattern matching performed by both the input actions.

Having specified the analysis it remains to be shown that the information computed by the analysis is correct. In the Flow Logic framework this is usually done by establishing a *subject reduction* property for the analysis:

Theorem 1 (Subject Reduction). *If* $(\hat{T}, \hat{\sigma}, \mathcal{I}) \models_N N$ *and* $L \vdash N \succ\!\!\longrightarrow_{\mathcal{I}} L' \vdash N'$ *then* $(\hat{T}, \hat{\sigma}, \mathcal{I}) \models_N N'$.

Proof. (Sketch) By induction on the structure of $L \vdash N \succ\!\!\longrightarrow_{\mathcal{I}} L' \vdash N'$ and using auxiliary results for the other judgements.

Now we return to the abstract system model for our example (Figure 10). To analyse it, we replace the two process variables J and U with processes as specified in Figure 14. The janitor process J moves from the janitor's workshop location JAN to the server room SRV where he picks up a the review for the insider paper from the printer (**in** ("review", "insiderpaper", $!r$) @PRT). The user U prints the review from PC1 via the print server PC2. The two interesting locations for the control-flow analysis are JAN and USR, where processes J and U are plugged in, respectively. When analysing U, the analysis starts by

$J \stackrel{\triangle}{=}$ **eval** (**in** (("review", "insiderpaper", !r)) @PRT) @SRV

$U \stackrel{\triangle}{=}$ **eval** (**eval** (**out** (("review", "insiderpaper", "accept")) @PRT) @PC2) @PC1

Fig. 14. Processes for the janitor and the user analysed in the abstract system model from Figure 10

analysing **eval** (**out** ($\cdots$) @PRT) @PC2, resulting in an analysis of the action **out** (("review", "insiderpaper", "accept")) @PRT. As specified in Figure 12, this results in the tuple ("review", "insiderpaper", "accept") being stored in $\hat{T}$(PRT), representing the fact that the user started a print job at the print server, and the resulting document ended up in the printer. The analysis of J results in analysing **in** (("review", "insiderpaper", !r)) @PRT, which tries to read a tuple matching the first two components from the tuple space at locations PRT. Since that is available after U has been analysed, the local variable r contains the string "accept", even though the janitor might not be authorised to access this data. Note that for sake of simplicity we do not have added security classifications to our model, but any mechanism could easily be added on top of the model and the analysis.

5   Related Work

Recently, insiders and the insider threat [13,14,3,2] have attracted increased attention due to the potential damage an insider can cause. Bishop [1] gives an overview of different definitions and provides unified definition, which is the basis for our work. By separating the reachability analysis from the actual threat, we are able to easily model other definitions of the insider threat, or insiders that are more capable.

While the aforementioned papers discuss the insider problem, only very little work can be found on the static analysis of system models with respect to a potential insider threat. Chinchani *et al.* [4] describe a modelling methodology which captures several aspects of the insider threat. Their model is also based on graphs, but the main purpose of their approach is to reveal possible attack strategies of an insider. They do so by modelling the system as a key challenge graph, where nodes represent physical entities that store some information or capability. Protections like, e.g., the cipher locks in our example, are modelled as key challenges. For legitimate accesses these challenges incur no costs, while for illegitimate accesses they incur a higher cost representing the necessary "work" to guess or derive the key. The difference to our approach is that they start with a set of target nodes and compute an attack that compromises these nodes. However, it is mostly unclear how the cost of breaking a key challenge is determined. We are currently working on incorporating probabilities into our model to express the likelihood of a certain capability being acquired by a malicious insider. It might be interesting to incorporate this into

Chinchani's approach and to execute our analysis on their graphs to compare these two approaches.

In a more general setting, fault trees have been used for analysing for system failures [7]. However, they have not been used to model attacks, but to compute the chance of combinations of faults to occur. Beside these, graphs have been used in different settings to analyse attacks on networks. Examples include privilege graphs [5,11] and attack graphs [15]. The major difference to our work is the level of detail in modelling static and dynamic properties of the system, and the ability to analyse the dynamic behaviour of actors.

6 Conclusion and Future Work

One of the most insidious problems in information security is that of protecting against attacks from an insider. Even though the problem is well recognised in the security community as well as in law-enforcement and intelligence communities, there has been relatively little focused research into developing models and techniques for analysing and solving (parts of) the problem. The main measure taken still is to audit log files *after* an insider incident has occurred.

We have presented a formal model that allows to *formally define* a notion of insider attacks and thereby enables to study systems and analyse the potential consequences of such an attack. Formal modelling and analysis is increasingly important in a modern computing environment with widely distributed systems, computing grids, and service-oriented architectures, where the line between insider and outsider is more blurred than ever.

The two components of our model—an abstract high-level system model based on graphs and the process calculus *acKlaim*—are expressive enough to allow easy modelling of real-world systems, and detailed enough to allow expressive analysis results. On the system model, we use reachability analysis to identify possible vulnerabilities and actions that an audit should check for, by computing locations that actors in the system can reach and/or access—independent of the actual actions they perform. On the abstract acKlaim model we perform a control-flow analysis of specific processes/actors to determine which locations a specific process may reach, which actions it may execute, and which data it may read. This can be compared to an after-the-fact audit of log files. To the best of our knowledge this is the first attempt in applying static analysis techniques to tackle the insider problem, and to support and pre-compute possible audit results. By separating the actual threat and attack from reachability, we can easily put existing models and formalisms on top of our model.

The main limitation of the analysis described in this paper is that we assume that all actions are logged. We are currently on adding logging to system specifications, and on extensions of this model to *malicious* insiders, who try to obtain keys as part of their actions in a system. Further we plan to extend both the system model and the precision and granularity of our analyses. In the policy model we are looking at how to integrate policies like *"only in the case of fire"* as mentioned in Section 2.1.

References

1. Bishop, M.: The Insider Problem Revisited. In: Proc. of New Security Paradigms Workshop 2005, Lake Arrowhead, CA, USA, Septenber 2005. ACM Press, NewYork (2005)
2. Caruso, V.L.: Outsourcing information technology and the insider threat. Master's thesis, Air Force Inst. of Technology, Wright-Patterson Air Force Base, Ohio (2003)
3. CERT/US Secret Service: Insider threat study: Illicit cyber activity in the banking and finance sector (August 2004) available at www.cert.org/archive/pdf/bankfin040820.pdf
4. Chinchani, R., Iyer, A., Ngo, H.Q., Upadhyaya, S.: Towards a theory of insider threat assessment. In: Proceedings of the 2005 International Conference on Dependable Systems and Networks, pp. 108–117. IEEE Computer Society Press, Los Alamitos (2005)
5. Dacier, M., Deswarte, Y.: Privilege graph: an extension to the typed access matrix model. In: Proceedings of the European Symposium On Research In Computer Security (1994)
6. Gollmann, D.: Insider Fraud. In: Christianson, B., Crispo, B., Harbison, W.S., Roe, M. (eds.) Security Protocols. LNCS, vol. 1550, pp. 213–219. Springer, Heidelberg (1999)
7. Gorski, J., Wardzinski, A.: Formalising fault trees. In: Redmill, F., Anderson, T. (eds.) Achievement and Assurance of Safety: Proceedings of the 3rd Safety-critical Systems Symposium, Brighton, pp. 311–328. Springer, Heidelberg (1995)
8. Hansen, R.R., Probst, C.W., Nielson, F.: Sandboxing in myKlaim. In: ARES'06. The First International Conference on Availability, Reliability and Security, Vienna, Austria, April 2006, IEEE Computer Society, Los Alamitos (2006)
9. Nicola, R.D., Ferrari, G., Pugliese, R.: KLAIM: a Kernel Language for Agents Interaction and Mobility. IEEE Transactions on Software Engineering 24(5), 315–330 (1998)
10. Nielson, H.R., Nielson, F.: Flow Logic: a multi-paradigmatic approach to static analysis. In: Mogensen, T.E., Schmidt, D.A., Sudborough, I.H. (eds.) The Essence of Computation. LNCS, vol. 2566, Springer, Heidelberg (2002)
11. Ortalo, R., Deswarte, Y., Kaâniche, M.: Experimenting with quantitative evaluation tools for monitoring operational security. IEEE Transactions on Software Engineering 25(5), 633–650 (1999)
12. Patzakis, J.: New incident response best practices: Patch and proceed is no longer acceptable incident response procedure. White Paper, Guidance Software, Pasadena, CA (September 2003)
13. Anderson, R.H., Brackney, R.C.: Understanding the Insider Threat. RAND Corporation, Santa Monica, CA, U.S.A., March 2005 (2005)
14. Shaw, E.D., Ruby, K.G., Post, J.M.: The insider threat to information systems. Security Awareness Bulletin No. 2-98, Department of Defense Security Institute September 1998 (1998)
15. Swiler, L., Phillips, C., Ellis, D., Chakerian, S.: Computer-attack graph generation tool (June 12, 2001)

Maintaining Information Flow Security Under Refinement and Transformation

Fredrik Seehusen[1,2] and Ketil Stølen[1,2]

[1] SINTEF Information and Communication Technology, Norway
[2] University of Oslo, Norway
{fse,kst}@sintef.no

Abstract. We address the problem of maintaining information flow security under refinement and transformation. To this end we define a schema for the specification of secure information flow properties and show that all security properties defined in the schema are preserved by a notion of refinement. Refinement is a process that requires human guidance and is in general not subject for automation. A transformation on the other hand, is an executable function mapping specifications to specifications. We define an interpretation of transformations and propose a condition under which transformations maintain security.

1 Introduction

We address the problem of maintaining information flow security during the process of making an abstract specification more concrete. This problem has received little attention, yet it is of relevance in any real-life scenario in which security analysis is carried out on the basis of a specification that abstracts away details of the full implementation. For example, it is of little help to know that Java code or some state machine specification is secure w.r.t. some property if validity of the property is not maintained by the compiler. Hence, we need means and a corresponding theory to ensure that the transformation from the abstract level to the more concrete level *maintains* the security of the abstract level.

Proving security once and for all is in general not possible. One reason for this is that the concrete level often includes peculiarities that do not have any abstract equivalent. Consequently security must be proven again at the concrete level to ensure that these additional peculiarities introduced via transformation do not violate security. Although additional verification is often needed at the concrete level, we still want to check and maintain security properties on the basis of the abstract specifications. There are three main reasons for this. First, analysis is in general more feasible at the abstract level since the concrete level may include too much detail to make analysis practical. Second, abstract specifications are in general more platform independent than concrete specifications. This means that analysis results are more reusable at the abstract levels. Third, abstract specifications tend to be more understandable than concrete specifications, hence it is in general easier to specify and check security requirements at abstract levels as opposed to the concrete levels.

In this paper we consider security in the sense of *secure information flow* properties (see e.g. [4,5,16]). The notion of secure information flow provides a way of specifying

T. Dimitrakos et al. (Eds.): FAST 2006, LNCS 4691, pp. 143–157, 2007.

security requirements by selecting a set of observers, i.e. abstractions of system entities, and then restricting allowed flow of information between the observers.

The process of making an abstract specification more detailed is known as *refinement*, and the relationship between information flow security and refinement has been researched for a fairly long time. In 1989 it was shown by Jacob [13] that secure information flow properties in general are not preserved by the standard notion of refinement. It has later been observed that the problem originates in the inability of most specification languages to distinguish between underspecification and unpredictability[1] [10,14,19]. We argue that this distinction is essential if secure information flow properties are to be preserved under refinement. To this end, both the standard notion of refinement and all secure information flow properties proposed in literature have to be redefined such that this distinction is taken into consideration. We show how to do this in a formalism similar to STAIRS [7,8,9] by defining a schema (based on [16]) for specifying secure information flow properties such that all properties defined in the schema are preserved by refinement.

Refinement is a relation on specifications that formalizes the process of stepwise development by the removal of underspecification. A transformation on the other hand is a computable function mapping specifications to specifications. For example, a compiler mapping a program to machine code is a kind of transformation. Currently, there is much ongoing work on transformation in relation to OMG's standardization activities on MDA (Model Driven Architecture) [18], where transformations characterize the mapping of PIM's (Platform Independent Model) to PSM's (Platform Specific Model). Motivated by this we give a semantic interpretation of transformations and propose a condition under which transformations maintain security.

In summary, the main contributions of this paper are: (1) the definition of a schema for specifying secure information flow properties that are preserved by the STAIRS notion of refinement. (2) The definition of a notion of secure transformation that preserves security properties defined in our schema.

This paper is structured as follows: Sect. 2 formalizes a notion of *system specification*. Sect. 3 describes what is meant by secure information flow. In Sect. 4 we present the STAIRS notion of refinement and propose a schema for specifying secure information flow properties that are preserved by this notion of refinement. In Sect. 5, we discuss security maintaining transformations. Sect. 6 provides conclusions and related work.

2   System Specifications

We model the input-output behavior of systems by finite sequences of *events* called *traces*. An event represents the *transmission* or the *reception* of a message. Formally, an event is a pair (k, m) consisting of a kind k and a message m. An event whose kind equals ! represents the transmission of a message, whereas an event whose kind equals ? represents the reception of a message. A message is a triple (a_1, a_2, s) consisting of a transmitter a_1, a receiver a_2, and a signal s representing the message body. Both

---

[1] Also termed *probabilistic non-determinism* [19].

transmitters and receivers are referred to as *agents*, i.e. system entities such as objects or components.

Definition 1. *The semantics of a system specification, denoted Φ, is a prefix-closed set of traces. A set of traces A is prefix-closed iff*

$$t \in A \wedge t' \sqsubseteq t \Rightarrow t' \in A$$

where $\sqsubseteq$ is the standard prefix ordering on sequences.

The reason why we require prefix-closure is that the definition of many secure information flow properties proposed in literature rely on this requirement [16,24].

In the sequel, we will for short write "specification" instead "the semantics of system specification" when it clear from the context what is meant.

2.1 Notational Convention

We define some notational conventions and standard operations. $\mathbb{P}(A)$ denotes the power set of A defined $\{X | X \subseteq A\}$. A^* denotes the set of all finite sequences over the set A. A sequence of *events*, i.e. a trace, is written $\langle e_1, e_2, ..., e_n \rangle$. The empty trace, i.e. the trace with no events is written $\langle \rangle$. The *projection* of a trace t on a set of events E, written $t|_E$, is obtained from t by deleting all elements not in E.

Further notational conventions are listed in Table 1. Here the notion $a \in A$ means that the set A is ranged over by a.

Table 1. Notational conventions

Set	Definition	Meaning	Set	Definition	Meaning
$a \in \mathcal{A}$		Set of agents.	$e \in \mathcal{E}$	$\{!, ?\} \times \mathcal{M}$	Set of events.
$o \in \mathcal{O}$	$\mathbb{P}(\mathcal{A})$	Set of observers.	$h \in \mathcal{H}$		Set of high-lvl. events.
$s \in \mathcal{S}$		Set of signals.	$l \in \mathcal{L}$		Set of low-lvl. events.
$m \in \mathcal{M}$	$\mathcal{A} \times \mathcal{A} \times \mathcal{S}$	Set of messages.	$t \in \mathcal{T}$	$\mathcal{E}^*$	Set of traces.

3   Information Flow Security

By secure information flow we understand a restriction on allowed flow of information between *observers*, i.e. sets of agents. Secure information flow can be described by a *flow policy* and a *secure information flow predicate*, referred to as a security predicate for short. The flow policy restricts information flow between observers, while the security predicate defines what is meant by information flow. Formally, a flow policy is a relation on observers

$$\not\rightarrow \subseteq \mathcal{O} \times \mathcal{O}$$

where $(o_1, o_2) \in \not\rightarrow$ requires that there shall be no information flow from o_1 to o_2.

For simplicity, we will in the sequel assume a fixed flow policy $\{(H, L)\}$ consisting of two observers only: H, the high-level observer and L, the low-level observer.

Security predicates that describe what is meant by information flow are expressed in terms of the observations that observers can make. Formally, the *observation* that an observer o can make of a trace t is obtained from t by deleting all events that can not be observed by o:

$$t|_{(\text{E}.o)}$$

Here E.o yields the set of all events that can be observed by o, i.e. all events that can be transmitted from or received by the agents in o:

$$\text{E}.o \triangleq \{(k, (a, a', m)) \in \mathcal{E} \mid (k =! \wedge a \in o) \vee (k =? \wedge a' \in o)\}$$

For short, we let $\mathcal{L}$ and $\mathcal{H}$ denote E.L and E.H, respectively.

To ensure that L cannot observe high-level events directly, we demand that $\mathcal{H} \cap \mathcal{L} = \emptyset$. This alone does not in general prevent information flow from H to L because L may *infer* confidential information from H based on the observations that L can make. A central notion in defining what is meant by inferences is that of *low-level indistinguishability*.

Definition 2. *Two traces t and t' are indistinguishable from L's point of view, written $t \sim_l t'$, iff*

$$t|_{\mathcal{L}} = t'|_{\mathcal{L}}$$

That is, iff L's observation of t is equal to L's observation of t'.

In the sequel we assume that L has complete knowledge of the specification Φ that describes the set of all possible behaviors represented by traces. This means that L may construct the set of all traces in Φ that are indistinguishable or compatible with a given observation. Formally, L may from the observation of any trace t, construct a so-called *low-level equivalence set* [24] (abbreviated LLES in the sequel):

$$\{t' \in \Phi \mid t \sim_l t'\}$$

In other words, if L makes an observation t, then L can infer that some trace in the LLES constructed from t has occurred, but not which one. Security predicates must demand that L shall not be able to deduce confidential information from the LLESs that L may construct. This is illustrated in the following example.

Example 1. Let $\Phi = \{\langle\rangle, \langle l_1\rangle, \langle h_1\rangle, \langle h_2\rangle, \langle h_1, l_1\rangle, \langle h_1, l_2\rangle, \langle h_2, l_2\rangle\}$, and assume that L may observe events l_1 and l_2 and that h_1 and h_2 are high-level events. Assume further a definition of security that states that L shall not with certainty be able to infer that a high-level event has occurred. If L makes the observation $\langle l_1\rangle$, then L may infer that either trace $\langle l_1\rangle$ or trace $\langle h_1, l_1\rangle$ have occurred. Since L cannot know which of these has occurred (because L cannot observe high-level events directly), and the former trace does not contain any high-level events, L cannot infer with certainty that a high-level event has occurred. If L on the other hand observes the trace $\langle l_2\rangle$, then L can infer that $\langle h_1, l_2\rangle$ or $\langle h_2, l_2\rangle$ have occurred. Again, L does not know which of these has occurred, but since both traces contain a high-level event and there are no other traces in Φ that are compatible with L's observation, L can infer with certainty that a high-level event has occurred. Hence, Φ is not secure w.r.t. our definition of security.

In order for Φ to be secure, one must demand that the LLESs that L can construct be *closed* w.r.t. some criterion [16]. In the above example, this amounts to demanding that there must be a trace with no high-level events in each LLES that L can construct.

3.1 Mantel's Assembly Kit

The schema we propose for describing security predicates is based on a schema proposed by Mantel [16]. He presents an assembly kit in which different notions of security can be defined. We give here a brief description of this assembly kit. The reader is referred to [16] for a more details.

In Mantel's framework, security properties are represented as *security predicates* where a security predicate SP is either a single *basic security predicate* BSP, or a conjunction of basic security predicates. Each basic security predicate BSP demands that for any trace t of the specification Φ there must be another trace t' that is indistinguishable from t from L's point of view, and which fulfills a condition Q, the *closure requirement* of BSP. The existence of t', however, is only required if a condition R, the *restriction* of BSP, holds. This results in the following schema for the formal definition of basic security predicates:

Definition 3. *Specification Φ satisfies the basic security predicate* $\mathrm{BSP}_{QR}(\Phi)$ *for restriction R and closure requirement Q iff*

$$\forall t \in \Phi \cdot R(\Phi, t) \Rightarrow \exists t' \in \Phi \cdot t \sim_l t' \wedge Q(t, t') \tag{1}$$

Example 2. The notion of security that is informally described in Ex. 1, may be defined by instantiating the schema as follows: $R \triangleq \mathrm{TRUE}$, and $Q \triangleq t'|_{\mathcal{H}} = \langle\rangle$. That is, for every trace t there must be a trace t' such that t' is indistinguishable from t w.r.t. L and such that t' does not contain any high-level events.

4 Refinement

Refinement is the process of making an abstract specification more concrete by removing underspecification. The standard notion of refinement [11] states that a system specification Φ' is a refinement of a system specification Φ iff

$$\Phi' \subseteq \Phi \tag{2}$$

Intuitively, there are at least as many implementations that satisfy Φ as there are implementations that satisfy Φ'. In this sense Φ' describes its set of implementations more accurately than Φ, ergo Φ' is less abstract than Φ.

The reason why secure information flow properties are not preserved by refinement becomes apparent when one considers again the manner in which these properties are defined (see Def. 3). That is, Φ is secure if some of its traces satisfy the closure requirement Q. However, by (2) there is no guarantee that a refinement of Φ will include those traces that satisfy Q, hence secure information flow properties are in general not preserved by refinement.

Intuitively, the cause of this problem is that security properties depend on unpredictability. E.g. the strength of ones password may be measured in terms of how hard it is for an attacker to guess the password one has chosen. The closure requirement Q may be seen as the security predicate's requirement of unpredictability, but traces that provide this unpredictability may be removed during refinement. This motivates a re-definition of the notions of specification and refinement where the distinction between underspecification and unpredictability is taken into consideration.

Definition 4. *A system specification, denoted Ω, is a set of trace sets. Each trace set in a specification is called an obligation. We demand that the set obtained by collapsing Ω into a set of traces must be prefix-closed, i.e. we demand*

$$t \in \widehat{\Omega} \wedge t' \sqsubseteq t \Rightarrow t' \in \widehat{\Omega}$$

where $\widehat{\Omega}$ is defined $\bigcup_{\phi \in \Omega} \phi$.

Definition 5. *System specification Ω' is a refinement of system specification Ω, written $\Omega \rightsquigarrow \Omega'$, iff*

$$(\forall \phi \in \Omega \cdot \exists \phi' \in \Omega' \cdot \phi' \subseteq \phi) \wedge (\forall \phi' \in \Omega' \cdot \exists \phi \in \Omega \cdot \phi' \subseteq \phi)$$

This corresponds to so-called limited refinement in STAIRS [20]. For an arbitrary obligation ϕ at the abstract level, there must be an obligation ϕ' at the concrete level such that ϕ' is a refinement of ϕ in the sense of the standard notion of refinement (see (2)). Moreover, each obligation at the concrete level must be a refinement of an obligation at the abstract level. The latter ensures that behavior that was not considered at the abstract level is not introduced at the concrete level.

The intuition is that the traces within the same obligation may provide underspecification, while the obligations provide unpredictability in the sense that an implementation is required to fulfill all obligations of a specification. Any valid implementation must potentially exhibit the behavior described by at least one trace in each obligation. By implementation we understand a specification with no underspecification. Given some program P, let $Traces(P)$ be the prefix-closed set of traces that can be generated by executing P, and let

$$[\![P]\!] \triangleq \{ \{t\} \mid t \in Traces(P) \}$$

Then P implements specification Ω iff

$$\Omega \rightsquigarrow [\![P]\!]$$

Example 3. Let $\Omega = \{\{\langle\rangle\}, \{\langle l \rangle\}, \{\langle l \rangle, \langle h_1 \rangle, \langle h_2 \rangle, \langle h_1, l \rangle, \langle h_2, l \rangle\}\}$, and assume that it is confidential that high-level events have occurred. Ω is secure in this respect; it is easy to verify that this holds for all implementations of Ω.

Lemma 1. $\rightsquigarrow$ *is transitive[2]:*

$$\Omega \rightsquigarrow \Omega' \wedge \Omega' \rightsquigarrow \Omega'' \Rightarrow \Omega \rightsquigarrow \Omega''$$

---

[2] The proofs of all the results in this paper can be in [22].

Instances of the schema of Def. 3 are in general not preserved by our notion of refinement. We need to modify the schema such that the distinction of unpredictability and underspecification is exploited. Instead of demanding that there is a trace t' that satisfies some criterion, we demand that there is an *obligation* ϕ such that all its traces satisfy that criterion.

Definition 6. *Specification Ω satisfies the basic security predicate* $\text{BSP}_{QR}(\Omega)$ *for restriction R and closure requirement Q iff*

$$\forall t \in \widehat{\Omega} \cdot R(\widehat{\Omega}, t) \Rightarrow \exists \phi \in \Omega \cdot \forall t' \in \phi \cdot t \sim_{\text{I}} t' \wedge Q(t, t')$$

The intuition of (Def. 6) is that obligations, as opposed to individual traces, may be seen as providing the unpredictability required by instances of the schema. Note that the schema may be instantiated by the same instances of R and Q that are presented in Mantel's paper.

In order to ensure that instances of the schema are preserved by refinement, we need to disallow some restrictions R whose truth value depend on the absence of traces. We therefore require that all restrictions R satisfy the following condition

$$(T' \subseteq T \wedge R(T', t)) \Rightarrow R(T, t) \tag{3}$$

for arbitrary traces t and trace sets T and T'. All instances of R presented in Mantel's paper satisfy condition (3).

Theorem 1. BSP_{QR} *is preserved by refinement for arbitrary restrictions R satisfying (3) and closure requirements Q:*

$$\Omega \rightsquigarrow \Omega' \wedge \text{BSP}_{QR}(\Omega) \Rightarrow \text{BSP}_{QR}(\Omega')$$

The notion of refinement introduced above corresponds to what is often referred to as property refinement or behavioral refinement [2]. Property refinement does not capture change in data-structure, i.e. the replacement of abstract event representations by concrete event representations. This is in contrast to refinement notions such as data refinement [12], interface refinement [2], or action refinement [23] which roughly speaking may be understood as property refinement modulo a translation between the concrete and the abstract data structure. Our notion of property refinement may be generalized into a notion of action refinement (actually event refinement in our case) using upwards and downwards simulation [3,12] in a fairly standard manner. To characterize under which conditions this notion of refinement is security preserving is, however, far from trivial. In the following, attention is restricted to a special case of this problem, namely under which conditions *transformations* are security preserving. A transformation may be understood a special case of action refinement where the concrete specification is generated automatically from the abstract specification.

5   Transformation

The notion of refinement addressed above is a binary relation on specifications that formalizes the process of stepwise development by removal of underspecification. A

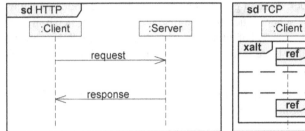
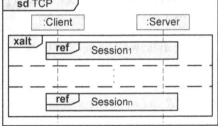

Fig. 1. HTTP to TCP

transformation on the other hand is an executable function taking an abstract syntactic specification as input and yielding a concrete syntactic specification as output. Thus transformation is a syntactic notion. Since security properties are defined on the semantics of specifications (i.e. on traces), we define a semantic interpretation of transformations which enables us to assert whether a transformation maintains security.

In Sect. 5.1, we give an example of a transformation that motivates our semantic interpretation of transformations given in Sect. 5.2. In Sect. 5.3, we propose a condition under which interpretations of transformations maintain security. Sect. 5.4 gives an example that clarifies some of the points made in Sect. 5.3.

5.1 Example: Transforming HTTP Specifications to TCP Specifications

The HTTP protocol is bound to the TCP protocol. One way of doing this binding during runtime is to create a new so-called TCP session for each HTTP request-response pair. A TCP-session consists of three phases: First a connection is established between the two sides of communication, then the HTTP request and response messages are segmented, encapsulated by TCP frames, and transmitted. Finally the connection is explicitly terminated.

A transformation that takes a specification that describes communication at the HTTP level and produces a specification that describes communication at the TCP level may be defined in accordance to how the HTTP protocol is bound to the TCP protocol. Such a transformation may be regarded as a transformation from the abstract to the concrete if one takes HTTP specifications as being at the abstract level and TCP specifications as being at the concrete level.

The UML interaction diagram on the left hand side of Fig. 1 describes a simple communication scenario at the HTTP level. The diagram on the right hand side is the result of applying a transformation from HTTP to TCP to the HTTP diagram. Here the so-called **xalt**-operator from STAIRS [8] specifies unpredictability[3] between different interaction scenarios. The **ref**-operator references other interaction diagrams that in this example describe different TCP-sessions. The reason why the HTTP request-response pair described in the diagram on the left hand side is translated to more than one TCP-session is that the TCP protocol must handle issues that are transparent at the HTTP

---

[3] Termed explicit non-deterministic choice in STAIRS.

level, e.g. message overtaking. One TCP session may for example describe the situation in which messages are received in the same order that they are transmitted, another may describe the situation in which this is not the case and so on. The reader is referred to [7,8,9,21] to see how UML interaction diagrams can be given trace semantics.

To assert whether the transformation from HTTP to TCP maintains security, we need to interpret the transformation in terms of how abstract traces (representing HTTP communication) are translated to concrete traces (representing TCP communication). There are three considerations that need to be taken into account when defining such an interpretation. First, an abstract trace may correspond to several concrete traces. The reasons for this is that TCP protocol must handle issues that are transparent at the HTTP level. Second, an abstract event may be decomposed into several concrete events because each HTTP package may be segmented into more than one TCP package during the TCP transmission phase. Third, there may be traces at the concrete level that have no abstract equivalent. To see this, let $\langle e \rangle$ represent the transmission of a HTTP package. Since a HTTP package may be segmented into several TCP packages, $\langle e \rangle$ may for example be translated into the trace $\langle e_1, e_2, e_3 \rangle$ where events e_1, e_2, and e_3 represent the transmission of TCP packages. Traces $\langle e_1 \rangle$ and $\langle e_1, e_2 \rangle$ may also be valid traces at the TCP level (these traces are in fact required to be present in a concrete specification since we assume that specifications are prefix-closed). Now, the TCP trace $\langle e_1, e_2, e_3 \rangle$ corresponds to $\langle e \rangle$ at the HTTP level since the TCP trace is *complete* in the sense that it represents the transmission of the entire HTTP message. But what about the TCP traces $\langle e_1 \rangle$ and $\langle e_1, e_2 \rangle$, do these traces correspond to $\langle e \rangle$ at the abstract level? The answer is no if the trace $\langle e \rangle$ is meant to represent the transmission of an entire HTTP package. The TCP traces $\langle e_1 \rangle$ and $\langle e_1, e_2 \rangle$ do not correspond to the empty HTTP trace ($\langle \rangle$) either, because the empty trace is meant (by any reasonable interpretation) to represent a scenario in which no communication occurs. From this we can conclude that, in general, there may be traces at the concrete level for which there are no corresponding traces at the abstract level.

5.2 Transformations from a Semantic Perspective

Syntactically, a transformation is an executable function translating abstract (syntactic) specifications to concrete (syntactic) specifications. Semantically, we interpret traces in terms of how abstract traces are translated to concrete traces.

In the following, let A denote some fixed but arbitrary abstract syntactic specification, T be a some transformation, and $T(A)$ denote the concrete specification obtained by applying T to A. Let Ω_a denote the semantics of A and Ω_c denote the semantics of $T(A)$. T is interpreted by a set of functions

$$F \subseteq \widehat{\Omega}_a \rightarrow \widehat{\Omega}_c$$

mapping traces in Ω_a to traces in Ω_c. The reason why we use a set of functions and not a single function is, as explained in the example, that a syntactic transformation may represent the same abstract trace by several concrete traces.

We say that the set of functions F is a *valid interpretation* of T w.r.t. A if Ω_c is a *translation* of Ω_a w.r.t. F as defined below. We first define the notion of translation for obligations, then we lift this notion to (semantic) specifications.

Definition 7. *Obligation ϕ_c is a translation of obligation ϕ_a w.r.t. function f, written $\phi_a \hookrightarrow_f \phi_c$, iff*

$$\phi_c \subseteq \{f(t) \,|\, t \in \phi_a\}$$

Definition 8. *Specification Ω_c is a translation of specification Ω_a w.r.t. interpretation F, written, $\Omega_a \hookrightarrow_F \Omega_c$, iff*

$$\forall f \in F \cdot \forall \phi_a \in \Omega_a \cdot \exists \phi_c \in \Omega_c \cdot \phi_a \hookrightarrow_f \phi_c$$

Our interpretation of transformations is similar to data refinement in that both notions roughly speaking may be understood as refinement modulo a translation of traces. More precisely:

Lemma 2. *Let Ω_c be contained in the image of Ω_a under the identity transformation id, then*

$$\Omega_a \hookrightarrow_{id} \Omega_c \Leftrightarrow \Omega_a \rightsquigarrow \Omega_c$$

Here $im(\Omega_a, F)$, the *image* of Ω_a under some F, is the set of obligations that are translations of obligations in Ω_a w.r.t. F:

$$im(\Omega_a, F) \triangleq \{\phi_c \,|\, \exists \phi_a \in \Omega_a \cdot \exists f \in F \cdot \phi_a \hookrightarrow_f \phi_c\} \tag{4}$$

A concrete specification is not necessarily contained in the image of the abstract specification it is translated from. The reason for this is, as explained in the previous example, that there may be concrete traces that do not have any abstract equivalent.

If F_1 and F_2 are interpretations, then $F_1 \circ F_2$ is understood as the interpretation obtained by functional point-to-point composition of all functions from F_1 and F_2. That is,

$$F_1 \circ F_2 \triangleq \{f_1 \circ f_2 \,|\, f_1 \in F_1 \wedge f_2 \in F_2\} \tag{5}$$

where $f_1 \circ f_2(t) = f_1(f_2(t))$.

Lemma 3. $\hookrightarrow$ *is transitive:*

$$\Omega_0 \hookrightarrow_{F_1} \Omega_1 \wedge \Omega_1 \hookrightarrow_{F_2} \Omega_2 \Rightarrow \Omega_0 \hookrightarrow_{F_2 \circ F_1} \Omega_2$$

We denote by $F^{-1}(t_c)$, the set of all traces in $\widehat{\Omega}_a$ that can be translated to t_c by the functions in F:

$$F^{-1}(t_c) \triangleq \{t_a \in \widehat{\Omega}_a \,|\, \exists f \in F \cdot f(t_a) = t_c\} \tag{6}$$

5.3   Secure Transformations

A transformation T maintains the security of an abstract specification A if there is a *valid secure interpretation* of T w.r.t. A. The notion of secure interpretation obviously depends on what is meant by secure, and should therefore be parameterized by security properties. In doing so, one must take into account that the security requirement at the abstract level may be syntactically and semantically different from the "corresponding" security requirement at the concrete level. One reason for this is that events at the abstract level may differ from the events at the concrete level. Another reason is that there may be concrete traces that do not have any corresponding abstract trace. The concrete security requirement must therefore handle traces that may not be taken into account by the security requirement at the abstract level.

The notion of secure interpretation is formally defined in the following

Definition 9. *Let* $\Omega_a \hookrightarrow_F \Omega_c$, *then the interpretation F is secure w.r.t. the abstract and concrete restrictions* R_a *and* R_c *and abstract and concrete closure requirements* Q_a *and* Q_c *if the following conditions are satisfied*

$$R_c(\widehat{\Omega}_c, t_c) \Rightarrow \exists t' \in F^{-1}(t_c) \cdot R_a(\widehat{\Omega}_a, t') \tag{7}$$

$$(R_c(\widehat{\Omega}_c, t_c) \wedge \forall t' \in \phi_a \cdot t_a \sim_I t' \wedge Q_a(t_a, t')) \Rightarrow \\ \exists \phi_c \in \Omega_c \cdot \forall t' \in \phi_c \cdot t_c \sim_I t' \wedge Q_c(t_c, t') \tag{8}$$

for all $t_c \in \widehat{\Omega}_c$, $\phi_a \in \Omega_a$, *and* $t_a \in F^{-1}(t_c)$.

Def. 9 may be understood to capture a rule that allows us to exploit that we have established Q_a at the abstract level when establishing Q_c at the concrete level. We believe that verifying (7) and (8) in most practical situations will be straightforward and more feasible than checking the security property at the concrete level directly.

Put simply, the first condition of Def. 9 just ensures that the transformation does not weaken the restriction R. The second condition ensures that the transformation does not strengthen the closure requirement Q and that low-level equality is preserved.

It follows from (7) that the concrete restriction R_c must filter away (i.e. yield false for) the concrete traces t_c that do not have any corresponding abstract trace. This is reasonable because one cannot take advantage of the fact that the abstract specification is secure when proving that t_c does not compromise security. It may therefore be the case that a new security analysis must be carried out at the concrete level for those traces that do not have an abstract equivalent.

When we relate Def. 9 to rules that describe date refinement in an assumption / guarantee or pre-post setting, we note that weakening/strengthening is the other way around. E.g., when refining a pre-post specification, one may weaken the pre-condition and strengthen the post-condition. The reason is that a pre-post condition is a specification that is refined into another specification while a restriction-closure predicate is a property that has been proved to hold for a specification that is translated to a concrete specification and whose validity should be maintained.

Theorem 2. *Let F be a interpretation that is secure w.r.t. restrictions* R_a *and* R_c, *and closure requirements* Q_a *and* Q_c, *then F maintains security in the following sense:*

$$\mathrm{BSP}_{Q_a R_a}(\Omega_a) \wedge \Omega_a \hookrightarrow_F \Omega_c \Rightarrow \mathrm{BSP}_{Q_c R_c}(\Omega_c)$$

5.4 Example: Why Security Requirements Change

Let Ω_a be an abstract specification consisting of two clients c_l and c_h that communicate with a server s via the HTTP protocol (see Fig. 2). Assume that c_l, based on its

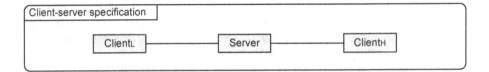

Fig. 2. Client-server example

observation of its communication with s and its knowledge of the system specification, should not be able to deduce information about the behavior of c_h. More formally, both the clients and the server can be represented as agents (recall the role of agents from Sect. 2). Thus the low-level observer is defined $\{c_l\}$ and the high-level observer is defined $\{c_h\}$. The security requirement on the HTTP level may be formalized by instantiating the schema of Def. 6 by some predicates R_a and Q_a.

Assume that F interprets a transformation from HTTP to TCP defined such that each event representing the transmission or reception of a HTTP message is translated into a complete (in the sense of the previous example) sequence of events describing the corresponding TCP messages. Let Ω_c be a translation of Ω_a w.r.t. F and assume that Ω_c also contains non-complete traces that do not correspond to any traces at the HTTP level.

Assume that Ω_a is secure (i.e. $\mathrm{BSP}_{R_a Q_a}(\Omega_a)$ is true) and that we want to check if the traces on the concrete level that have a corresponding abstract representation are secure w.r.t. our information flow property. In order to do this, we can create predicate on the concrete level that filters away those traces that do not have a corresponding abstract representation. More formally, the concrete restriction R_c is defined $R_c(\widehat{\Omega}, t) \triangleq R_a(\widehat{\Omega}, t) \wedge TCP\_OK(t)$ where TCP_OK is a predicate that yields true if the TCP trace t corresponds to a HTTP trace and false otherwise. Note that we are assuming that R_a may take HTTP traces as well as TCP traces as arguments. The concrete security property can now be obtained by instantiating the schema of Def. 6 by the predicates R_c and Q_a (since the closure requirement Q is left unchanged in this example).

If one wants to check that the TCP traces that do not correspond to any HTTP traces are secure w.r.t. some requirement, one cannot take advantage of the fact that Ω_a is secure. Therefore additional security analysis may be required w.r.t. these traces.

6   Conclusions and Related Work

In [21], we defined a secure information flow property in the semantics of STAIRS [7,8,9] and showed that this property was preserved by refinement and transformation. This paper simplifies and generalizes these results by considering, not only one, but many kinds of information flow properties. This paper also considers a more general notion of security preservation than considered in [21]. More precisely, this paper makes two contributions to the study of secure information flow. The first is a schema for specifying information flow properties that are preserved by the STAIRS notion of refinement. The second is the definition of a semantic interpretation of transformations and a condition under which transformations maintain security.

There are a number of papers related to information flow security and refinement. Jacob is the first person that we are aware of to show that secure information flow properties are not preserved by the traditional notion of refinement [13]. This became known as the *refinement paradox*. It has later been observed that this "paradox" is a manifestation of failing to clearly distinguish between underspecification and unpredictability. As far as we are aware of, this observation was first made in [19].

To the extent of our knowledge, the work of Heisel. et. al. [10] is similar to ours in that they both distinguish between underspecification and unpredictability and consider the notion of data refinement. The main differences between their work and ours are: (1) They work in a probabilistic setting, and thus their formalism differs from ours. (2) They do not consider information flow *properties* but a notion of confidentiality based on low-level indistinguishability only. (3) Their notion of confidentiality preserving refinement is different from ours in that they build the condition of confidentiality preservation into the definition of refinement. W.r.t. refinement, we have taken the dual approach of strengthening the notion of security.

The work of Jürjens [14,15] is also related to ours. Some of the main differences between his work and ours are: (1) His formalism differs from ours. (2) While Jürjens distinguishes between underspecification and unpredictability in order to define refinement preserving properties of confidentiality (secrecy) and integrity, he does not rely on this distinction in the definition of his information flow property. That is, the secure information flow property is satisfied iff each behavior refinement to a *deterministic* specification satisfies this property, i.e. he effectively closes the property under a notion of behavior refinement that does not distinguish between underspecification and unpredictability.

Three notable papers that addresses information flow security and refinement are [1,6,17]. The main difference between these papers and ours is that all these investigate conditions under which certain notions of refinement are security preserving without distinguishing between underspecification and unpredictability. Since this distinction is made in our formalism, we consider one notion of refinement only, and strengthen instead our notion of security in an intuitive manner. Hence, there is no need to propose conditions with which to check that a given refinements preserve security.

We are not aware of any work that explicitly address transformation and information flow security. Moreover, we are not aware of any work that show how to preserve secure information flow properties under a notion of refinement that takes the distinction of underspecification and unpredictability into consideration.

The main emphasis of this paper is on semantics. In future work, we will address syntactic transformations in more detail. We are also planning to address composition and transformation of security predicates. Eventually, we would like to develop a computerized tool that will check whether transformations maintain security.

Acknowledgments

This work has been funded by the Research Council of Norway through the project SE-CURIS (152839/220). We would like to thank the anonymous referees for their useful comments and suggestions.

References

1. Bossi, A., Focardi, R., Piazza, C., Rossi, S.: Refinement operators and information flow security. In: SEFM 2003. 1st International Conference on Software Engineering and Formal Methods, pp. 44–53. IEEE Computer Society Press, Los Alamitos (2003)
2. Broy, M., Stølen, K.: Specification and development of interactive systems. In: FOCUS on streams, interface, and refinement, Springer, Heidelberg (2001)
3. de Roever, W.-P., Engelhardt, K.: Data Refinement: Model-Oriented Proof Methods and their Comparison. In: Cambridge tracts on theoretical computer science, vol. 47, Cambridge University Press, Cambridge (1998)
4. Focardi, R., Gorrieri, R.: Classification of security properties (part i: Information flow). In: Focardi, R., Gorrieri, R. (eds.) Foundations of Security Analysis and Design. LNCS, vol. 2171, pp. 331–396. Springer, Heidelberg (2001)
5. Goguen, J.A., Meseguer, J.: Security policies and security models. In: IEEE Symposium on Security and Privacy, pp. 11–20. IEEE Computer Socity Press, Los Alamitos (1982)
6. Graham-Cumming, J., Sanders, J.W.: On the refinement of non-interference. In: Proceedings of the IEEE Computer Security Foundations Workshop, pp. 35–42. IEEE Computer Society Press, Los Alamitos (1991)
7. Haugen, Ø., Husa, K.E., Runde, R.K., Stølen, K.: Why timed sequence diagrams require three-event semantics. Research Report 309, Department of Informatics, University of Oslo (2004)
8. Haugen, Ø., Husa, K.E., Runde, R.K., Stølen, K.: STAIRS towards formal design with sequence diagrams. Journal of Software and Systems Modeling 4(4), 355–367 (2005)
9. Haugen, Ø., Stølen, K.: STAIRS – steps to analyse interactions with refinement semantics. In: Stevens, P., Whittle, J., Booch, G. (eds.) UML2003 - The Unified Modeling Language. Modeling Languages and Applications. LNCS, vol. 2863, pp. 388–402. Springer, Heidelberg (2003)
10. Heisel, M., Pfitzmann, A., Santen, T.: Confidentiality-preserving refinement. In: CSFW-14 2001. 14th IEEE Computer Security Foundations Workshop, pp. 295–306. IEEE Computer Society Press, Los Alamitos (2001)
11. Hoare, C.A.R.: Communicating Sequential Processes. Series in computer science. Prentice-Hall, Englewood Cliffs (1985)
12. Hoare, C.A.R., He, J., Sanders, J.W.: Prespecification in data refinement. Information Processing Letters 25(2), 71–76 (1987)
13. Jacob, J.: On the derivation of secure components. In: Proc. of the IEEE Symposium on Security and Privacy, pp. 242–247. IEEE Computer Society Press, Los Alamitos (1989)
14. Jürjens, J.: Secrecy-preserving refinement. In: Oliveira, J.N., Zave, P. (eds.) FME 2001. LNCS, vol. 2021, pp. 135–152. Springer, Heidelberg (2001)
15. Jürjens, J.: Secure systems development with UML. Springer, Heidelberg (2005)
16. Mantel, H.: Possibilistic definitions of security - an assembly kit. In: CSFW'00. IEEE Compuer Security Foundations Workshop, pp. 185–199. IEEE Computer Society Press, Los Alamitos (2000)
17. Mantel, H.: Preserving information flow properties under refinement. In: IEEE Symposium on Security and Privacy, pp. 78–91. IEEE Computer Society Press, Los Alamitos (2001)
18. Object Management Group.: Architecture Board ORMSC. Model Driven Architecture (MDA). Document number ormsc/2001-07-01 (2001)
19. Roscoe, A.: CSP and determinism in security modelling. In: IEEE Symposium on Security and Privacy, pp. 114–127. IEEE Computer Society Press, Los Alamitos (1995)
20. Runde, R.K., Haugen, Ø., Stølen, K.: Refining uml interactions with underspecification and nondeterminism. Nordic Journal of Computing 12(2), 157–188 (2005)

21. Seehusen, F., Stølen, K.: Information flow property preserving transformation of UML interaction diagrams. In: SACMAT 2006. 11th ACM Symposium on Access Control Models and Technologies, pp. 150–159. ACM Press, New York (2006)
22. Seehusen, F., Stølen, K.: Maintaining information flow security under refinement and transformation. Technical report SINTEF A311, SINTEF ICT (2006)
23. van Glabbeek, R.J., Goltz, U.: Refinement of actions and equivalence notions for concurrent systems. Acta Informatica 37(4/5), 229–327 (2001)
24. Zakinthinos, A., Lee, E.S.: A general theory of security properties. In: Proc. of the IEEE Computer Society Symposium on Research in Security and Privacy, pp. 94–102. IEEE Computer Society Press, Los Alamitos (1997)

A Classification of Delegation Schemes for Attribute Authority[*]

Ludwig Seitz, Erik Rissanen, and Babak Sadighi

SPOT, SICS
Box 1263, SE-16429 KISTA, Sweden
{ludwig, mirty, babak}@sics.se

Abstract. Recently *assertions* have been explored as a generalisation of certificates within access control. Assertions[1] are used to link arbitrary attributes (e.g. roles, security clearances) to arbitrary entities (e.g. users, resources). These attributes can then be used as identifiers in access control policies to refer to groups of users or resources.

In many applications attribute management does not happen within the access control system. External entities manage attribute assignments and issue assertions that are then used in the access control system. Some approaches also allow for the delegation of attribute authority, in order to spread the administrative workload. In such systems the consumers of attribute assertions issued by a delegated authority need a delegation verification scheme.

In this article we propose a classification for schemes that allow to verify delegated authority, with a focus on attribute assertion. Using our classification, one can deduce some advantages and drawbacks of different approaches to delegated attribute assertion.

1 Introduction

Attributes are currently regarded as the most generic way of referring to users and resources in access control systems. User identity, group memberships, security clearances, and roles can all be expressed using attributes. The eXtensible Access Control Markup Language (XACML)[1] uses attributes in order to specify applicable subjects, resources and actions in access control policies.

Access control systems are important components of distributed computing infrastructures (e.g. in Grid computing [2]). Often such infrastructures allow to share resources belonging to different entities, based on a mutually agreed access control policy. In order to enforce these policies locally for external users, the access control system needs to be capable to fetch attributes from external sources.

In complex cooperative scenarios, where different resources are administrated by different authorities and used by a variety of users, one can increase the efficiency of administration by delegating attribute authority. Delegation helps

---

[*] This work was carried out during the tenure of an ERCIM "Alain Bensoussan" Fellowship Programme.

[1] We use assertions synonymous for attribute certificates.

T. Dimitrakos et al. (Eds.): FAST 2006, LNCS 4691, pp. 158–169, 2007.

to spread the responsibility for specific security decisions to the people who are capable and in charge of taking them, instead of burdening a single administrator with it. This makes the system less error prone and makes it faster to implement attribute assignments on a local level.

In such a scenario, the problem arises how to verify whether an attribute assertion is valid and properly authorised. Various approaches for doing this exist, which all have different drawbacks and advantages.

In this article we present a method to classify different verification approaches based on two simple properties and present advantages and drawbacks of the various models based on our classification.

The remainder of this article is organised as follows: In section 2 we give a short overview of background knowledge necessary to reason about authority delegation. Section 3 presents related work. In section 4 we present our classification approach. We then discuss the advantages and drawbacks of the different models that can be obtained from the classification in section 5. Finally we summarise and give a conclusion in section 6.

2   Background

We assume an access control model, where every attribute has a *source of authority* (SOA), which is the initial entity that has the power to assign this attribute to other users. In our model a SOA can *delegate* administrative rights concerning the attribute, thus allowing other entities to act as *Attribute Authorities* (AA). Such a delegation allows an AA to assign attributes to entities and can also authorise further delegation of their authority. The delegation can be subject to conditions specified by its issuer, that constrain the authority it conveys.

The underlying delegation model that we implicitly use is more formally specified in the publications "Constrained Delegation" [3] and "Using Authority Certificates to Create Management Structures" [4].

3   Related Work

Attribute assertion has received intensive attention from the research community in the last years. As a result of this, two competing standards have emerged for issuing attribute assertions. Furthermore several systems using either one of these standards provide attribute assertion services. In this section we first discuss attribute assertion standards and then present some systems that use these standards to provide attribute assertion services.

3.1   Attribute Assertion Standards

The SAML [5] standard by the OASIS consortium defines an XML based syntax and protocols for requesting and providing different kinds of assertions, including attribute assertions. The current core specification of SAML does not address delegated assertions in any way. There are however proposals to use the existing extension points of SAML to address this issue. The first approach by Navarro et al. [6] is based on the same delegation model as our approach (see section 2). It uses assertion chains to verify delegated authority. The second approach by Wang et al. [7] uses a slightly different delegation model, however verification is also done with assertion chains.

RFC 3281 [8] defines a profile for attribute certificates (AC) based on the popular X.509 standard for authentication. The current profile specifically recommends not to support delegation because the administration and processing of AC chains is deemed to be too complex. Furthermore for each particular set of attributes only one SOA may exist that functions as AC issuer. However several systems using X.509 ACs have nevertheless implemented delegation mechanisms (c.f. next section).

3.2 Authority Delegation Approaches

The public key infrastructures (PKI) [9] have been dealing with a restricted form of attribute assertion since quite a while. Within PKI, the need for a delegation mechanism was quickly discovered. Therefore PKI implements a delegation mechanism based on *roots of trust* and *certificate chains*.

The PRIMA [10], [11] access control system, developed since 2003 at the Virginia Polytechnic Institute uses X.509 ACs to encode attribute assertions. PRIMA has implemented AC chain verification for delegation of attributes.

PERMIS [12] is a role based access control system that also uses X.509 ACs to provide attribute assertions (limited to role assignments). PERMIS makes use of a *Delegation Issuing Service* [13] in order to allow for delegation of attribute assertions. In this approach a delegation service issues attribute assertions on behalf of the attribute authorities. Three different modes of operation for this service have been proposed.

In the first mode[2], the service holds a delegation assertion from the SOA that gives it the right to issue attribute assertions on behalf of the other attribute authorities.

The second mode[3], the attribute authorities provide the service with delegation assertions that give the server the right to issue assertions on their behalf.

When using the third mode[4], the service does not have any delegation assertion and the verification of the attribute assertions it issues has to be done externally.

4 Modelling Delegated Attribute Assertion

Our approach for modelling delegated attribute assertion was to examine different possible schemes and to extract general properties. We first present the examined schemes and then the properties we have found.

---

[2] Called PMI, for Privilege Management Infrastructure.
[3] Called AC PKI mode, for Attribute Certificate and Public Key Infrastructure.
[4] Called PKI mode.

4.1 Examined Assertion Schemes with Delegation

We have considered four schemes for issuing and verifying delegated assertions, which we describe in the following sections. These may not cover all possible approaches, but they provide us with enough diversity to find two general properties. Furthermore all four of the schemes we have examined assume an *attribute push* approach, where the user somehow acquires assertions of his attributes and pushes them to the verifier. Equivalent models can easily be derived for an *attribute pull* approach, where the verifier pulls the relevant attributes of a user upon a request.

Shared key assertion. In the *shared key assertion* scheme, each attribute is represented by a single asymmetric key pair. The private key is used to sign assertions of the attribute and the public key is distributed to verifiers, so they can check the validity of these assertions.

The SOA of the attribute controls the private key, and can issue it to any entity he wishes to make an AA for this attribute. These AAs can further delegate attribute assertion to new AAs by disclosing the private key to them[5].

This scheme is represented in figure 1.

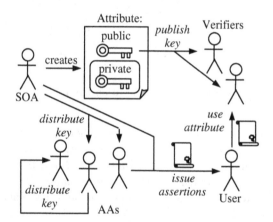

Fig. 1. Shared key attribute assertion and delegation

Sharing a group key is a common form of authority delegation. The security weaknesses are obvious and well known, but the simplicity of this mechanism makes it useful in some special cases (e.g. controlling access to a photocopying machine).

Assertion chaining. In the *Assertion chaining* scheme, every attribute is linked to a specific SOA. The relation of attribute to SOA is published to the

---

[5] Note that the SOA does not use his own private key for this, a special asymmetric key pair is generated to represent the attribute.

verifiers. The SOA can sign assertions with an asymmetric key pair that is some-how linked to his identity (e.g. by a X.509 public key certificate).

Furthermore the SOA and authorised AAs can delegate attribute assertion to other AAs by issuing attribute delegation assertions.

The verifier has to check that the initial certificate is signed by the SOA of the attribute and that the assertion chain is valid. The precise format of these delegation assertions and the verification algorithm for such assertion chains are out of the scope of this article.

PKI delegation, PRIMA and the AC PKI mode of the PERMIS Delegation Issuing Service correspond to this approach[6].

Figure 2 shows this assertion scheme.

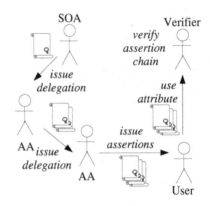

Fig. 2. Attribute assertion and delegation through assertion chains

Delegation server. In the *Delegation server* scheme, every attribute is linked to a specific delegation server, which is under control of the attribute's SOA. The delegation server maintains a list of authorised attribute AAs, which can also specify the power to further delegate attribute authority.

AAs issue attribute assertions using their personal asymmetric key pair for signatures.

Verifiers must check the validity of the assertions signature and then proceed to query the delegation server in order to determine if the AA that signed this assertion had the administrative power to do so.

The PMI mode of the PERMIS Delegation Issuing Service corresponds to this approach.

This assertion scheme is illustrated by figure 3.

Assertion server. The *Assertion server* scheme is somewhat similar to the Delegation server scheme, as it also features a specific server for each attribute. As in the previous scheme this server is under control of the attribute's SOA.

---

[6] However in PERMIS the last AA in a delegation chain is always the Delegation Issuing Service.

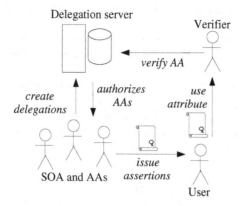

Fig. 3. Attribute assertion and delegation using a delegation server

However it not only stores the authorised attribute AA's, but also the attribute assignments they have issued.

The assertion server uses an asymmetric key pair in order to sign attribute assertions. The public key is previously published to the assertion verifiers.

Upon reception of an attribute assertion the verifier only has to check the validity of the assertion's signature and to make sure the signature key belongs to the corresponding assertion server.

We have implemented this scheme as an attribute provider for XACML PDPs[7]. It is based on the upcoming XACML 3.0 standard [14] and supports delegation of attribute authority as well as attribute hierarchies.

The PKI mode of the PERMIS Delegation Issuing Service also corresponds to this approach.

This scheme is illustrated by figure 4.

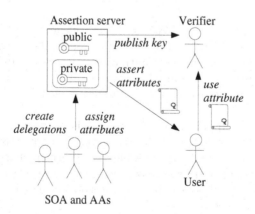

Fig. 4. Attribute assertion and delegation using an assertion server

---

[7] The sourcecode is available under http://www.sics.se/spot/assertion_server.html

4.2   General Properties of Assertion Schemes

If one examines the previously presented assertion schemes, one can find two general properties, which account for the similarities and the differences of these schemes.

The first property is *how attribute authorities are represented for verifiers*. There can either be *an individual representation* (i.e. each AA signs assertions with his own key) or a *group representation* where only a single AA persona is visible for the verifiers (i.e. there is only one key per attribute that is used to sign assertions). Figure 5 illustrates this property.

group representation of AAs:

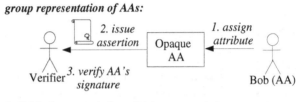

individual representation of AAs:

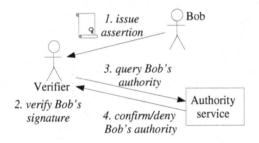

Fig. 5. Representation of AA's for the verifier

The second property is how *delegation statements* are issued. They can either be *pre-defined* (i.e. authority is transferred previously, independent of a specific request) or issued *on-demand* (i.e. authority is verified individually for each request). This property is illustrated in figure 6.

We can now assign property values to the previously presented assertion schemes as follows:

In the *Shared key* approach, each attribute is associated to one assertion signer: the asymmetric key pair of the attribute. Therefore only a group representation of AAs for the attribute is visible to the verifiers. Furthermore delegation statements are implicitly made by sharing the private key. Since this must happen before a delegated AA can issue an assertion, delegation statements must be considered pre-defined.

The *Assertion chaining* approach makes use of the individual asymmetric key pairs of the AAs in order to sign assertions. It has therefore an individual representation of AAs for the verifiers. In general delegation certificates would

pre–defined delegation statements:

SOA/AA→AA'   AA'→Verifier   Verifier
├──────────────┼────────────────┼──────────────────► time
delegation   attribute   assertion &
authority   is asserted   authority of AA'
is distributed   is verified

on–demand delegation statements:

SOA/AA   AA'→Verifier   Verifier   SOA →Verifier
├────────────┼──────────────┼──────────────┼──────► time
delegation   attribute   assertion   authority of AA' is
authority   is asserted   is verified   confirmed on–line
is stored

Fig. 6. Delegation statements about AA's for the verifier

be relatively long lived and delegation statements can therefore considered to be
pre-defined.

The approach using a *delegation server* also makes use of the individual asymmetric key pairs of the AAs to sign assertions. It is therefore classified as having individual AA representation. Delegation statements for an AA are checked by the delegation server on-demand, based on a request by a verifier.

When using an *assertion server* as in the fourth approach, we have a single asymmetric key pair signing all assertions and therefore a group representation of AAS for the assertion verifier. As the assertion server functions in the same way as the delegation server as far as delegation is concerned, it is also considered to issue delegation statements on-demand.

These results are summarised in table 1.

Table 1. Classifying delegated assertion schemes by *AA representation for verifiers* and issuing of *delegation statements*

	AA representation for verifiers	
delegation statements	*individual*	*group*
pre-defined	Shared key	Assertion chaining
on-demand	Assertion server	Delegation server

It is clear that the borders between these properties are not strictly speaking clear cut. One could imagine a *shared key* scheme where an attribute would be associated to several asymmetric key pairs. However this remains a group representation of AAs, unless you assign specific keys to specific AAs. In the latter case all of these keys would have to be published to the verifiers in a trusted way, which can then be seen as a variant of *assertion chaining*.

Another example would be if the delegation assertions used in *assertion chaining* would only be issued with a very short lifetime, supposedly for the use with a specific attribute assertion. Since either the verifier or the user would have to somehow gather these delegation assertions from a previously known authority, this can be seen as a variant of a *delegation server*.

5   Discussion

We now proceed to analyse the different properties found in the previous section, with regard to the following desired functionality of a scheme for delegated attribute assertion:

- Offline verification (i.e. the possibility to verify an assertion without having to contact a trusted third party in the verification process).
- Easy revocation of delegations and assertions.
- Possibility of non-cascading revocation of AA delegation rights (i.e. the assertions of an AA can stay valid after this AA's authority has been revoked)[8].
- Traceability of both delegations and assertions issued by AAs.
- Vulnerability and resilience against attacks.
- Possibility to create attribute hierarchies, where one attribute is considered to include another.

On-demand delegation statements prevent *offline verification*, since the service issuing the statements is a trusted third party that needs to be contacted in the process of verifying an AA's assertions. When using pre-defined delegation statements, attribute SOAs can publish the information necessary to verify an assertion issued by an AA (i.e. a delegation assertion), and verifiers having this information can do the verification offline.

The representation of AA for the verifiers does not affect the functionality of offline verification.

Revocation of assertions is only easy when using a group representation of AA and on-demand delegation statements. If AAs are individually represented, it is difficult to keep track of which assertions each individual AA has issued and therefore difficult to locate and revoke one.

If we have pre-defined delegation statements, it is difficult to keep track of AAs, especially if we consider the possibility of multiple delegation steps. It is therefore difficult to locate and revoke both delegations and assertions by delegated AAs.

If AAs are individually represented, it is difficult to have *non cascading revocation* of a delegation. In order to make this possible, one would need to keep a history of permissions over time, to check if an AA was authorised to issue an assertion at a certain point of time. This in turn requires a mechanism to prevent AAs from backdating their assertions (e.g. a trusted time stamping service).

---

[8] This is a desirable feature, if the actions of the AA before its authority was revoked are still considered to be correct and one does not want to redo all of them.

Table 2. The effect of the properties AA representation and Delegation statements on desirable functionality (read table as row-to-column relation)

	AA representation	delegation statements
Offline verification	Not affected	prevented by *on-demand* statements
Assertion revocation	Easy only for *group* representation and *on-demand* statements	
Noncascading revocation possible	Difficult for *individual* representation	Not affected
Traceability of AA actions	Easy only for *group* representation and *on-demand* statements	
Vulnerability and resilience	Greater risk with *group* representation	TTP required for *on-demand* statements
Attribute hierarchies possible	Easy dissemination of hierarchies for *group* representation and *on-demand* statements Imposing restrictions difficult with *group* representation and *pre-defined* statements	

With a group representation of AAs, assertions are not linked to a specific AA and therefore remain valid even if the authority of the issuing AA is revoked[9].

This functionality is not affected by the way how delegation statements are issued.

Traceability is similar to revocation, since it requires locating attribute and delegation assertions. Therefore the same considerations apply.

Issuing delegation statements on-demand requires a trusted third party (TTP) to be available online at every moment an attribute assertion is to be used. This is more *vulnerable* than an approach without TTPs since the TTP can become a bottleneck and also a single point of failure. Furthermore an attacker who subverts this TTP has complete control of the attributes that it manages. Pre-defined delegation statements make the system more robust, since there is no central service that attackers can target.

Having a group representation for AAs, creates a greater risk, since a service that produces assertions signed with the asymmetric key pair that represents this group, needs to be available for all AAs. Thus an attacker can take control of the entire system if he gains access to the private key of the group. Using an individual representation is more resilient, since only the subverted AAs keys need to be replaced.

None of the examined properties explicitly prevent *attribute hierarchies*. However a system designed like the *Assertion server* example makes it easier to collect such hierarchies and make them available to users and verifiers. In systems following the design of the *Shared key assertion* example, it is difficult to restrict

---

[9] This does not prevent the revocation of assertions issued by rogue AAs, it only allows to keep assertions valid even though the AA that issued them is not allowed to do so anymore.

a delegation in a way that would prevent an AA from creating a hierarchy. The other models would allow for such a design.

Table 2 summarises these observations.

6   Conclusion

In this article we have investigated the problem of verifying assertions issued by a delegated authority. We have extracted two criteria by which such verification schemes can be classified. From these criteria 4 different models for verification schemes result. We present an analysis of the drawbacks and advantages of these models. We do not give specific recommendations on which model is to be preferred over another one, since this strongly depends on the requirements of the actual application in which delegated attribute assertion is used. System designers can use our model to either evaluate different available products for use in their system or to design custom systems corresponding to their requirements.

References

1. Godik, S., Moses, T., (eds.).: eXtensible Access Control Markup Language (XACML). Standard, Organization for the Advancement of Structured Information Standards (OASIS) (2003) http://www.oasis-open.org/committees/xacml
2. Nagaratnam, N., Janson, P., Dayka, J., Nadalin, A., Siebenlist, F., Welch, V., Tuecke, S., Foster, I.: Security Architecture for Open Grid Services. Technical report, GGF OSGA Security Workgroup, Revised 6/5/2003 (2002), available from https://forge.gridforum.org/projects/ogsa-sec-wg
3. Bandmann, O., Dam, M., Firozabadi, B.S.: Constrained Delegation. In: Proceedings of 2002 IEEE Symposium on Security and Privacy, Oakland, CA, USA (2002)
4. Firozabadi, B.S., Sergot, M., Bandmann, O.: Using Authority Certificates to Create Management Structures. In: proceedings of Security Protocols, 9th International Workshop, Cambridge, UK, pp. 134–145 (2001)
5. Maler, E., Mishra, P., Philpott, R., (eds.).: The OASIS Security Assertion Markup Language (SAML) v1.1. Standard, Organization for the Advancement of Structured Information Standards (OASIS) (2003), http://www.oasis-open.org
6. Navarro, G., Firozabadi, B.S., Rissanen, E., Borrell, J.: Constrained delegation in XML-based Access Control and Digital Rights Management Standards. In: Proceedings of the IASTED International Conference on Communication, Network, and Information Security, New York, USA (2003)
7. Wang, J., Vecchio, D.D., Humphrey, M.: Extending the Security Assertion Markup Language to Support Delegation for Web Services and Grid Services. In: Proceedings of the International Conference on Web Services, Orlando, Florida, USA (2005)
8. Farrell, S., Housley, R.: An Internet Attribute Certificate Profile for Authorization. Request For Comments (RFC) 3281, Internet Egnineering Task Force (IETF) (2002), http://www.ietf.org/rfc/rfc3281.txt
9. PKIX Working Group: Public Key Infrastructure (X.509). Technical report, Internet Engineering Task Force (IETF) (2002), http://www.ietf.org/html.charters/pkix-charter.html

10. Lorch, M., Kafura, D.: Supporting Secure Ad-hoc User Collaboration in Grid Environments. In: Proceedings of the 3rd International Workshop on Grid Computing, Baltimore, MD, USA, pp. 181–193. Springer, Heidelberg (2002)

11. Lorch, M., Adams, D., Kafura, D., Koneni, M., Rathi, A., Shah, S.: The PRIMA System for Privilege Management, Authorization and Enforcement. In: Proceedings of the 4th International Workshop on Grid Computing, Phoenix, AR, USA, pp. 109–116. IEEE Computer Society, Los Alamitos (2003)

12. Chadwick, D., Otenko, A.: The PERMIS X.509 Role Based Privilege Management Infrastructure. In: Proceedings of the 7th ACM Symposium on Access Control Models and Technologies, Monterey, CA, USA, pp. 135–140. ACM Press, New York (2002)

13. Chadwick, D.: Delegation Issuing Service. In: NIST 4th Annual PKI Workshop, Gaithersberg, USA, 62–73 Available from: g.pdf (2005), http://middleware.internet2.edu/pki05/proceedings/chadwick-delegation-issuin

14. Rissanen, E., Lockhart, H., Moses, T., (eds.).: XACML v3.0 administrative policy. Standard, Organization for the Advancement of Structured Information Standards (OASIS) (2006), http://www.oasis-open.org/committees/xacml

Program Partitioning Using Dynamic Trust Models*

Dan Søndergaard[1], Christian W. Probst[1], Christian Damsgaard Jensen[1],
and René Rydhof Hansen[2]

[1] Informatics and Mathematical Modelling, Technical University of Denmark
s011283@student.dtu.dk, {probst,cdj}@imm.dtu.dk
[2] Department of Computer Science, University of Copenhagen
rrhansen@diku.dk

Abstract. Developing distributed applications is a difficult task. It is
further complicated if system-wide security policies shall be specified and
enforced, or if both data and hosts are owned by principals that do not
fully trust each other, as is typically the case in service-oriented or grid-
based scenarios. Language-based technologies have been suggested to
support developers of those applications—the *Decentralized Label Model*
and *Secure Program Partitioning* allow to annotate programs with security specifications, and to partition the annotated program across a set
of hosts, obeying both the annotations and the trust relation between
the principals. The resulting applications guarantee *by construction* that
safety and confidentiality of both data and computations are ensured.
In this work, we develop a generalised version of the splitting framework, that is parametrised in the trust component, and show the result
of specialising it with different trust models. We also develop a metric to
measure the quality of the result of the partitioning process.

1 Introduction

There is an increasing reliance on open computing environments; virtual organisations, supply chain management, grid computing, and pervasive computing
increase the need for spontaneous and dynamic formation of short term coalitions to solve a specific problem. The security implications of this evolution are
profound and new techniques must be developed to prevent violation of confidentiality and integrity in applications that execute on a widely distributed
computing platform, e.g., a computational grid infrastructure.

Developing applications for these distributed environments, however, is a difficult task. In scenarios where both data and hosts are owned by principals that
do not necessarily trust each other, as is typically the case in service-oriented or
grid-based scenarios, development is further complicated. Language-based technologies have been suggested to support developers of those applications—the

---

* This work has in part been supported by the EU research project #016004, *Software
Engineering for Service-Oriented Overlay Computers.*

T. Dimitrakos et al. (Eds.): FAST 2006, LNCS 4691, pp. 170–184, 2007.

Decentralized Label Model and *Secure Program Partitioning* allow to annotate programs with ownership and access control information, and to partition the annotated program across a set of hosts, obeying both the annotations and the trust relation between the principals. Starting from annotated *sequential* code, the resulting *distributed* applications guarantee *by construction* that safety and confidentiality of both data and computations are ensured. While this is a very powerful mechanism, the trust model used in the original framework [19,20] is very limited. We start in this work with developing a generalised version of the partitioning framework, that is parametrised in the trust component, and show the result of specialising it with different, increasingly dynamic and realistic trust models.

Another important aspect is the trust that principals in the system have in the partitioning generated by the splitter. Even though the sub-programs are guaranteed to obey the annotations as well as the confidentiality and integrity specifications by construction, principals will want a way to measure how well a certain partitioning fulfils all their constraints. Therefore we develop a metric to measure the quality of the result of the partitioning process.

The approach we base our work on is fundamentally different from simply securing regular algorithms by encrypting data. While there are algorithms that do operate on encrypted data [1,2,16], such algorithms are usually very specialised and in the general case it is not possible to transform an algorithm into an equivalent algorithm that operates on encrypted data. This means that users of grid applications must generally accept that both algorithm and data will be known to the computer that performs the calculations. It is therefore important to consider the segmentation of programs and data, in order to prevent sending sensitive data to the wrong, that is untrusted nodes (e.g., processing personal information, such as an electronic patient record, from a European citizen on a computer in the U.S.A. constitutes a possible violation of the European Data Protection Directive [8]).

This paper is structured as follows. The rest of this section introduces a running example, that we will use to illustrate different approaches. It is followed by a description of the splitting framework in Sec. 2. In Sec. 3 we develop a metric to judge the quality of a partitioning computed by the splitting framework, and in Sec. 4 we describe dynamic trust scenarios and their effect on the splitting process. Finally, Sec. 5 discusses related work and Sec. 6 concludes the paper and discusses future work.

1.1 Example

This section introduces our running example, that we will use to illustrate both the general framework and different trust models.

Consider the example of a pharmaceutical company that is in the process of developing a new drug. An important element of the drug discovery phase consists of high performance computing on large volumes of data, e.g., simulating chemical reactions, comparing gene sequences, etc. It is common for smaller pharmaceutical companies to specialise in particular types of drugs, resulting in many companies that belong to the same (pharmaceutical) trade association, but do not directly compete with each other. This is the typical scenario for a setting where one wants to develop applications that deal with data from companies that potentially distrust each other in handling some of their data, but are willing to share other parts. The fact that some companies are registered in the same country and belong to the same trade association may increase the initial confidence in their sites and serve as a recommendation in case no previous experience with that site has been recorded.

The case that we will use as example is that of two companies A and B who want to execute a gene sequencing. In order to save costs, they use the same provider C of such a service. In our setting, company A has a license agreement with C, such that they receive a gene once C has found a match. In contrast, B only receives the boolean result and would have to pay for actually obtaining the gene.

2   The Splitting Framework

This section describes the components of the original framework for Secure Program Partitioning as described by Myers *et al.* [19,20]. The main components are a security-typed programming language and a trust-based splitter. The partitioning process then essentially consists of two steps—*compiling* and *splitting*. The compiler processes the source code with security annotations as provided by a user, and the splitter tries to find a partitioning based on the trust relation of the principals. Fig. 1 shows the schematic overview of the framework. The input is an application written in a security-typed language. An example for a security-typed language is JIF [13] that extends Java with the Decentralised Label Model [14,15]. Before discussing the framework in more detail we introduce the notion of trust used in it.

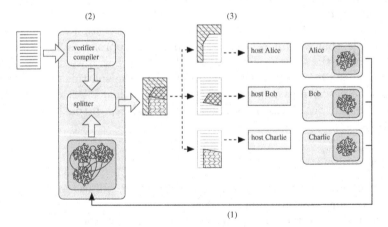

Fig. 1. The general splitting framework. Each principal in the system specifies a trust and an integrity graph (1), that is combined into the global trust graph and is used by the central splitter to partition the application across hosts in the net (2). Then the generated partitioning is distributed across the network and executed (3).

Fig. 2. Static trust graph for the example application. Solid edges denote confidentiality, while dashed edges denote integrity. The left graph depicts the initial static situation, the right hand graph the situation after Diana has joined the network.

2.1 Confidentiality and Integrity

Trust in the original framework is divided in the two components *confidentiality* and *integrity*. It is noteworthy that these two components are independent from each other.

Confidentiality is used to express that an actor A in the system has trust into another actor B as to keeping A's data confidential. This means that A is willing to store its data on a host operated by B. For the rest of this paper we tacitly identify a host with the user operating it. *Integrity* is used to express that an actor A assumes that results obtained from actor B have been computed correct. This means that A is willing to split computations on a host operated by B. Both confidentiality and integrity are complete and *non-transitive*, i.e., if A trusts B and B trusts C, then A does not automatically trust C.

A third measure that could easily be added is that of *availability* of a host in a distributed system. Principals could use this to express their trust in a certain host to be available to execute their computation. In contrast to confidentiality and integrity, which are subjective and hard to validate, availability is measurable in that one can check whether or not a host performed a certain operation. Therefore the availability assigned to a host could be increased or decreased over time. We are planning to further investigate this with our prototype implementation.

The two trust components confidentiality and integrity can be expressed as sets:

$$C_p = \{a_1 :, \ldots, a_n :\} \quad \text{and} \quad I_p = \{? : b_1, \ldots, b_n\} \tag{1}$$

where p, a_i, and b_i are principals in the system. Using this notation, C_p specifies, who has confidence in p, and I_p specifies who believes in p's integrity. For instance the trust graph on the left hand side of Fig. 2 can be expressed as

$$C_{Alice} = \{Alice :\} \qquad\qquad I_{Alice} = \{? : Alice\}$$
$$C_{Bob} = \{Bob :\} \qquad\qquad I_{Bob} = \{? : Bob\}$$
$$C_{Charlie} = \{Alice : ; Bob : ; Charlie :\} \quad I_{Charlie} = \{? : Alice, Bob, Charlie\}$$

For the graph on the right hand side of Fig. 2, the results for Alice, Bob, and Charlie remain the same, and for Diana one gets

$$C_{Diana} = \{Alice : ;\ Charlie :\} \qquad I_{Diana} = \{? : Diana, Charlie\}$$

Because the trust model is *non-transitive*, Bob does not trust Diana with regards to confidentiality.

2.2 Security-Typed Languages

This section introduces the necessary background on the Decentralized Label Model (DLM) and shows the annotated high-level source code for our example application (Fig. 3).

The central notion in the DLM is the *principal* ($p \in$ Principals), which represents any entity that can own data or operate on it (that is users, processes, hosts, etc.). Principals are used in two ways—on the one hand in expressing ownership and access rights of data, on the other hand to define the authority that the program at any given point in time has. In the example, principals are A and B, representing the pharmaceutical companies, and C, representing the service provider mentioned in Sec. 1.1.

Both ownership and access rights to data are expressed by *security labels* $L \in$ Labels $= \mathcal{P}(\text{Principals} \times \mathcal{P}(\text{Principals}))$, which can be written as sets. Each label specifies a set of owners for a piece of data and for each owner the principals that are allowed to access the data. In Fig. 3, the first part of the label of variable seq1 ($\{A : C\}$) indicates that the variable is owned by principal A and that A allows C to read it. Similarly, the label part $\{A : C; C : A\}$ at variable t1 indicates that this variable is owned by A and C, and each allows the other to read it. All components of a label L must be obeyed in accessing data labelled with L. Compound labels with several owners also arise during computations

```
sequence seq1 {A:C; ?:A};
sequence seq2 {B:C; ?:B};
gene g {C:A; ?:A,B};

bool t1 {A:C; C:A; ?:A};              // temporary variables
bool t2 {B:C; C:B; ?:B};
bool r1 {A:; ?:A};                    // return values
bool r2 {B:; ?:B};

t1 := scan(g, seq1);
t2 := scan(g, seq2);
r1 := declassify(t1,{A:; ?:A});
r2 := declassify(t2,{B:; ?:B});
```

Fig. 3. High level code for the example from Sec. 1.1. Companies A and B use a gene-sequencing service provided by C. While A has a license agreement with S that allows free access to genes (hence the label allowing A to read **g**), B only is allowed to read the result of the sequencing (and would have to pay for receiving the gene). For an explanation of the annotations c.f. Sec. 2.2.

using data tagged with only one owner, e.g., when invoking the method scan in Fig. 3 with arguments g labelled $\{C : A\}$ and seq2 labelled $\{B : C\}$. The resulting label $\{C : A, B : C\}$ allows only C to read data since the owner of data is automatically allowed to read it.

In addition to confidentiality information, labels can also contain *integrity* information. A label $\{? : p_1, \cdots, p_n\}$ specifies that principals p_1 through p_n believe that the data is correctly computed. As shown in Fig. 3, we combine confidentiality and integrity components in labels, and use the extraction functions $C(L)$ and $I(L)$, respectively.

Following [19,20] we write $L_1 \sqsubseteq L_2$ whenever L_1 is less restrictive than L_2. In the case of confidentiality this means that data labelled with L_1 allows *more* principals to read it than data labelled with L_2, and in the case of integrity this means that code labelled with L_1 is trusted by *less* principals than code labelled with L_2.

Before any attempt to split the program is made, the compiler verifies that the security labels are statically consistent. This initial verification ensures that all the security annotations are obeyed, for example that variables are not read by principals who lack the right to do so. For a detailed description see [19,20].

2.3   Splitting

Once the program has been verified, the next step is to compute a partitioning of the program onto available hosts in the network. Beside the security annotations in the code, the partitioning is based on the confidentiality and the integrity relation, which each principal specifies. As stated above, together these relations specify the amount of trust a principal has in the other principals in the system. The splitter takes the annotated program and these relations, and produces a split if possible. [19] discuss situations and counter-measures in situations that do not allow a split. The resulting sub-programs are then distributed on the individual hosts, and together implement the original program. In the generated sub-programs each field and statement has been assigned to a principal. In the rest of this section we briefly describe how this split is determined.

Assigning fields. In determining, whether a field of the program can be placed at a host h operated by principal p, the constraints $C(L_f) \sqsubseteq C_p$ and $I_p \sqsubseteq I(L_f)$ must be satisfied. The equations express that the principal p has at least as much confidentiality as the field f and at most as much integrity as the field. In the example (Fig. 3), the field seq1 has $C(\text{seq1}) = \{A, C\}$ and $I(\text{seq1}) = \{A\}$, resulting in host A being the only possible host this field can be scheduled to.

Assigning statements. A statement S can be assigned to a principal p if the principal has at least the confidentiality of all values used in the statement. Additionally the principal must have the integrity of all values defined. To ensure this, the two constraint $L_{in} = \bigsqcup_{v \in U(S)} L_v$ and $L_{out} = \bigsqcap_{l \in D(S)} L_l$ are enforced. Here, $U(S)$ denotes all values used in S, and $D(S)$ denotes all definitions in S. For a principal p to be able to execute S, the constraints $C(L_{in}) \sqsubseteq C_p$ and $I_p \sqsubseteq I(L_{out})$ must be satisfied. In the example (Fig. 3), the arguments to the second call to function scan have readers $\{A, C\}$ and $\{B, C\}$, resulting in C

being the only possible host. A similar result is obtained for integrity, therefore this statement is scheduled on host C.

Declassification. One problem with security-typed languages is that labels tend to become more and more restrictive in terms of allowed readers and required integrity. To circumvent this, explicit declassification has been introduced, which allows the programmer to specify a new label for a data item. Since a declassification statement is executed with a certain authority, all principals P whose authority is needed must trust the integrity of the execution reaching the declassification statement. This information is recorded in the label of the program counter, so we require $I(pc) \sqsubseteq \{? : P\}$. In the example program declassification is needed since the result of the gene scanning has to be sent back to the individual hosts, allowing them to read the data.

The result of the partitioning with respect to the two trust graphs from Fig. 2 is shown in Fig. 4.

2.4 Infrastructure

Before investigating splitting using more dynamic types of trust graphs, we briefly summarise the infrastructure used in our approach. As shown in Fig. 1, the system consists of a set of hosts and a central splitter. The splitter takes requests from clients, that send a program written in a security-typed language, and computes a partitioning of the program on the hosts in the system. The partitioning is guaranteed to obey all ownership and access control annotations present in the program. To compute the partitioning, the splitter uses a trust graph as specified by each client upon entering the network. This trust graph combines the two components *confidentiality* and *integrity* as described in Sec. 2.1. As a result, clients can rely on the fact that their data and code is only stored or executed on hosts that are operated by users who they trust to ensure confidentiality and/or integrity.

3 Quality of a Partitioning

The partitioning of the original program as computed by the splitter is guaranteed to obey all ownership- and access control-annotations, as well as the confidentiality and integrity specified by the principals. However, the original framework does not specify how to choose between several possible solutions for the constraint system generated from the program (Sec. 2). This section introduces a metric to judge the quality of a partitioning from the view point of a principal A. The idea is to judge the risk of a set of principals violating the confidentiality of data that is owned by A and has been partitioned to a host operated by B.

The mathematical foundation for this approach is Maurer's work on probabilistic trust [12], where trust values can be specified by numbers between 0 and 1, representing no and total trust, respectively. If we reconsider the static trust graph introduced in the previous section, we can annotate the confidence and integrity edges with probability 1, since the trust model is complete.

```
A: sequence seq1 {A:C; ?:A};        A: sequence seq1 {A:C; ?:A};
B: sequence seq2 {B:C; ?:B};        B: sequence seq2 {B:C; ?:B};
C: gene g {C:A; ?:A,B};             C: gene g {C:A; ?:A,B};

// temporary variables              // temporary variables
C: bool t1 {A:C; C:A; ?:A};         D: bool t1 {A:C; C:A; ?:A};
C: bool t2 {B:C; C:B; ?:B};         C: bool t2 {B:C; C:B; ?:B};
// return values                    // return values
A: bool r1 {A:; ?:A};               A: bool r1 {A:; ?:A};
B: bool r2 {B:; ?:B};               B: bool r2 {B:; ?:B};

C: t1 := scan(g, seq1);             D: t1 := scan(g, seq1);
C: t2 := scan(g, seq2);             C: t2 := scan(g, seq2);
C: r1 := declassify(t1,{A:; ?:A});  D: r1 := declassify(t1,{A:; ?:A});
C: r2 := declassify(t2,{B:; ?:B});  C: r2 := declassify(t2,{B:; ?:B});
```

Fig. 4. The result of splitting the example code from Fig. 3. The code on the left has been split using the left trust graph from Fig. 2, the code on the right has been split using the right trust graph in that figure. As a result of adding the host operated by Diana, statements that A has rights on have been partitioned to host D.

Now assume that a piece of data or code owned by principal A should be scheduled to a host h. How would A evaluate whether h is well-suited to host its data, or not. Again there are two components to this question. First of all, A will want to inspect which other principals might allow the splitter to partition their code to h. Any other code running on the host might result in an increased risk of A's data being leaked.

To compute the trust that a principal has in this *not* happening, we follow Maurer's formula. For a principal A's view we use his confidentiality graph CG_A. Like Maurer we are interested in computing the probability that particular subsets, from which the trust of A in another principal B's confidentiality can be derived, are contained in this view. The probability is

$$P(\nu \subseteq CG_p) = \prod_{S \in \nu} P(S)$$

To compute the overall trust that principal A has in B we use Maurer's formula and get

$$confidence(A, B) = \sum_{i=1}^{k} P(\nu_i \subseteq CG_A) \tag{2}$$

$$- \sum_{1 \le i_1 < i_2 \le k} P((\nu_{i_1} \cup \nu_{i_2}) \subseteq CG_A)$$

$$+ \sum_{1 \le i_1 < i_2 < i_3 \le k} P((\nu_{i1} \cup \nu_{i_2} \cup \nu_{i_3}) \subseteq CG_A)$$

$$- \cdots$$

Obviously, the risk that B leaks the data is the inverse of the confidence value, that is $1 - confidence(A, B)$.

In computing the probability that any of the principals that trust the host h will leak A's data we face the problem that these events are certainly not independent, so that it is hard to compute the probability for the case that this happens. However, the metric just needs to allow to compare different scenarios, but does not need to be a probability. So the first part of the metric computes the average of the inverse of all *conf* values as defined above:

$$leak(A, h) = \frac{\sum_{p \in C_h} (1 - confidence(A, p))}{|C_h|}$$

The higher the value of $leak(A, h)$ is, the less is the average confidence that A has in other principals that have confidence in host h. The second component is the confidence that principal A has in host h—this is a measure for how likely it is that h leaks data owned by A.

The metrics we suggest is defined as the quotient of these two numbers

$$M(A, h) = \frac{leak(A, h)}{confidence(A, h)}$$

The higher it is, the higher A judges the likelihood, that h will leak its data if stored on h. We voluntarily base the metrics only on the confidence values specified by A, since we consider the confidentiality of data to be of uttermost importance. One could easily extend the metrics to include integrity, or replace it altogether—our framework allows for easy experimentation with different metrics.

The metrics is used by the splitter whenever there are several hosts that data or code owned by a principal could be partitioned to. For example in the right hand side of Fig. 4 the metrics has been used to pick host D over C since the metrics values are smaller for the former.

4   Improving Dynamics

In dynamic distributed systems, the static trust model described in Sec. 2 is insufficient. Complete trust and *non-transitivity* are too simple concepts for most realistic trust scenarios. Additionally, the inability to handle dynamic networks makes the static trust model insufficient for dynamic distributed systems.

In order to make the Secure Program Partitioning applicable to more realistic applications, we extend the trust model in the rest of this paper to first handle dynamic extensions when hosts join or leave the network (Sec. 4.1), and to allow specification of partial or probability-based trust (Sec. 4.2).

Like in the static setting, the centralised splitter in the dynamic setting maintains a global trust graph, which contains trust relations (that is confidence and integrity values) of all principals.

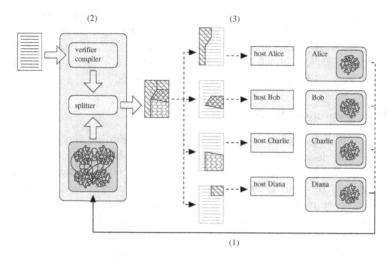

Fig. 5. Principal D joins the network. As a result, the trust graph is updated (1), the program is re-split (2), and if the splitting results in new sub-programs, the changed parts are re-distributed (3). In this scenario, part of the sub-program that had been scheduled to host A has been re-partitioned to run at host D (c.f. Fig. 1).

4.1 A Dynamic Network

In the dynamic scenario the set of available principals and the trust graph are no longer static [9]. When a principal p joins the network as depicted in Fig. 5, the principal is added to the set P_{active} of active principals. The joining principal informs the splitter of its trust relations, i.e., who it trusts. The splitter asks all the other principals about their confidence and integrity values with respect to the new principal and updates the trust graph with this information. It then decides if the program should be re-split, which happens if the trust of principals into the partitioning can be increased, as measured by the metrics.

When a principal p leaves the network, the program needs to be re-split if the leaving principal was storing data or code of the program. $p \in P_{split}$. The splitter will try to re-split the program. If this is not possible, the program cannot be executed. Execution is halted until the set of active principals, P_{active}, again can produce a legal split.

4.2 Dynamic Probabilistic Model

In the real world complete trust rarely exists. Therefore a binary trust model as the one proposed in [19] is too simple for many applications.

Instead we use probabilistic trust [12]. In this model, trust edges are annotated with probability values in the range 0 to 1, where 0 is complete distrust, and 1 complete trust. Trust is divided into confidentiality and integrity. Trust from a principal A to B is expressed as $P(TrustC_{A,B}) = \phi_{T_C}$ and $P(TrustI_{A,B}) = \phi_{T_I}$, where C and I denote confidentiality and integrity, respectively. The probability value essentially states, how probable it is that a principal is trustworthy.

Each principal can then specify what its lowest acceptable confidence level is, allowing principals to influence the safety of their data. A principal's confidence level might vary with how sensitive the information is.

4.3   Recommended Trust

Another modification to the original trust model is adding *recommended trust*. A principal can declare trust in another principals ability to recommend other principals by $p(RecC_{A,B,i}) = \phi_{R_C}$ and $p(RecI_{A,B,i}) = \phi_{R_I}$. Here i is the maximum allowable recommendation distance. For instance $i = 1$ will allow the principal to recommend only neighbouring principals in the trust graph. This is motivated by recommendations in, e.g., public-key infrastructures. We have left certificates out of our model to keep the presentation simpler, but of course frameworks like [12] can easily be put on top of our approach.

The trust graph now is constructed from a set of trust and recommendation statements, e.g.

$$TG = \{TrustC_{A,B}, TrustI_{A,B}, RecC_{A,B,1}, TrustC_{B,C}\}$$

The first step of calculating the confidence in a trust statement, e.g., that A trusts in B $(TrustC_{A,B})$, is to find all minimal paths from A to B. A minimal path is a path from A to B which is not a superset of any other path from A to B. Using minimal paths we define confidence similar to the definition of confidence in [12] using the same idea as in Sec. 3:

$$conf(Trust_{A,B}) = \sum_{i=1}^{k} P(\nu_i \subseteq TG) \tag{3}$$
$$- \sum_{1 \leq i_1 < i_2 \leq k} P((\nu_{i_1} \cup \nu_{i_2}) \subseteq TG)$$
$$+ \sum_{1 \leq i_1 < i_2 < i3 \leq k} P((\nu_{i_1} \cup \nu_{i_2} \cup \nu_{i_3}) \subseteq TG)$$
$$- \cdots$$

Then the probability that a path of trust statements is valid can be calculated by multiplying the probabilities of the individual statements:

$$P(\nu \subseteq TG) = \prod_{S \in \nu} P(S) \tag{4}$$

Our model differs from Maurer's [12] in that it deals with trust in confidentiality and integrity, not certificates. Maurer calculates the confidence in a certificate, while we calculate the confidence in a principal's trustworthiness. In practise this means that recommendations are fundamentally different. In a public key infrastructure a certificate relies on the principal who issued it. If the

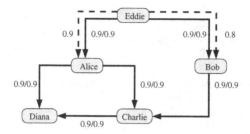

Fig. 6. A dynamic trust graph for the example application. Solid edges denote both confidentiality and integrity (we use the same values for both to simplify computations), while dashed edges denote trust in recommendation. The annotations on edges denote the probability measures assigned by principals.

principal issuing it has an invalid certificate, the issued certificate is also invalid. This dependency is used when calculating a recommendation path.

In our model, a principal might recommend a principal who is trustworthy, even though the recommender is not trustworthy. This means that the recommendation is not dependent on the recommender's trustworthiness.

4.4 Example with Probabilistic Trust Model

We now return to our example, now using the probabilistic model. A new principal F is added, and probabilities are added to the trust graph as show in Fig. 6.

All principals require that the confidence in a trust statement must be greater than or equal to 0.90. Now the confidence in the trust statements has to be calculated. To simplify calculations the probabilities of confidentiality and integrity have been chosen identical. Paths in the trust graph starting in A, B, or C, are unique, resulting, e.g., in

$$conf(Trust_{A,C}) = P(Trust_{A,C} \subseteq TG) = p(Trust_{A,C}) = 0.9$$

More interesting is the calculation of E's confidence in C and D. There exist two minimal paths $V_1 = \{Rec_{E,A,1}, Trust_{A,C}\}$ and $V_2 = \{Rec_{E,B,1}, Trust_{B,C}\}$. The probability for each path is calculated using (4):

$$P(V_1 \subseteq TG) = p(Rec_{E,A,1}) \cdot p(Trust_{A,C}) = 0.9 \cdot 0.9 = 0.81$$
$$P(V_2 \subseteq TG) = p(Rec_{E,B,1}) \cdot p(Trust_{B,C}) = 0.8 \cdot 0.9 = 0.72$$

Because the paths are disjoint, the combined probability becomes:

$$P((V_1 \cup V_2) \subseteq TG) = P(V_1 \subseteq TG) \cdot P(V_2 \subseteq TG)$$

The confidence can now be calculated using (4):

$$\begin{aligned} conf(Trust_{E,C}) &= P((V_1 \subseteq TG) \vee (V_1 \subseteq TG)) \\ &= P(V_1 \subseteq TG) + P(V_1 \subseteq TG) - P((V_1 \cup V_2) \subseteq TG) \\ &= 0.81 + 0.72 - 0.81 \cdot 0.72 = 0.9468 \end{aligned}$$

```
A: sequence seq1 {A:C; ?:A};
B: sequence seq2 {B:C; ?:B};
E: sequence seq3 {E:C; ?:E};
C: gene g {C:A; ?:A,B};

D: bool t1 {A:C; C:A; ?:A};        // temporary variables
C: bool t2 {B:C; C:B; ?:B};
C: bool t3 {E:C; C:E; ?:E};
A: bool r1 {A:; ?:A};              // return values
B: bool r2 {B:; ?:B};
E: bool r3 {C:; ?:C};

D: t1 := scan(g, seq1);
C: t2 := scan(g, seq2);
C: t3 := scan(g, seq3);
D: r1 := declassify(t1,{A:; ?:A});
C: r2 := declassify(t2,{B:; ?:B});
C: r3 := declassify(t3,{E:; ?:E});
```

Fig. 7. Extended version of the example from Fig. 3, using three client to the splitting service. The partitioning of the program is performed using the trust graph from Fig. 6.

Since there is only one path from F to E we get

$$conf(Trust_{E,D}) = 0.9 \cdot 0.9 = 0.81$$

Using these confidence values, the program can be split as shown in Fig. 7. Note that the calculations using E's data has been assigned to C as $0.9468 \geq 0.90$.

5   Related Work

Trust and explicit trust management has recently emerged as an important innovation in computer security [5]. Common trust management systems [3,4,7] implement a decentralised access control mechanism based on assertions, which may be contained in signed credentials. Assertions allow a principal to prove that she is sufficiently trusted to be granted certain privileges. Recent trust management frameworks, e.g., Trustbuilder [18], extend this access control framework with a mechanism that gradually discloses credentials in order to build the necessary level of trust without compromising the privacy of either party [10,17]. Security mechanisms based on the human notion of trust has also been proposed for pervasive computing [6,11]. We note that all these systems implement functionality that is orthogonal to our notions of dynamic trust graphs, and therefore can easily extend our system (and enhance the usability).

Regarding the splitting framework we have already covered the related work as we rely on Myers work [14,15,19,20] as the underlying foundation for our prototype implementation.

6   Conclusion and Future Work

We have presented an extension of a framework for secure program partitioning with a notion of dynamic trust and shown the results that this dynamics has on the computed partitioning. Given the increasing reliance on open computing environments, there also is an increased need for spontaneous and dynamic formation of short term coalitions to solve a specific problem. Our extensions make automatic partitioning of annotated code a viable technique to prevent violation of confidentiality and integrity in applications that execute on a widely distributed computing platform, e.g., a computational grid infrastructure. While the partitioning is already provided by the original infrastructure, only the added dynamics of network and trust make the technique applicable in this setting.

Another important addition of our work is the development of a metric to judge how well a partitioning to a specific host fulfils the requirements of a principal—on top of the guarantee that the sub-programs obey the annotations as well as the confidentiality and integrity specifications by construction. This allows a *qualitative* assessment of a partitioning on top of automated guarantees.

We plan to use our prototype implementation to experiment with more dynamic trust models and investigate more closely the interdependence between our metric, the computed partitioning, and the trust model. Another research avenue is to look closer at how to model *availability* as a measure of trust and specification, and to add some of the tools that allow trust management on top of our framework.

References

1. Abadi, M., Feigenbaum, J., Kilian, J.: On hiding information from an oracle. Journal of Computer and System Sciences 39(1), 21–50 (1989)
2. Blakley, G.R., Meadows, C.: A database encryption scheme which allows the computation of statistics using encrypted data. In: SSP '85. Proceedings of the 1985 Symposium on Security and Privacy, Los Angeles, Ca., USA, April 1990, pp. 116–122. IEEE Computer Society Press, Los Alamito (1990)
3. Blaze, M., Feigenbaum, J., Ioannidis, J., Keromytis, A.D.: The KeyNote trust management system. Internet Request for Comment RFC 2704, Internet Engineering Task Force, Version 2 (September 1999)
4. Blaze, M., Feigenbaum, J., Ioannidis, J., Keromytis, A.D.: The role of trust management in distributed systems security. In: Vitek, J. (ed.) Secure Internet Programming. LNCS, vol. 1603, pp. 185–210. Springer, Heidelberg (1999)
5. Blaze, M., Feigenbaum, J., Lacy, J.: Decentralized trust management. In: IEEE Computer Society, Technical Committee on Security and Privacy. Proceedings of the IEEE Symposium on Research in Security and Privacy, Oakland, CA, May 1996, IEEE Computer Society Press, Los Alamitos (1996)
6. Cahill, V., Gray, E., Seigneur, C.J.J.-M., Chen, Y., Shand, B., Dimmock, N., Twigg, A., Bacon, J., English, C., Wagealla, W., Terzis, S., Nicon, P., di Marzo Serugendo, G., Bryce, C., Carbone, M., Krukow, K., Nielsen, M.: Using trust for secure collaboration in uncertain environments. IEEE Pervasive Computing 2(3), 52–61 (2003)

7. Chu, Y.-H., Feigenbaum, J., LaMacchia, B.A., Resnick, P., Strauss, M.: REFEREE: Trust management for web applications. Computer Networks 29(8-13), 953–964 (1997)
8. European Parliament.: Directive 95/46/EC of the European Parliament and of the Council of 24 October 1995 on the protection of individuals with regard to the processing of personal data and on the free movement of such data (October 1995)
9. Hansen, R.R., Probst, C.W.: Secure dynamic program partitioning. In: Proceedings of Nordic Workshop on Secure IT-Systems (NordSec'05), Tartu, Estonia (October 2005)
10. Jones, V.E., Winsborough, W.H.: Negotiating disclosure of sensitive credentials, (December 09 1999)
11. Kagal, L., Finin, T.W., Joshi, A.: Communications - trust-based security in pervasive computing environments. IEEE Computer 34(12), 154–157 (2001)
12. Maurer, U.: Modelling a public-key infrastructure. In: Martella, G., Kurth, H., Montolivo, E., Bertino, E. (eds.) Computer Security - ESORICS 96. LNCS, vol. 1146, Springer, Heidelberg (1996)
13. Myers, A.C.: JFlow: Practical mostly-static information flow control. In: POPL, pp. 228–241 (1999)
14. Myers, A.C., Liskov, B.: A decentralized model for information flow control. In: Symposium on Operating Systems Principles, pp. 129–142 (1997)
15. Myers, A.C., Liskov, B.: Protecting privacy using the decentralized label model. ACM Transactions on Software Engineering and Methodology 9(4), 410–442 (2000)
16. Song, D.X., Wagner, D., Perrig, A.: Practical techniques for searches on encrypted data. In: IEEE Symposium on Security and Privacy, pp. 44–55 (2000)
17. Winsborough, W., Seamons, K., Jones, V.: Automated trust negotiation. Technical Report TR-2000-05, Department of Computer Science, North Carolina State University, April 24 2000. Monday, 24 April 2000 17:07:47 GMT
18. Winslett, M., Yu, T., Seamons, K.E., Hess, A., Jacobson, J., Jarvis, R., Smith, B., Yu, L.: The trustbuilder architecture for trust negotiation. IEEE Internet Computing 6(6), 30–37 (2002)
19. Zdancewic, S., Zheng, L., Nystrom, N., Myers, A.: Untrusted hosts and confidentiality: Secure program partitioning. In: Symposium on Operating Systems Principles, pp. 1–14 (2001)
20. Zdancewic, S., Zheng, L., Nystrom, N., Myers, A.C.: Secure program partitioning. ACM Transactions on Computer Systems 20(3), 283–328 (2002)

Locality-Based Security Policies*

Terkel K. Tolstrup[1], Flemming Nielson[1], and René Rydhof Hansen[2]

[1] Informatics and Mathematical Modelling, Technical University of Denmark
{tkt,nielson}@imm.dtu.dk
[2] Department of Computer Science, University of Copenhagen
rrhansen@diku.dk

Abstract. Information flow security provides a strong notion of end-to-end security in computing systems. However sometimes the policies for information flow security are limited in their expressive power, hence complicating the matter of specifying policies even for simple systems. These limitations often become apparent in contexts where confidential information is released under specific conditions.

We present a novel policy language for expressing permissible information flow under expressive constraints on the execution traces for programs. Based on the policy language we propose a security condition shown to be a generalized intransitive non-interference condition. Furthermore a *flow-logic* based static analysis is presented and shown capable of guaranteeing the security of programs analysed.

1 Introduction

The number of computing devices with built-in networking capability has experienced an explosive growth over the last decade. These devices range from the highly mobile to the deeply embedded and it has become standard for such devices to be "network aware" or even "network dependent" in the sense that these devices can use a wide variety of networking technologies to connect to almost any kind of computer network. Consequently modern software is often expected to utilise resources and services available over the network for added functionality and user collaboration. In such an environment where devices routinely contain highly sensitive or private information and where information flow is complex and often unpredictable it is very challenging to maintain the confidentiality of sensitive information. Predictably it is even more challenging to obtain formal guarantees or to formally verify that a given device or system does not leak confidential information. The problem is further exacerbated by the often complicated and ever changing security requirements of users. Examples include a user's medical records that should be inaccessible unless the user is at a hospital, or personal financial information that may be accessed by a bank or a financial advisor but not by the tax authorities except during a tax audit. The above examples expose one of the major drawbacks of traditional approaches to secure information flow,

---

* This work has in part been supported by the EU research project #016004, Software Engineering for Service-Oriented Overlay Computers.

T. Dimitrakos et al. (Eds.): FAST 2006, LNCS 4691, pp. 185–201, 2007.
© Springer-Verlag Berlin Heidelberg 2007

Localities

$\ell ::= l$ locality
$\quad\mid\ u$ locality variable

Nets

$N ::= l :: P$ single node
$\quad\mid\ l :: \langle et \rangle$ located tuple
$\quad\mid\ N_1 \parallel N_2$ net composition

Processes

$P ::= \mathbf{nil}$ null process
$\quad\mid\ a.P$ action prefixing
$\quad\mid\ P_1 \mid P_2$ parallel composition
$\quad\mid\ A$ process invocation

Actions

$a ::= \mathbf{out}(t)@\ell$ output
$\quad\mid\ \mathbf{in}(T)@\ell$ input
$\quad\mid\ \mathbf{read}(T)@\ell$ read
$\quad\mid\ \mathbf{eval}(P)@\ell$ migration
$\quad\mid\ \mathbf{newloc}(u)$ locality creation

Tuples

$T ::= F \mid F, T$ templates
$F ::= f \mid !x \mid !u$ template fields
$t ::= f \mid f, t$ tuples
$f ::= e \mid l \mid u$ tuple fields

Fields

$et ::= ef \mid ef, et$ evaluated tuple
$ef ::= V \mid l$ evaluated tuple field
$e ::= V \mid x \mid \ldots$ expressions

Fig. 1. Syntax

namely the lack of support for dynamic and flexible security policies. Even formulating, let alone formalising, an information flow policy for such diverse uses and changing requirements seems to be an insurmountable problem for the traditional approaches where lattice-based policies are formalised and enforced by *non-interference*. This has recently led researchers to look for better and more appropriate ways of specifying information flow policies and their concomitant notions of secure information flow, incorporating concepts such as *downgrading* (or *declassification*), *delimited release*, and *non-disclosure*.

In this paper we develop a novel notion of *locality-based security policies* in conjunction with a strong security condition for such policies: *History-based Release*. The locality-based security policies are powerful and flexible enough to be used in systems with a high degree of network connectivity and network based computing such as those described above. In this paper we model such systems in the μKlaim calculus, which is based on the *tuple space* paradigm, making it uniquely suited for our purposes. In addition we define what we believe to be the first tuple-centric notion of non-interference and show how History-based Release is a strict generalisation. Finally we construct a static analysis for processes modelled in μKlaim and demonstrate how it can be used to formally verify *automatically* that a given system is secure with respect to a given locality-based security policy. Such an analysis is an invaluable tool, both when designing and when implementing a complex system, and can be used to obtain security guarantees that are essential for critical systems.

2   The μKlaim Calculus

The Klaim family of process calculi were designed around the notion of a *tuple space*. In this paradigm systems are composed of a set of *nodes* distributed at

$$
\begin{aligned}
N_1 \parallel N_2 &\equiv N_2 \parallel N_1 \\
(N_1 \parallel N_2) \parallel N_3 &\equiv N_1 \parallel (N_2 \parallel N_3) \\
l :: P &\equiv l :: (P \mid \mathbf{nil}) \\
l :: A &\equiv l :: P \quad \text{if } A \overset{\triangle}{=} P \\
l :: (P_1 \mid P_2) &\equiv l :: P_1 \parallel l :: P_2
\end{aligned}
$$

$$
\begin{aligned}
\mathrm{match}(V, V) &= \epsilon \quad \mathrm{match}(!x, V) = [V/x] \\[4pt]
\mathrm{match}(l, l) &= \epsilon \quad \mathrm{match}(!u, l') = [l'/u] \\[4pt]
\frac{\mathrm{match}(F, ef) = \sigma_1 \qquad \mathrm{match}(T, et) = \sigma_2}{\mathrm{match}((F, T), (ef, et)) = \sigma_1 \circ \sigma_2}
\end{aligned}
$$

Fig. 2. Structural congruence   **Fig. 3.** Tuple matching

various *localities*. The nodes communicate by sending and receiving *tuples* to and from various tuple spaces based at different localities. Mobility in the Klaim calculi is modelled by remote evaluation of processes. In the standard tuple space model a tuple space is a resource shared among peers and therefore no attempt is made to restrict or control access to these.

The μKlaim calculus [8] comprises three parts: nets, processes, and actions. Nets give the overall structure in which tuple spaces and processes are located. Processes execute by performing actions. The syntax is shown in Fig. 1. Processes execute by performing an action, a, or by "invocation" of a process place-holder variable. The latter is used for iteration and recursion. Processes can be composed in parallel and finally a process can be the **nil**-process representing the inactive process. The following actions can be performed by a process. The **out**-action outputs a tuple into a tuple space at a specific locality; the **in** and **read** actions input a tuple from a specific tuple space and either remove it or leave it in place respectively; the **eval**-action remotely evaluates a process at a specified locality; and **newloc** creates a new locality.

The semantics for μKlaim, shown in Fig. 4, is a straightforward operational semantics and we shall not go into further detail here but refer instead to [8]. As is common for process calculi the semantics incorporates a structural congruence, see Fig. 2. In Fig. 3 the semantics for tuple matching, as used in the rules for the **in**- and **read**-actions, is shown. We assume the existence of a semantic function for evaluating tuples denoted as $[\![\cdot]\!]$.

Semantically we define an execution trace as the sequence of locations where processes are executed when evaluating the processes. Hence we write $L \vdash N \overset{l}{\longmapsto} L' \vdash N'$ when evaluating one step of a process located at the location l. Clearly the execution originates from an action being evaluated at the process space of location l. For the transitive reflexive closure we write $L \vdash N \overset{\omega}{\longmapsto}{}^* L' \vdash N'$ where $\omega \in \Omega$ is a string of locations.

3 Policies for Security

To protect confidentiality within a system, it is important to control how information flows so that secret information is prevented from being released on unintended channels. The allowed flow of information in a system is specified in a security policy. In this section we present a policy language based on graphs. Here vertices represent security domains, describing the resources available in the

$$\frac{\text{match}(\llbracket T \rrbracket, et) = \sigma}{l :: \mathbf{in}(T)@l'.P \parallel l' :: \langle et \rangle \xrightarrow{l} l :: P\sigma \parallel l' :: \mathbf{nil}}$$

$$\frac{\llbracket t \rrbracket = et}{l :: \mathbf{out}(t)@l'.P \parallel l' :: P' \xrightarrow{l} l :: P \parallel l' :: P' \parallel l' :: \langle et \rangle}$$

$$\frac{L \vdash N_1 \xrightarrow{l} L' \vdash N_1'}{L \vdash N_1 \parallel N_2 \xrightarrow{l} L' \vdash N_1' \parallel N_2}$$

$$\frac{\text{match}(\llbracket T \rrbracket, et) = \sigma}{l :: \mathbf{read}(T)@l'.P \parallel l' :: \langle et \rangle \xrightarrow{l} l :: P\sigma \parallel l' :: \langle et \rangle}$$

$$\frac{N \equiv N_1 \qquad L \vdash N_1 \xrightarrow{l} L' \vdash N_2 \qquad N_2 \equiv N'}{L \vdash N \xrightarrow{l} L' \vdash N'}$$

$$l :: \mathbf{eval}(Q)@l'.P \parallel l' :: P' \xrightarrow{l} l :: P \parallel l' :: P' \parallel l' :: Q$$

$$\frac{l' \notin L \qquad \lfloor l' \rfloor = \lfloor u \rfloor}{L \vdash l :: \mathbf{newloc}(u).P \xrightarrow{l} L \cup \{l'\} \vdash l :: P[l'/u] \parallel l' :: \mathbf{nil}}$$

Fig. 4. Operational semantics for μKlaim

net. A security domain is related to sets of resources available in the considered system.

This model allows for the granularity of the mapping from resources to security domains to be very fine-grained. For example we can introduce a security domain for each location. For improved precision we could partition the usage of a location into lifetime periods and introduce a domain for each, hence having more than one security domain for each location in the net. This would allow us to abstract from e.g. reuse of limited resources in the implementation. For further discussion of this see [23].

In our setting the tuple spaces are our resources, hence the localities are related to security domains. This allows us to reason about groups of localities together, as well as singling out specific localities and isolate these in their own security domains. The security policies therefore focus on the information flow between intended domains of localities. Consequently we assume that locations can be uniquely mapped to security domains.

Definition 1. *(Security Domains) For a given net we have a mapping from localities L to security domains V*

$$\underline{\cdot} : L \rightarrow V$$

We write $\underline{l}$ for the security domain of the location l.

Edges specify permitted flows of information. Information flow between resources can be restricted subject to fulfillment of constraints with respect to certain events taking place prior to the flow. Formally we propose the following definition of security polices.

Definition 2. *(Locality-based security policies) A security policy is a labelled graph $G = (V, \lambda)$, consisting of a set of vertices V representing security domains and a total function λ mapping pairs of vertices to labels $\lambda : V \times V \rightarrow \Delta$. We define $\mathbb{G}$ to be the set of policies. The structure, Δ, of labels is defined below.*

In a flow graph the set of vertices V represent security domains. A security domain indicates the usage of a resource in the system. The edges in the flow graph describe the allowed information flow between resources. Hence an edge from the vertex for security domain v_1 to the vertex for security domain v_2 indicates that information is allowed to flow between the resources in these domains subject to the label attached to the edge.

The edges in the flow graph are described by the function $\lambda : V \times V \rightarrow \Delta$. We write $v_1 \overset{\delta}{\rightsquigarrow} v_2$ for an edge from vertex v_1 to v_2 constrained by $\delta \in \Delta$, i.e. $\lambda(v_1, v_2) = \delta$. Information flow might be constrained by certain obligations that the system must fulfill before the flow can take place. Here we describe a novel constraint language that allows the security policy to be specific about intransitive information flows in the flow graph. Constraints are specified in the following syntax $\delta \in \Delta$:

$$\delta ::= true \mid false \mid v \mid \delta_1 \cdot \delta_2 \mid \delta_1 \wedge \delta_2 \mid \delta_1 \vee \delta_2 \mid \delta^*$$

A constraint may be trivially *true* or *false*. The constraint v enforces that flows occur at specific locations, thus that the flow is only permitted at locations that is part of the security domain v (i.e. $\underline{l} = v$). The constraint $\delta_1 \cdot \delta_2$ enforces that the flow is only allowed to occur if events described in δ_1 precedes events described in δ_2. Common logical operators $\wedge$ and $\vee$ are available to compose constraints. Finally Kleene's star * allows the policies to express cyclic behaviour.

We might omit the constraint, writing $v_1 \rightsquigarrow v_2$ for $v_1 \overset{true}{\rightsquigarrow} v_2$. Similarly we might omit an edge in a flow graph indicating that the constraint can never be fulfilled, i.e. $v_1 \overset{false}{\rightsquigarrow} v_2$.

Example 1. To illustrate the usage of flow graphs as security policies we here discuss the three examples given in Figure 5. The first flow graph (a) allows a flow from v_1 to v_2 and v_2 to v_3 but not from v_1 to v_3. That is neither directly nor through v_2! In this manner the intransitive and temporal nature of the policies allow us to have constraints on the order of information flows.

The second flow graph (b) allows the flow from v_1 to v_2, v_2 to v_3 and from v_1 to v_3 as well. The flow can be directly from v_1 to v_3 or through v_2. If we wish to restrict the flow to go through v_2 it could be done as in flow graph (c). We assume that $\underline{l}$ and $\underline{l}'$ map to security domains that no other locations are mapped to. Hence the last flow graph (c) restricts the flows between the security domains to certain locations. This ensures that for information to flow from v_1 to v_3 both locations need to participate. ∎

To give intuition to the above example policies we relate them back to the personal finance scenario mentioned in the introduction. In the following we let v_1, v_2, and

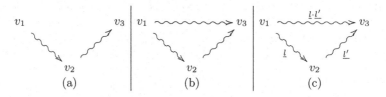

Fig. 5. Examples of flow graphs

v_3 denote the user, the user's financial advisor, and the tax authorities respectively. The first policy (Figure 5(a)) states that the user's financial information may be accessed by the financial advisor but *not* by the tax authorities while still allowing the financial advisor to send (other) information to the tax authorities. The second policy (Figure 5(b)) then states that the user's financial information may be accessed both by the financial advisor and by the tax authorities; this may be necessary during a tax audit. Finally the policy shown in (Figure 5(c)) defines a situation where the user's financial information may be accessed by both the financial advisor and the tax authorities but *only* through the financial advisor; this security policy ensures that the financial advisor can review all relevant information from the user before the tax authorities gain access to it.

A system is given by a net N and a security policy G together with a mapping $\underline{\cdot}$ and might be written N subject to $(G, \underline{\cdot})$. However, as the G and $\underline{\cdot}$ components are clear from context we choose not to incorporate the policies in the syntax of μKlaim.

3.1   Semantics of Constraints

In this subsection we present the semantics of our security policy language. The semantics is given as a translation to regular expressions over execution traces. The intuition is that if an execution trace is in the language of the regular expression derived by the semantics, then the constraint is fulfilled.

The main idea behind the locality-based security policies is that they specify constraints that must be fulfilled rather than the total behaviour of the system. This result in succinct policies. Therefore the semantics of constraints is based on an understanding of fulfilment of a constraint whenever an execution trace produces the locations specified. Hence if a trace that fulfills a constraint is preceded or succeeded by other traces the constraint remains fulfilled.

The *true* constraint is always fulfilled and hence is translated to the regular expression L^* accepting all execution traces. Similarly the constraint *false* cannot be fulfilled for any trace, and hence the generated language is $\emptyset$. The constraint v gives the language $L^* \cdot \{l \mid \underline{l} = v\} \cdot L^*$ as we wish to allow the flow only for executions taking place at l. The constraint $\delta_1 \cdot \delta_2$ indicates that the trace ω can be split into ω_1 and ω_2, where ω_1 must be in the language of δ_1, and respectively ω_2 must be in the language of δ_2. The constraints for $\delta_1 \wedge \delta_2$ and $\delta_1 \vee \delta_2$ are straightforward. One obvious definition of $[\![\delta^*]\!]$ is $[\![\delta]\!]^*$; however this

$$[true] = L^*$$
$$[false] = \emptyset$$
$$[v] = L^* \cdot \{l \mid \underline{l} = v\} \cdot L^*$$
$$[\delta_1 \cdot \delta_2] = [\delta_1] \cdot [\delta_2]$$
$$[\delta_1 \wedge \delta_2] = [\delta_1] \cap [\delta_2]$$
$$[\delta_1 \vee \delta_2] = [\delta_1] \cup [\delta_2]$$
$$[\delta^*] = L^* \cdot [\delta]^* \cdot L^*$$

Fig. 6. Semantics of constraints

choice would invalidate Lemma 1 below. Consequently, it is natural to define $[\delta^*] = L^* \cdot [\delta]^* \cdot L^*$ as then Lemma 1 continues to hold.

The semantics of the security policy language are given in Figure 6.

Lemma 1. *The semantical interpretation of constraint δ does not change by preceding or succeeding it by other traces $\forall \delta : [\delta] = L^* \cdot [\delta] \cdot L^*$.*

We define an ordering of constraints as the relation $\leq_\Delta \subseteq \Delta \times \Delta$, i.e. we say that δ is a restriction of δ' if $(\delta, \delta') \in \leq_\Delta$, normally we write $\delta \leq_\Delta \delta'$.

Definition 3. *We say that a constraint δ is a restriction of δ', written $\delta \leq_\Delta \delta'$ if we have $[\delta] \subseteq [\delta']$.*

Similarly we define a restriction relation between flow graphs.

Definition 4. *We say that a flow graph $G = (V, \lambda)$ is a restriction of $G' = (V', \lambda')$, written $G \leq G'$ if we have that*

$$V = V' \wedge \forall v_1, v_2 : \lambda(v_1, v_2) \leq_\Delta \lambda'(v_1, v_2)$$

4   Security Condition

To determine whether a program is secure or not, we need some condition for security. In this section we therefore present our definition of secure nets. The intuition is similar to that of non-interference, however we aim to generalize the traditional non-interference condition to permit release of confidential information, based on constraints on the history of the execution and it's present location. We call this condition *History-based Release*.

4.1   Security Condition

Before we formalize the main security condition we need to formalize what an attacker can observe. Consider an attacker that has access to a subset $\mathcal{V}$ of the tuplespaces that are available in the net under consideration. We formalize the observable part of a net by *nullifying* the tuple spaces that the attacker cannot observe.

Definition 5. *(V-observable) The V-observable part of a net N written $N|_V$ is*

$$(l :: P)|_V = l :: P$$

$$(l :: \langle et \rangle)|_V = \begin{cases} l :: \langle et \rangle & \text{if } l \in V \\ l :: nil & \text{otherwise} \end{cases}$$

$$(N_1 \parallel N_2)|_V = N_1|_V \parallel N_2|_V$$

Furthermore we assume that the attacker has knowledge of all the processes that exist in the net, and hence can reason about the absence of a tuple at a given location. Similar to the probabilistic attacker in [25] it is feasible to assume that two tuple spaces can be compared on all tuples. Thus for two nets N_1 and N_2 an attacker that observes at security domain V can compare the observable parts of the nets as $N_1|_V \sim N_2|_V$.

Definition 6. *(Observable equivalence) Two nets N_1 and N_2 are observably equivalent $N_1 \sim N_2$ iff*

$$\{\!\{ (l, \langle et \rangle) \mid N_1 = (\cdots \parallel l :: \langle et \rangle \parallel \cdots) \}\!\} = \{\!\{ (l, \langle et \rangle) \mid N_2 = (\cdots \parallel l :: \langle et \rangle \parallel \cdots) \}\!\}$$

where we write $\{\!\{ \cdot \}\!\}$ for a multi-set.

We define the function $\nabla : \mathcal{P}(V) \times \mathbb{G} \times \Omega \to \mathcal{P}(V)$ for extending a set of security domains with the domains that are permitted to interfere with the observed domains due to the fulfillment of constraints by the execution trace ω. The resulting set of security domains describe the permutted information flows during the execution.

Definition 7. *For a security policy G and a execution trace ω an observer at V can observe the localities*

$$\nabla(V, G, \omega) = V \cup \{ v_1 \mid v_2 \in V \wedge \omega \in [\![\lambda(v_1, v_2)]\!] \}$$

A less restrictive policy, ∇ will never reduce the observable part of the net. This allows us to establish the following fact.

Fact 1. *If $G \leq G'$ then $\nabla(V, G, \omega) \subseteq \nabla(V, G', \omega)$.*

We consider a program secure if in no execution trace, neither a single step nor a series of steps, will an attacker observing the system at the level of a set of security domains V be able to observe a difference at any locality, when all resources permitted to interfere with the locality is observably equivalent before the evaluation. We formalize the condition as a bisimulation over execution traces on nets.

Definition 8. *(Bisimulation) A (G, V)-bisimulation is a symmetric relation $\mathcal{R}$ on (the process part of) nets whenever*

$$L_1 \vdash N_1 \overset{\omega}{\rightsquigarrow}^* L_1' \vdash N_1' \wedge$$
$$L_1 \vdash N_1|_\emptyset \; \mathcal{R} \; L_2 \vdash N_2|_\emptyset \wedge$$
$$N_1|_{\nabla(V, G, \omega)} \sim N_2|_{\nabla(V, G, \omega)}$$

then there exists N_2', L_2' *and* ω' *such that*

$$L_2 \vdash N_2 \overset{\omega'}{\rightarrowtail}{}^* L_2' \vdash N_2' \wedge$$
$$L_1' \vdash N_1'|_\emptyset \; \mathcal{R} \; L_2' \vdash N_2'|_\emptyset \wedge$$
$$N_1'|_\mathcal{V} \sim N_2'|_\mathcal{V}$$

We use the fact that the observable part of a net projected on an empty set of security domains $L \vdash N|_\emptyset$ gives the process part of the net. The reason why we define the bisimulation in this way is to focus on the executable part and not the memory part.

The bisimulation follows the approach of Sabelfeld and Sands [22] in utilizing a *resetting of the state* between subtraces. This follows from modelling the attacker's ability to modify tuple spaces concurrently with the execution. Furthermore it accomodates the dynamically changing nature of the security policies due to the fulfillment of constraints, as seen in [13]. The definition is transitive but not reflexive. That the definition is not reflexive follows from observing that the net $l :: \mathbf{in}(!x)@l_H.\mathbf{out}(x)@l_L$ is not self-similar whenever information is not permitted to flow from l_H to l_L.

Fact 2. *If $G \le G'$ and $\mathcal{R}$ is a $(G, \mathcal{V})$-bisimulation then $\mathcal{R}$ is also a $(G', \mathcal{V})$-bisimulation.*

Definition 9. *A G-bisimulation is a relation $\mathcal{R}$ such that for all $\mathcal{V}$, $\mathcal{R}$ is a $(G, \mathcal{V})$-bisimulation. Denote the largest G-bisimulation $\approx_G$.*

Now we can define the security condition as a net being bisimilar to itself.

Definition 10. *(History-based Release) A net N is secure wrt. the security policy G if and only if we have $N \approx_G N$.*

Example 2. In the following we will consider a number of example programs that illustrate the strength of History-based Release. First consider the program

$$l :: \mathbf{in}(!x)@l_1.\mathbf{out}(x)@l_2$$

which reads a tuple from l_1 and writes it to l_2. With the policy $l_1 \overset{l}{\rightsquigarrow} l_2$, the program is secure, while changing the policy to $l_1 \overset{l'}{\rightsquigarrow} l_2$ makes the program insecure. The reason that the second program is insecure is because the bisimulation forces us to consider all possible traces, so even if the above program was modified to execute a process on l' concurrently with the one on l, the result would be the same. This corresponds to *intransitive non-interference* [14] (or *lexically scoped flows* according to [2]).

History-based Release goes beyond lexically scoped flows as the policy might constrain the history of a process. This is illustrated by the following example. Consider the security policy in Fig. 5(c) and assume that $l_1 = v_1$, $l_2 = v_2$ and $l_3 = v_3$, for which the program

$$l :: \mathbf{in}(!x)@l_1.\mathbf{out}(x)@l_2 \quad \| \quad l' :: \mathbf{in}(!y)@l_2.\mathbf{out}(y)@l_3$$

is secure. On the other hand the program

$$l :: \mathbf{in}(!x)@l_1.\mathbf{out}(x)@l_2 \quad \| \quad l' :: \mathbf{in}(!y)@l_1.\mathbf{out}(y)@l_3$$

is insecure because the process at l' might evaluate prior to the process at l. ∎

Example 3. Another concern is the handling of indirect flows. Consider the program

$$l :: \mathbf{in}(a)@l_1.\mathbf{in}(b)@l_2$$

and an attacker observing whether the tuple b is removed from location l_2 or not. Based on this the attacker will know if the process was capable of removing the tuple a from location l_1. Therefore History-based Release allows the program for the policy $l_1 \overset{l}{\rightsquigarrow} l_2$, but not for $l_1 \overset{false}{\rightsquigarrow} l_2$. This is due to the fact that information can be observed by the attacker through the absence of a tuple in a tuple space. ∎

Example 4. Finally we wish to look at an example program that is insecure in the traditional setting where lattices are used as security policies. Consider the program

$$l :: \mathbf{in}(!x)@l_2.\mathbf{out}(x)@l_3.\mathbf{read}(!y)@l_1.\mathbf{out}(y)@l_2$$

which is secure for the policy in Fig. 5(a) when $l_1 = v_1$, $l_2 = v_2$ and $l_3 = v_3$. This is because evaluating the program does not result in information flowing from l_1 to l_3. ∎

4.2   Consistency of History-Based Release

In this subsection we argue the consistency of the definition of History-based Release. In particular we will discuss two of the principles presented by Sabelfeld and Sands in [21]. In the following we consider declassification to refer to constraints that are not trivially evaluated to *true* or *false*.

Conservativity: *Security for programs with no declassification is equivalent to non-interference.*

Limiting all constraints on edges in the flow graphs to only being of the simple form *true*, *false* or v gives us intransitive non-interference. Removing all non-trivial constraints (i.e. only having the constraints *true* and *false*) results in traditional non-interference.

Monotonicity of release: *Adding further declassifications to a secure program cannot render it insecure.*

Adding declassifications to a program coresponds to making our security policies less restrictive. Hence we aim to show that a program will be secure for any policy at least as restrictive as the original policy, for which it can be shown secure.

Lemma 2. *(Monotonicity) If $G \leq G'$ then $N_1 \approx_G N_2 \Rightarrow N_1 \approx_{G'} N_2$.*

Proof: It follows from Fact 1 that $(N_1|_{\nabla(\mathcal{V},G',\omega)} \sim N_2|_{\nabla(\mathcal{V},G',\omega)}) \Rightarrow (N_1|_{\nabla(\mathcal{V},G,\omega)} \sim N_2|_{\nabla(\mathcal{V},G,\omega)})$. The Lemma follows from Fact 2 and observing that to show $N_1 \approx_{G'} N_2$ we have either $N_1|_{\nabla(\mathcal{V},G',\omega)} \sim N_2|_{\nabla(\mathcal{V},G',\omega)}$, in which case we can reuse the proof for $N_1 \approx_G N_2$, or otherwise the result holds trivially. ∎

$$E(\mathbf{nil}) = \emptyset$$
$$E(P_1 \mid P_2) = E(P_1) \cup E(P_2)$$
$$E(A) = E(P) \quad \text{if } A \triangleq P$$
$$E(\mathbf{out}^{\iota}(t)@\ell.P) = \{\iota\}$$
$$E(\mathbf{in}^{\iota}(T)@\ell.P) = \{\iota\}$$
$$E(\mathbf{read}^{\iota}(T)@\ell.P) = \{\iota\}$$
$$E(\mathbf{eval}^{\iota}(Q)@\ell.P) = \{\iota\}$$
$$E(\mathbf{newloc}^{\iota}(u).P) = \{\iota\}$$
(a)

$$\hat{\sigma}[\![V]\!] = \{V\}$$
$$\hat{\sigma}[\![x]\!] = \hat{\sigma}(x)$$
$$\hat{\sigma}[\![l]\!] = \{l\}$$
$$\hat{\sigma}[\![u]\!] = \hat{\sigma}(u)$$
$$\hat{\sigma}[\![f, t]\!] = \hat{\sigma}[\![f]\!] \times \hat{\sigma}[\![t]\!]$$
(b)

Fig. 7. (a) Exposed labels in a process. (b) Extension of $\hat{\sigma}$ to templates.

5 Security Analysis

In this section we present an approach for verifying systems fulfillment of confidentiality wrt. History-based Release specified in a security policy. The analyses are given in the *Flow Logic* framework [18]. Hence the security guarantee is static and performed prior to the deployment of the system considered.

The analyses are based on the approach of Kemmerer [12]. Thus we analyse a system in two steps. First in Section 5.1 we identify the local dependencies; this is done by modifying a *control flow analysis* by introducing a novel component for the synchronization of events allowing it to track implicit flows. Second in Section 5.2 we describe a closure condition of the local dependencies to find the global dependencies. These two steps are independent of the security policy given for the considered system, and only related to the program analysed. The final step is the comparison of the security policy and the flow graph extracted from the program and in Section 5.3 we argue that the security enforced by our approach is History-based Release.

5.1 Local Dependencies

The local dependencies are identified by a *control flow analysis*. In fact we modify the analysis presented in [10] by introducing a novel component for capturing synchronizations performed in Klaim processes. Hence we will only briefly describe the other components, before focusing on the extension. The analysis for the net N is handled by judgements of the form

$$(\hat{T}, \hat{\sigma}, \hat{C}) \models N : \hat{G}$$

The component $\hat{T} : L \to \mathcal{P}(t)$ is an abstract mapping that associates a location or location variable with the set of tuples that might be present at the tuple space. The component $\hat{\sigma} : T \to \mathcal{P}(t)$ is an abstract mapping holding all possible bindings of a variable or locality variable (or a pattern of these) that might be introduced during execution. Furthermore we introduce the abstract mapping $\hat{C} : Lab \to \mathcal{P}(L)$ that associates the label of an action to the set of localities that the process has previously synchronized with during its execution. The labels of actions are introduced below. Finally we collect an abstract flow graph in the component $\hat{G} : L \to \mathcal{P}(L \times L)$ for describing the flow between tuple spaces

$$\hat{\sigma} \vDash_i \epsilon : \hat{V}_\circ \triangleright \hat{V}_\bullet \qquad \text{iff} \quad \{\hat{et} \in \hat{V}_\circ \mid |\hat{et}| = i - 1\} \sqsubseteq \hat{V}_\bullet$$

$$\hat{\sigma} \vDash_i V, T : \hat{V}_\circ \triangleright \hat{W}_\bullet \quad \text{iff} \quad \hat{\sigma} \vDash_{i+1} T : \hat{V}_\bullet \triangleright \hat{W}_\bullet \ \wedge \ \{\hat{et} \in \hat{V}_\circ \mid prj_i(\hat{et}) = V\} \sqsubseteq \hat{V}_\bullet$$

$$\hat{\sigma} \vDash_i l, T : \hat{V}_\circ \triangleright \hat{W}_\bullet \quad \text{iff} \quad \hat{\sigma} \vDash_{i+1} T : \hat{V}_\bullet \triangleright \hat{W}_\bullet \ \wedge \ \{\hat{et} \in \hat{V}_\circ \mid prj_i(\hat{et}) = l\} \sqsubseteq \hat{V}_\bullet$$

$$\hat{\sigma} \vDash_i x, T : \hat{V}_\circ \triangleright \hat{W}_\bullet \quad \text{iff} \quad \hat{\sigma} \vDash_{i+1} T : \hat{V}_\bullet \triangleright \hat{W}_\bullet \ \wedge \ \{\hat{et} \in \hat{V}_\circ \mid prj_i(\hat{et}) = \hat{\sigma}(x)\} \sqsubseteq \hat{V}_\bullet$$

$$\hat{\sigma} \vDash_i u, T : \hat{V}_\circ \triangleright \hat{W}_\bullet \quad \text{iff} \quad \hat{\sigma} \vDash_{i+1} T : \hat{V}_\bullet \triangleright \hat{W}_\bullet \ \wedge \ \{\hat{et} \in \hat{V}_\circ \mid prj_i(\hat{et}) = \hat{\sigma}(u)\} \sqsubseteq \hat{V}_\bullet$$

$$\hat{\sigma} \vDash_i !x, T : \hat{V}_\circ \triangleright \hat{W}_\bullet \ \text{iff} \quad \hat{\sigma} \vDash_{i+1} T : \hat{V}_\bullet \triangleright \hat{W}_\bullet \ \wedge \ \hat{V}_\circ \sqsubseteq \hat{V}_\bullet \ \wedge \ prj_i(\hat{W}_\bullet) \sqsubseteq \hat{\sigma}(x)$$

$$\hat{\sigma} \vDash_i !u, T : \hat{V}_\circ \triangleright \hat{W}_\bullet \ \text{iff} \quad \hat{\sigma} \vDash_{i+1} T : \hat{V}_\bullet \triangleright \hat{W}_\bullet \ \wedge \ \hat{V}_\circ \sqsubseteq \hat{V}_\bullet \ \wedge \ prj_i(\hat{W}_\bullet) \sqsubseteq \hat{\sigma}(u)$$

Fig. 8. Abstract tuple matching

and the location at which the process was executed. We write $l \overset{l''}{\mapsto} l'$ when a flow from l to l' occurs at l''.

An indirect flow can occur by synchronizing with a tuple space before synchronizing with another, as the attacker might observe the absence of the second synchronization. For tracking these flows we label the actions in a program. We define the function $E : P \to \mathcal{P}(Lab)$ as the fixpoint of the *exposed* set of labels. This allows us to track which actions have been executed prior to the one considered at present. The function is presented in Fig. 7(a).

When analysing an action we must use $\hat{C}$ to find the locations that it synchronizes with. The reason is that these might block further execution, if their templates can not be matched anything available at the location. Hence if the attacker can observe the result of an action that follows the one considered he will learn of the existence (or absence) of the tuples matched. Therefore for all input or read actions the condition $\forall \iota_P \in E(P) : \hat{C}(\iota) \cup \hat{\sigma}(\ell) \subseteq \hat{C}(\iota_P)$ must be fulfilled, where ι is the label of the considered action, $\hat{\sigma}(\ell)$ is the set of locations synchronized with and P is the remaining part of the process.

All local information flows must be found in $\hat{G}$. Hence whenever an action results in a flow of information we check that it is in $\hat{G}$. There are two actions that result in flow of information. Clearly the **out** action will output information to the specified location, and whether or not this happens will give away whether previous synchronizations were successful or not. Similarly the **in** action will remove a tuple from the specified location, hence we ensure that a flow is recorded in $\hat{G}$. We do so by emposing the condition $[\hat{C}(\iota) \overset{l}{\mapsto} \hat{\sigma}(\ell)] \subseteq \hat{G}$, where ι is the label of the action considered and $\hat{\sigma}(\ell)$ is the set of influenced locations.

The rest of the components of the analysis are the same as in [10]. The analysis is specified in Fig. 9. In Fig. 7(b) we extend the component $\hat{\sigma}$ for application on templates and in Fig. 8 the analysis of abstract tuple matching is presented.

5.2   Global Dependencies

The analysis of global dependencies are inspired by the approach of Kemmerer [12]. This approach utilizes a transitive closure of the local dependencies. In our setting the local dependencies were identified by the control flow analysis presented above. However as we wish to take execution traces into account, we need to extend the closure, so that the edges are labelled with regular expressions. The goal of the closure will be to guarantee that the language of regular

$$(\hat{T}, \hat{\sigma}, \hat{C}) \vDash l :: P : \hat{G} \qquad \text{iff} \quad (\hat{T}, \hat{\sigma}, \hat{C}) \vDash^{\lfloor l \rfloor} P : \hat{G}$$

$$(\hat{T}, \hat{\sigma}, \hat{C}) \vDash l :: \langle et \rangle : \hat{G} \qquad \text{iff} \quad \langle et \rangle \in \hat{T}(\lfloor l \rfloor)$$

$$(\hat{T}, \hat{\sigma}, \hat{C}) \vDash (N_1 \parallel N_2) : \hat{G} \qquad \text{iff} \quad (\hat{T}, \hat{\sigma}, \hat{C}) \vDash N_1 : \hat{G} \wedge$$
$$(\hat{T}, \hat{\sigma}, \hat{C}) \vDash N_2 : \hat{G}$$

$$(\hat{T}, \hat{\sigma}, \hat{C}) \vDash^l \mathbf{nil} : \hat{G} \qquad \text{iff} \quad true$$

$$(\hat{T}, \hat{\sigma}, \hat{C}) \vDash^l P_1 \mid P_2 : \hat{G} \qquad \text{iff} \quad (\hat{T}, \hat{\sigma}, \hat{C}) \vDash^l P_1 : \hat{G} \wedge$$
$$(\hat{T}, \hat{\sigma}, \hat{C}) \vDash^l P_2 : \hat{G}$$

$$(\hat{T}, \hat{\sigma}, \hat{C}) \vDash^l A : \hat{G} \qquad \text{iff} \quad (\hat{T}, \hat{\sigma}, \hat{C}) \vDash^l P : \hat{G} \wedge$$
$$A \triangleq P$$

$$(\hat{T}, \hat{\sigma}, \hat{C}) \vDash^l \mathbf{out}^\iota(t)@\ell.P : \hat{G} \qquad \text{iff} \quad \forall l' \in \hat{\sigma}(\ell) : \hat{\sigma}[\![t]\!] \subseteq \hat{T}(l') \wedge$$
$$[\hat{C}(\iota) \xmapsto{l} \hat{\sigma}(\ell)] \subseteq \hat{G} \wedge$$
$$\forall \iota_P \in E(P) : \hat{C}(\iota) \subseteq \hat{C}(\iota_P) \wedge$$
$$(\hat{T}, \hat{\sigma}, \hat{C}) \vDash^l P : \hat{G}$$

$$(\hat{T}, \hat{\sigma}, \hat{C}) \vDash^l \mathbf{in}^\iota(T)@\ell.P : \hat{G} \qquad \text{iff} \quad \forall l' \in \hat{\sigma}(\ell) : \hat{\sigma} \vdash_1 T : \hat{T}(l') \triangleright \hat{W}_\bullet \wedge$$
$$[\hat{C}(\iota) \xmapsto{l} \hat{\sigma}(\ell)] \subseteq \hat{G} \wedge$$
$$\forall \iota_P \in E(P) : \hat{C}(\iota) \cup \hat{\sigma}(\ell) \subseteq \hat{C}(\iota_P) \wedge$$
$$(\hat{T}, \hat{\sigma}, \hat{C}) \vDash^l P : \hat{G}$$

$$(\hat{T}, \hat{\sigma}, \hat{C}) \vDash^l \mathbf{read}^\iota(T)@\ell.P : \hat{G} \qquad \text{iff} \quad \forall l' \in \hat{\sigma}(\ell) : \hat{\sigma} \vdash_1 T : \hat{T}(l') \triangleright \hat{W}_\bullet \wedge$$
$$\forall \iota_P \in E(P) : \hat{C}(\iota) \cup \hat{\sigma}(\ell) \subseteq \hat{C}(\iota_P) \wedge$$
$$(\hat{T}, \hat{\sigma}, \hat{C}) \vDash^l P : \hat{G}$$

$$(\hat{T}, \hat{\sigma}, \hat{C}) \vDash^l \mathbf{eval}^\iota(Q)@\ell.P : \hat{G} \qquad \text{iff} \quad \forall \iota_Q \in E(Q) : \hat{C}(\iota) \subseteq \hat{C}(\iota_Q) \wedge$$
$$\forall l' \in \hat{\sigma}(\ell) : (\hat{T}, \hat{\sigma}, \hat{C}) \vDash^{l'} Q : \hat{G} \wedge$$
$$\forall \iota_P \in E(P) : \hat{C}(\iota) \subseteq \hat{C}(\iota_P) \wedge$$
$$(\hat{T}, \hat{\sigma}, \hat{C}) \vDash^l P : \hat{G}$$

$$(\hat{T}, \hat{\sigma}, \hat{C}) \vDash^l \mathbf{newloc}^\iota(u).P : \hat{G} \qquad \text{iff} \quad \{\lfloor u \rfloor\} \subseteq \hat{\sigma}(\lfloor u \rfloor) \wedge$$
$$\forall \iota_P \in E(P) : \hat{C}(\iota) \subseteq \hat{C}(\iota_P) \wedge$$
$$(\hat{T}, \hat{\sigma}, \hat{C}) \vDash^l P : \hat{G}$$

Fig. 9. Flow analysis

expressions connected to an edge does indeed accept all the executions traces in which the information flow happens. Therefore a correct closure must guarantee that the resulting labelled graph has an edge from a node n_0 to another node n_k, whenever there exists a path possibly through other nodes in the local flow graph. Furthermore the labels in the resulting graph must accept a language that is a superset of all the languages in the local flow graphs.

Definition 11. *A correct closure $\hat{\mathcal{H}}$ of the flow graph $\hat{G}$, written $\hat{G} \trianglelefteq \hat{\mathcal{H}}$, is defined as $\hat{G} \trianglelefteq \hat{\mathcal{H}}$ iff*

$$\forall n_0 \xmapsto{l_1} n_1 \xmapsto{l_2} \cdots \xmapsto{l_k} n_k \in \hat{G} : \exists \delta : l_1 \cdots l_k \in [\![\delta]\!] \wedge n_0 \xrightarrow{\delta} n_k \in \hat{\mathcal{H}}$$

where $n_0 \xmapsto{l_1} n_1 \xmapsto{l_2} \cdots \xmapsto{l_k} n_k \in \hat{G}$ means $\forall i : n_{i-1} \xmapsto{l_i} n_i \in \hat{G}$.

One algorithm that can be used to compute the least $\hat{\mathcal{H}}$ such that $\hat{G} \trianglelefteq \hat{\mathcal{H}}$ is the *Pigeonhole Principle* presented in [11].

5.3 Static Security

We are confident that the static analyses presented above compute a flow graph $\hat{\mathcal{H}}$ for which the analyzed net comply with History-based Release.

Conjecture 1. *If $(\hat{T}, \hat{\sigma}, \hat{C}) \vDash N : \hat{G}$ and $\hat{G} \trianglelefteq \hat{\mathcal{H}}$ then $N \approx_{\hat{\mathcal{H}}} N$.*

In fact the analyses ensure that the analyzed net comply with History-based Release for any policy that is at least as restrictive as $\hat{\mathcal{H}}$.

Corollary 1. *If $(\hat{T}, \hat{\sigma}, \hat{C}) \vDash N : \hat{G}$, $\hat{G} \trianglelefteq \hat{\mathcal{H}}$ and $\hat{\mathcal{H}} \leq G$ then $N \approx_G N$.*

Proof: Follows from Lemma 2 and Conjecture 1. ■

6 Related Work

Traditionally policies for information flow security have been of the form of security lattices [1,6] where an underlying hierarchical structure on the principals in the system is assumed and reflected in the security lattice. Hence the principals are tied to security levels and an ordering of security levels indicate what information is observable to a principal. Security lattices have found a widespread usage in language-based approaches to information flow security, see e.g. [24,20].

In this paper we base our security policies on labelled graphs, i.e. without assigning an underlying ordering. Due to the lack of underlying ordering the expressiveness of the policies is increased, allowing for simplified specification of security policies for systems. One example is systems that let a principal act on resources in different security domains without causing a flow of information in between. The expressiveness gained is due to the transitive nature of the ordering in a lattice. Graphs have previously been used as information flow policies in [23]. Furthermore these policies relate back to resource matrices applied for e.g. covert channel identification [12,15].

Clearly the translation of a policy specified as a lattice to a labelled graph is straightforward. For each security level a security domain is introduced. Edges (labelled *true*) are added between security domains according to the ordering of the corresponding security levels.

The *Decentralized Label Model* by Myers and Liskov [17,16] is a framework for security policies that allows owners of information to specify who is permitted to read that information. The basis model is still a lattice and does not provide expressiveness similar to what is presented in this paper.

6.1 Semantical Security Conditions

The goal of specifying whether a system complies with what is stated in an information flow policy has been formally stated as *non-interference* [5,7]. Informally non-interference states that for all input to a system, that varies only on information not observable to the attacker, the resulting output will only vary on information not observable to the attacker. We showed in Section 4.2 that History-based Release generalises non-interference.

Non-Disclosure by Matos and Boudol [14] proposes extending the syntax of a ML-like calculus with specific constructs for loosening the security policy. These constructs have the form

$$\text{flow } A \prec B \text{ in } M$$

where M is an expression and A and B are security levels. The construct extends the security relation to permit information to flow from A to B in M and thereby permits *disclosure* of confidential information in lexically scoped parts of programs. The policies presented in this paper allow for flows to be scoped within a specified location, i.e. locations tied with a security domain. Clearly by introducing a security domain tied to a *fresh* location for each flow construct and constraining the information flow to only happen in execution traces containing the security domain we get scoped flows. Finally due to the transitive nature of underlying lattice structure in [14], we need to perform a transitive closure on the resulting graph to achieve the same effect in our policies. In this manner the *Non-Disclosure* property can be seen as a specialisation of the History-based Release property. Obviously the *Non-Disclosure* property does not have the expressiveness to handle constraints on execution traces.

Intransitive non-interference. Goguen and Meseguer [7] generalised non-interference to *intransitive non-interference* while observing that information flows might be permitted when properly filtered at specified security levels. The property was further investigated in [9,19] and adapted to a language-based setting by Mantel and Sands [13]. Mantel and Sands [13] formalise intransitive non-interference so that two goals are achieved. First the place in the program where information flow is limited through a syntactical extension of the language. Second the security level where information flows through is specified through an extension of the security lattice by an intransitive component.

History-based Release incorporates these concerns. The place in the program where information flow is guaranteed in the same way as described above for the non-disclosure property. Furthermore the locality-based security policies are intransitive due to being based on graphs rather than lattices.

Non-interference until by Chong and Myers [3,4] propose adding conditions to security policies based on lattices. This is done by introducing a special annotated flow into the security policies of the form $\ell_0 \overset{c_1}{\rightsquigarrow} \cdots \overset{c_k}{\rightsquigarrow} \ell_k$ which states that information can be gradually downgraded along with the fulfilment of the conditions $c_1, \ldots, c_k$. It is straightforward to represent the downgrading condition with History-based Release.

However, observe that once the conditions are fulfilled, information can flow directly from ℓ_0 to any of the security levels $\ell_1, \ldots, \ell_k$. Therefore *non-interference until* does not provide the intransitive guarantees of History-based Release. Another point is the temporal constraints that History-based Release enforce on execution traces. *Non-interference until* provides simple temporal guarantees, namely that conditions are fulfilled prior to downgrading, however neither the order of the fulfilment nor the conditions allow for temporal constraints.

Flow Locks. Recently Broberg and Sands [2] introduced the novel concept of *flow locks* as a framework for dynamic information flow policies. The policies are specified in syntactical constructs introduced in an ML-like calculus. The constructs are utilised in the opening and closing of flow locks, these locks are used in constraining the information flows in the policies. The policies have the form $\{\sigma_1 \Rightarrow A_1; \ldots; \sigma_n \Rightarrow A_n\}$ and are annotated to declarations of variables in the programs. These policies correspond to ours, where a policy needs to specify where information might flow globally during execution and is hence not transitively closed. The major difference is that our policies can include temporal constraints which cannot be expressed in the flow locks policies.

Another major difference between [2] and the present paper is the intuition behind the security condition. In the flow lock setting information can flow to security levels as specified in the policies, as long as necessary locks are opened beforehand. This differs from our definition in not being tied to the actual flow of information. E.g. once a lock is open information can flow from several levels and several times. Furthermore flow locks have no way of observing if a lock has been closed and opened again between two flows. In our setting the constraints on the execution trace must be fulfilled for every single flow, hence it is not sufficient that another process is executed at the right location, just before or after considered flow.

7   Conclusion

We have presented a novel concept of locality-based security policies for information flow security. These policies are based on labelled graphs and we have illustrated how this allows for a simpler specification of certain policies. Furthermore we have presented the History-based Release condition that formalise how temporal conditions and intransitive information flow are captured in the security policies.

A static analysis is presented as a mechanism for verification of systems. The analysis is divided into three parts. Since the first part is the only syntax-directed part and as it is independent of the security policy for the given system it can freely be exchanged. Hence allowing us to analyse other process calculi or even programming languages. Future investigation might consider possibilities of adapting History-based Release to hardware description languages where locations could be mapped to blocks in structural specifications.

References

1. Bell, D.E., LaPadula, L.J.: Secure computer systems: Mathematical foundations. Technical Report MTR-2547, vol. 1, MITRE Corp., Bedford, MA (1973)
2. Broberg, N., Sands, D.: Flow locks: Towards a core calculus for dynamic flow policies. In: Proc. European Symposium on Programming, pp. 180–196 (2006)
3. Chong, S., Myers, A.C.: Security policies for downgrading. In: CCS '04. Proceedings of the 11th ACM conference on Computer and communications security, New York, USA, pp. 198–209. ACM Press, New York (2004)

4. Chong, S., Myers, A.C.: Language-based information erasure. In: CSFW, pp. 241–254 (2005)

5. Cohen, E.S.: Information transmission in computational systems. ACM SIGOPS Operating Systems Review 11(5), 133–139 (1977)

6. Denning, D.E.: A lattice model of secure information flow. Comm. of the ACM 19(5), 236–243 (1976)

7. Goguen, J.A., Meseguer, J.: Security policies and security models. In: Proc. IEEE Symp. on Security and Privacy, pp. 11–20 (April 1982)

8. Gorla, D., Pugliese, R.: Resource access and mobility control with dynamic privileges acquisition. In: Baeten, J.C.M., Lenstra, J.K., Parrow, J., Woeginger, G.J. (eds.) ICALP 2003. LNCS, vol. 2719, pp. 119–132. Springer, Heidelberg (2003)

9. Haigh, J.T., Young, W.D.: Extending the Non-Interference Version of MLS for SAT. In: IEEE Symposium on Security and Privacy, pp. 232–239. IEEE Computer Society Press, Los Alamitos (1986)

10. Hansen, R.R., Probst, C.W., Nielson, F.: Sandboxing in myklaim. In: Proc. ARES'06 (2006)

11. Hopcroft, J.E., Motwani, R., Ullman, J.D.: Introduction to automata theory, languages, and computation, 2nd edn. Addison-Wesley, London (2001)

12. Kemmerer, R.A.: A practical approach to identifying storage and timing channels. In: IEEE Symposium on Security and Privacy, pp. 66–73 (1982)

13. Mantel, H., Sands, D.: Controlled declassification based on intransitive noninterference. In: Chin, W.-N. (ed.) APLAS 2004. LNCS, vol. 3302, pp. 129–145. Springer, Heidelberg (2004)

14. Matos, A.A., Boudol, G.: On declassification and the non-disclosure policy. In: Proc. IEEE Computer Security Foundations Workshop, pp. 226–240 (2005)

15. McHugh, J.: Covert Channel Analysis. Handbook for the Computer Security Certification of Trusted Systems (1995)

16. Myers, A.C.: Jflow: Practical mostly-static information flow control. In: POPL, pp. 228–241 (1999)

17. Myers, A.C., Liskov, B.: A decentralized model for information flow control. In: SOSP, pp. 129–142 (1997)

18. Nielson, H.R., Nielson, F.: Flow logic: A multi-paradigmatic approach to static analysis. In: The Essence of Computation, pp. 223–244 (2002)

19. Rushby, J.: Noninterference, Transitivity, and Channel-Control Security Policies. Technical Report CSL-92-02, SRI International (December 1992)

20. Sabelfeld, A., Myers, A.C.: Language-based information-flow security. IEEE J. Selected Areas in Communications 21(1), 5–19 (2003)

21. Sabelfeld, A., Sands, D.: Dimensions and principles of declassification. In: Proc. IEEE Computer Security Foundations Workshop. IEEE Computer Society Press, Los Alamitos (2005)

22. Sabelfeld, A., Sands, D.: Probabilistic noninterference for multi-threaded programs. In: CSFW, pp. 200–214 (2000)

23. Tolstrup, T.K., Nielson, F., Riis, H.: Information Flow Analysis for VHDL. In: Proc. Eighth International Conference on Parallel Computing Technologies. LNCS, Springer, Heidelberg (2005)

24. Volpano, D., Smith, G., Irvine, C.: A sound type system for secure flow analysis. J. Computer Security 4(3), 167–187 (1996)

25. Volpano, D.M., Smith, G.: Probabilistic noninterference in a concurrent language. Journal of Computer Security 7(1) (1999)

A Theorem-Proving Approach to Verification of Fair Non-repudiation Protocols

Kun Wei and James Heather

Department of Computing, University of Surrey, Guildford, Surrey GU2 7XH, UK
{k.wei,j.heather}@surrey.ac.uk

Abstract. We use a PVS embedding of the stable failures model of CSP to verify non-repudiation protocols, allowing us to prove the correctness of properties that are difficult to analyze in full generality with a model checker. The PVS formalization comprises a semantic embedding of CSP and a collection of theorems and proof rules for reasoning about non-repudiation properties. The well-known Zhou-Gollmann protocol is analyzed within this framework.

1 Introduction

Over the past decade, formal methods have been remarkably successful in their application to the analysis of security protocols. For example, the combination of CSP and FDR [10,8,12] has proved to be an excellent tool for modelling and verifying safety properties such as authentication and confidentiality. However, non-repudiation properties have not yet been mastered to the same degree since they must often be expressed as liveness properties and the vast bulk of work to date has been concerned only with safety properties.

Schneider has shown in [13] how to extend the CSP approach to analyze non-repudiation protocols. His proofs of correctness, based on the traces and the stable failures models of CSP as well as on rank functions, are constructed by hand. For safety properties, one usually assumes that one honest party wishes to communicate with another honest party, and one asks whether a dishonest intruder can disrupt the communications so as to effect breach of security. When considering non-repudiation, however, we are concerned with protecting one honest party against possible cheating by his or her interlocutor. Thus a non-repudiation protocol enables parties such as a sender Alice and a responder Bob to send and receive messages, and provides them with evidence so that neither of them can deny having sent or received these messages when they later resort to a judge for resolving a dispute.

There are two basic types of non-repudiation: *Non-repudiation of Origin (NRO)* provides Bob with evidence of origin that unambiguously shows that Alice has previously sent a particular message, and *Non-repudiation of Receipt (NRR)* provides Alice with evidence of receipt that unambiguously shows that Bob has received the message. Unforgeable digital signatures are usually the mechanism by which NRO and NRR can be obtained.

T. Dimitrakos et al. (Eds.): FAST 2006, LNCS 4691, pp. 202–219, 2007.
© Springer-Verlag Berlin Heidelberg 2007

However, a major problem often arises: there may come a point during the run at which either Alice or Bob reaches an advantageous position; for example, Alice may have collected all the evidence she needs before Bob has collected his, and Alice may then deliberately abandon the protocol to keep her advantageous position. Usually we will want to ensure that the protocol is *fair*.

- *Fairness* guarantees that neither Alice nor Bob can reach a point where he or she has obtained non-repudiation evidence, but where the other party is prevented from retrieving any required evidence that has not already been obtained.

Obviously fairness is the most difficult property to achieve in the design of such protocols, and several different solutions have been proposed. Two kinds of approach are discussed in [6], classified according to whether or not the protocol uses a third trusted party (TTP). The first kind of approach providing fairness in exchange protocols is based on either a *gradual exchange* [17] or *probabilistic protocol* [9]. Without the involvement of a TTP, a sender Alice gradually releases messages to a responder Bob over many rounds of a protocol, with the number of rounds chosen by Alice and unknown to Bob. Bob is supposed to respond for every message, and any failure to respond may cause Alice to stop the protocol. However, such protocols require that all parties have the same computational power, and a large number of messages must be exchanged. The other kind of approach uses a TTP to handle some of the evidence. Many fair non-repudiation protocols use the TTP as a delivery authority to establish and transmit some key evidence. The efficiency of such protocols depends on how much a TTP is involved in the communication, since heavy involvement of the TTP may become a bottleneck of communication and computation.

In the CSP model, fairness is naturally described as a liveness property. It is impossible for fairness to guarantee that both Alice and Bob can collect the required evidence simultaneously, since we are dealing with an asynchronous network, but it does guarantee that either of them must be able to access the evidence as long as the other party has obtained it. In this paper, we will verify the correctness of fairness of the Zhou-Gollmann protocol [20] using the process algebra CSP and its semantics embedding in a PVS theorem prover.

We have shown how to go some way towards verifying fairness of the ZG protocol using CSP and the FDR model checker in a recent paper [19]. However, in order to keep the problem tractable, it was necessary there to model a system with very small numbers of parties and messages; it was not possible to use the model-checking approach to prove fairness of the protocol in its full generality, or even for a system of a moderate size.

Evans and Schneider [4,13] give a useful start on this issue by using rank functions and the PVS embedding of the traces model of CSP to verify safety properties such as *NRO* and *NRR*. Our model, to some degree extending their work, can verify not only safety specifications, but also liveness specifications by means of embedding the stable failures model of CSP into the PVS theorem prover; in consequence, we can prove fairness, which cannot be tackled within their model.

In the remainder of this paper, we give a brief introduction to the CSP notation and to the embedding of CSP in PVS. We present the ZG protocol and its analysis, and then show the formalization of the protocol modelling and of its verification in PVS. Finally, we discuss and compare with other verification approaches for non-repudiation protocols.

2   CSP Notation

In CSP, a system can be considered as a process that might be hierarchically composed of many smaller processes. An individual process can be combined with events or other processes by operators such as prefixing, choice, parallel composition, and so on. There are four semantic models available—traces, stable failures, failures/divergences, and failures/divergences/infinite traces—and which one is chosen depends on what properties of the system one is trying to analyze. For safety properties, the traces model of CSP is enough. In this paper, we use the stable failures model of CSP to verify fairness in the ZG protocol. We will briefly illustrate the CSP language and the semantic models; for a fuller introduction, the reader is referred to [11,15].

Stop is a stable deadlocked process that never performs any events. The process $c \rightarrow P$ behaves like P after performing the event c. An event like c may be compounded; for example, one often used patten of events is $c.i.j.m$ consisting of a channel c, a sender i, a receiver j and a message m. The output $c!x \rightarrow P$ describes a process which is initially willing to output x along channel c, and then behave as P. The input $c?x : T \rightarrow P(x)$ denotes that it is initially ready to accept any value x of type T along channel c, and subsequently behave as $P(x)$.

The external choice $P_1 \square P_2$ may behave either like P_1 or like P_2, depending on what events its environment initially offers it. The traces of internal choice $P_1 \sqcap P_2$ are the same as those of $P_1 \square P_2$, but the choice in this case is non-deterministic.

The interface parallel $P_1 \underset{A}{\|} P_2$ is the process where all events in the set A must be synchronized, and other events can be performed independently by P_1 and P_2 respectively. An interleaving $P_1 \,|||\, P_2$ executes each part entirely independently and is equivalent with $P_1 \underset{\emptyset}{\|} P_2$.

A trace is defined to be a finite sequence of events. A refusal set is a set of events from which a process can fail to accept anything no matter how long it is offered; $refusals(P/t)$ is the set of P's refusals after the trace t; then (t, X) is a failure in which X denotes $refusals(P/t)$. If the trace t can make no internal progress, this failure is called a *stable failure*.

Liveness is concerned with behaviour that a process is guaranteed to make available, and can be inferred from stable failures; for example, if, for a fixed trace t, we have $a \notin X$ for all stable failures of P of the form (t, X), then a must be available after P has performed t.

Verification of property specifications is done by means of determining whether one process satisfies a specification. In the stable failures model, this equates to checking whether the traces and failures of one process are subsets of the traces and failures of the other:

$$P \text{ sat } S \Leftrightarrow \forall tr \in traces(P) \bullet S(tr) \wedge \forall (tr, X) \in failures(P) \bullet S(tr, X)$$

where $traces(P)$ collects all traces of the process P and $failures(P)$ denotes the set of stable failures of P.

For the properties we are considering, if S satisfies the property specification we are verifying, then P also holds such a property.

3   Embedding CSP Semantics in PVS

Full details of the embedding of the stable failures model of CSP in PVS for mechanizing proofs is presented in [18].

In the analysis of security protocols, we usually do not require modelling of successful termination; therefore, we here use a simplified version of the embedding of CSP in order to reduce the complexity of verification to some extent.

The stable failures model is represented by pairs (T, F) in which T is a set of traces that forms the semantics of a process in the traces model. The classic formalization of traces is to simply consider traces as lists of events. PVS has provided a predefined abstract datatype `list`. Thus, the type `trace` is defined as follows:

```
trace: TYPE = list[E]
```

where E is a parameter to denote the events appearing in the lists.

Table 1. CSP syntax

Operation	CSP	PVS
Stop	$Stop$	Stop
Prefix	$a \rightarrow P$	a >> P
External choice	$P_1 \square P_2$	P1 \/ P2
Internal choice	$P_1 \sqcap P_2$	P1 /\ P2
Interface parallel	$P_1 \underset{A}{\parallel} P_2$	Par(A)(P1,P2)
Interleave	$P_1 \mid\mid\mid P_2$	P1 // P2

Processes in the stable failures model consist of pairs (T, F) that satisfy various conditions, which can be found in [18], or in [11,15]. Some of CSP's main operators are listed in Table 1, with the standard CSP syntax and PVS's syntax. We also use the relation '<=' to denote satisfaction; for example, $P \text{ sat } S$ is represented as P<=S in PVS.

Recursive processes in CSP are defined in terms of equational definitions. We here formalize such processes by using the 'μ-calculus' theory to compute the least fixed point of a monotonic function[1]. We also have proved a general fixed point induction theorem to verify recursive processes. In order for fixed points to be useful, we have extended the least fixed point theory to represent mutually recursive processes and to prove whether a function has a unique fixed point.

In addition, we have proved a number of algebraic laws which are essential in the verification of properties of processes; these laws can also help us to verify the consistency of the CSP semantics. For more detailed explanations of the embedding of CSP in PVS, readers are advised to consult [18].

4   The Zhou-Gollmann Protocol

Zhou and Gollmann present a basic fair non-repudiation protocol using a lightweight TTP in [20], which supports non-repudiation of origin and non-repudiation of receipt as well as fairness. The main idea of the Zhou-Gollmann protocol is that a sender Alice delivers the ciphertext and the message key to Bob separately; the ciphertext is sent from the originator Alice to the recipient Bob, and Alice then sends the message key encrypted with her secret key to the TTP. Finally Alice and Bob may get their evidence from the TTP to establish the required non-repudiation. The notation below is used in the protocol description.

- M: message to be sent from A to B.
- K: symmetric key chosen by A.
- C: commitment (ciphertext) for message M encrypted with K.
- L: a unique label used to identify a particular protocol run.
- $f_{EOO}, f_{EOR}, f_{SUB}, f_{CON}$: flags indicating the purpose of a signed message.
- s_i: an asymmetric key used to generate i's digital signature.

After cutting down the plaintext part, the simplified protocol can be described as follows:

$$1. \ A \rightarrow B : \ s_A(f_{EOO}, B, L, C)$$
$$2. \ B \rightarrow A : \ s_B(f_{EOR}, A, L, C)$$
$$3. \ A \rightarrow TTP : \ s_A(f_{SUB}, B, L, K)$$
$$4. \ B \leftrightarrow TTP : \ s_T(f_{CON}, A, B, L, K)$$
$$5. \ A \leftrightarrow TTP : \ s_T(f_{CON}, A, B, L, K)$$

We briefly examine the protocol step by step to see how it works. Firstly, Alice composes a message including a flag, a unique label L, the receiver's name B and a ciphertext $C = K(M)$; Alice then signs the message with her private key and sends it to Bob. Secondly, Bob collects the message as one piece of evidence in which the label L identifies the run of the protocol, and then Bob responds with his signed message to provide A with evidence that B really has

---

[1] A monotonic function in this context is a function F such that if $Q \sqsubseteq P$ then $F(Q) \sqsubseteq F(P)$.

received C in this run. After she has got a response, Alice submits the encrypted message key K to the TTP. The TTP then decrypts it to get the K, generates the associated evidence encrypted with its private key and makes it available to Alice and Bob. Finally, Alice and Bob can fetch the evidence respectively.

The guarantee of fairness of such a protocol comes from an assumption that the channels between TTP and the parties are *resilient*; that is, messages may be delayed, but will eventually arrive in a finite amount of time. However, the channels between Alice and Bob can be unreliable; that is, the medium may delay, lose or misdirect messages.

5   CSP Modelling

Schneider in [13] gives an excellent overview of how to extend the CSP approach to analyze non-repudiation protocols. Because of the absence of mechanizing support, however, his proof of correctness has to be constructed by hand. Our version, whilst based on his analysis, is machine-assisted and makes various changes to the model in order to bring it closer a real-world implementation of the protocol.

Fairness says that if either A or B has managed to retrieve full evidence, the other party cannot be prevented indefinitely from retrieving the evidence. We cannot assert for verifying fairness that once A has obtained the evidence then B must have obtained the evidence as well, because there may be a delay between A's reception and B's reception. However, we can ensure that the evidence must be available to B, or that a specific action must be about to happen to enable B to get the evidence in the future.

To check a protocol like this one with CSP, we have to build models of the parties, the TTP and the medium and see how they can interfere with each other. Since the protocol is used to protect parties that do not trust each other, we do not adopt the traditional Dolev-Yao model [2], which provides a special intruder; instead, in our model, one of two communicating parties is an intruder. Fairness is only guaranteed to the party who runs in accordance with the protocol; for example, if A releases the symmetric key K before B responds, A will certainly place herself in a disadvantageous position.

It is also important, for a fully general proof, to allow other agents to participate on the network, since the protocol is expected to be correct no matter how many parties there are. We use a similar structure to that given by Schneider; the structure is shown in Figure 1.

The transmission of messages between parties is modelled by a CSP channel *trans*: the event *trans.i.j.m* denotes that party i transmits a message m to party j. Similarly, the receipt of messages is modelled as a channel *rec*: the event *rec.i.j.m* means that i receives a message m from j. The medium plays a role of the unreliable channel, whereas the the resilient channel is removed out of the medium and is used to directly link parties and the TTP. The communication in the resilient channel is modelled as *send* and *get*. In addition, the parties have an *evidence* channel which they use to announce the evidence.

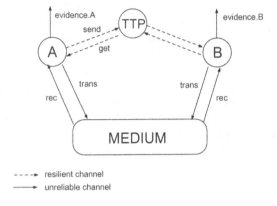

Fig. 1. Network for the ZG protocol

The entire network is generally represented as the parallel composition of these components:

$$NETWORK = ((\|\|_{i \in USER} Party_i) \underset{\{send,get\}}{\|} TTP)$$

$$\underset{\{trans,rec\}}{\|} Medium$$

In our scenario, we will treat A as a dishonest party, or a spy, and B as an honest party who always performs in accordance with the protocol; A and B may behave either as a sender or as a responder; A and B may run the protocol consecutively, and A may make use of the information deduced from B's messages to initiate a new run and may change her role at will. We also assume that more parities are able to communicate with A and B and consider the worst case that all parties except B are dishonest parties in the network. Therefore, such a network is further described as following:

$$NETWORK = (Party_B \|\|\| (\|\|_{i \in USER \setminus \{B\}} Spy_i)) \underset{\{send,get\}}{\|} TTP$$

$$\underset{\{trans,rec\}}{\|} Medium$$

5.1   Defining Honest Parties

The basic assumption underlying the definition is that the party B is not able to release his private key, reuse a label, or lose evidence he has already got. In our model, the party B can act either as a sender or as a responder.

$$Party_B = SEND \ \Box \ RESP$$

When acting as a sender, the party B running the protocol will then be described as follows:

$$SEND = \square_{i \in User} \; trans.B!i!s_B(f_{EOO}.i.L.C)$$

$$\rightarrow rec.B.i.s_i(f_{EOR}.B.L.C)$$

$$\rightarrow send.B.TTP.s_B(f_{SUB}.i.L.K)$$

$$\rightarrow get.B.TTP.s_T(f_{CON}.i.B.L.K) \rightarrow Party_B$$

Here we define that B is not included in the set $USER$. The responder process performs the protocol from the opposite perspective. B acting as a responder is described as follows:

$$RESP = \square_{j \in User} \; rec.B?j!s_j(f_{EOO}.B.L.C)$$

$$\rightarrow trans.B.j.s_B(f_{EOR}.j.L.C)$$

$$\rightarrow get.B.TTP.s_T(f_{CON}.j.B.L.K) \rightarrow Party_B$$

Obtaining the *evidence* channel to announce the evidence for an honest party is somewhat unnecessary since the $Party_B$ can get the evidence only through his interlocutor and the TTP. However, a dishonest party may obtain the evidence from someone else.

5.2   Creating a Spy

In our modelling of the non-repudiation protocol, we do not define a special party, a spy, as different from the legitimate parties. We assume that one of two communicating parties is a spy who may be able to deduce something of value from the messages it has received. The non-repudiation protocol is supposed to provide fairness for an honest party even if the other party is a spy.

The behaviour of a spy on the network is therefore described by the CSP process Spy:

$$Spy_i(S) = (\square_{m \in S} \; trans.i.!j!m \rightarrow Spy_i(S))$$

$$\square \; rec.i.?j?m \rightarrow Spy_i(Close(S \cup \{m\}))$$

$$\square \; (\square_{m \in S} \; send.i.TTP!m \rightarrow Spy_i(S))$$

$$\square \; get.i.TTP?m \rightarrow Spy_i(Close(S \cup \{m\}))$$

$$\square \; (\square_{m \in S} \; evidence.i?m \rightarrow Spy_i(S))$$

The spy is able to transmit anything over the network that can be deduced from the messages she has already learnt. She is also able to receive anything transmitted over the network.

The spy has an initial basic knowledge, such as public keys, labels and so on, and can build a number of legitimate messages before the start of the protocol. The $Close(S)$ function returns the set S closed up under these deduction rules. We here allow the spy to have three types of deduction based on constructing and extracting sequences, symmetric-key encryption and public-key encryption. For example, if she knows $\{K(M), K\}$, the spy can deduce M. However, the spy is supposed not to know other parties' private keys since they will never transmit these keys on the network.

5.3   Medium and TTP

The medium provides two types of message delivery service: one is an unreliable channel where messages might be lost, delayed and sent to any address; another one is a resilient channel where messages might be delayed, but will eventually arrive, and also be guaranteed not to arrive at the wrong address. The medium here is defined only for the unreliable channel, since the resilient channel will be integrated into the definition of the TTP.

$$Medium(S) = (\ trans!i!j!m \rightarrow Medium(S \cup \{m\})$$

$$\Box\ (\Box_{m \in S}\ rec?i?j?m \rightarrow Medium(S \backslash \{m\}))\ \Box\ idle \rightarrow Medium(S)$$

Note that the medium can deliver a message to the wrong destination, which means that it may lose messages in some sense. The $idle$ channel may cause messages to be delayed at random.

The trusted third party is expected to act in accordance with its role in the protocol; that is, the TTP accepts signed messages, generates new evidence and makes them available to associated parties. It is therefore modelled as follows:

$$TTP(S) = (\ send!i!TTP!m \rightarrow TTP(S \cup Evi(i, m)))$$

$$\Box\ (\Box_{e \in S}\ get?e \rightarrow TTP(S)))\ \Box\ idle \rightarrow TTP(S)$$

The TTP also plays the role of the resilient channel, along with the $idle$ channel that causes delays to message delivery. The $Evi(\{(i, m)\}))$ generates two copies of the evidence, for example, in this case they are $A.TTP.s_T$ $(f_{CON}.A.B.L.K)$ and $B.TTP.s_T(f_{CON}.A.B.L.K)$, so that only involved parties are able to have access to the evidence. It is important to note the underlying assumption hidden in this definition: the TTP always stores evidence it has generated and never discards it.

5.4   Specification

We here concentrate on fairness of the ZG protocol since Evans and Schneider [4,13] have provided rigorous verification of *Non-repudiation of Origin* and *Non-repudiation of receipt* in PVS by using the embedding of the traces model of CSP and rank functions.

Fairness is naturally expressed in the stable failures model of CSP. The essence of the idea is that if one of the two parties has obtained full evidence, then the other party either is already in possession of it or is able to access it. Since fairness is guaranteed only to a party who performs completely in accordance with the protocol, we here give only two specifications according to the different roles of B.

First, we deal with the case where B acts as a responder; that is, if A has proof of receipt, then B must be in a position to obtain proof of origin. Thus the formal specification is given as follows:

$$
\begin{aligned}
FAIR1(tr, X) \cong\ & evidence.A.s_T(f_{CON}.A.B.L.K) \in tr \\
& \land\ evidence.A.s_B(f_{EOR}.A.L.C) \in tr \\
& \Rightarrow \\
& rec.B.A.s_A(f_{EOO}.B.L.C) \in tr \\
& \land\ (get.B.TTP.s_T(f_{CON}.A.B.L.K) \in tr \\
& \quad \lor\ get.B.TTP.s_T(f_{CON}.A.B.L.K) \notin X)
\end{aligned}
$$

and the requirement on the system is that

$$NETWORK \quad \mathbf{sat} \quad FAIR1(tr, X)$$

The above specification states that if A holds full evidence, then B must either be able to get the evidence or have already obtained the evidence.

Secondly, we deal with the case in which B acts as a sender; that is, if A has proof of origin, then B must be in a position to obtain proof of receipt. It is therefore modelled as follows:

$$
\begin{aligned}
FAIR2(tr, X) \cong\ & evidence.A.s_T(f_{CON}.A.B.L.K) \in tr \\
& \land\ evidence.A.s_B(f_{EOO}.A.L.C) \in tr \\
& \Rightarrow \\
& rec.B.s_A(f_{EOR}.B.L.C) \in tr \\
& \land\ (get.B.TTP.s_T(f_{CON}.A.B.L.K) \in tr \\
& \quad \lor\ get.B.TTP.s_T(f_{CON}.A.B.L.K) \notin X)
\end{aligned}
$$

and the specification is:

$$NETWORK \quad \mathbf{sat} \quad FAIR2(tr, X)$$

We now need to verify the two assertions above by translating the specifications into PVS notation.

6   The Fairness Model in PVS

The fairness property requires that if A has obtained full evidence, then B either is already in possession of it or is able to access it; for example, in the

$FAIR1$ specification, if A has got $s_B(f_{EOR}.A.L.C)$ and $s_T(f_{CON}.A.B.L.K)$, then either both messages $s_A(f_{EOO}.B.L.C)$ and $s_T(f_{CON}.A.B.L.K)$ must have been appeared in the trace of B or the event $get.B.TTP.s_T(f_{CON}.A.B.L.K)$ cannot be prevented from appearing in the trace of B.

In order to establish such properties, it is useful to construct some general properties. We here use the assertion that the network satisfies the $FAIR1$ specification as an example to show how to prove the fairness property in PVS.

According to the description of $FAIR1$, we split it into two lemmas:

Lemma 1

$$NETWORK \ \textbf{sat} \ evidence.A.s_B(f_{EOR}.A.L.C) \in tr$$
$$\Rightarrow rec.B.A.s_A(f_{EOO}.B.L.C) \in tr$$

and

Lemma 2

$$NETWORK \ \textbf{sat} \ evidence.A.s_B(f_{EOR}.A.L.C) \in tr$$
$$\wedge \ evidence.A.s_T(f_{CON}.A.B.L.K) \in tr$$
$$\Rightarrow get.B.TTP.s_T(f_{CON}.A.B.L.K) \in tr$$
$$\vee \ get.B.TTP.s_T(f_{CON}.A.B.L.K) \notin X$$

Obviously, the $FAIR1$ is proved if Lemma 1 and Lemma 2 hold. We will prove the above two lemmas respectively.

The fairness property is concerned with the fact that certain events should occur only under particular circumstances. We here first introduce an important specification derived from Schneider's rank function theory as follows:

$$R \ \text{precedes} \ T \ \hat{=} \ tr \upharpoonright R = \langle \rangle \Rightarrow tr \upharpoonright T = \langle \rangle$$
$$\text{no} \ R \ \hat{=} \ tr \upharpoonright R = \langle \rangle$$

which states that if some events from T occur in a trace, then some events from R must have been appear earlier in the trace. The Lemma 1 can be naturally represented by such a property.

Schneider [14] has provided a well-developed approach using the rank function theory and the CSP traces model to establish such properties for authentication properties. Evan [4] has also constructed the proof of NRO and NRR of the ZG protocol in PVS. Since the proof of the Lemma 1 has nearly been done in their previous work, we here just migrate it to our stable failures model and rewrite all proofs. For example, the definition `pcd(R,T)` and some rules are given in Figure 2 where `proj` corresponding to $\upharpoonright$ is the projection operation.

The basic idea in the rank function theory is that we use a function ρ to map the network's message space to two values: 0 and 1. For example, we assume that every message in T has rank 0 and other messages have rank 1; if every component of the network maintains[2] positive rank when prevented from outputting R, we may assert that nothing in T can occur unless something in R

---

[2] If only messages of positive rank are input, then any output message must have positive rank.

```
property_pcd[E:TYPE]:THEORY
   ...
   a: VAR E
   t: VAR trace[E]
   R,T,X,A: VAR set[E]
   P,Q: VAR process[E]

   pcd(R,T): [set[trace[E],set[[trace[E],set[E]]]]
       =( {t| proj(t,T) = null IMPLIES proj(t,R)= null},
          {(t,X)|true})

   no(R): [set[trace[E]],set[[trace[E],set[E]]]]
       = ( { t | proj(t,R)=null }, {(t,X) | true } )
   ...
   pcd_parallel: LEMMA P <= pcd(R,T) AND subset?(T,A)
                              IMPLIES Par(A)(P,Q) <= pcd(R,T)

   pcd_interleave: LEMMA P <= pcd(R,T) AND Q <= pcd(R,T)
                              IMPLIES P//Q <= pcd(R,T)

   pcd_interleave1: LEMMA P <= pcd(R,T) AND Q <= no(T)
                              IMPLIES P//Q <= pcd(R,T)
   ...
END property_pcd
```

Fig. 2. Proof rules for precedes

occurs previously. The rank function approach is discussed more fully in [14] and the proof is detailedly introduced in [3,4], and no further discussion is given in the paper.

Using the rank function approach, we have proved the following key property:

Lemma 3

$$NETWORK \;\; \boldsymbol{sat} \;\; evidence.A.s_B(f_{EOR}.A.L.C) \in tr$$
$$\Rightarrow trans.B.A.s_B(f_{EOR}.A.L.C) \in tr$$

The key property is that if A has obtained the evidence $s_B(f_{EOR}.A.L.C)$ then B must have sent it; in other words, a message signed by s_B must have rank 0 in this case. Such a rank function is established in PVS as Figure 3.

The network also satisfies another property:

Lemma 4

$$NETWORK \;\; \boldsymbol{sat} \;\; rec.B.A.s_A(f_{EOO}.B.L.C) \in tr$$
$$\Rightarrow trans.B.A.s_B(f_{EOR}.A.L.C) \in tr$$

```
rho(m) : RECURSIVE int =
  CASES m OF
    text(z)     : 1,
    label(z)    : 1,
    user(z)     : 1,
    flag(z)     : 1,
    public(z)   : 1,
    symm(z)     : 1,
    secret(z)   : IF z = b THEN 0 ELSE 1 ENDIF,
    conc(z1, z2) : min(rho(z1), rho(z2)),
    code(k, z)  : IF k = secret(b) AND
              z = conc4(feor,a,l,m) THEN 0 ELSE rho(z) ENDIF
  ENDCASES
 MEASURE m BY <<
```

Fig. 3. Rank function for Lemma 3

Proof. In the behaviour of $Party_B$, the event $rec.B.A.s_A(f_{EOO}.B.L.C)$ always precedes $trans.B.A.s_B(f_{EOR}.A.L.C)$ since he is an honest party. Therefore the network inherits the property from the $Party_B$ according to the rules `pcd_parallel` and `pcd_interleave1` listed in Figure 2.

In addition, the 'precedes' can be transitive; therefore, the Lemma 1 is proved by the Lemma 3 and Lemma 4.

To finish the proof of the fairness property, we then introduce the second property as follows:

$$T \text{ is unpreventable after } R \ \hat{=} \ \sigma(tr \upharpoonright R) = R$$
$$\Rightarrow \ (X \cap T) \backslash \sigma(tr \upharpoonright T) = \emptyset$$

which \ is a different operation. The property shows that if all events from the set R occur in a trace, then the event from T either has appeared earlier in the trace or is not included in the refusal set X after performing this trace. Such a property corresponding to the second part of the $FAIR1$ specification is here used to prove that $get.B.TTP.s_T(f_{CON}.A.B.L.K)$ is unpreventable after A has got the full evidence. The definition of `upt(T,R)` and some important rules are given in Figure 4. We also define `s_pcd(R,T)` as a more strict definition of the 'precedes' property which requires if all elements of T occur in a trace then all elements of R must have occurred in the trace.

The Lemma 2 is too tricky to be reached simply by applying the rules listed in Figure 4. The solution is to rewrite the $NETWORK$ process as follows:

$$NETWORK = (Party_A \ ||| \ Party_B)$$
$$\underset{\{trans,rec,send,get\}}{||} \ (Medium \ ||| \ TTP)$$

```
property_upt[E:TYPE]:THEORY
...
 a: VAR E
 t: VAR trace[E]
 R,T,X,A: VAR set[E]
 P,Q: VAR process[E]

 upt(T,R):[set[trace[E],set[[trace[E],set[E]]]]
    =( {t|true},
        {(t,X)| sigma(proj(t,R))=R IMPLIES
            difference(intersection(X,T), sigma(proj(t,T)))
            = emptyset })

 s_pcd(R,T):[set[trace[E],set[[trace[E],set[E]]]]
    =( {t| sigma(proj(t,T))=T IMPLIES sigma(proj(t,R))=R},
        {(t,X) | true } )
...
 upt_parallel: LEMMA P <= upt(T,R) AND Q <= upt(T,X) AND
                     subset?(union(R,X),A) AND subset?(T,A)
                     IMPLIES Par(A)(P,Q) <= upt(T,union(R,X))

 upt_interleave: LEMMA P <= upt(T,R) AND Q <= no(R)
                                  IMPLIES P//Q <= upt(T,R)
 upt_pcd_transitive: LEMMA  P <= upt(T,X) AND P <= s_pcd(X,R)
                                  IMPLIES P <= upt(T,R)
...
END property_upt
```

Fig. 4. Proof rules for unpreventable

Obviously, this new definition is equivalent to the original one, but makes the proof become rather easier when combined with the following lemmas.

Lemma 5

$$Medium \;|||\; TTP \; \textbf{\textit{sat}} \; get.A.TTP.s_T(f_{CON}.A.B.L.K) \in tr$$
$$\Rightarrow get.B.TTP.s_T(f_{CON}.A.B.L.K) \in tr$$
$$\lor get.B.TTP.s_T(f_{CON}.A.B.L.K) \notin X$$

Proof. Once the TTP has received a legitimate submission, the evidence is always available to the parties involved. Hence, $get.B.TTP.s_T(f_{CON}.A.B.L.K)$ is always unpreventable after $get.A.TTP.s_T(f_{CON}.A.B.L.K)$ has occurred. The assertion that the TTP satisfies the property has been proved by directly using the general induction theorem. The interleaving of the medium and TTP holds it as well by means of the rule `upt_interleave` listed in Figure 4.

Lemma 6

$$Party_A \parallel\!\parallel Party_B \ \textbf{sat} \ trans.B.A.s_B(f_{EOR}.A.L.C) \in tr$$
$$\Rightarrow get.B.TTP.s_T(f_{CON}.A.B.L.K) \in tr$$
$$\vee \ get.B.TTP.s_T(f_{CON}.A.B.L.K) \notin X$$

Proof. The $Party_B$ has to perform $get.B.TTP.s_T(f_{CON}.A.B.L.K)$ after he responds to A with $s_B(f_{EOO}.A.L.C)$, so that $get.B.TTP.s_T(f_{CON}.A.B.L.K)$ is unpreventable.

Lemma 7

$$NETWORK \ \textbf{sat} \ trans.B.A.s_B(f_{EOR}.A.L.C) \in tr$$
$$\wedge \ get.A.TTP.s_T(f_{CON}.A.B.L.K) \in tr$$
$$\Rightarrow get.B.TTP.s_T(f_{CON}.A.B.L.K) \in tr$$
$$\vee \ get.B.TTP.s_T(f_{CON}.A.B.L.K) \notin X$$

Proof. This is proved relying on the rule `upt_parallel` with the Lemma 5 and Lemma 6 since the union of two 'preceding' events respectively in two different processes is a subset of the interface of their parallel then the unpreventable property still holds in the parallel composition.

Furthermore, the Lemma 2 is proved in terms of the Lemma 7 and two properties that $trans.B.A.s_B(f_{EOR}.A.L.C)$ precedes $evidence.A.s_B(f_{EOR}.A.L.C)$ and $get.A.TTP.s_T(f_{CON}.A.B.L.K)$ precedes $evidence.A.s_T(f_{CON}.A.B.L.K)$ in the network. The rule `upt_pcd_transitive` plays an important role in the above proof that if the process P satisfies the fact that a set of events T are unpreventable after a set of events X, whereas X precedes a set of events R, then P satisfies that T is unpreventable after R.

This completes the proof; we have formalized all this in PVS. The proof of the *FAIR2* specification has also been formally completed in a similar way, making use of the above lemmas.

It is also important, for a fully general proof, to allow other agents to participate on the network, since the protocol is expected to be correct no matter how many parties there are. We have also extended our model to more general situations; for example, the case where B may engage in concurrent runs.

7   Discussion

In this paper, we have modelled and verified the Zhou-Gollmann non-repudiation protocol with respect to correctness of fairness, which requires that neither of two parties can establish evidence of origin or evidence of receipt while still preventing the other party from obtaining such evidence. Proving fairness in a theorem prover can help us to extract some general understanding of how to design such a kind of protocol. For instance, from the Lemma 5 and Lemma 6, we can clearly see that least two factors should be considered: one is that the TTP should always make the evidence available to the parties involved when it has received a legitimate submission; the other is that B cannot be prevented from accessing the evidence when he has responded to the first part of evidence from A.

Although the Zhou-Gollmann protocol is rather simple, our formal verification shows that it does provide strong fairness under the assumptions described in this paper. However, there is an attack [5] if we slightly change our assumptions. Suppose that we allow the TTP and B to lose the evidence, and A first completes a protocol run with B and possesses $s_B(f_{EOR}.A.L.C)$ and $s_T(f_{CON}.A.B.L.K)$; a couple of weeks later, A then uses the same symmetric key and label but sends a new plaintext message to initiate a new run; A ends the run by obtaining the new EOR and presenting it with $s_T(f_{CON}.A.B.L.K)$ to a judge; A might be lucky enough to discover that TTP and B have discarded their old evidence.

Incorporating this assumption into our model would mean that the correctness of the fairness property cannot be proved because of the presence of the hidden attacks. For example, Lemma 5 would not hold any more if B could lose the evidence. In investigating why these lemmas can no longer be proven, it is likely that one would uncover the attack.

We here give a suggestion that all evidence should have incorporated into it a tag provided by the TTP, such as timestamp, so as to make it clear when the two parts of the evidence match each other.

Some related work can be found in the literature concerning verification of non-repudiation protocols using different approaches. Zhou et al. in [21] firstly use 'BAN-like' belief logic to check only safety properties of the non-repudiation protocols. Schneider [13] gives an excellent overview of the CSP modelling and proves the correctness of properties using stable failures and rank functions; however, the proofs are constructed by hand. Evans [4] extends Schneider's work to prove safety properties such as NRO and NRR in the PVS theorem prover. Shmatikov and Mitchell in [16] verify fairness as a monotonic property using Murφ; that is, if fairness is broken at one point of the protocol, the protocol will remain unfair. This approach also cannot deal with liveness properties. Kremer and Raskin [7] use the finite state model checker MOCHA to verify non-repudiation and fair exchange protocols. This approach, which is rather different from ours here, can also cope with liveness properties as well as safety properties. However, they have modelled networks in which A and B can engage in only one run of the protocol. In addition, Abadi and Blanchet [1] formalize and verify the key security properties of a cryptographic protocol for certified email that has many commonalities with the Zhou-Gollmann protocol. Most of verification work is done with an automatic protocol verifier, however such a tool has not been verified and finished.

We have proved the fairness property of the Zhou-Gollmann protocol in its full generality in the case of two parties that are able to perform multiple runs or concurrent runs, along with an unbounded number of other dishonest parties. Admittedly, verifying a system like this requires considerable work. However,

PVS is a deductive system in which all completed proofs can be used in later proofs. In the course of constructing this proof, we have amassed many lemmas and theorems that will make proving properties of similar systems substantially less time-consuming, both for us and for others.

We aim to extend our model to cover a larger size of network running the Zhou-Gollmann protocol; for example, we will deal with the network allowing multiple concurrent runs. We also wish to challenge the analysis of certain sophisticated systems or security protocols.

References

1. Abadi, M., Blanchet, B.: Computer-Assisted Verification of a Protocol for Certified Email. In: Cousot, R. (ed.) SAS 2003. LNCS, vol. 2694, pp. 316–335. Springer, Heidelberg (2003)
2. Dolev, D., Yao, A.C.: On the security of public key protocols. IEEE Transactions on Information Theory 29(2) (1983)
3. Dutertre, B., Schneider, S.A.: Embedding CSP in PVS: an application to authentication protocols. In: Gunter, E.L., Felty, A.P. (eds.) TPHOLs 1997. LNCS, vol. 1275, Springer, Heidelberg (1997)
4. Evans, N.: Investigating Security through Proof. PhD thesis, Royal Holloway, University of London (2003)
5. Gürgens, S., Rudolph, C.: Security analysis of (un-) fair non-repudiation protocols. In: Abdallah, A.E., Ryan, P.Y A, Schneider, S. (eds.) FASec 2002. LNCS, vol. 2629, pp. 97–114. Springer, Heidelberg (2003)
6. Kremer, S., Markowitch, O., Zhou, J.: An intensive survey of non-repudiation protocols. Technical Report 473 (2002)
7. Kremer, S., Raskin, J.-F.: A game-based verification of non-repudiation and fair exchange protocols. In: Larsen, K.G., Nielsen, M. (eds.) CONCUR 2001. LNCS, vol. 2154, Springer, Heidelberg (2001)
8. Lowe, G.: Breaking and fixing the Needham-Schroeder public-key protocol using FDR. In: Margaria, T., Steffen, B. (eds.) TACAS 1996. LNCS, vol. 1055, pp. 147–166. Springer, Heidelberg (1996)
9. Markowitch, O., Roggeman, Y.: Probabilistic non-repudiation without trusted third party. In: Second Workshop on Security in Communication Network 99 (1999)
10. Roscoe, A.W.: Modelling and verifying key-exchange protocols using CSP and FDR. In: Proceedings of 8th IEEE Computer Security Foundations Workshop (1995)
11. Roscoe, A.W.: The Theory and Practice of Concurrency. Prentice-Hall International, Englewood Cliffs (1998)
12. Ryan, P., Schneider, S., Goldsmith, M., Lowe, G., Roscoe, B.: The Modelling And Analysis Of Security Protocols. Addison Wesley, London (2000)
13. Schneider, S.A.: Formal analysis of a non-repudiation protocol. In: Proceedings of the 11th IEEE Computer Security Foundations Workshop (1998)
14. Schneider, S.A.: Verifying authentication protocols in CSP. IEEE TSE, 24(9) (September 1998)
15. Schneider, S.A.: Concurrent and real-time systems: the CSP approach. John Wiley & Sons, West Sussex, England (1999)
16. Shmatikov, V., Mitchell, J.C.: Analysis of abuse-free contract signing. In: Frankel, Y. (ed.) FC 2000. LNCS, vol. 1962, pp. 174–191. Springer, Heidelberg (2001)

17. Tedrick, T.: How to exchange half a bit. In: CRYPTO, pp. 147–151 (1983)
18. Wei, K., Heather, J.: Embedding the stable failures model of CSP in PVS. In: accepted by Fifth International Conference on Integrated Formal Methods, Eindhoven, The Netherlands (2005)
19. Wei, K., Heather, J.: Towards verification of timed non-repudiation protocols. In: Dimitrakos, T., Martinelli, F., Ryan, P.Y A, Schneider, S. (eds.) FAST 2005. LNCS, vol. 3866, Springer, Heidelberg (2006)
20. Zhou, J., Gollmann, D.: A fair non-repudiation protocol. In: Proceedings of the IEEE Symposium on Research in Security and Privacy, Oakland, CA, pp. 55–61. IEEE Computer Society Press, Los Alamitos (1996)
21. Zhou, J., Gollmann, D.: Towards verification of non-repudiation protocols. In: Proceedings of 1998 International Refinement Workshop and Formal Methods Pacific, pp. 370–380, Canberra, Australia (September 1998)

A Formal Specification of the MIDP 2.0 Security Model*

Santiago Zanella Béguelin[1], Gustavo Betarte[2], and Carlos Luna[2]

[1] INRIA Sophia Antipolis, 06902 Sophia Antipolis Cedex, France
Santiago.Zanella@sophia.inria.fr
[2] InCo, Facultad de Ingeniería, Universidad de la República, Montevideo, Uruguay
{gustun,cluna}@fing.edu.uy

Abstract. This paper presents, to the best of our knowledge, the first formal specification of the application security model defined by the Mobile Information Device Profile 2.0 for Java 2 Micro Edition. The specification, which has been formalized in Coq, provides an abstract representation of the state of a device and the security-related events that allows to reason about the security properties of the platform where the model is deployed. We state and sketch the proof of some desirable properties of the security model. Although the abstract specification is not executable, we describe a refinement methodology that leads to an executable prototype.

1 Introduction

Mobile devices (e.g. cell phones) often have access to sensitive personal data, are subscribed to paid services and are capable of establishing connections with external entities. Users of such devices may, in addition, download and install applications from untrusted sites at their will. Since any security breach may expose sensitive data, prevent the use of the device, or allow applications to perform actions that incur a charge for the user, it is essential to provide an application security model that can be relied upon – the slightest vulnerability may imply huge losses due to the scale the technology has been deployed.

Java 2 Micro Edition (J2ME) is a version of the Java platform targeted at resource-constrained devices which comprises two kinds of components: configurations and profiles. A configuration is composed of a virtual machine and a set of APIs that provide the basic functionality for a particular category of devices. Profiles further determine the target technology by defining a set of higher level APIs built on top of an underlying configuration. This two-level architecture enhances portability and enables developers to deliver applications that run on a wide range of devices with similar capabilities. This work concerns the topmost level of the architecture which corresponds to the profile that defines the security model we formalize.

---

* This work is partially funded by the IST program of the European Commission, FET under the *MOBIUS* project, the INRIA-Microsoft Joint Research Laboratory, and STIC-AmSud under the *ReSeCo* project.

T. Dimitrakos et al. (Eds.): FAST 2006, LNCS 4691, pp. 220–234, 2007.

The Connected Limited Device Configuration (CLDC) is a J2ME configuration designed for devices with slow processors, limited memory and intermittent connectivity. CLDC together with the Mobile Information Device Profile (MIDP) provides a complete J2ME runtime environment tailored for devices like cell phones and personal data assistants. MIDP defines an application life cycle, a security model and APIs that offer the functionality required by mobile applications, including networking, user interface, push activation and persistent local storage. Many mobile device manufacturers have adopted MIDP since the specification was made available. Nowadays, literally millions of MIDP enabled devices are deployed worldwide and the market acceptance of the specification is expected to continue to grow steadily.

In the original MIDP 1.0 specification [1], any application not installed by the device manufacturer or a service provider runs in a sandbox that prohibits access to security sensitive APIs or functions of the device (e.g. push activation). Although this sandbox security model effectively prevents any rogue application from jeopardizing the security of the device, it is excessively restrictive and does not allow many useful applications to be deployed after issuance.

MIDP 2.0 [2] introduces a new security model based on the concept of protection domain. Each API or function on the device may define permissions in order to prevent it from being used without authorization. Every installed application is bound to a unique protection domain that defines a set of permissions granted either unconditionally or with explicit user authorization. Untrusted applications are bound to a protection domain with permissions equivalent to those in a MIDP 1.0 sandbox. Trusted applications may be identified by means of cryptographic signatures and bound to more permissive protection domains. This model enables applications developed by trusted third parties to be downloaded and installed after issuance of the device without compromising its security.

Some effort has been put into the evaluation of the security model for MIDP 2.0; Kolsi and Virtanen [3] and Debbabi et al. [4] analyse the application security model, spot vulnerabilities in various implementations and suggest improvements to the specification. Although these works report on the detection of security holes, they do not intend to prove their absence. The formalization we overview here, however, provides a formal basis for the verification of the model and the understanding of its intricacies.

We developed our specification using the Coq proof assistant [5,6]. A detailed description of the specification is presented in Spanish in [7]; a shorter, preliminary version of this paper appeared in InCo's technical report series [8]. Both documents, along with the full formalization in Coq may be obtained from http://www-sop.inria.fr/everest/personnel/Santiago.Zanella/MIDP.

The rest of the paper is organized as follows, Section 2 describes some of the notation used in this document, Section 3 overviews the formalization of the MIDP 2.0 security model, Section 4 presents some of its verified properties along with outlines of their proofs, Section 5 proposes a methodology to refine the specification and obtain an executable prototype and finally, Section 6 concludes with a summary of our contributions and directions for future work.

2   Notation

We use standard notation for equality and logical connectives ($\wedge$, $\vee$, $\neg$, $\rightarrow$, $\forall$, $\exists$). Implication and universal quantification may be encoded in Coq using dependent product, while equality and the other connectives can be defined inductively. Anonymous predicates are introduced using lambda notation, e.g. ($\lambda\, n$. $n = 0$) is a predicate that when applied to n, is true iff n is zero.

We extensively use record types; a record type definition

$$R \stackrel{\text{def}}{=} \{ field_1 : A_1, \ldots, field_n : A_n \} \tag{1}$$

generates a non-recursive inductive type with just one constructor, namely mkR, and projections functions $field_i : R \rightarrow A_i$. We write $\langle a_1, \ldots, a_n \rangle$ instead of $mkR\ a_1 \ldots a_n$ when the type R is obvious from the context. Application of projections functions is abbreviated using dot notation (i.e. $field_i\ r = r.field_i$). For each field $field_i$ in a record type we define a binary relation $\equiv_{field_i}$ over objects of the type as

$$r_1 \equiv_{field_i} r_2 \stackrel{\text{def}}{=} \forall\, j, j \neq i \rightarrow r_1.field_j = r_2.field_j \tag{2}$$

We define an inductive relation I by giving introduction rules of the form

$$\frac{P_1 \cdots P_m}{I\ x_1 \ldots x_n}\ rule \tag{3}$$

where free occurrences of variables are implicitly universally quantified.

We assume as predefined inductive types the parametric type $option\ T$ with constructors $None : option\ T$ and $Some : T \rightarrow option\ T$, and the type $seq\ T$ of finite sequences over T. We denote the empty sequence by $[\,]$ and the constructor that appends an element a to a sequence s in infix form as in $s \frown a$. The symbol $\oplus$ stands for the concatenation operator on sequences.

3   Formalization of the MIDP 2.0 Security Model

In this section we present and discuss the formal specification of the security model. We introduce first some types and constants used in the remainder of the formalization, then we define the set of valid device states and security-related events, give a transition semantics for events based on pre- and postconditions and define the concept of a session.

3.1   Sets and Constants

In MIDP, applications (usually called MIDlets) are packaged and distributed as suites. A suite may contain one or more MIDlets and is distributed as two files, an application descriptor file and an archive file that contains the actual Java classes and resources. A suite that uses protected APIs or functions should declare the corresponding permissions in its descriptor either as required for its correct functioning or as optional.

Let *Permission* be the total set of permissions defined by every protected API or function on the device and *Domain* the set of all protection domains. Let us introduce, as a way of referring to individual MIDlet suites, the set *SuiteID* of valid suite identifiers. We will represent a descriptor as a record composed of two predicates, *required* and *optional*, that identify respectively the set of permissions declared as required and those declared as optional by the corresponding suite,

$$Descriptor \stackrel{\text{def}}{=} \{required, optional : Permission \rightarrow Prop\} \qquad (4)$$

A record type is used to represent an installed suite, with fields for its identifier, associated protection domain and descriptor,

$$Suite \stackrel{\text{def}}{=} \{id : SuiteID, domain : Domain, descriptor : Descriptor\} \qquad (5)$$

Permissions may be granted by the user to an active MIDlet suite in either of three modes, for a single use (oneshot), as long as the suite is running (session), or as long as the suite remains installed (blanket). Let *Mode* be the enumerated set of user interaction modes $\{oneshot, session, blanket\}$ and $\leq_m$ an order relation such that

$$oneshot \leq_m session \leq_m blanket \qquad (6)$$

We will assume for the rest of the formalization that the security policy of the protection domains on the device is an anonymous constant of type

$$Policy \stackrel{\text{def}}{=} \{ \; allow : Domain \rightarrow Permission \rightarrow Prop, \\ user \; : Domain \rightarrow Permission \rightarrow Mode \rightarrow Prop \; \} \qquad (7)$$

which for each domain specifies at most one mode for a given permission,

$$(\forall \; d \; p, allow \; d \; p \rightarrow \forall \; m, \neg user \; d \; p \; m) \; \wedge \\ (\forall \; d \; p \; m, user \; d \; p \; m \rightarrow \neg allow \; d \; p \; \wedge \forall \; m', user \; d \; p \; m' \rightarrow m = m') \qquad (8)$$

and such that *allow d p* holds when domain d unconditionally grants the permission p and *user d p m* holds when domain d grants permission p with explicit user authorization and maximum allowable mode m (w.r.t. $\leq_m$). The permissions effectively granted to a MIDlet suite are the intersection of the permissions requested in its descriptor with the union of the permissions given unconditionally by its domain and those given explicitly by the user.

3.2 Device State

To reason about the MIDP 2.0 security model most details of the device state may be abstracted; it is sufficient to specify the set of installed suites, the permissions granted or revoked to them and the currently active suite in case there is one. The active suite, and the permissions granted or revoked to it for the session are grouped into a record structure

$$SessionInfo \stackrel{\text{def}}{=} \{ \; id \qquad\qquad\qquad : SuiteID, \\ granted, revoked : Permission \rightarrow Prop \; \} \qquad (9)$$

The abstract device state is described as a record of type

$$State \stackrel{\text{def}}{=} \{ \; suite \qquad\qquad : Suite \rightarrow Prop, \\ session \qquad\qquad : option \; SessionInfo, \qquad\qquad (10) \\ granted, revoked : SuiteID \rightarrow Permission \rightarrow Prop \; \}$$

where *suite* is the characteristic predicate of the set of installed suites.

Example 1. Consider a MIDlet that periodically connects to a webmail service using HTTPS when possible or HTTP otherwise, and alerts the user whenever they have new mail. The suite containing this MIDlet should declare in its descriptor as required permissions p_push, for accessing the PushRegistry (for timer-based activation), and p_http, for using the HTTP protocol API. It should also declare as optional the permission p_https for accessing the HTTPS protocol API. Suppose that upon installation, the suite (whose identifier is id) is recognized as trusted and is thus bound to a protection domain dom that allows access to the PushRegistry API unconditionally but by default requests user authorization for opening every HTTP or HTTPS connection. Suppose also that the domain allows the user to grant the MIDlet the permission for opening further connections as long as the suite remains installed. Then, the security policy satisfies:

$$allow \; dom \; p\_push \; \wedge user \; dom \; p\_http \; blanket \; \wedge user \; dom \; p\_https \; blanket \quad (11)$$

If st is the state of the device, the suite is represented by some $ms : Suite$ such that $st.suite \; ms$ and $ms.id = id$ hold. Its descriptor $ms.descriptor$ satisfies

$$ms.descriptor.required \; p\_push \; \wedge ms.descriptor.required \; p\_http \; \wedge \\ ms.descriptor.optional \; p\_https \qquad\qquad\qquad\qquad (12)$$

The MIDlet will have unlimited access to the PushRegistry applet, but will have to request user authorization every time it makes a new connection. The user may chose at any time to authorize further connections by granting the corresponding permission in *blanket* mode, thus avoiding being asked for authorization each time the applet communicates with the webmail service.   □

The remainder of this subsection enumerates the conditions that must hold for an element $s : State$ in order to represent a valid state for a device.

1. A MIDlet suite can be installed and bound to a protection domain only if the set of permissions declared as required in its descriptor are a subset of the permissions the domain offers (with or without user authorization). This

compatibility relation between $des : Descriptor$ and $dom : Domain$ can be stated formally as follows,

$$des \wr dom \overset{\text{def}}{=} \forall\, p : Permission, \tag{13}$$
$$des.required\; p \rightarrow allow\; dom\; p\ \vee \exists\, m : Mode, user\; dom\; p\; m$$

Every installed suite must be compatible with its associated protection domain,

$$SuiteCompatible \overset{\text{def}}{=} \tag{14}$$
$$\forall\, ms : Suite, s.suite\; ms \rightarrow ms.descriptor \wr ms.domain$$

2. Whenever there exists a running session, the suite identifier in $s.session$ must correspond to an installed suite,

$$CurrentInstalled \overset{\text{def}}{=} \forall\, ses : SessionInfo, s.session = Some\; ses \rightarrow \tag{15}$$
$$\exists\, ms : Suite, s.suite\; ms \wedge ms.id = ses.id$$

3. The set of permissions granted for the session must be a subset of the permissions requested in the application descriptor of the active suite. In addition, the associated protection domain policy must allow those permissions to be granted at least in $session$ mode,

$$ValidSessionGranted \overset{\text{def}}{=} \forall\, ses : SessionInfo, s.session = Some\; ses \rightarrow$$
$$\forall\, p : Permission, ses.granted\; p \rightarrow$$
$$\forall\, ms : Suite, s.suite\; ms \rightarrow ms.id = ses.id \rightarrow$$
$$(ms.descriptor.required\; p\ \vee ms.descriptor.optional\; p)\ \wedge$$
$$(\exists\, m : Mode, user\; ms.domain\; p\; m\ \wedge session \leq_{\mathrm{m}} m)$$
$$\tag{16}$$

4. Every installed suite shall have a unique identifier,

$$UniqueSuiteID \overset{\text{def}}{=} \forall\, ms_1\; ms_2 : Suite, \tag{17}$$
$$s.suite\; ms_1 \rightarrow s.suite\; ms_2 \rightarrow ms_1.id = ms_2.id \rightarrow ms_1 = ms_2$$

5. For every installed suite with identifier id, the predicate $s.granted\; id$ should be valid with respect to its descriptor and associated protection domain ($ValidGranted\; s$). We omit the detailed formalization of this condition.
6. A granted permission shall not be revoked at the same time and viceversa ($ValidGrantedRevoked\; s$). We omit the detailed formalization.

3.3 Events

We define a set $Event$ for those events that are relevant to our abstraction of the device state (Table 1). The user may be presented with the choice between accepting or refusing an authorization request, specifying the period of time their

Table 1. Events

Name	Description	Type
start	Start of session	$SuiteID \rightarrow Event$
terminate	End of session	$Event$
request	Permission request	$Permission \rightarrow option\ UserAnswer \rightarrow Event$
install	MIDlet suite installation	$SuiteID \rightarrow Descriptor \rightarrow Domain \rightarrow Event$
remove	MIDlet suite removal	$SuiteID \rightarrow Event$

choice remains valid. The outcome of a user interaction is represented using the type $UserAnswer$ with constructors

$$ua\_allow, ua\_deny : Mode \rightarrow UserAnswer \tag{18}$$

The behaviour of the events is specified by their pre- and postconditions given by the predicates Pre and Pos respectively. Preconditions (Table 2) are defined in terms of the device state while postconditions (Table 3) are defined in terms of the before and after states and an optional response which is only meaningful for the *request* event and indicates whether the requested operation is authorized,

$$\begin{aligned} Pre &: State \rightarrow Event \rightarrow Prop \\ Pos &: State \rightarrow State \rightarrow option\ Response \rightarrow Event \rightarrow Prop \end{aligned} \tag{19}$$

Table 2. Event preconditions. The precondition of the *request* event is omitted for reasons of space

---

$Pre\ s\ (start\ id) \overset{\text{def}}{=}$
    $s.session = None\ \land \exists\ ms : Suite, s.suite\ ms \land ms.id = id$
$Pre\ s\ terminate \overset{\text{def}}{=} s.session \neq None$
$Pre\ s\ (install\ id\ des\ dom) \overset{\text{def}}{=}$
    $des \wr dom \land \forall\ ms : Suite, s.suite\ ms \rightarrow ms.id \neq id.$
$Pre\ s\ (remove\ id) \overset{\text{def}}{=}$
    $(\forall\ ses : SessionInfo, s.session = Some\ ses\ \rightarrow ses.id \neq id)\ \land$
    $\exists\ ms : Suite, s.suite\ ms \land ms.id = id$

Example 2. Consider an event representing a permission request for which the user denies the authorization. Such an event can only occur when the active suite has declared the requested permission in its descriptor and is bound to a protection domain that specifies a user interaction mode for that permission (otherwise, the request would be immediately accepted or rejected). Furthermore, the requested permission must not have been revoked or granted for the

Table 3. Event postconditions. The postcondition for the *request* event is omitted for reasons of space.

$Pos\ s\ s'\ r\ (start\ id) \overset{\text{def}}{=}$
$\quad r = None\ \wedge s \equiv_{session} s'\ \wedge \exists\ ses',\ s'.session = Some\ ses'\ \wedge ses'.id = id\ \wedge$
$\quad \forall\ p : Permission, \neg ses'.granted\ p\ \wedge \neg ses'.revoked\ p$

$Pos\ s\ s'\ r\ terminate \overset{\text{def}}{=} r = None\ \wedge s \equiv_{session} s'\ \wedge s'.session = None$

$Pos\ s\ s'\ r\ (install\ id\ des\ dom) \overset{\text{def}}{=}$
$\quad r = None\ \wedge\ (\forall\ ms : Suite, s.suite\ ms \rightarrow s'.suite\ ms)\ \wedge$
$\quad (\forall\ ms : Suite, s'.suite\ ms \rightarrow s.suite\ ms\ \vee ms = \langle id, dom, des \rangle)\ \wedge$
$\quad s'.suite\ \langle id, dom, des \rangle\ \wedge s'.session = s.session\ \wedge$
$\quad (\forall\ p : Permission, \neg s'.granted\ id\ p \wedge \neg s'.revoked\ id\ p)\ \wedge$
$\quad (\forall\ id_1 : SuiteID, id_1 \neq id \rightarrow$
$\qquad s'.granted\ id_1 = s.granted\ id_1\ \wedge s'.revoked\ id_1 = s.revoked\ id_1)$

$Pos\ s\ s'\ r\ (remove\ id) \overset{\text{def}}{=} r = None\ \wedge s \equiv_{suite} s'\ \wedge$
$\quad (\forall\ ms : Suite, s.suite\ ms \rightarrow ms.id \neq id \rightarrow s'.suite\ ms)\ \wedge$
$\quad (\forall\ ms : Suite, s'.suite\ ms \rightarrow s.suite\ ms \wedge ms.id \neq id)$

---

rest of the session or the rest of the suite's life,

$Pre\ s\ (request\ p\ (Some\ (ua\_deny\ m))) \overset{\text{def}}{=}$
$\quad \exists\ ses : SessionInfo, s.session = Some\ ses\ \wedge$
$\qquad \forall\ ms : Suite, s.suite\ ms \rightarrow ms.id = ses.id \rightarrow$
$\qquad (ms.descriptor.required\ p\ \vee ms.descriptor.optional\ p)\ \wedge \qquad\qquad (20)$
$\qquad (\exists\ m_1 : Mode, user\ ms.domain\ p\ m_1)\ \wedge$
$\qquad \neg ses.granted\ p\ \wedge\ \neg ses.revoked\ p\ \wedge$
$\qquad \neg s.granted\ ses.id\ p\ \wedge \neg s.revoked\ ses.id\ p$

When $m = session$, the user revokes the permission for the whole session, therefore, the response denies the permission and the state is updated accordingly,

$Pos\ s\ s'\ r\ (request\ p\ (Some\ (ua\_deny\ session))) \overset{\text{def}}{=}$
$\quad r = Some\ denied\ \wedge s \equiv_{session} s'\ \wedge$
$\quad \forall\ ses : SessionInfo, s.session = Some\ ses \rightarrow$
$\qquad \exists\ ses' : SessionInfo, \qquad\qquad\qquad\qquad\qquad\qquad\qquad\qquad (21)$
$\qquad s'.session = Some\ ses'\ \wedge ses' \equiv_{revoked} ses\ \wedge ses'.revoked\ p\ \wedge$
$\qquad (\forall\ q : Permission, q \neq p \rightarrow ses'.revoked\ q = ses.revoked\ q)$

3.4   One-Step Execution

The behavioural specification of the execution of an event is given by the $\hookrightarrow$ relation with the following introduction rules:

$$\frac{\neg Pre\ s\ e}{s \xrightarrow{e/None} s}\ npre \qquad \frac{Pre\ s\ e \quad Pos\ s\ s'\ r\ e}{s \xrightarrow{e/r} s'}\ pre$$

$$\qquad\qquad\qquad\qquad\qquad\qquad\qquad\qquad\qquad\qquad\qquad (22)$$

Whenever an event occurs for which the precondition does not hold, the state must remain unchanged. Otherwise, the state may change in such a way that the event postcondition is established. The notation $s \xrightarrow{e/r} s'$ may be read as "the execution of the event e in state s results in a new state s' and produces a response r".

3.5   Sessions

A session is the period of time spanning from a successful *start* event to a *terminate* event, in which a single suite remains active. A session for a suite with identifier id (Fig. 1) is determined by an initial state s_0 and a sequence of steps $\langle e_i, s_i, r_i \rangle$ $(i = 1, \ldots, n)$ such that the following conditions hold,

- $e_1 = start\ id$;
- $Pre\ s_0\ e_1$;
- $\forall\ i \in \{2, \ldots, n-1\}, e_i \neq terminate$;
- $e_n = terminate$;
- $\forall\ i \in \{1, \ldots, n\}, s_{i-1} \xrightarrow{e_i/r_i} s_i$.

$$s_0 \xrightarrow{start\ id/r_1} s_1 \xrightarrow{e_2/r_2} s_2 \xrightarrow{e_3/r_3} \cdots \xrightarrow{e_{n-1}/r_{n-1}} s_{n-1} \xrightarrow{terminate/r_n} s_n$$

Fig. 1. A session for a suite with identifier id

To define the session concept we introduce before the concept of partial session. A partial session is a *session* for which the *terminate* event has not yet been elicited; it is defined inductively by the following rules,

$$\frac{Pre\ s_0\ (start\ id) \quad s_0 \xrightarrow{start\ id/r_1} s_1}{PSession\ s_0\ ([\ ] \frown \langle start\ id, s_1, r_1 \rangle)}\ psession\_start \tag{23}$$

$$\frac{PSession\ s_0\ (ss \frown last) \quad e \neq terminate \quad last.s \xrightarrow{e/r} s'}{PSession\ s_0\ (ss \frown last \frown \langle e, s', r \rangle)}\ psession\_app \tag{24}$$

Now, sessions can be easily defined as follows,

$$\frac{PSession\ s_0\ (ss \frown last) \quad last.s \xrightarrow{terminate/r} s'}{Session\ s_0\ (ss \frown last \frown \langle terminate, s', r \rangle)}\ session\_terminate \tag{25}$$

4   Verification of Security Properties

This section is devoted to establishing relevant security properties of the model. Due to space constraints, proofs are merely outlined; however, all proofs have been formalized in Coq and are available as part of the full specification.

4.1   An Invariant of One-Step Execution

We call one-step invariant a property that remains true after the *execution* of every event if it is true before. We show next that the validity of the device state, as defined in Section 3.2, is a one-step invariant of our specification.

Theorem 1. *Let Valid be a predicate over State defined as the conjunction of the validity conditions in Sect. 3.2. For any s s' : State, r : option Response and e : Event, if Valid s and s $\xrightarrow{e/r}$ s' hold, then Valid s' also holds.*

Proof. By case analysis on $s \xrightarrow{e/r} s'$. When *Pre s e* does not hold, $s = s'$ and s' is valid because s is valid. Otherwise, *Pos s s' r e* must hold and we proceed by case analysis on e. We will only show the case *request p (Some (ua_deny session))*, obtained after further case analysis on a when $e = request\ p\ (Some\ a)$.

The postcondition (21) entails that $s \equiv_{session} s'$, that the session remains active, and that $ses' \equiv_{revoked} ses$. Therefore, the set of installed suites remains unchanged ($s'.suite = s.suite$), the set of permissions granted for the session does not change ($ses'.granted = ses.granted$) and neither does the set of permissions granted or revoked in *blanket* mode ($s'.granted = s.granted$, $s'.revoked = s.revoked$). From these equalities, every validity condition of the state s' except *ValidGrantedRevoked s'* follows immediately from the validity of s. We next prove *ValidGrantedRevoked s'*.

We know from the postcondition of the event that

$$\forall\ q, q \neq p \rightarrow ses'.revoked\ q = ses.revoked\ q \tag{26}$$

Let q be any permission. If $q \neq p$, then from (26) follows $ses'.revoked\ q = ses.revoked\ q$ and because q was not granted and revoked simultaneously before the event, neither it is afterwards. If $q = p$, then we know from the precondition (20) that p were not granted before and thus it is not granted afterwards. This proves *ValidGrantedRevoked s'* and together with the previous results, *Valid s'*. □

4.2   Session Invariants

We call session invariant a property of a step that holds for the rest of a session once it is established in any step. Let P be a predicate over T, we define *all P* as an inductive predicate over *seq T* by the following rules:

$$\frac{}{all\ P\ [\ ]}\ all\_nil \qquad \frac{all\ P\ ss \quad P\ s}{all\ P\ (ss \frown s)}\ all\_snoc \tag{27}$$

Theorem 2. *Let s_0 be a valid state and ss a partial session starting from s_0, then every state in ss is valid,*

$$all\ (\lambda\ step\ .\ Valid\ step.s)\ ss \tag{28}$$

Proof. By induction on the structure of *PSession* s_0 *ss*.

- When constructed using *psession_start*, *ss* has the form $[\,]\frown\langle start\ id, s_1,\ r_1\rangle$ and $s_0 \xrightarrow{start\ id/r_1} s_1$ holds. We must prove

$$all\ (\lambda\ step\ .\ Valid\ step.s)\ ([\,]\frown\langle start\ id, s_1,\ r_1\rangle) \qquad (29)$$

By applying *all_app* and then *all_nil* the goal is simplified to *Valid* s_1 and is proved from $s_0 \xrightarrow{start\ id/r_1} s_1$ and *Valid* s_0 by applying Theorem 1.
- When it is constructed using *psession_app*, *ss* has the form $ss_1 \frown last \frown \langle e, s', r\rangle$ and $last.s \xrightarrow{e/r} s'$ holds. The induction hypothesis is

$$all\ (\lambda\ step\ .\ Valid\ step.s)\ (ss_1 \frown last) \qquad (30)$$

and we must prove $all\ (\lambda\ step\ .\ Valid\ step.s)\ (ss_1 \frown last \frown \langle e, s', r\rangle)$. By applying *all_app* and then (30) the goal is simplified to *Valid* s'. From (30) we know that *last.s* is a valid state. The goal is proved from $last.s \xrightarrow{e/r} s'$ and *Valid last.s* by applying Theorem 1. $\qquad\square$

The above theorem may be easily extended from partial sessions to sessions using Theorem 1 one more time. State validity is just a particular property that is true for a partial session once it is established, the result can be generalized for other properties as shown in the following lemma.

Lemma 1. *For any property P of a step satisfying*

$$\forall\ (s\ s' : State)(r\ r' : option\ Response)(e\ e' : Event),$$
$$e' \neq terminate \to s \xrightarrow{e'/r'} s' \to P\ \langle e, s, r\rangle \to P\ \langle e', s', r'\rangle\ , \qquad (31)$$

if PSession s_0 $(ss \frown step \oplus ss_1)$ *and P step, then all P* ss_1 *holds.*

Perhaps a more interesting property is a guarantee of the proper enforcement of revocation. We prove that once a permission is revoked by the user for the rest of a session, any further request for the same permission in the same session is refused.

Lemma 2. *The following property satisfies* (31),

$$(\lambda\ step\ .\ \exists\ ses, step.s.session = Some\ ses \land ses.revoked\ p) \qquad (32)$$

Theorem 3. *For any permission p, if PSession* s_0 $(ss \frown step \frown step_1 \oplus ss_1)$, $step_1.e = request\ p\ (Some\ (ua\_deny\ session))$ *and Pre* $step.s\ step_1.e$, *then*

$$all\ (\lambda\ step\ .\ \forall\ o, step.e = request\ p\ o \to step.r \neq Some\ allowed)\ ss_1 \qquad (33)$$

Proof. Since *Pos* $step.s\ step_1.s\ step_1.r\ step_1.e$ must hold, p is revoked for the session in $step_1.s$. From Lemmas 1 and 2, p remains revoked for the rest of the session. Let $e = request\ p\ o$ be an event in a step $step_2$ in ss_1. We know that p is revoked for the session in the state before $step_2.s$. If the precondition for e does not hold in the state before[1], then $step_2.r = None$. Otherwise, e must be *request p None* and its postcondition entails $step_2.r = Some\ denied$. $\qquad\square$

---

[1] Actually, it holds only when $o = None$.

5 Refinement

In the formalization described in the previous sections we have specified the behaviour of events implicitly as a binary relation on states instead of explicitly as a state transformer. Moreover, the described formalization is higher-order because, for instance, predicates are used to represent part of the device state and the transition semantics of events is given as a relation on states. The most evident consequence of this choice is that the resulting specification is not executable. What is more, the program extraction mechanism provided by Coq to extract programs from specifications cannot be used in this case. However, had we constructed a more concrete specification at first, we would have had to take arbitrary design decisions from the beginning, unnecessarily restricting the allowable implementations and complicating the verification of properties of the security model.

We will show in the rest of this section that it is feasible to obtain an executable specification from our abstract specification. The methodology we propose produces also a proof that the former is a refinement of the latter, thus guaranteeing soundness of the entire process. The methodology is inspired by the work of Spivey [9] on operation and data refinement, and the more comprehensive works of Back and von Wright [10] and Morgan [11] on refinement calculus.

5.1 Executable Specification

In order to construct an executable specification it is first necessary to choose a concrete representation for every object in the original specification not directly implementable in a functional language. In particular, the transition relation that defines the behaviour of events implicitly by means of their pre- and postconditions must be refined to a function that deterministically computes the outcome of an event. At this point, it is unavoidable to take some arbitrary decisions about the exact representation to use. For example, a decidable predicate P on A might be represented as a function from A to a type isomorphic to *bool*, as an exhaustive list of the elements of A that satisfies the predicate (when P has finite support), or in some other equally expressive way. For every type T in the abstract specification, we will denote its concrete model as $\overline{T}$. Let $a : A$ and $\overline{a} : \overline{A}$, we will indicate that $\overline{a}$ is a refinement of a as $a \sqsubseteq \overline{a}$.

In our case, every predicate to be refined is decidable and is satisfied only by a finite subset of elements in its domain (they are all characteristic predicates of finite sets). Let P be one of such predicates on a set A and let l be a list of elements of $\overline{A}$, we will say that l refines P whenever

$$\begin{aligned}(\forall\, a, P\, a \to \exists\, \overline{a}, \overline{a} \in l \ \wedge \ a \sqsubseteq \overline{a}) \ \wedge \\ (\forall\, \overline{a}, \overline{a} \in l \to \exists\, a, P\, a \ \wedge \ a \sqsubseteq \overline{a})\end{aligned} \tag{34}$$

where $x \in l$ means that there exists at least one occurrence of x in l. When A and $\overline{A}$ coincide, $\sqsubseteq$ is the equality relation on A, and the condition (34) simplifies to $\forall\, a, P\, a \leftrightarrow a \in l$. Let $a : A$ and $\overline{a} : \overline{A}$ be such that $a \sqsubseteq \overline{a}$, we define

$$
\begin{aligned}
(None : option\ A) &\sqsubseteq (None : option\ \overline{A}) \\
Some\ a &\sqsubseteq Some\ \overline{a}
\end{aligned}
\tag{35}
$$

The above concrete representations can be used to obtain a concrete model for the device state and the security-related events:

$$
\overline{State} := \{\ suite \qquad\qquad\qquad : list\ \overline{Suite}, \\
session \qquad\qquad\qquad : option\ \overline{SessionInfo}, \\
granted, revoked : SuiteID \rightarrow list\ Permission\ \}
\tag{36}
$$

$$
\begin{aligned}
\overline{start} &: SuiteID \rightarrow \overline{Event} \\
\overline{terminate} &: \overline{Event} \\
\overline{request} &: Permission \rightarrow option\ UserAnswer \rightarrow \overline{Event} \\
\overline{install} &: SuiteID \rightarrow \overline{Descriptor} \rightarrow Domain \rightarrow \overline{Event} \\
\overline{remove} &: SuiteID \rightarrow \overline{Event}
\end{aligned}
\tag{37}
$$

The refinement relation $\sqsubseteq$ can be naturally extended to states, events and the rest of the types used in the formalization.

5.2 Soundness

Having chosen a concrete representation for the objects in the specification, everything is set for specifying the behaviour of events as a function

$$
interp : \overline{State} \rightarrow \overline{Event} \rightarrow \overline{State} \times (option\ Response)
\tag{38}
$$

The soundness of the *interp* function w.r.t. the transition relation $\hookrightarrow$ is given by the following simulation condition, illustrated in Fig. 2.

$$
\forall\, (s : State)\, (\overline{s} : \overline{State})\, (e : Event)\, (\overline{e} : \overline{Event})\, (r : option\ Response), \\
s \sqsubseteq \overline{s} \rightarrow e \sqsubseteq \overline{e} \rightarrow \\
let\ (\overline{s}', r) := interp\ \overline{s}\ \overline{e}\ in\ \exists\, s' : State, s' \sqsubseteq \overline{s}'\ \wedge\ s \xrightarrow{e/r} s'
\tag{39}
$$

It can be shown that the refinement relation $\sqsubseteq$ on states satisfies

$$
\forall\, \overline{s} : \overline{State}, \exists\, s : State, s \sqsubseteq \overline{s}
\tag{40}
$$

Thus, the existential quantifier in (39) may be replaced by a universal quantifier to obtain the stronger (but sometimes easier to prove) condition:

$$
\forall\, (s\ s' : State)\, (\overline{s} : \overline{State})\, (e : Event)\, (\overline{e} : \overline{Event})\, (r : option\ Response), \\
s \sqsubseteq \overline{s} \rightarrow e \sqsubseteq \overline{e} \rightarrow \\
let\ (\overline{s}', r) := interp\ \overline{s}\ \overline{e}\ in\ s' \sqsubseteq \overline{s}'\ \rightarrow s \xrightarrow{e/r} s'
\tag{41}
$$

With a function *interp* satisfying either (39) or (41) and a concrete initial state $\overline{s_0}$ that refines an initial abstract state s_0, the Coq program extraction mechanism can be used to produce an executable prototype of the MIDP 2.0 security model in a functional language such as OCaml, Haskell or Scheme.

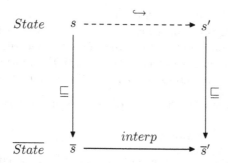

Fig. 2. Simulation relation between *interp* and the relation $\hookrightarrow$. Given states s, $\bar{s}$ and events e, $\bar{e}$ such that $s \sqsubseteq \bar{s}$ and $e \sqsubseteq \bar{e}$, for every state $\bar{s}'$ and response r computed by *interp* there must exist a corresponding abstract state s' refined by $\bar{s}'$ reachable from s by the $\hookrightarrow$ relation with the same response.

6   Conclusions

The informal specification in [2] puts forward an application security model that any MIDP 2.0 enabled device must satisfy. Although analyses of particular implementations have been proved useful for discovering vulnerabilities, so far the problem of the verification of the security model has not been addressed. We believe our contribution constitutes an excellent starting point for a thorough verification of the model, which would give a higher assurance level than the techniques applied so far.

We have produced, to the best of our knowledge, an unprecedented verifiable formalization of the MIDP 2.0 security model and have also constructed the proofs of several important properties that should be satisfied by any implementation that fulfils its specification. It is unclear from the MIDP 2.0 specification exactly how other mechanisms interact with the security model. Our formalization is precise and detailed enough to study, for instance, the interference between the security rules that control access to the device resources and mechanisms such as application installation. These issues have not been treated anywhere else.

We have also proposed a refinement methodology that might be used to obtain a sound executable prototype of the security model. Although we do not show it here, we have followed this methodology with a restricted set of events. Judging by the success of this experience, we strongly believe it is feasible to obtain a prototype for the whole set.

The specification has been completed in 4 man-months and comprises around 2200 lines, about 1000 of which are dedicated to proofs. In its construction, two simplifying assumptions have been made:

1. the security policy is static;
2. up to one suite may be active at a time.

Actually, most existing implementations (if not all) enforce these assumptions. However, the MIDP 2.0 specification does not and therefore, it would be interesting to explore the consequences of relaxing them by extending the formalization. An orthogonal direction is to divert from the MIDP 2.0 specification, enriching the model to allow more expressive policies. We imagine two possibilities:

1. abandon the unstructured model of permissions in favour of a hierarchical one;
2. generalize user interaction modes.

The former would allow group of permissions to be revoked or granted according to a tree structure, perhaps exploiting the already hierarchical naming of permissions in MIDP. The latter would allow richer policies such as granting a permission for a given number of uses or sessions. In a recent, as yet unpublished work, Besson, Dufay and Jensen [12] describe a generalized model of access control for mobile devices that follows these directions to some extent.

References

1. JSR 37 Expert Group: Mobile Information Device Profile for Java 2 Micro Edition. Version 1.0. Sun Microsystems, Inc. (2000)
2. JSR 118 Expert Group: Mobile Information Device Profile for Java 2 Micro Edition. Version 2.0. Sun Microsystems, Inc. and Motorola, Inc. (2002)
3. Kolsi, O., Virtanen, T.: MIDP 2.0 security enhancements. In: Proceedings of the 37th Annual Hawaii International Conference on System Sciences, Washington, DC, USA. IEEE Computer Society, Los Alamitos (2004) 90287.3
4. Debbabi, M., Saleh, M., Talhi, C., Zhioua, S.: Security analysis of wireless Java. In: Proceedings of the 3rd Annual Conference on Privacy, Security and Trust (2005)
5. The Coq Development Team: The Coq Proof Assistant Reference Manual – Version V8.0. (2004)
6. Bertot, Y., Castéran, P.: Interactive Theorem Proving and Program Development. Coq'Art: The Calculus of Inductive Constructions. In: Texts in Theoretical Computer Science, Springer, Heidelberg (2004)
7. Zanella Béguelin, S.: Especificación formal del modelo de seguridad de MIDP 2.0 en el Cálculo de Construcciones Inductivas. Master's thesis, Universidad Nacional de Rosario (2006)
8. Zanella Béguelin, S., Betarte, G., Luna, C.: A formal specification of the MIDP 2.0 security model. Technical Report 06-09, Instituto de Computación, Facultad de Ingeniería, Universidad de la República, Uruguay (2006)
9. Spivey, J.M.: The Z Notation: A Reference Manual. In: International Series in Computer Science, Prentice Hall, Hemel Hempstead, Hertfordshire, UK (1989)
10. Back, R.J., von Wright, J.: Refinement Calculus: A Systematic Introduction. In: Graduate Texts in Computer Science, Springer, Heidelberg (1998)
11. Morgan, C.: Programming from specifications. Prentice-Hall, Inc, Upper Saddle River, NJ, USA (1990)
12. Besson, F., Dufay, G., Jensen, T.: A formal model of access control for mobile interactive devices. In: Gollmann, D., Meier, J., Sabelfeld, A. (eds.) ESORICS 2006. LNCS, vol. 4189, Springer, Heidelberg (2006) (to appear)

A Comparison of Semantic Models for Noninterference*

Ron van der Meyden and Chenyi Zhang

University of New South Wales and
National ICT Australia, Sydney, Australia

Abstract. The literature on definitions of security based on causality-like notions such as noninterference has used several distinct semantic models for systems. Early work was based on state-machine and trace-set definitions; more recent work has dealt with definitions of security in two distinct process algebraic settings. Comparisons between the definitions has been carried out mainly within semantic frameworks. This paper studies the relationship between semantic frameworks, by defining mappings between a number of semantic models and studying the relationship between notions of noninterference under these mappings.

1 Introduction

"Noninterference" is a term loosely applied in the literature to a class of formal security properties motivated from considerations of information flow and causality. Since it was invented in [1], several distinct schools have produced a variety of generalizations of the original notion, each based on their own approach to modelling systems. Existing definitions of noninterference can be roughly classified by whether they are framed in the semantic context of state-based automaton models [1,2,3,4,5,6], trace-based models [7,8,9,10], or process algebraic based models (further divisible into CSP [11] and CCS [12] based variants) [13,14,15].

There have been a number of survey works and studies of the relationships between these definitions in the individual schools [15,13] but, on the whole, comparisons have been carried out within rather than across semantic frameworks. So far the only cross-domain contribution to our knowledge is [16], in which language-based security has been connected with a particular process algebraic property by a one-way translation. In this paper, we attempt to bridge some of the gaps by considering the relationships between the various classical semantic models and some of the proposed notions of noninterference. We consider three types of models: two automaton-like models (introduced in Sect. 2) and a process algebraic framework (discussed in Sect. 5). The semantic intuitions underlying these frameworks are somewhat different. The automaton models have notions of "action" and of "observation", the latter being a function of state in one case and associated to actions in the other. The process algebraic framework

---

* National ICT Australia is funded through the Australian Government's *Backing Australia's Ability* initiative, in part through the Australian Research Council.

is seemingly more general, but diverges from the intuitions of the automaton models in that it treats both actions (outputs) and observations (inputs) uniformly as "active". However, the state-observed automaton models rather than the process algebraic models are what is used in current work in operating systems verification [17,18] — the application originally motivating the literature on noninterference — so it is desirable to precisely understand the relationship between these frameworks. We address this question by defining formal mappings (see Sects. 4 and 5) between the semantic frameworks. We study whether a variety of definitions of noninterference (introduced for the automaton models in Sect. 3) in the different frameworks correspond under these mappings.

2   State-Based Models

The original system models used in the literature on noninterference modelled systems as a type of deterministic or nondeterministic automaton, with outputs for each of the security domains. Similarly to the Moore-Mealy distinction for finite state automata, we find two types of models, depending on whether outputs are associated to states [5,6] or actions [1,4]. The original definitions assumed deterministic systems, but the focus of subsequent work has been on how to generalize the definitions to nondeterministic systems. In general, these systems are input-enabled, in the sense that any action can be taken at any time.

A nondeterministic *action-observed* state machine is a tuple of the form $M = \langle S, s_0, next, dom, A \rangle$, where S is a set of states, $s_0 \in S$ is the initial state, A is a set of actions, $dom : A \to D$ associates with each action a security domain from the set of security domains D, and $next : S \times A \to \mathcal{P}(O \times S)$ is a transition function. Here O is a set of observations that can be made when performing an action. Given a state $s \in S$, and an action $a \in A$, the set $next(s, a)$ is required to be non-empty. A tuple $(o, t) \in next(s, a)$ intuitively represents that on action a it is possible to make a transition from state s to state t and produce output o. Such a machine is *deterministic* if $next(s, a)$ is a singleton for all states s and actions a. In this case, the function $next$ may be replaced by two functions $step : S \times A \to S$ and $out : S \times A \to O$ such that $next(s, a) = \{(out(s, a), step(s, a))\}$ to obtain the state machine definition one finds, e.g., in [4]. A run of an action-observed system is a sequence $r = s_0(a_1, o_1)s_1(a_2, o_2)s_2 \ldots (a_n, o_n)s_n \in S((A \times O)S)^*$ such that for all $1 \leq i \leq n$, $(o_i, s_i) \in next(s_{i-1}, a_i)$. A state $s \in S$ is said to be reachable if it occurs in some run. We write $\mathbb{M}_{na}$ for the set of all nondeterministic action-observed state machines and $\mathbb{M}_a$ for the set of deterministic action-observed state machines, where, in both cases, all states are reachable[1].

A nondeterministic *state-observed* state machine is a tuple of the form $M = \langle S, s_0, next, obs, dom, A \rangle$ where S is a set of states; $s_0 \in S$ is the initial state; the function $next : S \times A \to \mathcal{P}(S) \setminus \{\emptyset\}$ is a transition function, such that $next(s, a)$

---

[1] This restriction is of significance because the definitions and results below that concern unfolding relations are sensitive to unreachable states. A system may always be restricted to its reachable component, and this operation should, intuitively, not have an impact on its security. Thus this restriction is without loss of generality.

defines the set of states to which it is possible to make a transition when action $a \in A$ is performed at a state $s \in S$; the function $dom : A \rightarrow D$ associates a security domain with each action, and the function $obs : S \times D \rightarrow O$ describes the observation made in each state by each security domain. For readability, we 'curry' the function obs by writing $obs_u(s)$ for $obs(s, u)$ for $u \in D$ and $s \in S$. Such a state machine is deterministic if $next(s, a)$ is a singleton for all states s and actions a. In this case we may define a function $step : S \times A \rightarrow S$ by $next(s, a) = \{step(s, a)\}$. A run of a state-observed system is a sequence $r = s_0 a_1 s_1 a_2 s_2 \ldots a_n s_n \in S(AS)^*$ such that for all $1 \leq i \leq n$, $s_i \in next(s_{i-1}, a_i)$. (Here we omit representation of the observations since these may be recovered using the function obs.) A state $s \in S$ is said to be reachable if it occurs in some run. We write $\mathbb{M}_{ns}$ for the set of all nondeterministic state-observed machines, and $\mathbb{M}_s$ for the set of all deterministic state-observed machines where, in both cases, all states are reachable.

The most significant apparent difference between state and action observed machines is that, in the former, all agents make an observation when an action is performed, whereas in the latter, only the agent performing the action does so. Since the execution model is asynchronous, this means that whereas in action observed systems, other agents would, unless they themselves act, have no knowledge that any agent has performed an action, they may come to have this information in state observed systems even without acting. However, such a situation would often be a reason for the system to be declared insecure. The action-observed setting somewhat resembles the process algebraic setting of [19] where agents have to perform actions to synchronise with the system to achieve the effect of 'observation', but differs from it in that it bundles actions together with observations whereas [19] has separate notions of 'input' and 'output' actions.

3 Security Properties on State-Based Models

We now recall from the literature a number of security properties in the two types of state-based systems. We study the relationships between these properties in Sect. 4.

Historically, one of the first information flow properties was (transitive) noninterference [1,20], defined with respect to deterministic machines. We base our discussion on the presentation of Rushby [4], which has been followed in many other works. Rushby defines both state-observed and action-observed systems, but treats them independently and does not consider any direct relations between the two. The classical definitions were cast in terms of *security policies* describing permitted information flows between an arbitrary collection of agents. Much of the subsequent literature restricts attention to the policy $L \leq H$ with two agents High (H) and Low (L), with information permitted to flow from Low to High but not from High to Low. For uniformity, we also make this restriction here, and let $A_H = \{a \in A \mid dom(a) = H\}$ and $A_L = \{a \in A \mid dom(a) = L\}$.

As noted above, in both state-observed and action-observed deterministic systems, we have a function $step : S \times A \rightarrow S$ to represent the deterministic state evolution as a result of actions. To represent the result of executing a sequence of actions, define the operation $\circ : S \times A^* \rightarrow S$, by $s \circ \epsilon = s$ and $s \circ (\alpha \cdot a) = step(s \circ \alpha, a)$ for $s \in S$, $\alpha \in A^*$ and $a \in A$.

With respect to the simple policy $L \leq H$, the definition of noninterference can be described in terms of the operation $purge_L : A^* \rightarrow A^*$ on sequences of actions that restricts the sequence to the subsequence of actions of L. Intuitively, the purged High actions are not allowed to lead to any effects observable to L. This is formalised as follows in the definitions of noninterference following [4], one for each type of system.

Definition 1

1. *A system in* $\mathbb{M}_{na}$ *satisfies noninterference if it is deterministic and for all* $\alpha \in A^*$ *and* $a \in A_L$, *we have* $out(s_0 \circ \alpha, a) = out(s_0 \circ purge_L(\alpha), a)$. *We write* NI_a *for the set of such systems.*
2. *A system in* $\mathbb{M}_{ns}$ *satisfies noninterference if it is deterministic and for all* $\alpha \in A^*$, *we have* $obs_L(s_0 \circ \alpha) = obs_L(s_0 \circ purge_L(\alpha))$. *We write* NI_s *for the set of such systems.*

The definitions of noninterference in the two types of system are very similar. We show below that they can be seen to be equivalent in a precise sense.

One way of understanding the statement that H does not interfere with L in a deterministic system is as stating that every sequence of H actions is compatible with the actions and observations of L. This leads to the proposal to take a similar notion as the formulation of noninterference in nondeterministic systems: an approach known as nondeducibility [21]. Nondeducibility is defined in a quite general way, in terms of a pair of *views* of runs. We focus here on a commonly used special case: Low's nondeducibility of High's actions.

We take an agent u's view $view_u(r)$ of a run r to be the maximal state of information that it can have in an asynchronous system: its sequence of actions and observations reduced modulo stuttering. We begin by extending the agent's observations to runs. In action-observed systems we define the extended observation function $Obs_u^a : S((A \times O)S)^* \rightarrow (AO)^*$ for $u \in D$ by $Obs_u^a(s) = \epsilon$ and

$$Obs_u^a(r \cdot (a, o) \cdot s') = \begin{cases} Obs_u^a(r) \cdot a \cdot o & \text{if } dom(a) = u \\ Obs_u^a(r) & \text{otherwise.} \end{cases}$$

Here, taking the stance that an agent is aware of each action that it performs (so that if it performs an action twice, obtaining the same output, it knows that it has performed the action twice) we do not need to apply a stuttering reduction, and take $view_u(r) = Obs_u^a(r)$. In state-observed systems, the agent makes an observation at each state, and we define $Obs_u^s : S(AS)^* \rightarrow O^+(AO^+)^*$ by $Obs_u^s(s) = obs_u(s)$, and

$$Obs_u^s(\delta \cdot a \cdot s) = \begin{cases} Obs_u^s(\delta) \cdot a \cdot obs_u(s) & \text{if } dom(a) = u \\ Obs_u^s(\delta) \cdot obs_u(s) & \text{otherwise.} \end{cases}$$

Here the agent may make the same observation several times in a row, without an intervening action by that agent. This indicates that another agent has acted. To eliminate this timing-based reasoning, in order to make the definition compatible with the assumption of asynchrony, we may take the view to be $view_u(r) = Cond(Obs_u^s(r))$ where $Cond$ is the function on sequences that removes consecutive repetitions.

To state the definition of nondeducibility, we also require a function to extract the sequence of actions performed by an agent. We write $Act_u(r)$ for the sequence of actions performed by agent u in run r, and $Act(r)$ the sequence of all actions in r. We say that a sequence β is a *possible view* for agent u in a system M if there exists a run r of M such that $view_u(r) = \beta$.

Definition 2. *A system M satisfies Nondeducibility on Inputs if for every $\alpha \in A_H^*$, and every possible L view β in M, there exists a run r of M with $Act_H(r) = \alpha$ and $view_L(r) = \beta$. Write NDI_s and NDI_a for the set of systems in M_{ns} and M_{na} (respectively) satisfying nondeducibility on inputs.*

Wittbold and Johnson [2] argued that systems classified as secure by nondeducibility on inputs may nevertheless permit flows of information flow from High to Low. They present a system in which by selecting its actions according to a particular strategy, High may directly control Low's observations. They propose an alternate definition they call "nondeducibility on strategies" which behaves more satisfactorily on the example.

The framework in which they work is synchronous state machines with simultaneous actions. Nevertheless, it is possible to formulate a similar definition in the asynchronous models defined above. In state-observed systems, we define an asynchronous High strategy to be a function $\pi : O^+(A_HO^+)^* \to A_H \cup \{\epsilon\}$ mapping each possible high view to a choice of High action or the "noop" action ϵ. We say that a run $s_0a_1s_1 \ldots a_ns_n$ is consistent with π if $dom(a_i) = H$ implies $a_i = \pi(view_H(s_0a_1s_1 \ldots a_{i-1}s_{i-1}))$, for each $i = 1 \ldots n$. Similarly, in action-observed systems, we define an asynchronous High strategy to be a function $\pi : (A_HO)^* \to A_H \cup \{\epsilon\}$. A run $s_0(a_1,o_1)s_1 \ldots (a_n,o_n)s_n$ is consistent with π if $dom(a_i) = H$ implies $a_i = \pi(view_H(s_0(a_1,o_1)s_1 \ldots (a_{i-1},o_{i-1})s_{i-1}))$. Given a system $M \in \mathsf{M}_{na}$ or $M \in \mathsf{M}_{ns}$ and a strategy π of the appropriate type, define

$$Aview_L(M,\pi) = \{view_L(r) \mid r \text{ is a run of } M \text{ consistent with } \pi\}.$$

Definition 3. *M is secure wrt Nondeducibility on Strategies (written $M \in NDS_a$ or $M \in NDS_s$, according as $M \in \mathsf{M}_{na}$ or $M \in \mathsf{M}_{ns}$) if for all High strategies π, π', $Aview_L(M,\pi) = Aview_L(M,\pi')$.*

It is evident that every possible low level observation arises from some high level action sequence, and hence from some high level strategy (perform *that* sequence of actions). Hence if every high level strategy is compatible with every low level observation, then every high level input sequence is compatible with every low level observation. That is, nondeducibility on strategies implies nondeducibility on inputs. In fact the converse holds as well.

Theorem 1. $NDS_a = NDI_a$ and $NDS_s = NDI_s$.

A very similar result has previously been noted in a process algebraic setting by Focardi and Gorrieri[2]. Theorem. 1 could in fact be obtained as a consequence of their results and translation results from state and action observed systems that we present in Sect. 5. Note that, by Wittbold and Johnson's example [2], the equivalence does *not* hold in synchronous systems.

A number of the definitions in the literature on noninterference for nondeterministic systems are closely related to the following notion, that was originally motivated as a way of facilitating proofs of noninterference for deterministic systems.

Definition 4. *An* unwinding relation *for a system $M \in \mathbb{M}_a$ is an equivalence relation $\sim_L$ on the states of M satisfying the following conditions, for all states s, t and actions a:*[3]

- *Output Consistency$_a$: if $a \in A_L$ and $s \sim_L t$ then $out(s,a) = out(t,a)$;*
- *Locally Respects: if $a \in A_H$ then $s \sim_L step(s,a)$;*
- *Step Consistency: if $a \in A_L$ and $s \sim_L t$ then $step(s,a) \sim_L step(t,a)$.*

An unwinding relation for a system $M \in \mathbb{M}_s$ is an equivalence relation satisfying Locally Respects, Step Consistency, and the following variant of Output Consistency.

- *Output Consistency$_s$: if $s \sim_L t$ then $obs_L(s) = obs_L(t)$.*

The relationship between unwinding conditions and noninterference is given by the following classical results:

Theorem 2. [20,4]

1. *If there exists an unwinding relation for $M \in \mathbb{M}_{na}$ ($M \in \mathbb{M}_{ns}$), then $M \in NI_a$ ($M \in NI_s$).*
2. *If $M \in NI_a$ ($M \in NI_s$) then there exists an unwinding relation for M.*

The following is a natural generalization of Definition 4 to nondeterministic systems. (Note that Output Consistency has been incorporated into SC in the unwinding relation for $\mathbb{M}_{na}$.)

Definition 5. *An* unwinding relation *for a system $M \in \mathbb{M}_{na}$ is an equivalence relation $\sim_L$ on the states of M such that for all states s, s', t, actions a, and outputs o,*

- *LR_a: if $a \in A_H$ and $(o,t) \in next(s,a)$ then $s \sim_L t$,*

---

[2] See [19] on p.20-21: Theorem 3.27 states $NDCIT = NNIIT$, and Corollary 3.29 states $NNIIT = TNDI \cap IT$. The definition of TNDI resembles that of NDI, and the definition of NDCIT resembles that of NDS.

[3] We present a slight modification of the usual definition, which would have an equivalence relation $\sim_u$ for each agent u, satisfying a similar set of conditions for each u. For the policy $L \leq H$ we can take $\sim_H$ to be the universal relation, which automatically satisfies the necessary conditions.

- SC_a: if $a \in A_L$ and $s \sim_L s'$ and $(o, t) \in next(s, a)$, then there exists a state t' such that $(o, t') \in next(s', a)$ and $t \sim_L t'$.

An unwinding relation for a system $M \in \mathsf{M}_{ns}$ is an equivalence relation satisfying

- OC_s: if $s \sim_L t$ then $obs_L(s) = obs_L(t)$.
- LR_s: if $a \in A_H$ and $t \in next(s, a)$ then $s \sim_L t$,
- SC_s: if $a \in A_L$ and $s \sim_L s'$ and $t \in next(s, a)$, then there exists $t' \in next(s', a)$ such that $t \sim_L t'$.

Several definitions of noninterference can be expressed in terms of this generalized notion of unwinding. The following is essentially from [5], and a similar definition is given in [6].

Definition 6. $M \in \mathsf{M}_{ns}$ satisfies Behavioral Nondeterministic Security ($M \in BNS_s$) if the relation $\sim_L$ on the states of M defined by $s \sim_L t$ if $obs_L(s) = obs_L(t)$ is an unwinding relation.

Intuitively, this definition says that L's future observations depend only on L's current observation and L's future actions. This is particularly appropriate when we interpret L's observation as L's complete state, and wish to express that H is unable to interfere with this state. A related intuition in action observed systems is that L's future observations should depend only on L's most recent observation. The literature does not appear to contain any such definition for action observed systems, perhaps because states do not necessarily encode the most recent observation. However, by means of a transformation of the system we may obtain a behaviourally equivalent[4] system in which states do encode the information required.

Definition 7. Let $UF : \mathsf{M}_{na} \to \mathsf{M}_{na}$ be the unfolding function such that for each $M = \langle S, s_0, next, A, dom \rangle$ the system $UF(M)$ is the restriction of the system $\langle S', s'_0, next', A, dom \rangle$ to its set of reachable states, where

- $S' = S \times (D \to O \cup \{\varepsilon_0\})$;
- $s'_0 = (s_0, f_0)$ where f_0 is the function with $f_0(u) = \varepsilon_0$ for all $u \in D$
- $next' : S' \times A \to \mathcal{P}(O \times S')$ is defined as $next'((s, f), a) = \{(o, (s', f[dom(a) \mapsto o])) \mid (o, s') \in next(s, a)\}$.

Here ε_0 is a special output denoting no 'real' output has been observed to this moment. We use the notation $f[u \mapsto o]$ for the function g that is identical to f except that $g(u) = o$.

The intuition of this mapping is that introduces an extra component in the state that remembers the most recent output for each agent. (The price is to blow up the state space for all these observational possibilities.) This information is extractable by the functions $lastobs_u : S' \to O$ defined by $lastobs_u((s, f)) = f(u)$ for $(s, f) \in S'$ and $u \in D$. We may now give a definition of Behavioural Nondeterministic Security on action observed systems that captures the intuition that L behaviour should depend only on L's most recent observation.

---

[4] This can be made precise by means of an appropriate notion of bisimulation on action observed systems.

Definition 8. $M \in \mathbb{M}_{na}$ *satisfies* Behavioral Nondeterministic Security ($M \in BNS_a$) *if on* $UF(M)$ *the relation* $\sim_L$ *defined by* $s \sim_L t$ *if* $lastobs_L(s) = lastobs_L(t)$ *is an unwinding relation.*

Whereas Definition 6 and 8 obtain a definition of noninterference by asserting that a *particular* relation is unwinding, the following does so by requiring the existence of an unwinding relation.

Definition 9. $M \in \mathbb{M}_{na}$ ($M \in \mathbb{M}_{ns}$) *satisfies* restrictiveness, *written* $M \in RES_a$ ($M \in RES_s$), *if there exists an unwinding relation for* M.

The use of McCullough's [7] term "restrictiveness" in this definition is non-obvious. We justify it later when we discuss McCullough's work in the context of the process algebraic definitions treated in Sect. 5.

Proposition 1. *The following inclusions are proper:* $BNS_a \subset RES_a \subset NDI_a$ *and* $BNS_s \subset RES_s \subset NDI_s$.

4   Transformations Between State-Based Models

We now turn to our main interest in this paper, which is to study the relationship between security properties defined over different semantic models. For this, we require translations between the two types of models. The intuition underlying the two models introduced above, that agents can both act on and observe their environment is the same, and the modelling of the dynamics of actions is very closely related. Thus, the major issue in translation is how to deal with the observations. To transform action-observed systems into state-observed systems is not too difficult: the essence has already been introduced in the unfolding construction used for BNS_a (Definition 7), and we need only modify this construction by erasing observations from the transitions.

Definition 10. *Let* $F_{as} : \mathbb{M}_{na} \rightarrow \mathbb{M}_{ns}$ *be the translation function such that for each* $M = \langle S, s_0, next, A, dom \rangle$, *if* $UF(M) = \langle S', s'_0, next', A, dom \rangle$ *and* $lastobs_u : S' \rightarrow O$ *are the associated mappings to observations* O, *we have* $F_{as}(M) = \langle S', s'_0, next'', obs, A, dom \rangle$, *where*

$$next''(s, a) = \{t \mid (o, t) \in next'(s, a)\}$$

and $obs(s, u) = lastobs_u(s)$.

The range of F_{as} is a proper subset of $\mathbb{M}_{ns}$, because in any $F_{as}(M)$, for any $u, v \in D$, u can not modify v's observation before v gives any input. It is plain that if M is deterministic, then so is $F_{as}(M)$, so also $F_{as} : \mathbb{M}_a \rightarrow \mathbb{M}_s$.

It is also possible to translate state observed systems to action observed systems. An apparent obstacle, however, is that whereas in action-observed systems, an action gives a new observation only to the agent performing the action, an action in a state-observed system may also give a new observation to others.

In the following definition, we handle the need to model these additional effects by mapping the state observations to *potential* observations, that would be obtained if the agent were to look at the state. Thus, we define a translation that equips each agent u with a new action $look_u$ that enables the agent to obtain its observation from the current state, without changing that state.

Definition 11. Let $F_{sa} : \mathbb{M}_{ns} \to \mathbb{M}_{na}$ be the function such that for each $M = \langle S, s_0, next, obs, A, dom \rangle$, we have $F_{sa}(M) = \langle S, s_0, next', A', dom' \rangle$, where:

1. $A' = A \cup \{look_u \mid u \in D\}$,
2. $next' : S \times A' \to \mathcal{P}(O \times S)$ is defined by
   (a) $next'(s, a) = \{(o, t) \mid t \in next(s, a) \land o = obs_{dom(a)}(t)\}$ for $a \in A$,
   (b) $next'(s, look_u) = \{(obs_u(s), s)\}$ for $u \in D$,
3. $dom' = dom \cup \{\langle look_u, u \rangle \mid u \in D\}$.

We note that this translation produces a system with significantly more runs and views than the original state-observed system. This comes about because agents may, by failing to perform a *look* action, omit to make an observation they would have made in the state-observed system, or may perform a *look* action multiple times in the same state. The former, in particular, means that there exist runs in which agents have a "state of information" that would not have occurred in the state observed system. We would not expect, therefore, that all 'information theoretic' properties will be preserved by these translations. However, we may prove that the properties discussed above correspond under the translations:

Theorem 3. Let $\mathcal{P}$ be any of the properties NI, NDI, NDS, BNS, RES. Then

1. for all $M \in \mathbb{M}_{na}$, we have $M \in \mathcal{P}_a$ iff $F_{as}(M) \in \mathcal{P}_s$, and
2. for all $M \in \mathbb{M}_{ns}$, we have $M \in \mathcal{P}_s$ iff $F_{sa}(M) \in \mathcal{P}_a$.

This result can be understood as confirming the following key intuition concerning security properties and observations: a system is insecure if an agent is able to obtain prohibited information. Thus, modifying a system by permitting additional runs in which agents make *fewer* observations and *uninformative* (e.g. repeat) observations does not change the satisfaction of the security property.

5   Transformations to a Process Algebraic Model

Since the development of the original noninterference definitions, research has moved to how these definitions may be generalised to systems defined in process algebra. Work in this area has been conducted within the framework of the process algebra CSP [11], surveyed in [15], as well as the framework of a variant called SPA of the process algebra CCS [12], surveyed in [13]. We focus here on the latter, which it is closer to the models considered above in that it distinguishes inputs and outputs (corresponding loosely to actions and observations). It is also cast in terms of a common semantic underpinning for both the CSP and CCS approaches, viz., labelled transition systems.

Definition 12. *A labelled transition system (LTS) is a quadruple* $M = \langle P, p_0,$
$\rightarrow, \mathcal{L} \rangle$ *where* $\mathcal{L}$ *is the set of event labels,* P *is the set of processes (or states),*
p_0 *is the initial process (or state), and* $\rightarrow \subseteq P \times (\mathcal{L} \cup \{\tau\}) \times P$ *is the transition*
relation.

A run of M is a sequence $p_0 \xrightarrow{l_1} p_1 \xrightarrow{l_2} p_2 \ldots p_{n-1} \xrightarrow{l_n} p_n$, and the states that occur
in a run are said to be reachable. The corresponding *trace* of L is the sequence
of labels $l_1 \ldots l_n$ with any occurrences of τ deleted. We write $T(M)$ for the set of
traces of M. We write $\mathbb{L}$ for the set of all $LTSs$ in which all states are reachable.

In CCS, there is also a self-inverse bijection $\overline{\cdot} : \mathcal{L} \to \mathcal{L}$ and the set of events $\mathcal{L}$
is partitioned into a set I of input events and the set $O = \{\overline{a} | a \in I\}$ of output
events. Intuitively, the input event a may synchronise with the output event $\overline{a}$
when composing processes. We write $\mathbb{L}^{IO}(I)$ for the set of all LTS's with inputs
I and corresponding set of outputs $O = \{\overline{a} | a \in I\}$, or simply $\mathbb{L}^{IO}$ when I is clear.

In order to study security definitions, Focardi and Gorrieri [19] enhance CCS
by an orthogonal partitioning of the space of events into High and Low events.
Combining the two distinctions, the set $\mathcal{L}$ of all events is thereby partitioned
into High inputs (denoted HI), High outputs (HO), Low inputs (LI) and Low
outputs (LO). They call the resulting process calculus SPA.

Apparently, labelled transition systems are more general than the state machine models discussed above, in that inputs are not always enabled. Super-
ficially, SPA's labelled transition systems seem closest to action-observed state
machines, inasmuch as both inputs (actions) and outputs (observations) are associated to transitions. Given the equivalences discussed above, we therefore focus
on translating action-observed machines into SPA. However, whereas action-
observed machines combine an action and an observation into a single state
transition, SPA separates the two notions. This leaves open several plausible
translations from $\mathbb{M}_{na}$ to $\mathbb{L}^{IO}$. One follows an approach like that used above
for the translation from $\mathbb{M}_{na}$ to $\mathbb{M}_{ns}$, and treats the observations as optional
events which do not change the state. We assume in the following that the sets
of possible H and L observations in an action observed system are disjoint. This
is without loss of generality, since we may always rename the H observations,
which does not affect any of the notions of security, since these do not refer to
H observations. Similarly, we assume the sets of actions and observations are
disjoint. (Note the H and L actions are already separated by the function *dom*.)

Definition 13. *Define* $F_{al}^1 : \mathbb{M}_{na} \to \mathbb{L}^{IO}$, *such that if* $M = \langle S, s_0, next, dom, A \rangle$,
then $F_{al}^1(M)$ *is the restriction to its reachable states of* $\langle P, p_0, \rightarrow, \mathcal{L} \rangle$ *where*

1. $P = S \times (O \cup \{\varepsilon_H, \varepsilon_L\})^D$,
2. $p_0 = (s_0, f_0)$ *where* f_0 *is the function with* $f_0(L) = \varepsilon_L$ *and* $f_0(H) = \varepsilon_H$,
3. $\mathcal{L} = I \cup O$ *with* $I = A$,
4. $(s, f) \xrightarrow{l} (t, g)$ *iff either* $l = a \in A$ *and for some* $o \in O$ *we have* $(o, t) \in$
   $next(s, a)$ *and* $g = f[dom(a) \mapsto o]$, *or* $(t, g) = (s, f)$ *and* $l = f(u)$ *for some*
   $u \in D$ *and* $f(u) \in O$.

Another approach to the translation, which keeps observations obligatory, is to
introduce for each state s and action a a new state (s, a) to represent that the

action a has been taken from state s, but the corresponding observation has not yet been made.

Definition 14. Let $F_{al}^2 : \mathbb{M}_{na} \to \mathbb{L}^{IO}$ such that for $M = \langle S, s_0, next, dom, A \rangle$, we have $F_{al}(M) = \langle P, p_0, \to, \mathcal{L} \rangle$ where

1. $P = S \cup (S \times A)$,
2. $p_0 = s_0$,
3. $\mathcal{L} = I \cup O$ with $I = A$,
4. $\to = \{(s, a, (s, a)) \mid s \in S, \ a \in A\} \cup \{((s, a), o, t) \mid (o, t) \in next(s, a)\}$.

Focardi and Gorrieri discuss the condition of input-totality in the context of relating their definitions of security on SPA processes to classical definitions. An LTS $M \in \mathbb{L}^{IO}(I)$ is *input total* if for all $s \in P$ and for all $a \in I$, there exists $t \in P$ such that $s \xrightarrow{a} t$. It is apparent that for all $M \in \mathbb{M}_{na}$, the LTS $F_{al}^1(M)$ is input total, but the LTS $F_{al}^2(M)$ is *not* input total, since inputs are not accepted in the intermediate states (s, a). We will discuss below the impact this difference has on the relationship between definitions of security in $\mathbb{M}_{na}$ and $\mathbb{L}^{IO}$.

We now state a number of the definitions of security discussed by Focardi and Gorrieri. Given a trace t of an LTS in $\mathbb{L}^{IO}$, we write $low(t)$ for the subsequence of labels in $LI \cup LO$, $high(t)$ for the subsequence of labels in $HI \cup HO$, and $highinput(t)$ for the subsequence of labels in HI. We extend these functions to apply pointwise to sets of traces. We call a sequence in $low(T(M))$ a *possible low view* of M.

Definition 15. $M \in \mathbb{L}^{IO}$ is secure wrt Nondeterministic Noninterference ($M \in NNI_l$) if for every possible low view $\alpha \in low(T(M))$, there exists a trace $t \in T(M)$ such that $low(t) = \alpha$ and $highinput(t) = \epsilon$ is the null sequence.

This definition permits the trace t to contain high outputs. The following stronger definition prohibits this.

Definition 16. $M \in \mathbb{L}^{IO}$ is secure wrt Strong Nondeterministic Noninterference ($M \in SNNI_l$) if for every possible low observation $\alpha \in low(T(M))$, there exists a trace $t \in T(M)$ such that $low(t) = \alpha$ and $high(t) = \epsilon$ is the null sequence.

The following is a formulation of nondeducibility on inputs in $\mathbb{L}^{IO}$.

Definition 17. $M \in \mathbb{L}^{IO}$ is secure wrt Nondeducibility on Inputs ($M \in NDI_l$) if for every $\alpha \in HI^*$, for every possible low view $\beta \in low(T(M))$, there exists a trace $t \in T(M)$ such that $low(t) = \beta$ and $highinput(t) = \alpha$.

Finally, we have a definition that is motivated as a generalization of nondeducibility on strategies. This can be phrased[5] in terms of a process composition with synchronization on High events, which we formulate as follows. Given LTSs $M_1 = \langle P_1, p_1, \to_1, \mathcal{L}_1 \rangle$ and $M_2 = \langle P_2, p_2, \to_2, \mathcal{L}_2 \rangle$, define the composition $M_1 \|_H M_2 = \langle P, p_0, \to, \mathcal{L} \rangle$ with states $P = P_1 \times P_2$, initial state $p_0 = (p_1, p_2)$,

---

[5] We simplify the presentation of Focardi and Gorrieri to minimize the amount of process algebraic notation that we need to introduce.

labels $\mathcal{L} = \mathcal{L}_1 \cup \mathcal{L}_2$, and transitions defined by $(s,t) \xrightarrow{l} (s',t')$ if either $l \in LI \cup LO$ and one of $s \xrightarrow{l} s'$ and $t = t'$ or $s = s'$ and $t \xrightarrow{l} t'$, or else $l = \tau$ and there exists events l_1, l_2 in $HI \cup HO$ such that $l_1 = \overline{l_2}$ and $s \xrightarrow{l_1} s'$ and $t \xrightarrow{l_2} t'$.

Definition 18. *$M \in \mathbb{L}^{IO}$ is secure wrt Nondeducibility on Compositions ($M \in NDC_l$) if for every $M' \in \mathbb{L}^{IO}$ that has labels in $HI \cup HO$ only, we have $low(T(M)) = low(T(M\|_H M'))$.*

Focardi and Gorrieri also consider the following variant $NDCIT$ (or $NDC_l \cap IT$), which constrains the LTS's in question to be input-enabled. We define this in terms of a looser notion $NDC(IT)_l$, to separate input-totality of the system itself from input-totality of the composed systems.

Definition 19. *$M \in \mathbb{L}^{IO}(HI \cup LI)$ is secure wrt Nondeducibility on Compositions with Input Total systems ($M \in NDC(IT)_l$) if for every input-total $M' \in \mathbb{L}^{IO}(HI)$, we have $low(T(M)) = low(T(M\|_H M'))$.*

Intuitively, restricting M' to be input-total ensures M' cannot block any H output events from M in the composed system $M\|_H M'$. Investigating the relationship between the definitions of security in action-observed systems and $\mathbb{L}^{IO}$, under the transformations defined above, we obtain the following.

Theorem 4. *For all systems $M \in \mathbb{M}_{na}$ we have $M \in NDI_a$ iff $F_{al}^1(M) \in NDI_l$ iff $F_{al}^2(M) \in NDI_l$.*

Thus, both transformations produce LTS representations of the system that are equivalent with respect to the property of nondeducibility on input. Since nondeducibility on strategies is equivalent to nondeducibility on input on $\mathbb{M}_{na}$, this result gives us a way of checking the former property through a mapping to $\mathbb{L}^{IO}$. However, it remains of interest to check whether the notion of nondeducibility defined on $\mathbb{L}^{IO}$ corresponds to that on $\mathbb{M}_{na}$. This is particularly so as Focardi and Gorrieri show that the placement of nondeducibility on composition with respect to the other properties is somewhat sensitive to the class of systems to which it is applied, and the class of systems used in the compositions. Focardi and Gorrieri prove the following relationships: [19] $NDC_l = SNNI_l \subset NNI_l$, and $NDI_l \subset NNI_l$, and $NDI_l \not\subseteq NDC_l$ and $NDC_l \not\subseteq NDI_l$ and $NDC_l \cap IT = NNI_l \cap IT = NDI_l \cap IT$. We add to this the following result about input total systems:

Proposition 2. *$NDC_l \cap IT = NDC(IT)_l \cap IT$.*

That is, on input-total systems, input-total High processes have the same discriminative powers as all processes. Using the fact that F_{al}^1 produces input-total LTS's, the equivalence of NDS_a and NDI_a and the facts from the previous two propositions, we obtain a direct correspondence between nondeducibility on strategies and several notions of nondeducibility on composition.

Corollary 1. *For $M \in \mathbb{M}_{na}$, we have $M \in NDS_a$ iff $F_{al}^1(M) \in NDCIT_l$ iff $F_{al}^1(M) \in NDC(IT)_l$ iff $F_{al}^1(M) \in NDC_l$.*

This means that on input-total systems, and hence on the range of F_{al}^1, the distinct notions NDC_l, $NDC(IT)_l$, $NDCIT_l$, NDI_l and NNI_l collapse. We find a similar correspondence for F_{al}^2 (except that $NDCIT_l$ is excluded here since $F_{al}^2(M)$ is not input-total.)

Theorem 5. *For $M \in M_{na}$, we have $F_{al}^2(M) \in NDI_l$ iff $F_{al}^2(M) \in NDC_l$ iff $F_{al}^2(M) \in NDC(IT)_l$.*

We now turn to McCullough's notion of 'restrictiveness', already mentioned above. There are two versions of 'restrictiveness' introduced in McCullough's early works. The former [22] is a trace-based definition, while the latter is essentially defined on labelled transition systems [7,23]. In [23] McCullough mentions both definitions and concludes that the one on labelled transition systems is a stronger notion. The cleanest presentation of the LTS version occurs in [23]. Here we present this definition in the pattern used for unwinding properties for the automaton models above.

Definition 20. *Define a McCullough unwinding relation for an LTS M without τ transitions to be an equivalence relation $\sim$ on the states of M such that*

- *for all states s, s', t and input sequences α and α' such that $\alpha|LI = \alpha'|LI$, $s \xrightarrow{\alpha} s'$ and $s \sim t$ there exists a state t' such that $s' \sim t'$ and $t \xrightarrow{\alpha'} t'$;*
- *for all states s, s', t and output sequences α such that $s \xrightarrow{\alpha} s'$ and $s \sim t$, there exists a state t' and an output sequence α' such that $\alpha|LO = \alpha'|LO$, $t \xrightarrow{\alpha'} t'$, and $s' \sim t'$.*

Using this notion, the following is equivalent to McCullough's definition.

Definition 21. *An LTS M is restrictive ($M \in RES_l$) if it is input-total, it has no τ transitions, and there exists a McCullough unwinding relation for M.*

Focardi and Gorrieri [19] have proposed a definition of restrictiveness in the context of all LTS's, but in addition to dealing with τ transitions, their definition requires that a distinction be made between high and low level τ transitions, for reasons that are not made clear. Since our translations do not produce LTSs with τ transitions, the above restricted definition suffices for our present purposes.

Further, Focardi and Gorrieri classify their definition of restrictiveness with the other trace-based properties they consider. We point out that a better comparison is with the separate hierarchy of bisimulation based definitions of security they define. The following is one of the notions in this hierarchy.

Definition 22. *$M \in \mathbb{L}^{IO}$ satisfies strong bisimulation non-deducibility on compositions ($SBNDC$) if for every $p \in P$ reachable from p_0, if $p \xrightarrow{h} p'$ for some $h \in H$ then $(p\backslash H) \approx_B (p'\backslash H)$.*

Here, $\approx_B$ is the weak bisimulation, and '$\backslash$' is the restriction operator, with the usual definitions in CCS [12]. We may show the following, which justifies the use of the term restrictiveness in Definition 9.

Theorem 6. *If* $M \in \mathbb{M}_{na}$ *then* $M \in RES_a$ *iff* $F^1_{al}(M) \in RES_l$ *iff* $F^1_{al}(M) \in$ *SBNDC.*

For completeness, we also characterise the notion BNS [5] discussed above, within LTS. The intuition for BNS is that that Low's future pattern of observations depends only on the current Low state. To obtain a notion of Low state in LTS's, we take the perspective that an agent is able to perceive the set of observations being offered it in each state. (This makes the most intuitive sense when these transitions are self-transitions. It is also quite reasonable if different observations represent, e.g., the values of different variables that the agent may read.) For a state p of an LTS $\langle P, p_0, \rightarrow, \mathcal{L} \rangle$, define $obs_L(p)$ to be the set of $o \in LO$ such that there exists $p' \in P$ with $p \xrightarrow{o} p'$.

Definition 23. *An LTS* M *is in* BNS_l *if the relation* $\sim_L$, *defined on* M *by* $p \sim_L q$ *if* $obs_L(p) = obs_L(q)$, *is a McCullough unwinding.*

The intuition for the relation $\sim_L$ on LTS's (equivalence of the set of possible observations) is somewhat different from that used in the definition of BNS_a (equivalence of the most recent L observation). However, in $F^1_{al}(M)$, the (unique) next possible observation is in fact that which would have been obtained from the most recent L action. Thus, it is not surprising to find the following equivalence.

Theorem 7. *If* $M \in \mathbb{M}_{na}$ *then* $M \in BNS_a$ *iff* $F^1_{al}(M) \in BNS_l$.

6   Conclusion

We have studied the relationships between a variety of definitions of noninterference under a number of mappings between different semantic frameworks. Our results show that similar properties in different models do correspond in a precise sense, but highlight some subtleties: e.g., more properties are preserved when the obligatory observations in the state-observed model are treated as optional when mapped to the other models. Of particular interest, given our motivation from operating systems verification, is that the strongest process algebraic notion, $SBNDC$, is still weaker on the automaton models than the notion BNS_s which seems closest to the models and properties used in the operating systems verification literature [17,18]. However, this literature involves issues such as separation policy, scheduling and synchrony that go beyond asynchronous models and the specific policy $L \leq H$ we have treated in this paper. We intend to address these issues in future work.

References

1. Goguen, J., Meseguer, J.: Security policies and security models. In: IEEE Symp. on Security and Privacy, pp. 11–20 (1982)
2. Wittbold, J.T., Johnson, D.M.: Information flow in nondeterministic systems. In: Proc. IEEE Symp. on Security and Privacy, pp. 144–161 (1990)
3. Millen, J.K.: Hookup security for synchronous machine. In: Proc. CSFW'90, pp. 84–90 (1990)

4. Rushby, J.: Noninterference, transitivity, and channel-control security policies. Technical report, SRI international (1992)
5. Bevier, W.R., Young, W.D.: A state-based approach to noninterference. In: Proc. CSFW'94, pp. 11–21 (1994)
6. Oheimb, D.: Information flow control revisited: Noninfluence = Noninterference + Nonleakage. In: Samarati, P., Ryan, P.Y A, Gollmann, D., Molva, R. (eds.) ESORICS 2004. LNCS, vol. 3193, pp. 225–243. Springer, Heidelberg (2004)
7. McCullough, D.: Noninterference and the composability of security properties. In: Proc. IEEE Symp. on Security and Privacy, pp. 177–186 (1988)
8. McLean, J.: A general theory of composition for trace sets closed under selective interleaving functions. In: Proc. IEEE Symp. on Security and Privacy, pp. 79–93 (1994)
9. Zakinthinos, A., Lee, E.: A general theory of security properties. In: Proc. IEEE Symp. on Security and Privacy, pp. 94–102 (1997)
10. Mantel, H.: Possibilistic definitions of security – an assembly kit. In: Proc. CSFW'00, pp. 185–199 (2000)
11. Hoare, C.: Communicating Sequential Processes. Prentice Hall, Englewood Cliffs (1985)
12. Milner, R.: Communication and Concurrency. Prentice-Hall, Englewood Cliffs (1989)
13. Focardi, R., Gorrieri, R.: Classification of security properties. In: Focardi, R., Gorrieri, R. (eds.) Foundations of Security Analysis and Design. LNCS, vol. 2171, pp. 331–396. Springer, Heidelberg (2001)
14. Roscoe, A.: CSP and determinism in security modelling. In: Proc. IEEE Symp. on Security and Privacy, pp. 114–221 (1995)
15. Ryan, P.Y.A.: Mathematical models of computer security. In: Focardi, R., Gorrieri, R. (eds.) Foundations of Security Analysis and Design. LNCS, vol. 2171, pp. 1–62. Springer, Heidelberg (2001)
16. Focardi, R., Rossi, S., Sabelfeld, A.: Bridging language-based and process calculi security. In: Sassone, V. (ed.) FOSSACS 2005. LNCS, vol. 3441, pp. 299–315. Springer, Heidelberg (2005)
17. Greve, D., Wilding, M., van Fleet, W.: A separation kernel formal security policy. In: ACL2 Workshop (2003)
18. Martin, W., White, P., Taylor, F., Goldberg, A.: Formal construction of the mathematically analyzed separation kernel. In: Proc. 15th IEEE Int. Conf. on Automated Software Engineering (ASE'00) (2000)
19. Focardi, R., Gorrieri, R.: A classification of security properties for process algebras. Journal of Computer Security 1, 5–33 (1995)
20. Goguen, J., Meseguer, J.: Unwinding and inference control. In: IEEE Symp. on Security and Privacy (1984)
21. Sutherland, D.: A model of information. In: Proc. 9th National Computer Security Conference, pp. 175–183 (1986)
22. McCullough, D.: Specifications for multi-level security and a hook-up property. In: Proc. IEEE Symp. on Security and Privacy, pp. 161–166 (1987)
23. McCullough, D.: A hookup theorem for multi-level security. IEEE Transactions on Software Engineering 16(6), 563–568 (1990)

Hiding Information in Multi Level Security Systems

Danièle Beauquier[1] and Ruggero Lanotte[2]

[1] LACL CNRS FRE 2673, Université Paris 12 Val de Marne
[2] Dipartimento di Scienze della Cultura, Politiche e dell'Informazione
Università dell'Insubria

Abstract. In this paper we analyze the possibility for malicious agents to transmit an information possibly hidden in a Multi Level Security System via a covert
channel. We give a framework for which we get two decidability results. Firstly,
given a code and a system one can decide whether the system allows a covert
channel for this code. Secondly, one can decide whether there exists a code to
transmit one bit of information, the code is computable as well as the strategies
of the two partners.

1 Introduction

Security in systems (see [2], [3] and [4]) must ensure a state of inviolability from hostile
actions. Hence, unauthorized agents should not be able to have access to secret information. Detecting and preventing illegal information leak is particularly important for
multi-level security (MLS) systems. In these systems the access is controlled in such a
way that no high level information is allowed to pass to lower level users, but low level
information is available to high level users. The challenge here is to check whether
agents having classified information may leak information to agents with lower classification via the use of shared resources.

One way to violate a security policy is the use of covert channels. The notion of
covert channel was first introduced by Lampson (see [12]). A *covert channel* is a transmission channel that is used to transfer data with the purpose of violating security policy. The idea is that an agent uses the resources and functionalities of a system changing
its performance with the purpose of sending a (secrete) information to another agent.
Analyzing covert channels is one branch of current information flow security research.
A new approach to covert channel analysis and capacity estimation and can be found
in [25].

A communication channel can be used also to transmit *hidden* information, it is usually referred as a *steganographic* channel ([23]). In [29] there was a first formalization
of steganographic channel by modelling the prisoners problem. In this problem, two
prisoners in the jail plan to escape together. All communications between them are
monitored, hence, they must hide the escape plan messages in innocuous looking data.

This landmark begun the studies on subliminal channels. Subliminal since the information is transmitted by a channel used to send information in a cryptosystem. The
history of subliminal channel can be found in [30], further studies can be found in [28]
and [32].

T. Dimitrakos et al. (Eds.): FAST 2006, LNCS 4691, pp. 250–269, 2007.
© Springer-Verlag Berlin Heidelberg 2007

These studies have found applications in several fields like military and intelligence, digital cash and copyright marking (for a survey see [23]).

There are two main differences between ordinary covert channels and steganographic covert channels. Opposite to steganographic channels, when studying covert channels no attention is paid to hiding their existence. Secondly, a covert channel is tacitly assumed to emit data for an unlimited time, which is not the case for steganographic channels : a message hidden in an image for example has a size which is obviously limited by the size of the image.

The covert channels we study in this paper refer to both of these properties, namely an encoding is used (hence in some way we can model also hiding information) and the size of the transmitted message is bounded. The systems we consider are Multi Level Systems. We use the classical partition of agents in *high agents* (having access to secrete information) and *low agents* (having access only to public information). Each agent can perform actions classified as high or low according to the class of the agent which performs these actions. Depending on the performed action, the system changes its state in a non deterministic way.

The high agent wants to communicate to the low agent an information (sometimes hidden in the messages allowed by the protocol) by using a channel allowed by the system under consideration. High and low agents agree on a certain code built from what the low agent can see about the behavior of the system. Hence each information is associated with a certain sequence of symbols that the low agent can see. When the high agent wants to send a certain information, he performs the strategy associated with that information. The goal of this strategy is to get a sequence visible by the low agent which corresponds to one of the possible encodings of this information, whatever is the choice of the system.

We prove that given a code and a system, it is decidable to check whether this code generates a channel and, if it is the case, it is possible to compute the strategies of both agents to send and receive information. Moreover, we give an algorithm which decides given a system whether there exists a code to transmit one bit of information. The algorithm provides also the code and the strategies when the answer is positive.

After some notations given in the next section, we describe our model in section 3. Section 4 is devoted to the decidability result. We illustrate our model with an example in section 5 and describe in the last section our future work.

2 Related Work

Several studies have been done on covert channels. As an example, in [6] and [8] covert channels are studied from the point of view of non interference. Non interference means that a high level agent cannot influence the system in such a way that a low level agent can see the effects. Other techniques to detect covert channels have been proposed, which are based on typing, process algebra, axiomatic approaches, etc (see [24]),[13],[1] and [21]). Covert timing channels have also been studied. For example, in [7] results on information flow shown in [6] are extended to a timed setting and in [22] timing covert channels for real time data base systems are studied. Timed Z-channel are studied in [18]. In [16] covert channels are described as finite state machines, noiseless and memoryless covert channels are studied in [17]. Other examples can be found in [20] and [15].

Unlike these works, our paper focuses on the code that can be chosen by an attacker to send information in a timed setting, the approach is based on the definition of strategies and the problem is solved by using game theory.

In [10] the authors have considered a coding and transmission strategy for a covert channel using a single choice node (namely, a configuration of the system sensible to the actions of the attacker). In [11] an algorithm based on game theory is proposed for this approach. Differently from our study, these papers give a sufficient condition for the existence of a covert channel.

Other papers consider notions of security properties based on strategies. As an example, in [34] a security property called Nondeducibility on Strategies is introduced. This property is satisfied if the low level agent cannot exclude any strategy of the high level agent by reading his visible part of the execution. Similar properties are defined in [14] (where a system appears the same to the low level agent, for every possible high level users interacting with him) and also in [33] (where a stronger version of NS is considered.).

These definitions assume that the low level agent is passive. Here we consider a cooperation between the low and the high level agents where the low level agent chooses a strategy which permits to the high level agent to send information. Moreover, in the papers mentioned a security property that a system can satisfy is defined. In our paper, instead, we focus on the definition of the code of the transmission and on the capacity on the channel.

3   Basic Notations

Let Σ be a finite set of symbols. The set of finite (resp. infinite) strings over the alphabet Σ is denoted by Σ^* (resp. Σ^ω). The empty word is denoted ϵ. Let $\Sigma^\infty = \Sigma^* \cup \Sigma^\omega$ and $\Sigma^+ = \Sigma^* \setminus \{\epsilon\}$.

For every $\alpha \in \Sigma^\infty$, with $|\alpha|$ we denote the length of α. If α is an infinite string, then $|\alpha| = \infty$. Moreover, if $|\alpha| \geq 1$ and $|\alpha| \neq \infty$, then with $last(\alpha)$ we denote the last symbol appearing in α, more precisely, $last(\alpha) = a$ if $\alpha = \beta a$ for some β and $a \in \Sigma$.

Given a string α and a natural number n such that $n \leq |\alpha|$, then with $\alpha|_n$ we denote the string β such that $|\beta| = n$ and $\alpha = \beta\gamma$, for some string γ.

Given two strings $\alpha_1, \alpha_2 \in \Sigma^\infty$, we say that α_1 is *a proper prefix of* α_2 (written $\alpha_1 < \alpha_2$) if $\alpha_2 = \alpha_1\beta$ for some $\beta \in \Sigma^+$. Moreover, we say that α_1 is *a prefix of* α_2 (denoted $\alpha_1 \leq \alpha_2$) if either $\alpha_1 = \alpha_2$ or $\alpha_1 < \alpha_2$.

Let Σ be an alphabet; with $Pair(\Sigma)$ we denote the alphabet $2^\Sigma \times \Sigma$.

Given a string $\alpha \in \Sigma^\infty$ and a set of symbols $A \subseteq \Sigma$, with $\Pi_A(\alpha)$ we denote the subsequence of α one gets by erasing symbols which are not in A.

Let $\Delta \subseteq \Sigma^\infty$ be a set of strings. With $Pref(\Delta)$ (resp. $PPref(\Delta)$) we denote the set of finite prefixes of Δ: $\{\alpha \in \Sigma^* \mid \alpha \leq \beta$ for some $\beta \in \Delta\}$ (resp. the set of proper prefixes of Δ: $\{\alpha \in \Sigma^* \mid \alpha < \beta$ for some $\beta \in \Delta\}$). The set Δ *is prefix free* if $\Delta \cap PPref(\Delta) = \emptyset$.

The cardinality of a set X is denoted $|X|$.

4 The Model

In this section we describe the model we use for the system and the covert channel.

4.1 The System

Following [26], we model non deterministic systems using action (or event) systems.

The system is modelled as a finite non deterministic transition system where the actions of the low and high agents modify the state of the system. We model the elapsing of time with a special action denoted $tick$. The agents know the entire specification of the system but during an execution they have a partial information, in particular they do not know what is the current state of the system and the low agents see only the actions of their level.

Definition 1. *A timed system S is a tuple (Q, q_0, Act, δ) where*

- *Q is a finite set of states partitioned into two sets Q_{Low} and Q_{High} that are disjoint finite sets of low and high states respectively.*
- *$q_0 \in Q$ is the initial state.*
- *Act is a finite set of symbols partitioned into two sets Low and $High$ that are two disjoint finite sets of low and high actions, respectively. We assume that the special symbol $tick$ representing the elapsing of one time unit without any low or high action being performed is not in Act.*
- *δ is the set of transitions that is partitioned into two sets δ_{Low} and δ_{High} such that $\delta_{Low} \subseteq Q_{Low} \times (Low \cup \{tick\}) \times Q$ is the set of low transitions and $\delta_{High} \subseteq Q_{High} \times (High \cup \{tick\}) \times Q$ is the set of high transitions. Moreover, one cannot avoid time elapsing, for this reason we assume that for every state $q \in Q$ there is at least one transition (q, a, q') in δ, $a \in Act \cup \{tick\}$. It means that even if no action in Act is possible, the tick action is available in that case.*

The timed system S is *deterministic* if, given a state q and an action $a \in Act \cup \{tick\}$, there is at most one transition from q labelled with a, more precisely, for any $q \in Q$ and $a \in Act \cup \{tick\}$, it holds that $|\{(q, a, q') \mid (q, a, q') \in \delta\}| \leq 1$.

Given a state q, with $Act(q)$ we denote the set of actions performable from q, more precisely, $Act(q) = \{a \in Act \cup \{tick\} \mid (q, a, q') \in \delta \text{ for some } q' \in Q\}$.

A *path* for a timed system $S = (Q, q_0, Act, \delta)$ starting from $q \in Q$ is a (possibly infinite) sequence of transitions $\delta_1 \delta_2 \ldots \delta_n \ldots$ where for any i, $\delta_i = (q_i, a_i, q_{i+1}) \in \delta$. The path is also written $q_1 \xrightarrow{a_1} q_2 \ldots q_n \xrightarrow{a_n} q_{n+1} \ldots$.

The set of finite paths of S is denoted with $Path$ and the set of finite paths starting from q is denoted with $Path(q)$. We denote with $last(\omega)$ (resp. $first(\omega)$) the last (resp. first) state of a finite path ω, i.e. if $\omega = q_1 \xrightarrow{a_1} q_2 \ldots q_n \xrightarrow{a_n} q_{n+1}$ then $last(\omega) = q_{n+1}$ and $first(\omega) = q_1$.

With $Path_{Low}$ (resp. $Path_{High}$) we denote the set of paths ω in $Path$ such that $last(\omega) \in Q_{Low}$ (resp. Q_{High}).

Given two finite paths $\omega = \delta_1 \delta_2 \ldots \delta_n$ and $\omega' = \delta'_1 \delta'_2 \ldots \delta'_p$ such that $last(\omega) = first(\omega')$, the sequence $\delta_1 \delta_2 \ldots \delta_n \delta'_1 \ldots \delta'_p$ is a path denoted with $\omega\omega'$.

4.2 Covert Channels

In this subsection we explain how the low and high users can collaborate to create a hidden covert channel inside the system. The interpretation of the behavior of the system is as follows. At each step the choice of the action to perform is made by the high (resp. low) agent if the state is a high (resp.) low one. After that, the system resolves the non determinism. In this way, there is a possibility of cooperation between a low and a high agent if they agree by advance on some code. The two agents can decide in advance of some partition (the code) of the set of visible sequences seen by the low agent into 2^n classes. In this way the low agent is able to receive the encoding of a message of length n from the high agent. This message corresponds to the class containing the sequence of actions he observes. The problem is to know whether for a given code, the high agent is able to force the system to produce a sequence of actions whose visible part belongs to the class chosen by the high agent.

As usual we assume that the low agent cannot see high actions but he sees the *tick* steps. Actually, it is reasonable that when time elapses for an agent, then it elapses for all the agents. Since we consider instantaneous actions, obviously, the low agent cannot distinguish whether the high agent performs one or more actions in a given time slot (it is the designer of the system who decides the number of actions that can occur in a given time slot).

This semantics is a classical one considered in several papers defining discrete time models, see as an example [7] where the same semantics is adopted in a process algebra framework.

One way to get a covert channel in such a situation is to decide that the low agent will apply a strategy fixed by advance, and that the high agent will apply a strategy which depends on the message he intends to send. The problem can be interpreted as a game of the two partners against the non deterministic choices of the system.

Example 1. Fig. 1 and Fig 2 are two timed systems. In Fig. 1, low states are states $0, 2, 3, 6, 7$ and in Fig 2 low states are states $0, 3, 4, 5, 6$.

We will see below that the first system does not contain a covert channel for any code, because whatever is the choice of the high agent the low level will observe the same behavior, and then the low agent cannot infer any choice of the high agent. The second system has a covert channel of one bit at least because depending on the choice of the high agent the low agent will observe different behaviors.

From now on with Low_t, $High_t$ and Act_t we respectively denote the sets $Low \cup \{tick\}$, $High \cup \{tick\}$ and $Act \cup \{tick\}$.

Let $\omega = q_1 \xrightarrow{a_1} q_2 \ldots q_n \xrightarrow{a_n} q_{n+1}$ be a path. The *sequence of choices in ω* w.r.t. Act_t is the sequence $(A_1, a_1) \ldots (A_n, a_n)$ in $Pair(Act_t)^*$ such that for $i \in [1, n]$, $A_i = Act(q_i)$. This sequence represents what was seen by the high agent, namely, what were the choices made by the high and the low agents. In particular the high agents does not know the current state of the system.

The situation for the low agent is different since he sees only the low events.

Let $\omega = q_1 \xrightarrow{a_1} q_2 \ldots q_n \xrightarrow{a_n} q_{n+1}$ be a path. Let $i_1 < i_2 < \cdots < i_k$ be the sequence of indices j in $[1, n]$ such that $a_j \in Low_t$. The *sequence of choices in ω* w.r.t. Low_t is the sequence $(B_1, a_{i_1}) \ldots (B_k, a_{i_k})$ in $Pair(Low_t)^*$ such that:

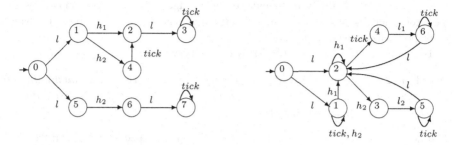

Fig. 1.   **Fig. 2.**

for $j \in [1, k]$, if $q_{i_j} \in Q_{Low}$, then $B_j = Act(q_{i_j})$ otherwise $B_j = \emptyset$.

Notice that in this last case $a_{i_j} = tick$, because if q_{i_j} is a high state, the low agent can see the choice of the high agent only if it is a tick.

The *sequence of choices in* a path ω w.r.t. Low_t will be denoted by $\Pi_{Low_t}(\omega)$.

Let $\omega_1, \omega_2 \in Path$; we write $\omega_1 \approx_{Low} \omega_2$ if ω_1 and ω_2 have the same sequence of choices w.r.t. Low_t and $Act(last(\omega_1)) = Act(last(\omega_2))$. This equivalence relation $\approx_{Low}$ expresses the fact that two paths in the same equivalence class are undistinguishable from the point of view of the low agent. With $[\omega]_{Low}$ we denote the class $\{\omega' \in Path \mid \omega \approx_{Low} \omega'\}$. On the same way, we write $\omega_1 \approx_{High} \omega_2$ if ω_1 and ω_2 have the same sequence of choices w.r.t. Act_t and $Act(last(\omega_1)) = Act(last(\omega_2))$.

A *Low-strategy* is a function $f : Path_{Low} \to Low_t$ satisfying:

- $f(\omega) \in Act(last(\omega))$
- if $\omega \approx_{Low} \omega'$, then $f(\omega) = f(\omega')$.

The idea is that the low agent performs the same choice for the paths with the same visible part w.r.t. Low_t because his choice can depend only on what he can see.

Symmetrically, a *High-strategy* is a function $r : Path_{High} \to High_t$ satisfying:

- $r(\omega) \in Act(last(\omega))$
- if $\omega \approx_{High} \omega'$, then $r(\omega) = r(\omega')$.

With Str_{Low_t} and Str_{High_t} we denote, respectively, the set of *Low*-strategies and *High*-strategies.

A *strategy of S* is a partial function $g : Path \times Act_t \to Q$ such that, for any path finite ω and any $a \in Act(last(\omega))$, $g(\omega, a)$ is defined and $(last(\omega), a, g(\omega, a)) \in \delta$. It means that the system S resolves the non determinism, by choosing the transition to use at some point performing some action. With Str_S we denote the set of strategies of S.

For any $f \in Str_{Low_t}$, $r \in Str_{High_t}$ and any finite path ω, with $next(\omega, f, r)$ we denote the symbol $f(\omega)$ if $last(\omega) \in Q_{Low}$ and $r(\omega)$ if $last(\omega) \in Q_{High}$. It represents the next action which will occur after the execution of path ω according to the respective low and high strategies f and r.

Moreover, given $g \in Str_S$, with $path(f, r, g)$ we denote the infinite path $\omega = q_1 \xrightarrow{a_1} \cdots \xrightarrow{a_n} q_{n+1} \cdots$ such that, for any n, it holds that $q_{n+1} = g(\omega|_{n-1}, a_n)$ and $a_n =$

$next(\omega|_{n-1}, f, r)$. Actually, if strategies of the low agent, the high agent and the system are fixed, then the systems becomes deterministic and has a unique behavior which corresponds to the path $path(f, r, g)$.

The sequence $\Pi_{Low_t}(path(f, r, g))$ will be abbreviated into $\Pi_{Low_t}(f, r, g)$.

Definition 2. *Let ψ be a subset of $Pair(Low_t)^+$, and $f \in Str_{Low_t}$. A winning strategy with respect to f and ψ is a strategy $r \in Str_{High_t}$ such that for any $g \in Str_S$, it holds that $\Pi_{Low_t}(f, r, g)$, has a prefix in ψ.*

A strategy for the high agent is a winning strategy with respect to f and ψ if whatever is the strategy of the system, if the low agent applies the strategy f and the high agent applies the strategy r then the behavior of the system will have a projection on the low level which has a prefix in ψ.

Definition 3. *A n-code is a family $\{\psi_1, \ldots, \psi_{2^n}\}$ of disjoint non empty finite subsets of $Pair(Low_t)^+$ such that $\left(\bigcup_{i=1}^{2^n} \psi_i\right)$ is prefix free.*

Definition 4. *Let S be a timed system. There exists a covert channel of n bits for S if there exists an n-code $\psi_1, \ldots, \psi_{2^n}$ and a strategy $f \in Str_{Low_t}$ such that for any $i \in [1, 2^n]$ there exists a winning strategy with respect to f and ψ_i.*

Actually, if the low agent applies strategy f and the high agent applies strategy r_i then whatever is the strategy of the system, the behavior of the system will have a projection on the low level which has a prefix in ψ_i. And since $\left(\bigcup_{i=1}^{2^n} \psi_i\right)$ is prefix free, as soon as this prefix occurs, the low agent knows that no longest prefix can belong to another $\psi_{i'}$.

We note that this permits therefore to send hidden information. Let $M = \{m_1, \ldots, m_k\}$ be a set of messages expressing the possible value of a certain information. As an example, M can be the set $\{Yes, Not\}$ or the range of possible values of some secrete stored data. The idea is that the high agent during his execution wants to send hiddenly to the low agent some message of M. Let $\psi_1, \ldots, \psi_{2^n}$ be a n-code with $n \geq log(k)$. The high and low agents agree that $\psi_1, \ldots, \psi_k$ correspond respectively to the messages $m_1, \ldots, m_k$. Hence, if the high agent wants to send hiddenly the value m_j, he will apply a strategy which forces the low agent to realize a sequence in ψ_j.

Example 2. The system of Fig. 1 does not allow an n-code for any $n \geq 1$ for the reason invoked above. Actually, the only manner for the high agent to send information to the low agent is to perform the tick action. But $\psi_0 = \{(\{l\}, l)(\emptyset, tick)\}$, $\psi_1 = \{(\{l\}, l)(\{l\}, l)\}$ is not a 1-code, since the state reached from state 0 after the action l is chosen by the system and not by the high agent. Thus if the system chooses to go in state 5, then the observation of the low level is always $(\{l\}, l)(\{l\}, l)$ and the high level cannot send the bit 0.

Nevertheless this system is usually considered insecure. Actually, if the low agent observes the $(\{l\}, l)(\emptyset, tick)$ surely h_2 is performed by the high agent. But we are not interested in this paper to this type of information flow.

The second example, namely the system of Fig. 2 allows an 1-code. The pair $\psi_0 = \{(\{l\}, l)(\emptyset, tick)\}$, $\psi_1 = \{(\{l\}, l)(\{l_2\}, l_2)\}$ is a 1-code. Actually, the strategy f of the low level is trivial. The winning strategy r_0 with respect to f and ψ_0 is as follows:

$r_0(q_0 \xrightarrow{l} q_2) = r_0(q_0 \xrightarrow{l} q_1) = tick$ (the two paths are $\approx_{High}$-equivalent so the value for r_0 must be the same).

So whatever is the strategy g of the system, $(\{l\}, l)(\emptyset, tick)$ will be a prefix of $\Pi_{Low_t}(f, r_0, g)$, i.e. the low agent will observe this string.

The winning strategy r_1 with respect to f and ψ_0 is as follows:

- $r_1(q_0 \xrightarrow{l} q_2) = r_1(q_0 \xrightarrow{l} q_1) = h_1$
- $r_1(q_0 \xrightarrow{l} q_2 \xrightarrow{h_1} q_2 = r_1(q_0 \xrightarrow{l} q_1 \xrightarrow{h_1} q_2) = h_2$

Whatever is the strategy g of the system, $(\{l\}, l)(\{l_2\}, l_2)$ will be a prefix of $\Pi_{Low_t}(f, r_1, g)$, i.e. the low agent will observe this string.

One can notice that we have defined r_0 and r_1 not everywhere but only on the paths which are "realized" when these strategies are executed. The value of r_0 and r_1 on other paths is not important.

4.3 Deadlocking the Timed System

In the definition given before, we do not give the possibility to the high agent to deadlock the system to communicate information. We note that we consider a system to be deadlocked if the low agent can no longer perform any action in Low.

In the following definition we show how to modify the system S in order to consider also information flow by mean of deadlock.

Definition 5. *Given a timed system $S = (Q, q_0, Act, \delta)$ with S_{dead} we denote the timed system $(Q', q_0', Act', \delta')$*

- *$Q' = Q \cup \{dl\}$. The state dl is a low state; So we have $Q'_{Low} = Q_{Low} \cup \{dl\}$ and $Q'_{High} = Q_{High}$. The state dl is reached when the high agent decides to deadlock the system.*
- *$q_0' = q_0$.*
- *$Act' = Act \cup \{\top\}\}$. The sets of low and high actions are respectively Low and $High \cup \{\top\}\}$. The action $\top$ represents the fact that the high system stops its communication with the system S with the purpose of deadlocking S.*
- *$\delta' = \delta \cup \delta_1 \cup \{(dl, tick, dl)\}$ such that:*
  $\delta_1 = \{(q, \top, dl) \mid q \in Q_{High}\}$.

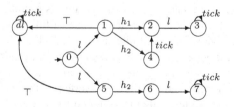

Fig. 3.

Example 3. The system of Fig. 1 allowing deadlock is represented in Fig. 3. The system now allows a covert channel of one bit. As an example $\psi_0 = \{(\{l\}, l)(\{tick\}, tick)\}$, $\psi_1 = \{(\{l\}, l)(\{l\}, l)\}$ is a 1-code. Actually after the choice of the system in the initial state the high agent can block the system in order to realize ψ_0, and in order to realize ψ_1 he chooses h_1 if this action is available, otherwise he chooses h_2.

5   Two Algorithms for Detecting a Covert Channel

In this section we prove that for a given code one can decide whether a system has a covert channel. Moreover, we show how to find a 1-code.

5.1   Checking an n-Code

From now on, we use the system of Figure 2 as a running example. Hence, each example of this section refers to that system.

First of all we observe that the value assumed by a high strategy is not important when considering a path whose sequence of choices is not a proper prefix of a sequence in ψ. Hence, we formalize this fact before proving the main theorem stating the decidability of checking n-codes.

Definition 6. *Let $f \in Str_{Low_t}$ and $r \in Str_{High_t}$ be a winning strategy with respect to some finite prefix free set $\psi \subset Pair(Low_t)^+$. We define $Domain(r)$ as the set of $\omega \in Path_{High}$ such that $\omega \in Path(f, r)$ and $\Pi_{Low_t}(\omega) \in PPref(\psi)$.*

Clearly, the value of r outside its domain does not influence the fact that r is a winning strategy. More precisely:

Lemma 1. *Let $f \in Str_{Low_t}$ and $r \in Str_{High_t}$ be a winning strategy with respect to f and some finite prefix free set $\psi \subset Pair(Low_t)^+$.*

If $r' \in Str_{High_t}$ is such that $r'_{|Domain(r)} = r_{|Domain(r)}$ then r' is a winning strategy with respect to f and ψ and $Domain(r) = Domain(r')$.

Let $f \in Str_{Low_t}$ and consider some finite prefix free set $\psi \subset Pair(Low_t)^+$. In order to decide whether there exists a winning strategy with respect to f and ψ, we translate the problem into a *2-player game*.

We recall briefly the main idea of a two player game. A two player game is composed by *two players* P_0 and P_1 and a *game graph* that is a tuple (V_0, V_1, Act, E) where V_0 and V_1 are two disjoint sets of vertices, Act is a finite set of symbols, and, $E \subseteq (V_0 \cup V_1) \times Act \times (V_0 \cup V_1)$ is a finite set of edges. For $i = 0, 1$, when a vertex in V_i is reached the next edge to follow is chosen by the player P_i. A player chooses the next edge with respect to a strategy that is a function from paths to edges. A strategy is memoryless if it depends only on the last vertex of the path. A player wins when the other player is in a vertex without exiting edges. A player has a winning strategy starting from a certain vertex when he wins the game for any strategy adopted by the other player.

The following Lemma is a well known result [9].

Lemma 2. *Let G be a game graph. One can decide whether a player has a winning strategy from some vertex in linear time w.r.t. the size of the game graph G. Moreover if there exists a winning strategy there exists a memoryless one and it can be computed also in linear time.*

Let us describe the two player game associated to our problem.

Given a timed system $S = (Q, q_0, Act, \delta)$, with $post(q, a)$ we denote the set $\bigcup_{(q,a,q')}\{q'\}$. We can easily extend this definition to sets $D \subseteq Q$ as $post(D, a) = \bigcup_{q \in D}\{post(q, a)\}$. Moreover, with $Act(D)$ we denote the set $\bigcup_{q \in D}\{Act(q)\}$, and, with $split(D)$ we denote the partition $\{D_1, \ldots, D_m\}$ of D such that, for any $q, q' \in D$, it holds that $Act(q) = Act(q')$ iff there exists j such that $q, q' \in D_j$.

We consider the game graph $G(S, f, \psi) = (V_0, V_1, Act \cup \{\epsilon\}, E)$ where

- V_0 is the set of triples $(D, \alpha, 0)$ such that:
  - either $D \subseteq Q_{Low}$ or $D \subseteq Q_{High}$ and $q, q' \in D \implies Act(q) = Act(q')$;
  - α is in $PPref(\psi)$;
- V_1 is the set of triples $(D, \alpha, 1)$ such that:
  - $D \subseteq Q$;
  - α is in $Pref(\psi)$;
- the set of edges E is defined as follows:
  - For any vertex $(D, \alpha, 0) \in V_0$ such that $\alpha \in PPref(\psi)$ and $D \subseteq Q_{High}$ if $h \in Act(D)$, there exists an edge with label h and target $(post(D, h), \alpha, 1)$.
  - For any vertex $(D, \alpha, 0) \in V_0$ such that $\alpha \in PPref(\psi)$ and $D \subseteq Q_{High}$, if $tick \in Act(D)$ there exists an edge with label $tick$ and target $(post(D, tick), \alpha(\emptyset, tick), 1)$.
  - For any vertex $(D, \alpha, 0) \in V_0$ such that $\alpha \in PPref(\psi)$ and $D \subseteq Q_{Low}$, there exists an edge with label l and target $(post(D, l), \alpha(Act(D), l), 1)$ iff l is the symbol chosen by f when considering a path with sequence of choices equal to $\alpha(Act(D))$.
  - for any vertex $(D, \alpha, 1) \in V_1$ and $D' \in split(D)$, there exists an edge with label ϵ and target $(D', \alpha, 0)$;

We explain below how this graph simulates the behavior of the system when the low level applies the strategy f.

A vertex $s = (D, \alpha, 0)$ in V_0 stores in its first component D all the possible reached states in S due to the non determinism of S for a fixed set of actions in Act_t, and in its second component α the sequence of choices w.r.t. Low_t. If $D \subseteq Q_{Low}$ there is only one transition from s which corresponds to the application of strategy f. If $D \subseteq Q_{High}$ there are several transitions from s which correspond to the different possible strategies of the high level. Transitions from states in V_0 simulate the choices of the low and the high agents. So player P_0 corresponds to the low and high agents.

Transitions $(D, \alpha, 1) \xrightarrow{\epsilon} (D', \alpha, 0)$ where $D' \in split(D)$ are used to simulate the non determinism of the system with the control that the decisions of the high (or low) level are the same for two states q and q' such that $Act(q) = Act(q')$. Therefore transitions from states of V_1 simulate the strategy of the system S and correspond to the choices of player P_1.

There are two types of vertices without exiting edges. Those which are in V_0 correspond to the situation when no more action is possible which permits to keep a sequence of choices w.r.t. Low_t which is in $Pref(\psi)$. In that case the player P_1 wins the game. Exiting edges which are in V_1 correspond to the situation when the system has realized a sequence of choices w.r.t. Low_t which is in ψ. In that case the player P_0 wins the game.

As a matter of fact, our problem is reducible to a two player game in the following sense:

Theorem 1. *Let S be a timed system, $f \in Str_{Low_t}$ and ψ be a finite prefix free set included in $Pair(Low_t)^+$. There exists a winning strategy with respect to f and ψ in S iff player P_0 has a winning strategy in the game graph $G(S, f, \psi)$. Moreover, to check whether there exists a winning strategy with respect to f and ψ in S is decidable in exponential time w.r.t. the size of S. If the system is deterministic, then it is decidable in polynomial time w.r.t. the size of $|S|$ and the size of $|\psi|$.*

Moreover we can estimate the complexity of the problem:

Theorem 2. *Let S be a timed system. To check whether there exists a covert channel in S for a given n-code is decidable in exponential time w.r.t. the size of S and the size of the n-code. If the system is deterministic, then it is decidable in exponential time w.r.t. the size of the n-code.*

In order to prove these two theorems we need auxiliary lemmas.

In the following Lemmas we associate to each path in S which is *compatible with the set ψ*, some path in G and we prove that P_1 wins the game iff there is a winning strategy with respect to f and ψ.

We say that a path ω in S starting from q_0 is *compatible with the set ψ* if $\Pi_{Low_t}(\omega) \in PPref(\psi)$ or $\Pi_{Low_t}(\omega) \in \psi$ and the last transition of ω is labeled by an action in Low_t. Notice that this action can be a *tick* and can be performed in that case by the high level. Let us associate to each path ω compatible with the set ψ a path $\theta(\omega)$ starting from the initial state of G as follows:

if ω has a length equal to zero, the same is true for $\theta(\omega)$, otherwise

let $\omega = q_0 \xrightarrow{a_0} q_1 \ldots q_n \xrightarrow{a_n} q_{n+1}$ and let $(D, \alpha, 0)$ be the last state of $\theta(\omega')$ where $\omega' = q_0 \xrightarrow{a_0} q_1 \ldots q_{n-1} \xrightarrow{a_{n-1}} q_n$,

1. if $\Pi_{Low_t}(\omega) \in PPref(\psi)$ then $\theta(\omega)$ is obtained by adding to $\theta(\omega')$ two transitions:
   $$(D, \alpha, 0) \xrightarrow{a_n} (post(D, a_n), \alpha', 1) \xrightarrow{\epsilon} (D_j, \alpha', 0)$$
   where D_j and α' are defined by:
   - $D_j \in split(post(D, a_n)$ and $q_{n+1} \in D_j$
   - $\alpha' = \alpha$ if $q_n \in Q_{High}$ and $a_n \neq tick$
   - $\alpha' = \alpha(\emptyset, tick)$ if $q_n \in Q_{High}$ and $a_n = tick$
   - $\alpha' = \alpha(Act(D), a_n)$ if $q_n \in Q_{Low}$.
2. if $\Pi_{Low_t}(\omega) \in \psi$ and $a_n \in Low_t$ then $\theta(\omega)$ is obtained by adding to $\theta(\omega')$ the transition $(D, \alpha, 0) \xrightarrow{a_n} (post(D, a_n), \alpha', 1)$ where α' satisfies:

- $\alpha' = \alpha(\emptyset, tick)$ if $q_n \in Q_{High}$ and $a_n = tick$
- $\alpha' = \alpha(Act(D), a_n)$ if $q_n \in Q_{Low}$.

Notice that in this latter case, the last state of $\theta(\omega)$ has no exiting edge. So we have the property:

Lemma 3. *Let r be a winning strategy with respect to f and ψ. For every strategy g of S and every prefix ω of $path(f, r, g)$ such that $\Pi_{Low_t}(\omega) \in \psi$ then $\theta(\omega)$ is a winning path for player P_0.*

And as a consequence we have:

Lemma 4. *If there exists a winning strategy with respect to f and ψ in S then there exists a winning strategy γ for player P_0 in the game graph $G(S, f, \psi)$.*

Conversely,

Lemma 5. *If there exists a winning strategy for player P_0 in the game graph $G(S, f, \psi)$, then there exists a winning strategy with respect to f and ψ for S.*

Proof. Let γ be a winning strategy for player P_0. We use γ to define a winning strategy r with respect to f and ψ for S. Due to Lemma 1, it is useless to define r on paths such that $\Pi_{Low_t}(\omega) \notin PPref(\psi)$. Let $r(\omega) = \gamma(\theta(\omega))$ for every $\omega \in PPref(\psi)$. By construction if $\omega_1 \approx_{High} \omega_2$ then $r(\omega_1 = r(\omega_2))$, so r is a high strategy. Moreover since γ is a winning strategy for player P_0, clearly for every strategy $g \in Str_S$, $\Pi_{Low}(f, r, g)$ has a prefix in ψ and so r is a winning strategy.

Proof of Theorem 1
Using Lemmas 4 and 5 there exists a winning strategy with respect to f and ψ iff the game $G(S, f, \psi)$ has a winning strategy for player P_0.

By Lemma 2 in linear time with respect to the size of G one can decide whether player P_0 has a winning strategy and if it is the case, compute a memoryless winning strategy for this player.

Since the size of $Pref(\psi)$ is polynomial in $|\psi|$, the number of vertices of G is exponential only w.r.t. Q. Therefore, one can decide in exponential time w.r.t. Q and in polynomial time with respect to $|\psi|$ whether there exists a winning strategy with respect to f and ψ. If the system is deterministic obviously the size of the game graph is polynomial in $|Q|$, $|Act|$ and $|\psi|$.   □

Proof of Theorem 2
Let $\{\psi_1, \ldots, \psi_{2^n}\}$ be a n-code. For each strategy $f \in Str_{Low_t}$, one can decide for each $i \in [1..2^n]$ whether there is a winning strategy with respect to f and ψ_i using Theorem 1. Moreover the "useful" part of f is its restriction to the set $F = \{[\omega]_{Low} \mid \omega \in Path_{Low}, \Pi_{Low_t}(\omega) \in Pref(\bigcup_{i=1}^{2^n} \psi_i)\}$.

That is if two strategies f and f' coincide on F then there is a winning strategy with respect to f and ψ_i for every $i \in [1, 2^n]$ iff there is a winning strategy with respect to f' and ψ_i for every $i \in [1, 2^n]$. The set F is finite and the number of possible values of f is computable and is exponential in the size of the n-code, and therefore using Theorem 1 to check whether there exists a covert channel in S for the n-code $\{\psi_1, \ldots, \psi_{2^n}\}$ is decidable in exponential time w.r.t. the size of S and the n-code.

If the system is deterministic, by Theorem 1, it is decidable in exponential time w.r.t. the size of the n-code.   □

Example 4. In Fig. 4 we show the game graph of the system in Fig. 2 where ψ is equal to $\{(\{l\}, l)(\emptyset, tick)\}$. In this case f is unique. Circles represent the cases in which the mark is 0 and hence represent vertices in V_0 (played by low/high agents). Boxes represent the cases in which the mark is 1 and hence represent vertices in V_1 (played by the system). States $(\{4\}, (\{l\}, l)(\emptyset, tick), 1)$ and $(\{1, 4\}, (\{l\}, l)(\emptyset, tick), 1)$ are the winning states for the low/high agents. State $(\{3\}, (\{l\}, l), 0)$ is the winning state for the system.

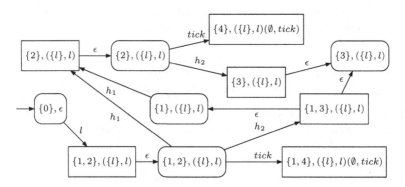

Fig. 4. Game graph for system in Fig. 2

Note that even for deterministic systems we have an exponential complexity bound. But, if each set composing the n-code has exactly one element the problem complexity is exponential only in the size of S. If S is deterministic the problem complexity becomes polynomial.

Corollary 1. *Let S be a timed system and $\{\psi_1, \ldots, \psi_{2^n}\}$ be an n-code such that $|\psi_i| = 1$, for any i. To check whether $\{\psi_1, \ldots, \psi_{2^n}\}$ is a covert channel in S is decidable in exponential time w.r.t. the size of S. If the system is deterministic, then it is decidable in polynomial time w.r.t. the size of S and the n-code.*

Proof. The strategy f is fixed by the n-code in the set $F = \{[\omega]_{Low} \mid \Pi_{Low_t}(\omega) \in Pref(\bigcup_{i=1}^{2^n} \psi_i)\}$.   □

It can be of interest to consider for which class it is possible to have a n-code where each set has exactly one element. The following proposition states that it is always possible for deterministic systems, implying that the decidability is potentially polynomial for deterministic systems.

Proposition 1. *If S is deterministic and $\{\psi_1, \ldots, \psi_{2^n}\}$ is an n-code for S, there exists an n-code $\{\psi'_1, \ldots, \psi'_{2^n}\}$ for S such that $\psi'_i \subseteq \psi_i$ and $|\psi'_i| = 1$, for any i.*

Proof. Derives directly from the fact that $|Str_S| = 1$, since S is deterministic. Indeed, there exists only one string α_i in each ψ_i which is a prefix of $\Pi_{Low_t}(path(f, r_i, g))$ where g is the unique strategy of the system. Thus one can take $\psi'_i = \{\alpha_i\}$.   □

5.2 Finding a 1-Code

An interesting question is to decide whether a given system has a n-code for a fixed n. We give here a positive answer to this problem for $n = 1$.

Let S be a system and $\{\psi_0, \psi_1\}$ be a 1-code for S. It means that the high agent can send one bit of information to the low agent. We show that if such a code exists there exists one with a size bounded by some function of the size of S.

Lemma 6. *Let S be a system and $\{\psi_0, \psi_1\}$ be a 1-code for S. Let $l \in Pair(Low_t)$ and $u \in Pair(Low_t)^+$ such that $ul \in \psi_0$ and $u \notin PPref(\psi_1)$ then $\{\psi_0 \cup \{u\} \setminus \{ul\}, \psi_1\}$ is a 1-code for S.*

Proof. Let f be a low strategy and r_0, r_1 be winning high strategies for f and the code $\{\psi_0, \psi_1\}$. Clearly, without changing f, r_0 and r_1 remain winning strategies for the new code. $\square$

Lemma 7. *Let S be a system and $\{\psi_0, \psi_1\}$ be a 1-code for S. Let $u \in PPref(\psi_0 \cup \psi_1)$. If there does not exist two different strings v, w such that $uv \in \psi_0$ and $uw \in \psi_1$ then there exists a smaller 1-code for S.*

Proof. Assume that for every v such that $uv \in \psi_0 \cup \psi_1$, actually uv belongs to ψ_0 (the other case is treated in a similar way). Then all these uv can be removed from ψ_0 and replaced with u. Let ψ_0' be the new set we get in this way. Clearly, if f is a low strategy and r_0, r_1 are winning high strategies w.r.t. f for ψ_0 and ψ_1 respectively, then r_0, r_1 are also winning high strategies w.r.t. f for ψ_0' and ψ_1 respectively. $\square$

Lemma 8. *Let S be a system which admits a 1-code. There exists a 1-code $\{\psi_0, \psi_1\}$ such that every proper prefix of $\psi_0 \cup \psi_1$ is a proper prefix of ψ_0 and a proper prefix of ψ_1.*

Proof. It is a direct consequence of the previous Lemma (Recall that ψ_0 and ψ_1 are prefix-free). $\square$

The following Lemma expresses the fact that one can take a code where all strings are "useful".

Lemma 9. *Let S be a system and $\{\psi_0, \psi_1\}$ be a 1-code for S. There exist a pair $\{\psi_0', \psi_1'\}$ and a low strategy $f \in Str_{Low_t}$ such that there exist winning strategies r_0, r_1 w.r.t. f for ψ_0' and ψ_1' respectively satisfying the following property: for every $u \in \psi_i'$ there exists a strategy $g \in Str_S$ such that u is a prefix of $\Pi_{Low_t}(path(f, r_i, g))$*

Proof. If for $i = 0, 1$ we remove from ψ_i all the strings u for which there does not exist a strategy $g \in Str_S$ such that u is a prefix of $\Pi_{Low_t}(path(f, r_i, g))$ the new pair $\{\psi_0', \psi_1'\}$ is still a 1-code for S. $\square$

Let $\omega = q_1 \xrightarrow{a_1} \ldots$ in $Path$. A strategy $g \in Str_S$ is *compatible* with ω if for every $n \geq 0$, $g(\omega|_n, a_{n+1}) = last(\omega_{n+1})$.

Let us introduce now some definitions in order to prove that if a system admits a 1-code, there exists one with a size bounded by a function of the size of S, which implies, using theorem 2 the decidability of the existence and the computation of a 1-code.

The idea is to attach to each prefix of $\psi_0 \cup \psi_1$ where $\{\psi_0, \psi_1\}$ is a 1-code a finite information about the runs which contain this prefix.

Let $f \in Str_{Low}$ and $r_0, r_1 \in Str_{High}$. Let $P(f, r_0, r_1)$ be the set $Path_{Low} \cap Pref(path(f, r_0) \cup path(f, r_1))$

For all $\omega \in P(f, r_0, r_1)$, let us define

$C(\omega) = \{(q, l) \in Q_{Low} \times Low_t \mid \exists \omega' \in P(f, r_0, r_1)$ s.t. $\omega' \approx_{High} \omega \; f(\omega') = l$ and $last(\omega') = q\}$.

The finite set $C(\omega)$ represents all the possible pairs (q, l) associated to paths $\omega' \in Path_{Low}$ which are $\approx_{High}$ equivalent to ω, where q is the last state of ω' and l is the action chosen by f for ω'. Thus $C(\omega)$ collects all the possible values (q, l) for paths in $Path_{Low}$ which have the same observable sequence for a high level agent.

$\mathcal{D}(\omega) = \{C(\omega') \mid \omega' \in P(f, r_0, r_1)$ and $\omega' \approx_{Low} \omega\}$

Let $u \in Pair(Low_t)^*$. We attach to u some information given by:

$State(u) = \{\mathcal{D}(\omega) \mid \omega \in P(f, r_0, r_1)$ and $\Pi_{Low_t}(\omega) = u\}$.

As for $LowPair$, the idea is that, if $State(uv) = State(u)$, then the strings uvz of the 1-code can be substituted by uz.

Example 5. Let $\alpha = (\emptyset, tick)(\{l_1\}, l_1)(\{l\}, l)$. We note that $\psi_0 = \{(\{l\}, l)\alpha(\emptyset, tick)\}$ and $\psi_1 = \{(\{l\}, l)\alpha(\{l_2\}, l_2)\}$ is a 1-code for the system of Fig. 2. Moreover, we have that $State((\{l\}, l)\alpha) = State((\{l\}, l)) = \{\{(q_3, l_2)\}\}$. Hence, α can be cut. Actually, we have already shown that $\psi_0 = \{(\{l\}, l)(\emptyset, tick)\}$ and $\psi_1 = \{(\{l\}, l)(\{l_2\}, l_2)\}$ is a 1-code for the system.

Let $N = |Q| \times (|Low| + 1)$. Then $State(u)$ is bounded by the constant 2^{2^N}, if S is non deterministic, and 2^N if S is deterministic.

We define the *size* of a finite subset of $Pair(Low_t)^*$ as the maximal length of its strings.

Lemma 10. *Let S be a system and $\{\psi_0, \psi_1\}$ be a 1-code for S. There exists a 1-code of size at most 2^{2^N}. If S is deterministic, then there exists a 1-code of size at most 2^N.*

Proof. Let r_0 and r_1 be winning strategies with respect to some low strategy f for ψ_0 and ψ_1 respectively. Using Lemmas 6, 7, 8 and 9 one can assume that the 1-code $\{\psi_0, \psi_1\}$ satisfies the following properties :

1. if $u \in PPref(\psi_i)$ then $u \in PPref(\psi_{\bar{i}})$ (if $i = 0, \bar{i} = 1$ and if $i = 1, \bar{i} = 0$)
2. for every $u \in \psi_i$ there exists a strategy $g \in Str_S$ such that u is a prefix of $\Pi_{Low_t}(path(f, r_i, g))$.

Let $M = 2^{2^N}$. If the size of the 1-code $\{\psi_0, \psi_1\}$ is greater than M there exists a string uvw of $Pref(\psi_0) \cap Pref(\psi_1)$ where v is non empty and $State(u) = State(uv)$ (note that if S is deterministic is sufficient 2^N). We now build smaller sets ψ_0', ψ_1' a new low strategy f' and new high strategies r_0' and r_1'.

- Sets ψ_0' and ψ_1' are defined as follows:
  $\psi_0' = (\psi_0 \setminus uvPair(Low_t)^*) \cup \{uz \mid uvz \in \psi_0\}$
  $\psi_1' = (\psi_1 \setminus uvPair(Low_t)^*) \cup \{uz \mid uvz \in \psi_1\}$.
  Actually in ψ_0 and in ψ_1, the strings which have uv as a prefix are replaced by strings obtained by "cutting" the factor v.

- The new strategy f' is derived from f as follows:

  For every finite path $\omega \in P(f, r_0, r_1)$:

  If u is not a prefix of $\Pi_{Low_t}(\omega)$ or if $\Pi_{Low_t}(\omega) = u$ then $f'(\omega) = f(\omega)$.

  Otherwise let $\omega_1 \in Path_{Low}$ the unique path such that $\omega = \omega_1\omega_2$ and $\Pi_{Low_t}(\omega_1) = u$. Let $q = last(\omega_1)$. Since $State(u) = State(uv)$ there exists a path $\theta(\omega_1)$ such that $\Pi_{Low_t}(\theta(\omega_1)) = uv$, $last(\theta(\omega_1)) = q$, $f(\theta(\omega_1)) = f(\omega_1)$, $C(\omega_1) = C(\theta(\omega_1))$ and $\mathcal{D}(\omega_1) = \mathcal{D}(\theta(\omega_1))$. The choice of $\theta(\omega_1)$ is not arbitrary, that is we respect both equivalences $\approx_{High}$ (note that $\approx_{High}$ is a refinement of $\approx_{Low}$). More precisely if $C(\omega_1') = C(\omega_1)$, then we choose a $\theta(\omega_1')$ such that $C(\theta(\omega_1')) = C(\theta(\omega_1))$. Then define $f'(\omega) = f(\theta(\omega_1)\omega_2)$.

  If $\omega \notin P(f, r_0, r_1)$, define f' in any way regular for relation $\approx_{Low}$.

  We prove that f' defines a low strategy, i.e. if $\omega' \approx_{Low} \omega$ then $f'(\omega') = f'(\omega)$. We have just to prove it in the case when u is a proper prefix of $\Pi_{Low_t}(\omega)$.

  If u is a proper prefix of $\Pi_{Low_t}(\omega)$ then ω' and ω can be written in a unique way:

  $\omega = \omega_1\omega_2$ with $\Pi_{Low_t}(\omega_1) = u$ and $\omega_1 \in Path_{Low}$,

  $\omega' = \omega_1'\omega_2'$ with $\Pi_{Low_t}(\omega_1') = u$ and $\omega_1' \in Path_{Low}$,

  with $\omega_1 \approx_{Low} \omega_1'$.

  So there exists a path $\theta(\omega_1)$ such that $f'(\omega) = f(\theta(\omega_1)\omega_2)$ and $f'(\omega') = f(\theta(\omega_1)\omega_2')$. Since $\theta(\omega_1)\omega_2'$ and $\theta(\omega_1)\omega_2$ are $\approx_{Low}$-equivalent we have $f'(\omega') = f'(\omega)$.

- Let us now define the new high strategies r_i'.

  * Let $\omega \in Path_{High} \cap (Pref(path(f, r_i)))$.

    If u is not a prefix of $\Pi_{Low_t}(\omega)$ or if $\Pi_{Low_t}(\omega) = u$ then $r_i'(\omega) = r_i(\omega)$.

    Otherwise we take the same decomposition $\omega = \omega_1\omega_2$ as above and the same $\theta(\omega)$. Then define $r_i'(\omega) = r_i(\theta(\omega)\omega_2)$.

  * Let $\omega \notin Path_{High} \cap Pref(path(f, r_i))$, define r_i' in any way regular for relation $\approx_{High}$.

We prove that r_i' defines a high strategy, i.e. if $\omega' \approx_{High} \omega$, then $r_i'(\omega') = r_i'(\omega)$. We have just to prove it in the case when u is a proper prefix of $\Pi_{Low_t}(\omega)$.

If u is a proper prefix of $\Pi_{Low_t}(\omega)$ then ω' and ω can be written in a unique way:

$\omega = \omega_1\omega_2$ with $\Pi_{Low_t}(\omega_1) = u$ and $\omega_1 \in Path_{Low}$

$\omega' = \omega_1'\omega_2'$ with $\Pi_{Low_t}(\omega_1') = u$ and $\omega_1' \in Path_{Low}$

in such a way that $\omega_1 \approx_{High} \omega_1'$. So the path $\theta(\omega_1)$ is $\approx_{High}$ equivalent to $\theta(\omega_1)$, thus $\theta(\omega_1)\omega_2$ is $\approx_{High}$ equivalent to $\theta(\omega_1)\omega_2'$ and $r_i'(\omega) = r_i(\theta(\omega_1)\omega_2) = r_i(\theta(\omega_1')\omega_2') = r_i(\omega')$.

We have to prove now that r_i' is a winning strategy for f' with respect to ψ_i'.

Let $g \in Str_S$ and $\omega = path(f', r_i', g)$. Assume that $Pref(\Pi_{Low_t}(\omega)) \cap \psi_i' = \emptyset$. Let u_0 be the longest prefix of $\Pi_{Low_t}(\omega)$ which is a prefix of ψ_i'.

There are two cases:

1. u is a prefix of u_0
2. u_0 is a proper prefix of u or u and u_0 are incomparable for the prefix order

Case 1. We have to discuss according to $\Pi_{Low_t}(\omega) = u_0$ or not.

If $\Pi_{Low_t}(\omega) = u_0$, we write $\omega = \omega_0 \omega_1 \omega'$ with $\Pi_{Low_t}(\omega_0) = u$, $last(\omega_0) \in Q_{Low}$ and $\Pi_{Low_t}(\omega_0\omega_1) = u_0 = uu'$. The path ω_0 is defined in a unique way, and we choose ω_1 as short as possible.

Then ω_0 is a prefix of $path(f, r_i, g)$. Moreover for every ω_2 such that $\omega_2 \leq \omega_1$,

if $\omega_0\omega_2 \in Path_{Low}$ then $f'(\omega_0\omega_2) = f(\theta(\omega_0)\omega_2)$, and

if $\omega_0\omega_2 \in Path_{High}$ then $r'_i(\omega_0\omega_2) = r_i(\theta(\omega_0)\omega_2)$

with $\Pi_{Low_t}(\theta(\omega_0)) = uv$.

Thus take a strategy $g' \in Str_S$ which is compatible with $\theta(\omega_0)\omega_1\omega'$. We have that $\theta(\omega'_0)\omega_1\omega' = path(f, r_i, g')$. Since uu' is a proper prefix of ψ'_i then uvu' is a proper prefix of ψ_i. There exists a finite path $\theta(\omega_0)\omega_1\omega_2$ in $Path_{Low}$ such that $f(\theta(\omega_0)\omega_1\omega_2) = l \in Low_t$, $B = Act(last(\theta(\omega_0)\omega_1\omega_2))$, $\Pi_{Low_t}(\omega_0\omega_1\omega_2) = uvu'$, and $uvu'(l, B)$ is a prefix of $\Pi_{Low}(\theta(\omega_0)\omega_1\omega')$. But $f(\omega_0\omega_1\omega_2) = l$ and $g(\omega_0\omega_1\omega_2, l) = g'(\theta(\omega_0)\omega_1\omega_2, l)$. So $uu'(l, B)$ must be a prefix of $\Pi_{Low}(\omega_0\omega_1\omega')$. Contradiction.

If $\Pi_{Low_t}(\omega) \neq u_0$.

We write $\omega = \omega_0\omega_1\omega'$ with $\Pi_{Low_t}(\omega_0) = u$, $last(\omega_0) \in Q_{Low}$, $\Pi_{Low_t}(\omega_0\omega_1) = u_0 = uu'$, and $last(\omega_0\omega_1) \in Q_{Low}$. Paths ω_0 and ω_1 are defined in a unique way. Let $B = Act(last(\omega_0\omega_1))$, $l = f'(\omega_0\omega_1)$. Then $uu'(B, l)$ is a prefix of $\Pi_{Low_t}(\omega)$ and $uu'(B, l)$ is not a prefix of ψ'_i.

As before, take a strategy $g' \in Str_S$ which is compatible with $\theta(\omega_0)\omega_1\omega'$. We have that $\theta(\omega_0)\omega_1\omega' = path(f, r_i, g')$. Since $uu'(B, l)$ is not a prefix of ψ'_i then $uvu'(B, l)$ is not a prefix of ψ_i. But $uvu'(B, l)$ is a prefix of $\Pi_{Low_t}(path(f, r_i, g'))$. Contradiction.

Case 2. We have $u_0 \in Pref(\psi_i)$. Moreover for every finite prefix ω_l of ω which is in $Path_{Low}$ one has $f'(\omega_l) = f(\omega_l)$ and for every finite prefix ω_h of ω which is in $Path_{High}$ one has $r'_i(\omega_h) = r_i(\omega_h)$. So $\omega = path(f, r_i, g)$. But since r_i is a winning strategy for f with respect to ψ_i, $\Pi_{Low_t}(\omega)$ has a prefix u_1 in ψ_i. So $u_0 \leq u_1$ and $u_1 \in \psi'_i$. Contradiction with $Pref(\Pi_{Low_t}(\omega)) \cap \psi'_i = \emptyset$.

By lemma 10, to find a 1-code, it is sufficient to enumerate all the 1-codes. Hence we have the following theorem.

Theorem 3. *Let S be a system; it is decidable in triple exponential time to find a 1-code for S. If S is deterministic, then it is decidable in double exponential time.*

6   A Case Study

Here is a classical example in which shared files stored in a cache can create a covert timed channel ([12]).

Let a system with a disk of space M and a cache of space N. Obviously, we assume that $N \leq M$. The security policy implemented by the system is that low and high agents can only read files. To read a file from the cache costs t_c time units. If the file is not in the cache, beforehand it must be read from the disk and stored in the cache. This operation costs t_d, and hence, to read a file not in the cache costs $t_c + t_d$.

Consider the following policy of management of the cache: when a request for a file not in the cache occurs, the file less recently refereed in the cache is overwritten.

With $ReadL_i$ (resp. $ReadHw_i$) we denote the request of the low agent (resp. high agent) for the file i. With $NopH$ we denote the fact that the high agent requires no file.

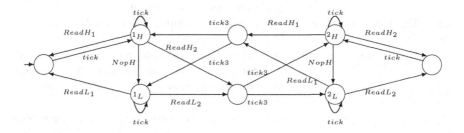

Fig. 5. A cache model

Symbol $NopH$ is necessary to allow the system to pass from high to low states, and hence, to accept high/low requests.

In figure 5 we model the cache where $M = 2$, $N = 1$ $t_c = 1$ and $t_d = 2$. With $tick^n$ we denote the sequence of n ticks. State 1_H (resp. 1_L) is a high state (resp. low state) representing the fact that file 1 is stored in the cache, and states 2_H (resp. 2_L) is a high state (resp. low state) representing the fact that file 2 is stored in the cache. Initially the cache contains the file 1 and to start the system needs 1 time unit.

Obviously, the high agent can transmit information by storing files in the cache and hence by changing the answer of the system to a request of the low agent.

Let $[tick] = (\emptyset, tick)$ and $[ReadL_1] = (\{tick, ReadL_1, ReadL_2\}, ReadL_1)$.

As an example, a 1-code is:

- $\psi_0 = \{[tick][ReadL_1]\}$
- $\psi_1 = \{[tick][tick][tick][tick][ReadL_1]\}$

Actually to realize ψ_0 (resp. ψ_1) the high agent must choose the request $NopH$ (resp. the request $ReadH_2$) when the set of choices is $\{tick, NopH, ReadH_1, ReadH_2\}$. On the other hand the low agent chooses always the request $ReadL_1$.

We note that the system is deterministic and hence to check that $\{\psi_0, \psi_1\}$ is a 1-code can be done in polynomial time.

In this manner, we can we easily define a n-code, for any $n \geq 2$. Actually, we have shown how the high agent can communicate 1 bit to the low agent. This is possible since the low agent can understand whether the file 1 is or is not in the cache. Hence, an n-code can be written by considering a sequence of n requests of the low agent for the file 1. Each set composing the n-code is a possible sequence of length n of presence/absence of the file 1 in the cache. So, we have 2^n possible cases. Hence, to communicate a certain sequence of n bits, the high agent performs a sequences of requests that respects the chosen sequence of length n of presence/absence of the file 1.

7   Conclusion

In this paper we have described how one can exploit and get round a multi level security system to get a hidden covert channel. We have proved that it is decidable to check whether a system allows a covert channel for a given n-code on one hand and on the other hand to to check whether a system allows a covert channel for one bit of information. This latter algorithm provides in case of a positive answer the 1-code and the strategies to apply for the low and high user respectively.

As a future work we want to extend our second algorithm to the case of a n-code which permits a hidden covert channel for a fixed n. We conjecture also that this code can be expressed as a regular expression which is a function of the number n of bits one wants to transmit.

Instead of of a hierarchical concept of classes of users, a distributed one is also relevant in some situations. In that case the rules are symmetric for high and low users, and the high agent observes only high actions. The questions which are solved in this paper are open under these hypothesis.

References

1. Andrews, G.R., Reitmans, R.P.: An axiomatic approach to information flows in programs. ACM transactions on Programming languages and Systems 2, 56–76 (1980)
2. Bell, D.E., La Padula, J.J.: Secure computer systems: mathematical foundations, Mitre technical report 2547, MITRE, vol. I (1973)
3. Bell, D.E., La Padula, J.J.: Secure computer systems: a mathematical model, MITRE technical report 2547, MITRE, vol. II (1973)
4. Bell, D.E., La Padula, J.J.: Secure computer systems: unified exposition and multics interpretation, Mitre technical report 2997, MITRE, vol. I (1975)
5. Fisky, G., Fisk, M., Papadopoulos, C., Neil, J.: Eliminating Steganography in Internet Traffic with Active Wardens. In: Petitcolas, F.A.P. (ed.) IH 2002. LNCS, vol. 2578, pp. 18–35. Springer, Heidelberg (2003)
6. Focardi, R., Gorrieri, R.: Classification of Security Properties (Part I: Information Flow). In: Focardi, R., Gorrieri, R. (eds.) Foundations of Security Analysis and Design. LNCS, vol. 2171, pp. 331–396. Springer, Heidelberg (2001)
7. Focardi, R., Gorrieri, R., Martinelli, F.: Real Time information Flow Analysis. IEEE JSAC 21, 20–35 (2003)
8. Goguen, J., Meseguer, J.: Security policies and security models. In: Proc. IEEE Symposium on Security and Privacy Proceedings, pp. 11–20 (1982)
9. Grädel, E.: Finite model theory and descriptive complexity. In: Finite Model Theory and Its Applications, Springer, Heidelberg (2003) (to appear)
10. Hélouët, L., Jard, C., Zeitoun, M.: Covert channels detection in protocols using scenarios. In: SPV 2003 (2003)
11. Hélouët, L., Zeitoun, M., Degorre, A.: Scenarios and Covert channels, another game. In: Proc. of Games in Design and Verification, ENTCS, pp. 93–116 (2005)
12. Lampson, B.: A note on the confinement problem. Communication of the ACM 16, 613–615
13. Lowe, G.: Quantifying information flow. In: Gollmann, D., Karjoth, G., Waidner, M. (eds.) ESORICS 2002. LNCS, vol. 2502, pp. 18–31. Springer, Heidelberg (2002)
14. Martinelli, F.: Partial Model Checking and Theorem Proving for Ensuring Security Properties. In: Proc. of IEEE CSFW, pp. 44–52 (1998)
15. McHugh, J.: Covert Channel Analysis: A Chapter of the Handbook for the Computer Security Certification of Trusted Systems (1995), available at
    http://chacs.nrl.navy.mil/publications/handbook/
16. Millen, J.K.: Finite-State Noiseless Covert Channels. In: Proc. of IEEE CSFW, pp. 81–86 (1989)

17. Moskowitz, I.S., Miller, A.R.: Simple Timing Channels. In: Proc. of IEEE Computer Symposium on Research in Security and Privacy, pp. 56–64 (1994)
18. Moskowitz, I.S., Greenwald, S.J., Kang, M.H.: An Analysis of the Timed-Z Channel. In: Proc. of IEEE Computer Symposium on Security and Privacy, pp. 2–11 (1996)
19. Murdoch, S.J., Zielinski, P.: Covert Channels for Collusion in Online Computer Games. In: Fridrich, J. (ed.) IH 2004. LNCS, vol. 3200, pp. 355–369. Springer, Heidelberg (2004)
20. National Computer Security Center.: A Guide to Understanding Covert Channel Analysis of Trusted Systems NCSC-TG-30 (1993), available at
    http://www.radium.ncsc.mil/tpep/library/rainbow/
21. Sabelfeld, A., Myers, A.C.: Language-based information flow security. IEEE Journal on selected areas in communications, 21 (2003)
22. Son, S.H., Mukkamala, R., David, R.: Integrating Security and Real-Time Requirements using Covert Channel Capacity. IEEE Trans. Knowledge and Data Eng. 12, 865–879 (2000)
23. Petitcolas, F.A.P., Anderson, R.J., Kuhn, M.G.: Information Hiding-A Survey. In: Proc. of the IEEE Special issue on protection of multimedia content, vol. 87, pp. 1062–1078 (1999)
24. Volpano, D., Smith, G.: Eliminating covert flows with minimum typings. In: Proc. IEEE CSF, pp. 156–168 (1997)
25. Wang, Z., Lee, R.: New Constructive Approach to Covert Channel Modeling and Channel Capacity Estimation. In: Zhou, J., Lopez, J., Deng, R.H., Bao, F. (eds.) ISC 2005. LNCS, vol. 3650, pp. 498–505. Springer, Heidelberg (2005)
26. Zakinthinos, A., Lee, E.S.: A general theory of security properties. In: Proc. of IEEE Symposium on Security and Privacy, pp. 74–102 (1997)
27. Shannon, C.E.: Communication theory of secrecy systems. Bell System Technical Journal 28, 656–715 (1949)
28. Simmons, G.J.: Contemporary Cryptology. In: The Science of Information Integrity, IEEE Press, New York (1992)
29. Simmons, G.J.: The prisoners' problem and the subliminal channel. In: Prod. of Workshop on Communications Security, pp. 51–67. IEEE Press, Orlando, Florida (1984)
30. Simmons, G.J.: The history of subliminal channels. IEEE Journal of Selected Areas in Communications 16, 452–462 (1998)
31. Anderson, R.J., Vaudenay, S., Preneel, B., Nyberg, K.: The Newton channel, Proc. of Workshop on Information Hiding. In: Anderson, R. (ed.) Information Hiding. LNCS, vol. 1174, pp. 151–156. Springer, Heidelberg (1996)
32. Simmons, G.J.: Subliminal channels: Past and present. European Transaction on Telecommunications 5, 459–473 (1994)
33. van der Meyden, R., Wilke, T.: Synthesis of Distributed Systems from Knowledge-Based Specifications. In: Abadi, M., de Alfaro, L. (eds.) CONCUR 2005. LNCS, vol. 3653, pp. 562–576. Springer, Heidelberg (2005)
34. Wittbold, J.T., Johnson, D.M.: Information flow in nondeterministic systems. In: Proc. of IEEE Symposium on Security and Privacy, pp. 144–161 (1990)
35. Wittbold, J.T., Johnson, D.M.: Results concerning the bandwidth of subliminal channels. IEEE Journal of Selected Areas in Communications 16, 463–473 (1998)

A New Trust Model Based on Advanced D-S Evidence Theory for P2P Networks*

Chunqi Tian, Shihong Zou, Wendong Wang, and Shiduan Cheng

State Key Laboratory of Networking and Switching
Beijing University of Posts and Telecommunications
Beijing, P.R. China, 100876
tianchunqi@163.com, {zoush, wdwang, chsd}@bupt.edu.cn

Abstract. Building trust relationship between peers in a large-scale distributed P2P file-sharing system is a fundamental and challenging research topic. Recommendation based trust mechanism is widely employed to establish the trust relationship. However, most existing approaches can not efficiently deal with inconsistent or conflicting recommendation information, and uncertainty of information. Dempster-Shafer (D-S) evidence theory is preponderant in tackling uncertainty of information, but classical combination rule always results in unreasonable results especially when evidences severely conflict each other. In this paper, we improve the combination rule for D-S evidence theory and develop a novel trust model based on it. For the problem of security, some measures are also proposed to defense against several malicious attacks. Experimental results show that the proposed model can significantly improve the successful transaction rate of P2P networks and effectively detect malicious behaviors in P2P networks.

1 Introduction

Peer-to-peer file-sharing networks have many benefits over standard client-server approaches to distributing data, including increased robustness, scalability. However, the open and anonymous nature of these networks leads to a complete lack of responsibility for the content a peer puts on the network, opening the door to abuses of these networks by malicious peers. Therefore, it is necessary to build trust relationship between peers in the distributed large-scale P2P networks.

Trust represents an integrated evaluation of behavior and capacity of a peer in the viewpoint of another peer. Current researches on trust mostly focus on setting up the reliable trust management model for P2P networks. There exist a large number of trust models that commit themselves to computing a trust value for a source provider. Such systems typically assign each node a trust value based on the transactions it has performed with others. For example, XRep [1,2] provides a protocol complementing

---

* This work was supported by the National Basic Research Program of China (Grant No. 2003CB314806 and 2006CB701306), the National Natural Science Foundation of China (No. 90204003 and 60472067).

T. Dimitrakos et al. (Eds.): FAST 2006, LNCS 4691, pp. 270–284, 2007.
© Springer-Verlag Berlin Heidelberg 2007

current Gnutella protocol by allowing peers to keep track of and share information about the reputation of other peers and resources. EigenRep proposed by Kamvar et al [3] is another reputation management system for P2P networks. Their trust evaluation stems from the concept of transitive trust. They assume the existence of a small number of trustworthy peers whose opinions on other peers are known to be trusted. The reputation-based trust mechanisms in P2P systems [5-7] are similar with social networks in which a peer issues a query for another peer's reputation to its friends before they will transact and depends on its friends' referrals to build trust relationship. However, there are some disadvantages in these schemes and we sum up as follows: first, though some methods [6,7] differentiate referrals' reliability, they do not incorporate multi-characteristic to rate these referrals or only give some experiential evaluation without any theoretic bases; second, most existing reputation mechanisms need clear positive or negative rating ([1-3,5,7]) ,but this condition is difficult to achieve in actual networks; third, the certainty of trust relationship is only considered in these mechanisms, but in fact trust relationship is very complex and dynamic, so uncertainty of trust ought to be considered [15].

With these research problems in mind, we develop a trust management framework for unstructured peer-to-peer systems, with emphasis on efficiently aggregating referrals which include conflicts and inconsistency, as well controlling such possible attacks and threats as denigration, collusion, and strategic attacks. Our contribution can be summarized in the following four aspects:

First, we present an advanced D-S combination rule that can efficiently combine various evidences even though these evidences badly conflict each other.

Second, we propose a decentralized trust model—AET^2M, an Advanced D-S Evidence Theory based Trust Model. Furthermore, we address a feedback credibility based algorithm to effectively build a basic probability assignment function (BPA) of a peer and give a evaluation evidence of uncertainty. Moreover, some methods for resisting such malicious attacks as denigration, collusion and behavior oscillating are presented.

Third, we present a set of experiments that show the effectiveness of our trust model in detecting malicious behavior of service providers.

This paper is organized as follows. In section 2, we review some existing works. Section 3 presents the advanced D-S combination rule and AET^2M. Some experiment results are illustrated in section 4. In section 5, we conclude our work.

2 Related Works

XRep [1,2] proposed by Cornelli et al. adopts a binary rating system and is based on the Gnutella query broadcasting method using TTL limit. Their focus is to provide a protocol complementing existing P2P protocols, as demonstrated on top of Gnutella. However, there are no formalized trust metric and no experimental results in the paper validating their approach.

Another work is EigenRep [3]. Their algorithm again focuses on a Gnutella like P2P file sharing network. They addressed the collusion problem by assuming there are peers in the network that can be pre-trusted. While the algorithm showed promising results against a variety of threat models, we argue that the implementation of the algorithm is very complex and requires strong coordination and synchronization of peers.

Wang and Vassileva [4] propose a Bayesian network-based trust model that uses reputation built on recommendations. They differentiate two types of trust: trust in the host's capability to provide the service and trust in the host's reliability in providing recommendations.

Xiong and Liu [5] present a reputation-based trust supporting framework. They introduce three basic parameters and two adaptive parameters. They incorporate the concepts of a trust value and the similarity with oneself to compute credibility and satisfaction.

Song [7] proposes a trust model that used fuzzy logic inference to compute the local trust value of a peer and aggregate the recommendation information. Fuzzy logic provides rules for reasoning with linguistic trust metrics.

Yu and Singh present in [6] a mathematical theory of evidence to evaluate and spread the trustworthiness ratings of agents. Main contribution is to introduce evidence to express the local trust value of a given peer. However, there are a few disadvantages in this paper, for example, directly applying D-S evidence theory that can give rise to unreasonable results when evidences are not independent each other to combine referrals, not considering evidence reliability when the local trust values are aggregated and so on.

3   Advanced D-S Evidence Theory Based Trust Model for P2P Networks

D-S theory of evidence [8,9] is a framework for such purposes that have found applications in diverse areas such as expert systems, information retrieval, computer vision, pattern matching, and automatic target recognition and so on. The D-S theory could narrow down a hypothesis set with the accumulation of evidence and it allows for a representation of the "ignorance" due to the uncertainty in the evidence. When the ignorance reaches the value zero, the D-S model reduces to the standard Bayesian model. Thus, the D-S theory could be considered as a generalization of the theory of probability. Here for brief purpose we will not state D-S theory of evidence and its combination rule in detail. For expositions on the D-S theory, see the seminal monograph [9], also [10] and [11].

3.1   Advanced Combination Rule for D-S Theory of Evidence

There exist many problems when directly using D-S theory of evidence to fuse data, as can be found by researches. The main reasons are as below:

1.   The combination condition is strict and require that evidences be independent each other. In P2P networks, there are always collusive peers who collude and depend on each other to disturb the P2P system and referrals from collusive peers are interrelated. Directly combining these evidences will easily induce unreasonable results.
2.   Focal element's exploration arises easily and computation complexity increases in exponential means.

3. Unable to deal with conflicting evidences and distinguish the scale of subset in which evidence is.

Bearing those in mind, we take such steps as de-correlation, as can be seen in [16], to weaken these conditions and further apply them to model trust relationship between peers in P2P networks.

The basic D-S combination rule can fuse evidences from different evidence sources. However, there exist some shortcomings especially when evidences conflict each other badly and the combination results may be unacceptable. Therefore, Yager [10] presented a new combination rule. In Yager's combination rule, the probability of conflicting evidences is completely distributed to the unknown proposition. Yager's combination rule is better than that of D-S evidence theory in capability. However, the combination results are not desirable in case of three or more evidences.

A new combination formula was presented in [11], by defining evidence credibility and distributing conflicting information partly to unknown region, partly to weighted combination. Though it averted a conflict, the result was not all-sided since it discarded the conflicting information which was sometimes very important. Absorbing method was proposed in [12], distributing conflicting probability to maximal focal element of BPA and not considering the effect of conflict on other focal elements. Therefore, it could produce an illogical result.

We point out that in the combination rule conflicting evidences are partial useful even though they badly conflict each other, and further conflicting information can not be discarded simply. Based on the opinion, we put forward an efficient combination rule depicted as formula (1), that is, the conflicting probability that evidences support is distributed to every proposition according to its average supported degree. The new combination rule improves the reliability and rationality of the combination results. Even though evidences conflict one another highly, good combination results are also obtained.

$$\begin{cases} m(\Phi) = 0 \\ m(A) = \sum_{\cap A = A_i \ 1 \le i \le n} \prod_{1 \le i \le n} m_i(A_i) + k \cdot f(A), \forall A \ne \Phi \cdot \end{cases} \qquad (1)$$

Where $k = \sum_{\cap A_i = \Phi \ 0 \le i \le n} \prod m_i(A_i) = 1 - \sum_{\cap A_i \ne \Phi \ 0 \le i \le n} \prod m_i(A_i)$, $f(A) = \dfrac{\sum_{1 \le i \le n} m_i(A)}{S_e}$, $S_e = \sum_{1 \le i \le n} m_i(X)$, X is the collect of all the focal element of n evidences.

Aiming at the advanced combination rule, we have done a large number of experiments. The results shows that in comparison with some existing rules our combination rule not only converges at consistent information quickly but also yields a more reasonable consequence, no matter how much the number of evidences is or the number of focal elements in the evidences is.

3.2 Description of Downloading for P2P Networks

Before depicting our model, we list three principles for the design. First, Peer will always trust itself. Second, bad behavior makes the trustworthiness value drop faster and good behavior increases the value slower. Third, it will be bad peer prone if a peer continually behaves badly.

P2P networks are overlaying networks that consist of a large number of nodes. For convenience, we use file-sharing systems as example in the whole paper. In the following, we call the peer to request file and rate other peers *rater*, the peer to response and be evaluated *ratee*, and the peer that sends the trustworthiness value of the known peers to others the recommender.

According to the quality of services provided by cooperating peers (*ratee*), we classify services into four categories, as shown in Table 1. We formalize the quality set as $Q = \{G, C, I, M\}$. This coarse-grain classification is flexible enough to apply to any resource sharing. More subclasses can be introduced if necessary. Both I and M services are bad services, and will cause the *rater* to decrease the *ratee*'s score.

Table 1. Description of file downloading

File Quality	Description
G (Good)	The file is as good as expected.
C (Common)	The file is correct, but with some degradation
I (Inauthentic)	The file is inauthentic
M (Malicious)	The file is malicious (e.g. virus or Trojan Horse)

In a reputation system, a peer makes decisions based on its experience and other peers' referrals. The peer i rate another peer j after they directly transact with each other. Local trust value of j is evaluated by i in the light of the quality of files that j have provided. But to evaluate the trustworthiness of j comprehensively, i can not rely on only direct experience. In a referral process, i issues a query for j's reputation, other peers who have interacted with j— termed recommenders—may response to query and give their feedbacks that are interaction experience with j to i. I then can incorporate the knowledge of other peers according to its acquaintanceship degree to them.

3.3 Credibility

Trustworthiness of a peer is a temporal value, because the behavior of the peer will change dynamically. The old trustworthiness value may totally misrepresent one peer's quality after some time. To solve this problem, an adaptive time window is used in this paper to depict peer's transaction behavior. Only the behaviors of the *ratee* inside the window are taken into consideration. With the window shifting forward, (we suppose that the forward window end-time is backward window start-time), the value reflects the fresh statistics of the *ratee*'s recent behaviors. The window size plays an important role in the credibility calculation. The smaller the window size is, the more the shorter-term assessment is favorite by the trustworthiness calculation.

In our model a peer locally stores the proportion lists of four types of files (G, C, I, M) downloaded from the peers that it has interacted with. For instance, if peer i has a number of interactions with peer j during the period $[t_{start}, t_{end}] = [W_1, W_2 \cdots W_n]$, where $W_k (1 \leq k \leq n)$ denote the kth time window, the first transaction must happen inside

W_1 and current transaction lies in W_n. Suppose the transaction results of peer i with peer j inside W_k is described as $\{r_{ij}^k(G), r_{ij}^k(C), r_{ij}^k(I), r_{ij}^k(M)\}$.

It is indispensable to differentiate the effect of transaction period on computing the trust value of a peer in current trust models since individual behavior changes over time. To solve the problem, a time based evaluation method that fresher interactions are more important than old ones is adopted widely, namely, assigning more weights to recent interactions and less weight to previous interactions. We present a decay function to achieve the same goal, furthermore, decay function is more operable, more easy controllable, more flexible than weight application.

Decay function f is in fact a timing discount function and is depicted as $f(k) = f_k = \rho^{n-k}, 0 < \rho < 1, 0 \le k \le n$, where f_k is a function value, also is decay factor for the kth time window. As can be seen from the definition of decay function, the weight for the first interaction is $f_1 = \rho^{n-1}$, that is, decay degree is maximal; the current interaction's weight is $f_n = 1$, namely, decay degree is 0.

Suppose the interaction result of peer i and peer j for the current time window W_n is $\{r_{ij}^n(G), r_{ij}^n(C), r_{ij}^n(I), r_{ij}^n(M)\}$, if for the time window W_{n-1}, the one is $\{r_{ij}^{n-1}(G), r_{ij}^{n-1}(C), r_{ij}^{n-1}(I), r_{ij}^{n-1}(M)\}$, incorporating both the results using decay function f is

$$\left\{\left(r_{ij}^n + f_{n-1}r_{ij}^{n-1}\right)(G), \left(r_{ij}^n + f_{n-1}r_{ij}^{n-1}\right)(C), \left(r_{ij}^n + \frac{1}{f_{n-1}}r_{ij}^{n-1}\right)(I), \left(r_{ij}^n + \frac{1}{f_{n-1}}r_{ij}^{n-1}\right)(M)\right\}.$$ Note that

decay function act as penalty function which is represented by the reciprocal of decay factor $\frac{1}{f_{n-1}}$ (>1) when I and M happen. In the same way, incorporating all interactions

results is $\left\{\left(\sum_{k=1}^{n} f_k r_{ij}^k\right)(G), \left(\sum_{k=1}^{n} f_k r_{ij}^k\right)(C), \left(\sum_{k=1}^{n} \frac{1}{f_k} r_{ij}^k\right)(I), \left(\sum_{k=1}^{n} \frac{1}{f_k} r_{ij}^k\right)(M)\right\}$.

Credibility is the percentage of the rate of diverse files to overall rate. As to above

example, credibility in G, C, I, M is respectively $\left(\sum_{k=1}^{n} f_k r_{ij}^k\right)(G) \Big/ S_{GCIM}$, $\left(\sum_{k=1}^{n} f_k r_{ij}^k\right)(C) \Big/ S_{GCIM}$,

$\left(\sum_{k=1}^{n} \frac{1}{f_k} r_{ij}^k\right)(I) \Big/ S_{GCIM}$, $\left(\sum_{k=1}^{n} \frac{1}{f_k} r_{ij}^k\right)(M) \Big/ S_{GCIM}$ where $S_{GCIM} = \left(\sum_{\substack{k=1 \\ T=G,C}}^{n} f_k r_{ij}^k\right)(T) + \left(\sum_{\substack{k=1 \\ T=I,M}}^{n} \frac{1}{f_k} r_{ij}^k\right)(T)$.

In our model, credibility is computed when a peer receives a query for referral about another peer, furthermore, in the current time window if other peers request the referrals about the same peer, the computed credibility is valid. Upon acquiring the credibility in G, C, I, M, we may build BPA function of a peer using it.

3.4 Modeling BPA Function of a Peer

We have classified file quality into four categories G, C, I, M and so the frame of discernment is $\Theta = \{G, C, I, M\}$. When peer i has transacted with peer j, we assume that its credibility in $\theta_j \in \Theta$ ($j = 1,2,3,4$) is α_{ij}, satisfying $\sum_{j=1}^{4} \alpha_{ij} = 1$.

Using the credibility, we can model the support degree of peer i to θ_j, moreover, the latter should be a single increasing function of the former. We simplify the relationship into a linear function:

$$m(\{\theta_j\}|R_i) = \lambda \alpha_{ij}, 0 < \lambda \leq 1 . \tag{2}$$

Because α_{ij} satisfies the condition $\sum_{j=1}^{4} \alpha_{ij} = 1$, the constraint $\sum_{j=1}^{4} m(\{\theta_j\}|R_i) \leq 1$ is tenable.

In order to turn m into a BPA function, we must complement a definition:

$$m(\Theta|R_i) = 1 - \sum_{j=1}^{4} m(\{\theta_j\}|R_i) . \tag{3}$$

Therefore, $m(\bullet|R_i)$ function defined by formulae (2) and (3) is a basic probability assignment function whose focal elements include at most $\{\theta_j\}$ ($j=1,2,3,4$) and discernment frame Θ.

We will simplify the BPA function of a recommender. Suppose $m_i^j = m(\{\theta_j\}|R_i)$, $m_i^0 = m(\Theta|R_i)$ for a recommender R_i, $i=1,2,\cdots r$, $\theta_j \in \Theta$, $j=1,2,3,4$, so the BPA functions of such r recommenders can be described by the following matrix:

$$M = \begin{bmatrix} m_1^0 & m_1^1 & \cdots & m_1^4 \\ m_2^0 & m_2^1 & \cdots & m_2^4 \\ & & \vdots & \\ m_r^0 & m_r^1 & \cdots & m_r^4 \end{bmatrix} . \tag{4}$$

Where the ith row denote the ith recommender's BPA function, R_i, $i=1,2,\cdots r$.

3.5 Evidence Inference Algorithm and Combination Method

Now we will combine such r BPA functions into an integrated function. First of all, de-correlation of evidences must be executed so as to be independent of each other. Being characteristic of a common property, these BPA functions include at most such focal elements as $\{\theta_j\}$, $\theta_j \in \Theta$ ($j=1,2,3,4$) and discernment frame Θ. Therefore, our combination algorithm is a lineal increasing computation, which efficiently decreases computation complexity and also preferably solves the problem of the explosion of focal elements.

Suppose the collection of all the recommenders is $I(i) = \{R_1, R_2, \cdots R_i\}, i=1,2,\cdots r$, so the former i rows in the recommendation matrix can be depicted as below:

$$m_{I(i)}^j = m(\{\theta_j\}|I(i)), \theta_j \in \Theta, j=1,2,3,4 . \tag{5}$$

$$m_{I(i)}^0 = m(\Theta|I(i)), j=1,2,3,4 . \tag{6}$$

Combining these BPA functions by the advanced combination rule, we can educe the following formula:

$$m_{I(i)}^j = \sum_{\cap A_t=\{\theta_j\}} \prod_{1\le t\le i} m_t^{A_t} + k_{I(i)} \cdot f_{I(i)}(\theta_j), \theta_j \in \Theta, j=1,2,3,4 . \tag{7}$$

$$m_{I(i)}^0 = \prod_{1\le t\le i} m_t^0 + k_{I(i)} \cdot f_{I(i)}(\Theta) . \tag{8}$$

Where $k_{I(i)} = \sum_{\cap A_t=\Phi} \prod_{1\le t\le i} m_t^{A_t}$, $f_{I(i)}(\theta_j) = \dfrac{\sum_{t=1}^{i} m_t^j}{\sum_{t=1}^{i+1} m_t^X}$, X is the collection of all focal

elements of $I(i) = \{R_1, R_2, \cdots R_i\}$. When $i=r$ comes into existence, we will obtain a combined BPA function denoted as m, so $m(\{\theta_j\}) = m_{I(r)}^j$, $m(\Theta) = m_{I(r)}^0$, $\theta_j \in \Theta$, $j=1,2,3,4$. This m function is just the combined BPA function of all the recommendation evidences.

Because the focal elements of referral evidences are only the single element and discernment frame in our P2P trust model, the complexity of referral information is $r \cdot (i+1) = O(ri)$ (i denote the cardinality of Θ) if there exist r evidences .That is to say, information complexity is a linear relationship with the number of evidences.

The computation complexity of combining r evidences is $r \cdot O(i^2) = O(ri^2)$, that is, computation complexity is also a linear relationship with the number of evidences.

3.6 Local Rating

The recommendation based P2P trust models always include two steps: one is local rating, the other is aggregating ratings. A peer's local rating about another peer is based on direct interactions each other. The local rating is generated every time when an interaction takes place. We describe both the ratings in detail in the following sections.

In AET^{2}M, the local rating of peer j in the viewpoint of peer i is expressed in the form of an evidence that i supports in term of quality of the files downloaded from peer j. For example, the local rating is $R_{ij} = m_{ij} = \{m_{ij}(G), m_{ij}(C), m_{ij}(I), m_{ij}(M), m_{ij}(\Theta)\}$, where m is a BPA function over $\Theta = \{G, C, I, M\}$.

3.7 Aggregating Ratings and Trust Value Evaluating Method

Upon receiving overall referrals, *rater* will fuse them into a specific evidence by advanced combination rule. However, main challenge is that recommenders' reputation is different and the referral from the peer with high reputation is more reliable than that with low reputation. Therefore, we should differentiate these referrals and assign different weights to them. We think that the first few peers to join a network are often known to be trustworthy, since the designers and early users of a P2P network are likely to have less motivation to destroy the networks they build. (These peers form a collective named pre-trusted peers). If the referrals come from these peers, they are regarded reliable. For convenience, suppose the weights of the referrals from pre-trusted peers are w_k and other referrals' weight is w_i ($w_i < w_k$), moreover, the lower the reputation value of a peer is, the less the weight of its referral is. We define the peers' BPA function as:

$$m(\{\theta_j\}|R_i) = \frac{w_i}{w_k}\lambda\alpha_{ij}, \ m(\Theta|R_i) = 1 - \sum_{j=1}^{4} m(\{\theta_j\}|R_i) \ , \ j = 1,2,3,4 \ . \tag{9}$$

On obtaining the BPAs of all referrals, peer i (*rater*) will combine these evidences in terms of formula (7).

The combined evidence is not a specific value but a joint support list for G, C, I, M, Θ and further we have found through a large number of experiments that combined evidence offers very little support to Θ. In our model, the evaluation rule for the trust value of peer j (*ratee*) in the viewpoint of peer i (*rater*) is in the light of relative degree of support which combined evidence offers to G, C, I, M, Θ. The details are as follows: (suppose the degree to which combined evidence supports G, C, I, M, Θ is a, b, c, d respectively).

1. If the degree of support that combined evidence offers to I and M is not beyond a threshold ($Threshold_I > Threshold_M$), the peer is thought of as a trustworthy node; otherwise an untrustworthy one.
2. If there are two credible peers, their trust value is judged by the support degree of G and C according to $a + \frac{b}{\eta}$ ($\eta > 1$). The larger $a + \frac{b}{\eta}$ is, the higher the trust value of the peer is.
3. When both the peers are credible and further the support degree of G and C is same, the following result is obvious: the lager $c + \gamma d$ ($\gamma > 1$) is, the less credible the peer is.

As can be seen from above, we can conclude that the way in which the trust value of a peer is rated is flexible and multi-scale in comparison with some existing trust model in which the trust value of a peer is defined as a specific, single value.

3.8   The Approach to Resisting Denigration, Collusion and Oscillating

Denigration will happen when this type of malicious peers are asked for the trustworthy of these peers with which they have transacted and they always provide a untrue, negative ratings for the peers.

Malicious peers form a malicious collective by assigning a high trust value to another malicious peer in the network. Collusive peers provide inauthentic files to peers outside when selected as download source and provide denigrated ratings for these peers.

Compared with some existing models, trust value of a peer is not a specific value but a combined evidence that peers, ever having transacted with it, support its transaction behavior in AET^2M. Furthermore, the evaluation of trust value is elastic and multi-scale. We have found that a small quantity of denigrations or exaggerations have a slight effect on an established result through a large number of experiments. This fact also embodies the predominance of D-S theory of evidence in soft evaluation aspect.

We have taken several measures to defense against denigration and collusion in the following.

Firstly, we de-correlate the evidences from all the recommenders before combining them. The reasons lie in two aspects: one is that combination rule require that evidences should be independent of one another, the other is that we aim at prevent peers from colluding.

Secondly, we pre-treat all evidences before combining them in accordance with their similarity. If similarity degree of an evidence with the combined evidence is less than a given threshold, the evidence is regarded as an invalid one and is discarded.

Thirdly, we differentiate the referral according to a recommender's reputation. As shown in formula (9), if a recommender is a discredited one, its referral is discounted, that is to say, the lower the recommender's reputation is, the more the referral is at a discount. Therefore, the low-reputation peer denigrates its competitor or exaggerates its complice very difficultly.

Finally, we prescribe that if there are some evidences which support I or M type of files beyond a given threshold, *rater* may ask *ratee* for transaction records. By checking the records, *rater* will ignore the referral if it finds I or M rating is given to *ratee* frequently. In addition, if *rater* has performed a large number of transactions with *rate*, and furthermore referral information is different from direct transaction records, *rater* may neglect the referral and think much of direct trust.

We can efficiently restrain malicious peers from denigrating and colluding by means of these measures and favorable effect is found in the consequent simulations.

There are more realistic malicious peers that are knowledgeable of the rules of the game and may adaptively decide on a strategy in order to maximize their expected payoff in P2P networks. There are a number of ways in which such peers can attempt to fool the system and obtain higher payoffs. For example, they can build a good reputation and then start cheating occasionally at a rate that gives them a higher payoff, but still allows them to maintain an acceptable reputation. Or, they could oscillate between periods of building and then milking their reputation.

To cope with such potential dynamic behaviors of peers, our adaptive time window based algorithm to better react to the oscillating behaviors. The basic idea is to adaptively use a smaller time window to reflect the peer's most recent behavior when the peer is dropping its performance over a threshold. Concrete steps are depicted as below (suppose peer i, *rater*, is transacting with peer j, *ratee*).

Firstly, peer i must check whether I and M types of files uploaded by peer j exceed a given threshold in the current time window *win* or not.

Secondly, if the rate r_I, r_M of I and M files uploaded by peer j in the current time window *win* exceed each threshold (both thresholds are different and in general $Threshold_{r_I} > Threshold_{r_M}$). *Rater* will computes another rate r_I', r_M' using a recent subset of the feedback taken by a small time window W_s smaller than W. The second value, r_I' or r_M', will be returned as the final value if it is larger than the first value by a certain threshold, which likely indicates the peer is dropping its performance recently. Otherwise, the first value, r_I, r_M will be returned.

By choosing a proper adaptive small window, this method can detect the abnormity of peer behavior in time, and make the credibility of the peer drop quickly as long as few fake transactions happen. Simultaneity, it makes the credibility of a peer hard to build, easy to drop, namely, the credibility cannot be quickly increased by a small number of good transactions, but it will quickly drop if the peer starts cheating.

4 Experiment Results

In this section, we will assess the performance of our scheme as compared to a P2P network where YuBin scheme and EigenRep is implemented. We shall demonstrate the scheme's performance under a variety of threat models. All three schemes are implemented based on Query Cycle Simulator [13,14]. There are 100 query cycles in one experiment and the results are averaged over 3 runs.

4.1 Simulation Environment

In each query cycle, a peer i in the network may be actively issuing a query, inactive, or even down and not responding to queries passing by. Upon issuing a query, a peer waits for incoming responses, selects a download source among those peers that responded and starts downloading the file until gets the authentic file or tries all the download sources. Then the query cycle finishes and the data is collected.

In simulation we assume that there are 1000 peers in the network among which malicious peers vary between 100 and 500 and the query message is flooded with TTL=5. Normal peers are in the uptime with the uniform random distribution over [0%, 100%] and issue queries in the uptime with the uniform random distribution over [0%, 50%], while malicious peers are always up and always issue queries. In addition, different types of peers also vary in their behavior of responding queries and providing files. For good peers, the probability to provide authentic files is 96%, while simple malicious peers will respond to all queries they have received and provide inauthentic files with the probability of 70% for all download requests. To tackle node overload problem, we prescribe that ratio of request download from a peer with high trust value is 80%.

The content distribution model is the same as that in [14]. In this model each file is characterized by the content category c and the popularity rank r within this category. c and r both follow the Zipf distribution. Distributions used in the model are based on the measurement of real-world P2P networks. Normal peers issue queries in accordance with their interests while malicious peers issue queries randomly just to harm other peers or disturb the system. In our simulation environment, there are 5000 numbers of files in all and 50 content categories are hold in the network.

In our experiments, we consider different threat models, where a threat model describes the behavior of a malicious peer in the network. Malicious peers' behavior will be described as follows:

- Simple malicious peers. This type of malicious peers always provide an inauthentic file when selected as download source, we call these SM.
- Denigrating peers. This type of malicious peers always denigrates the peers with which they have transacted and provide a denigrated ratings when asked for the trustworthy of these peers .we call these DM.
- Collusive peers. Malicious peers are explained in Section 3.8. Collusive camouflage is a fact that collusive peers provide an authentic file to good peers outside the collective in a probability when selected as download source in an attempt to hide their malicious intention, we call these CC.

● Strategic peers. This type of malicious peers can build a good reputation and then start cheating occasionally at a variable rate, but still allows them to maintain an acceptable reputation. Or, they could oscillate between periods of building and then milking their reputation.

4.2 Successful Transaction Rate (STR)

We compare the successful transaction rate (STR) of our scheme with YuBin scheme and EigenRep under SM, DM, Collusive, CC and strategy. The metrics, successful transaction rate, is ratio of the number of successful transaction over overall transaction numbers, is used to evaluate the efficiency of trust model.

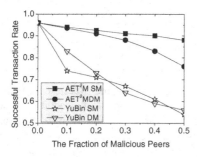
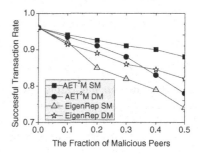

Fig. 1. STR under SM and DM   **Fig. 2.** STR under SM and DM

Simple Malicious Peers and Denigrating Peer. The successful transaction rates of three models under SM and DM are shown in Fig.1 and Fig.2. When there is no malicious peer in the system, STR of three schemes are all 96%. With the fraction of malicious peers increasing, STRs of three schemes descend, but our model descends most slightly. YuBin scheme drop rapidly and STR is only about 55% when the fraction of malicious peers is 50%. This is because on the one hand it directly uses original D-S combination rule to combine evidences, on the other hand it does not distinguish transaction date and does not punish malicious behavior, so its computation of trust value is rough. It can possibly regard bad peers from which to download file as good peers by error, which get invalid transaction numbers increase inevitably. Not taking into consideration under SM that malicious peers provide authentic file in certain probability, EigenRep can not punish these peers and therefore the successful transaction rates fall more heavily. In comparison with YuBin scheme and EigenRep, the successful transaction rates of our model remain high all long when the fraction of malicious peers is 50%.

Collusive Malicious Peers. The successful transaction rates of three models under Collusive are shown in Figure 3, and total number of malicious peers performing collusion was increased in steps of 10%. The successful transaction rate in EigenRep, which does not take into account collusive attacks, descends evidently with malicious peers increasing. YuBin scheme's STR is falling almost linearly and STR is only 20%

when the rate of collusive peers arrives at 50%. Compared to both schemes, our trust model is designed to tackle collusive attacks, therefore to large extend is proved robust against collusive cheating.

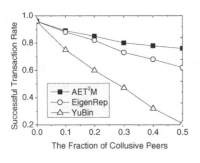
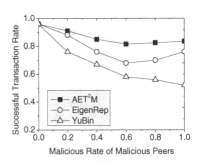

Fig. 3. STR under Collusive   **Fig. 4.** STR under CC

Figure 4 shows an interesting result. For this experiment, fraction of malicious providers in the system was fixed to 25%. The fraction of transactions in which malicious providers offer inauthentic services was varied, starting from 0%, increasing in steps of 10%. However, in a CC system we can see that their attack will be more effective when they provide inauthentic services intermittently. When the services are always inauthentic, reports on malicious providers' behavior between good providers and malicious providers will be entirely polarized. If malicious providers offer good services frequently, reports issued by good peers and malicious peers will have less difference compared to the previous case. We believe this may increase the effectiveness of their attack. As we can see in Figure 4, YuBin system suffers the most under CC. As malicious providers offer inauthentic services more frequently, however, EigenRep and our system tend to perform better. This is because when malicious peers provide inauthentic files in a low probability, they can gather high trust even from good peers, namely, trust mechanism can not distinguish whether the peers are good or not. From this experiment we can find that our scheme is not sensitive to the fraction of inauthentic services that collusive peers provide in the system and so is influenced mildly.

Strategic Peers. We also compare the successful transaction rate of the system with the complex strategy peers with EigenRep and YuBin scheme. Considering the operability of the experiment, we simplify this type of strategic peers, whereas the case is representative. In simulation, suppose the peer whose trust value is less than 0.5 is untrustworthy, and a strategic peer provides true files in a probability of 20% when its trust value is beyond 0.6 and in 60% probability when its trust value is less than 0.6.

4.3 The Efficiency of Resistance Against Oscillating Peers

To address dynamic behaviors of peers, we propose a simple adaptive small-window based algorithm to better react to the behaviors. The goal of this experiment is to show how adaptive small-window algorithm works against strategic dynamic personality of peers. We simulated a community with 200 good peers, but a malicious peer with oscillating behavior. We simulated a changing pattern in which the peer first builds its reputation, then performs fake transactions with others peers and so its reputation is milked, finally it again tries to retrieve its reputation as much as before.

The experiment proceeds as peers randomly perform transactions with each other and a good peer is selected to compute the trust value of the malicious peer periodically. We compare adaptive small window algorithm to basic approach that uses a fixed time window.

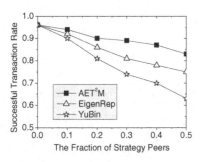
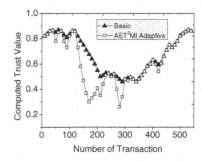

Fig. 5. STR under strategy   **Fig. 6.** The trust value of an oscillating peer

Fig.6 shows the computed trust value of peer u by adaptive metric and basic metric against the type of changing pattern. In the basic model, the peer gains by milking the reputation, but it also has to pay the same amount of cost to build it back. In our model adaptive, a peer is quickly detected for its bad behavior, but it cannot simply increase its trust value quickly by acting well for a short period so the cost of rebuilding reputation is actually higher than the gain of milking it.

5 Result

The paper presents a framework for trust management in distributed P2P networks. By virtue of an advanced D-S combination rule, we efficiently enhance the aggregating performance especially when referrals include conflicting or inconsistent information. Further, we address some methods for resisting such malicious attacks as denigration, collusion and behavior oscillating. The simulation results show that the proposed trust model can improve the successful transaction rate as well as help malicious peer detection and can be applied to a large-scale distributed system.

References

1. Damiani, E., di Vimercati, S.D.C., Paraboschi, S., Samarati, P.: A reputation-based approach for choosing reliable resources in peer-to-peer networks. In: Proceedings of the 9th ACM conference on Computer and communications security, pp. 207–216. ACM Press, NewYork (2002)
2. Cornelli, F., Damiani, E., di Vimercati, S.D.C., Paraboschi, S.: Choosing reputable servents in a P2P network. In: Proceedings of the 11th Int'l World Wide Web Conf., pp. 441–449. ACM Press, Hawaii (2002)

3. Kamvar, S.D., Schlosser, M., Garcia-Molina, H.: The EigenTrust Algorithm for Reputation Management in P2P Networks. In: Proceedings of the 12th International conference of WWW, Budapest, Hungary (2003)
4. Wang, Y., Vassileva, J.: Trust and Reputation Model in Peer-to-Peer Networks. In: Proceedings of the Third International Conference on Peer-to-Peer Computing(P2P'03) (2003)
5. Xiong, L., Liu, L.: PeerTrust: Supporting Reputation-Based Trust for Peer-to-Peer Electronic Communities. IEEE Transactions on Knowledge and Data Engineering 16, 843–857 (2004)
6. Yu, B., Singh, M.P.: An Evidential Model of Distributed Reputation Management. In: Falcone, R., Barber, S., Korba, L., Singh, M.P. (eds.) AAMAS 2002. LNCS (LNAI), vol. 2631, Springer, Heidelberg (2003)
7. Song, S.S., Hwang, K., Zhou, R.F.: Trusted P2PTransactions with Fuzzy Reputation Aggregation. IEEE Internet Computing 2, 18–28 (2005)
8. Dempster, A.P.: Upper and lower probabilities induced by a multi—valued mapping. Ann Mathematical Statistics (1967)
9. Shafer, G.: A mathematical theory of evidence, pp. 10–28. Princeton University Press, Princeton, NJ (1976)
10. Yager.: On the Dempster-Shafer framework and new combination rules. Information Science 41, 93–137 (1989)
11. Sun, Q., Ye, X.Q., Gu, W.K.: A new composition method for evidence theory. Chinese Journal of Electronics 28, II7–119 (2002)
12. Xu, H., Semt, P.: Some strategies for explanations in evidence reasoning. IEEE Trans.on Syst.,Man and Cybern Part A: Systems Human 28, 599–607 (1996)
13. http://p2p.stanford.edu/www/demos.htm
14. Schlosser, M., Condie, T., Kamvar, S.: Simulating a File-Sharing P2P Network. In: First Workshop on Semantics in P2P and Grid Computing (December 2002)
15. Sun, Y., Han, Z., Yu, W., Ray, K.J.: A trust evaluation framework in distributed network: vulnerability analysis and defense against attacks. In: IEEE Infocom 2006, Barcelona, Spain (2006)
16. Zhang, D.G., Xu, G.Y., Shi, Y.C.: Extended method of evidence theory for pervasive computing. Chinese Journal of Computers 27, 918–927 (2004)

Author Index

Basin, David 80
Beauquier, Danièle 250
Betarte, Gustavo 220
Bistarelli, Stefano 1
Borgström, Johannes 16
Brændeland, Gyrd 31

Cheng, Shiduan 270

Dall'Aglio, Marco 1
Daubignard, M. 47
Deng, Yuxin 65

Grinchtein, Olga 16

Hankes Drielsma, Paul 80
Hansen, René Rydhof 127, 170, 185
Heather, James 202

Janvier, R. 47
Jensen, Christian Damsgaard 170

Kramer, Simon 16
Krukow, Karl 96

Lakhnech, Y. 47
Lanotte, Ruggero 250
Luna, Carlos 220

Matteucci, Ilaria 112
Mazaré, L. 47
Mödersheim, Sebastian 80

Nielsen, Mogens 96
Nielson, Flemming 127, 185

Pang, Jun 65
Peretti, Pamela 1
Probst, Christian W. 127, 170

Rissanen, Erik 158

Sadighi, Babak 158
Seehusen, Fredrik 143
Seitz, Ludwig 158
Søndergaard, Dan 170
Stølen, Ketil 31, 143

Tian, Chunqi 270
Tolstrup, Terkel K. 185

van der Meyden, Ron 235
Viganò, Luca 80

Wang, Wendong 270
Wei, Kun 202
Wu, Peng 65

Zanella Béguelin, Santiago 220
Zhang, Chenyi 235
Zou, Shihong 270

Lecture Notes in Computer Science

Sublibrary 4: Security and Cryptology

Vol. 4734: J. Biskup, J. López (Eds.), Computer Security – ESORICS 2007. XIV, 628 pages. 2007.

Vol. 4727: P. Paillier, I. Verbauwhede (Eds.), Cryptographic Hardware and Embedded Systems - CHES 2007. XIV, 468 pages. 2007.

Vol. 4691: T. Dimitrakos, F. Martinelli, P.Y.A. Ryan, S. Schneider (Eds.), Formal Aspects in Security and Trust. VIII, 285 pages. 2007.

Vol. 4677: A. Aldini, R. Gorrieri (Eds.), Foundations of Security Analysis and Design. VII, 325 pages. 2007.

Vol. 4657: C. Lambrinoudakis, G. Pernul, A M. Tjoa (Eds.), Trust and Privacy in Digital Business. XIII, 291 pages. 2007.

Vol. 4637: C. Krügel, R. Lippmann, A. Clark (Eds.), Recent Advances in Intrusion Detection. XII, 337 pages. 2007.

Vol. 4622: A. Menezes (Ed.), Advances in Cryptology - CRYPTO 2007. XIV, 631 pages. 2007.

Vol. 4593: A. Biryukov (Ed.), Fast Software Encryption. XI, 467 pages. 2007.

Vol. 4586: J. Pieprzyk, H. Ghodosi, E. Dawson (Eds.), Information Security and Privacy. XIV, 476 pages. 2007.

Vol. 4582: J. López, P. Samarati, J.L. Ferrer (Eds.), Public Key Infrastructure. XI, 375 pages. 2007.

Vol. 4579: B. M. Hämmerli, R. Sommer (Eds.), Detection of Intrusions and Malware, and Vulnerability Assessment. X, 251 pages. 2007.

Vol. 4575: T. Takagi, T. Okamoto, E. Okamoto, T. Okamoto (Eds.), Pairing-Based Cryptography – Pairing 2007. XI, 408 pages. 2007.

Vol. 4521: J. Katz, M. Yung (Eds.), Applied Cryptography and Network Security. XIII, 498 pages. 2007.

Vol. 4515: M. Naor (Ed.), Advances in Cryptology - EUROCRYPT 2007. XIII, 591 pages. 2007.

Vol. 4499: Y.Q. Shi (Ed.), Transactions on Data Hiding and Multimedia Security II. IX, 117 pages. 2007.

Vol. 4464: E. Dawson, D.S. Wong (Eds.), Information Security Practice and Experience. XIII, 361 pages. 2007.

Vol. 4462: D. Sauveron, K. Markantonakis, A. Bilas, J.-J. Quisquater (Eds.), Information Security Theory and Practices. XII, 255 pages. 2007.

Vol. 4450: T. Okamoto, X. Wang (Eds.), Public Key Cryptography – PKC 2007. XIII, 491 pages. 2007.

Vol. 4437: J.L. Camenisch, C.S. Collberg, N.F. Johnson, B.A. Hamilton, P. Sallee (Eds.), Information Hiding. VIII, 389 pages. 2007.

Vol. 4392: S.P. Vadhan (Ed.), Theory of Cryptography. XI, 595 pages. 2007.

Vol. 4377: M. Abe (Ed.), Topics in Cryptology – CT-RSA 2007. XI, 403 pages. 2006.

Vol. 4341: P.Q. Nguyên (Ed.), Progress in Cryptology - VIETCRYPT 2006. XI, 385 pages. 2006.

Vol. 4332: A. Bagchi, V. Atluri (Eds.), Information Systems Security. XV, 382 pages. 2006.

Vol. 4329: R. Barua, T. Lange (Eds.), Progress in Cryptology - INDOCRYPT 2006. X, 454 pages. 2006.

Vol. 4318: H. Lipmaa, M. Yung, D. Lin (Eds.), Information Security and Cryptology. XI, 305 pages. 2006.

Vol. 4307: P. Ning, S. Qing, N. Li (Eds.), Information and Communications Security. XIV, 558 pages. 2006.

Vol. 4301: D. Pointcheval, Y. Mu, K. Chen (Eds.), Cryptology and Network Security. XIII, 381 pages. 2006.

Vol. 4300: Y.Q. Shi (Ed.), Transactions on Data Hiding and Multimedia Security I. IX, 139 pages. 2006.

Vol. 4298: J.K. Lee, O. Yi, M. Yung (Eds.), Information Security Applications. XIV, 406 pages. 2007.

Vol. 4296: M.S. Rhee, B. Lee (Eds.), Information Security and Cryptology – ICISC 2006. XIII, 358 pages. 2006.

Vol. 4284: X. Lai, K. Chen (Eds.), Advances in Cryptology – ASIACRYPT 2006. XIV, 468 pages. 2006.

Vol. 4283: Y.Q. Shi, B. Jeon (Eds.), Digital Watermarking. XII, 474 pages. 2006.

Vol. 4266: H. Yoshiura, K. Sakurai, K. Rannenberg, Y. Murayama, S.-i. Kawamura (Eds.), Advances in Information and Computer Security. XIII, 438 pages. 2006.

Vol. 4258: G. Danezis, P. Golle (Eds.), Privacy Enhancing Technologies. VIII, 431 pages. 2006.

Vol. 4249: L. Goubin, M. Matsui (Eds.), Cryptographic Hardware and Embedded Systems - CHES 2006. XII, 462 pages. 2006.

Vol. 4237: H. Leitold, E.P. Markatos (Eds.), Communications and Multimedia Security. XII, 253 pages. 2006.

Vol. 4236: L. Breveglieri, I. Koren, D. Naccache, J.-P. Seifert (Eds.), Fault Diagnosis and Tolerance in Cryptography. XIII, 253 pages. 2006.

Vol. 4219: D. Zamboni, C. Krügel (Eds.), Recent Advances in Intrusion Detection. XII, 331 pages. 2006.

Vol. 4189: D. Gollmann, J. Meier, A. Sabelfeld (Eds.), Computer Security – ESORICS 2006. XI, 548 pages. 2006.

Vol. 4176: S.K. Katsikas, J. López, M. Backes, S. Gritzalis, B. Preneel (Eds.), Information Security. XIV, 548 pages. 2006.

Vol. 4117: C. Dwork (Ed.), Advances in Cryptology - CRYPTO 2006. XIII, 621 pages. 2006.

Vol. 4116: R. De Prisco, M. Yung (Eds.), Security and Cryptography for Networks. XI, 366 pages. 2006.

Vol. 4107: G. Di Crescenzo, A. Rubin (Eds.), Financial Cryptography and Data Security. XI, 327 pages. 2006.

Vol. 4083: S. Fischer-Hübner, S. Furnell, C. Lambrinoudakis (Eds.), Trust and Privacy in Digital Business. XIII, 243 pages. 2006.

Vol. 4064: R. Büschkes, P. Laskov (Eds.), Detection of Intrusions and Malware & Vulnerability Assessment. X, 195 pages. 2006.

Vol. 4058: L.M. Batten, R. Safavi-Naini (Eds.), Information Security and Privacy. XII, 446 pages. 2006.

Vol. 4047: M.J.B. Robshaw (Ed.), Fast Software Encryption. XI, 434 pages. 2006.

Vol. 4043: A.S. Atzeni, A. Lioy (Eds.), Public Key Infrastructure. XI, 261 pages. 2006.

Vol. 4004: S. Vaudenay (Ed.), Advances in Cryptology - EUROCRYPT 2006. XIV, 613 pages. 2006.

Vol. 3995: G. Müller (Ed.), Emerging Trends in Information and Communication Security. XX, 524 pages. 2006.

Vol. 3989: J. Zhou, M. Yung, F. Bao (Eds.), Applied Cryptography and Network Security. XIV, 488 pages. 2006.

Vol. 3969: Ø. Ytrehus (Ed.), Coding and Cryptography. XI, 443 pages. 2006.

Vol. 3958: M. Yung, Y. Dodis, A. Kiayias, T.G. Malkin (Eds.), Public Key Cryptography - PKC 2006. XIV, 543 pages. 2006.

Vol. 3957: B. Christianson, B. Crispo, J.A. Malcolm, M. Roe (Eds.), Security Protocols. IX, 325 pages. 2006.

Vol. 3956: G. Barthe, B. Grégoire, M. Huisman, J.-L. Lanet (Eds.), Construction and Analysis of Safe, Secure, and Interoperable Smart Devices. IX, 175 pages. 2006.

Vol. 3935: D.H. Won, S. Kim (Eds.), Information Security and Cryptology - ICISC 2005. XIV, 458 pages. 2006.

Vol. 3934: J.A. Clark, R.F. Paige, F.A.C. Polack, P.J. Brooke (Eds.), Security in Pervasive Computing. X, 243 pages. 2006.

Vol. 3928: J. Domingo-Ferrer, J. Posegga, D. Schreckling (Eds.), Smart Card Research and Advanced Applications. XI, 359 pages. 2006.

Vol. 3919: R. Safavi-Naini, M. Yung (Eds.), Digital Rights Management. XI, 357 pages. 2006.

Vol. 3903: K. Chen, R. Deng, X. Lai, J. Zhou (Eds.), Information Security Practice and Experience. XIV, 392 pages. 2006.

Vol. 3897: B. Preneel, S. Tavares (Eds.), Selected Areas in Cryptography. XI, 371 pages. 2006.

Vol. 3876: S. Halevi, T. Rabin (Eds.), Theory of Cryptography. XI, 617 pages. 2006.

Vol. 3866: T. Dimitrakos, F. Martinelli, P.Y.A. Ryan, S. Schneider (Eds.), Formal Aspects in Security and Trust. X, 259 pages. 2006.

Vol. 3860: D. Pointcheval (Ed.), Topics in Cryptology – CT-RSA 2006. XI, 365 pages. 2006.

Vol. 3858: A. Valdes, D. Zamboni (Eds.), Recent Advances in Intrusion Detection. X, 351 pages. 2006.

Vol. 3856: G. Danezis, D. Martin (Eds.), Privacy Enhancing Technologies. VIII, 273 pages. 2006.

Vol. 3786: J.-S. Song, T. Kwon, M. Yung (Eds.), Information Security Applications. XI, 378 pages. 2006.

Vol. 3108: H. Wang, J. Pieprzyk, V. Varadharajan (Eds.), Information Security and Privacy. XII, 494 pages. 2004.

Vol. 2951: M. Naor (Ed.), Theory of Cryptography. XI, 523 pages. 2004.

Vol. 2742: R.N. Wright (Ed.), Financial Cryptography. VIII, 321 pages. 2003.